THE SECRET LIFE OF BOB HOPE

Also by Arthur Marx and published by Robson Books

My Life With Groucho

THE SECRET LIFE
OF BOB HOPE

Arthur Marx

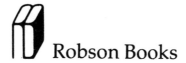
Robson Books

To: *Lois*
Cece
Gabe
&
Brandy

First published in Great Britain in 1994 by Robson Books Ltd, Bolsover House, 5-6 Clipstone Street, London W1P 7EB

Copyright © 1993 Arthur Marx
The right of Arthur Marx to be identified as author of this work has been asserted by him in accordance with the Copyright, Designs and Patents Act 1988

British Library Cataloguing in Publication Data
A catalogue record for this title is available from the British Library

ISBN 0 86051 897 3

Due to the make-up of this book the following pages are blank:16, 28, 82, 96, 114, 134, 146, 154, 172, 202, 206, 220, 260, 300, 318, 326, 338, 368, 410, 424, 434, 444.

Printed in Finland by W.S.O.Y.

INTRODUCTION

When the chief kidnapper of Frank Sinatra Jr. was on trial in the mid-sixties, an FBI man testified that the gang had originally planned to abduct one of Bob Hope's children, but abandoned the idea, because—in his words—"Hope is such a good American and has done so much in entertaining the troops."

With a reputation, even in the underworld, that he is an "untouchable" it's easy to understand why Bob Hope has been pressured, on several occasions during his long life, to give up show business and run for public office. After all, if the late George Murphy, a mediocre song and dance man, could be elected to the United States Senate, and another actor could be President for eight years, Bob Hope ought to be a shoo-in for any office he aspired to. Or so the politicians believed.

But Hope is too shrewd a handler of his own destiny to get involved in politics himself. He much prefers to be a friend of presidents, senators and others in high office, quipping, "I don't need to be in politics—I'm already in show business."

As always, he can be counted on to answer a serious question with a joke. But perhaps there's more to his avoidance of direct involvement in politics than can be gleaned from his simple one-liner.

No doubt Hope is well aware that, once a candidate throws

his hat into the political arena, his behind-the-scenes behavior is likely to be subjected to the severest examination by the media. And Hope is smart enough to know that his personal life would never stand up to the kind of scrutiny that has been the bane of Gary Hart and Teddy Kennedy, and more recently of George Bush and Bill Clinton in their 1992 election campaigns.

Hope's womanizing, one of inside Hollywood's worst-kept secrets, would make Hart, Kennedy, Bush and Clinton look like pikers in the philandering derby. His character and his attitudes, his Midas-like greed, his anti-environmentalist stance, and his callous dismissing of longtime, loyal associates would not play well in the headlines either.

For all his frailties, Bob Hope is one of the most popular comedians ever, not to mention the richest. Right up through 1993 his TV programs, though becoming a little tired, had turned up regularly in the top ten of the Nielsen ratings, and his personal wealth, depending on which magazine you believe, *Forbes* or *Time*, is estimated to be anywhere from $200 to $600 million. In addition, his name, according to a recent poll, ranks beside the Pope and Mickey Mouse in worldwide recognition.

How did Hope manage to reach such heights and still keep his public image so clean? How did he conceal his double life from those in the news media most likely to blab? Never mind how he managed to stay married to the same woman since 1935. In Hope's seven decades of stardom, there's hardly been a breath of scandal connected to his name—outside of show business, that is. However, in Hope's inner circle of writers, directors, producers, advisers, agents, business managers, girl-friends, publicity men, golfing and fishing companions, secre-taries and leading ladies, it's widely known that there's a lot more to those sexy innuendoes and lecherous laughter-evoking leers directed at the beautiful women on his shows than the average fan suspects or would dare to imagine.

Still, few of Hope's intimates are willing to talk about his seamier side. What's the Hope secret? How did he manage all these years to keep a lid on the same kind of behavior that has sunk Gary Hart and Teddy Kennedy, and that was gradually leaked out about other prominent figures, including Franklin D. Roosevelt, JFK, Lyndon Johnson, Princess Di and Prince Charles, Bill Clinton and Gennifer Flowers?

Is he so well loved that no one wants to blow the whistle on him? Or is he such a powerful icon by now that even those who dislike him are afraid to cross him? Or is it some of both?

Admittedly, a whole lot more people love Bob Hope than hate him. But even among those who dislike him, or at least have a reason to, or are on the other side of the fence politically, or don't think he's a great comedian, there is an ambivalent feeling about him that's difficult to explain. Call it respect or call it fear, no one wants to tell the whole truth about him.

When I asked the late Joyce Haber, novelist and one-time entertainment gossip columnist for the *Los Angeles Times*, how it was possible for Hope to keep his private life so private all these years, she told me, "We all knew about Bob and his women, but never wrote about those things when I was on the paper. We never even mentioned the Rock Hudson thing, though we all knew he was gay, and being gay wasn't something you shouted from the rooftops in those days. But now it's different. You write or talk about anything or anybody as long as it sells papers or gets ratings on the talk shows."

Except when it involves Bob Hope.

To my knowledge there have only been two occasions when Hope's philandering has been publicly exposed: once in a 1956 *Confidential* magazine article detailing his relationship with actress Barbara Payton, and once in 1991 when a former secretary told what she knew of his secret life to the *Globe*. But even the people who saw those articles in the supermarket journals have a tendency to shrug them off as either apocryphal or just the rumblings of a disgruntled ex-employee. Even if there was a certain amount of truth to their revelations, what of it? Didn't most husbands cheat at one time or another? And, besides, who wouldn't want to have a fling with Miss World or Raquel Welch?

Only people who know the real Bob Hope recognize the truth and are aware that that was just the top of the shadow being exposed. To the people reading the tabloids while standing at the checkout line at the food market, Bob Hope was still the lighthearted, breezy, attractive leading man comic who always kept them laughing, who still could sing "Thanks for the Memory" better than anyone, who rarely got the girl in the "Road" pictures, and who unselfishly gave of his time through the years to entertaining U.S. troops, no matter how far away from his wife and family it took him during the holiday seasons. In short, he remained the symbol of everything good about America—Mom, and apple pie and the flag and baseball and hot dogs and the Oscar and of course our men in uniform.

And the funny part is, Bob Hope wasn't even born in the U.S.A.

1

Bob Hope's famous ski-snoot first saw daylight on May 29, 1903 in Eltham, England, a small suburb about ten kilometers outside of London.

At least that's the date given in his official biographies. That would make him ninety in 1993. The late Jay Burton, a gag writer who worked for Hope in 1948, believed he was born a couple of years prior to that.

In 1948 Burton was with the comedian in San Francisco, playing one of his numerous benefits. The two were at the same hotel, and had rooms across the hall from each other.

Around six-thirty the morning after the benefit, Burton opened his door to go downstairs for breakfast. As he did, Hope, in his pajamas, opened his door to pick up the morning paper which had been left there for him. Over Hope's shoulder Burton could see the figure of a young lady in the bed. Burton knew she wasn't Hope's wife, Dolores, because she hadn't come on the trip.

Noticing Burton, Hope smiled guiltily at him, and exclaimed, "Forty-seven's too old to be doing this." Then he quickly stepped back inside his room and closed the door.

Whether Hope meant he was too old to be getting up at six-thirty, or too old to be taking the risk of having an affair, Burton wasn't sure. Which is beside the point anyway. The point is: if he admitted to being forty-seven in 1948, that would mean he was born in 1901 instead of 1903.

Since there is usually a disparity of a few years between what most stars claim as their age and how old they really are, Hope's fudging of his birth year by so little could indicate a show of class. And class is one thing he's always had plenty of.

Where it came from is anybody's guess. Perhaps, it's in his genes, or maybe from the fact that he had a loving mother, who brought him up with the right set of values.

But considering his humble beginnings, that he had six brothers to contend with, an alcoholic father who was an erratic provider at best, a mother who had her hands full taking care of such a large brood, and a rough-and-tumble street gang he kept company with as a teenager in Cleveland, Ohio, one has to marvel that Hope emerged from his environment with any class at all.

His father, William Henry Hope, known as Harry to family, was a stonemason. He was a fairly successful one when he married Hope's mother, Avis Townes, on April 25, 1891, in Cardiff, Wales.

Avis Townes was the orphaned daughter of a Welsh sea captain who, along with his wife, had been drowned in a shipwreck. She was fifteen when she met and was swept off her tiny feet by the handsome Harry when he came to town with his father, a master stonemason, to join a work gang building the new stone docks on the southeast coast of Wales.

A petite young lady with short brown hair, brown eyes and an indomitable spirit, Avis had been raised by well-to-do foster parents in nearby Barry. She was extremely attractive and was gifted musically as well. Her foster parents encouraged her talent by giving her singing, spinet and harp lessons.

Her biggest talent seemed to be for bearing children. A year after she and Harry settled down in a comfortable house in Monmouthshire, Wales, Avis gave birth to a son named Ivor. She encored with James Francis II in July of the next year. And Emily came along in July of 1895.

When Harry's stonemason job ended, he moved the family

back to Barry, where he'd first met Avis. There she gave birth to a fourth child, Frederick Charles. There wasn't enough work in Barry, so again Harry and family left Barry to move on—this time to Lewisham, England. There he prospered for a time, but began to drink excessively at the local pub and to squander his money on gambling—mainly, horse playing.

Hard luck, compounded by Harry's gullibility, ate up the rest of the family's savings. A friend had talked Harry into investing in a stable of race horses, but the friend turned out to be no friend at all when he disappeared with the money.

Adding to their miseries, while Avis was pregnant for a fifth time, Emily died of diphtheria. A fourth son, William John, was born to the Hopes soon after that, but Harry was desolate over the death of Emily and started drinking more heavily than ever.

By the turn of the century, stonemasons were becoming less and less in demand. Bricks had taken the place of quarry-stones, and bricklaying, which paid less, was taking the place of stonecutting.

In desperation, Harry moved the family once again—this time to 44 Craighton Road, in Eltham, and into one of a row of cheap houses originally built by Harry's father, James. Work in Eltham was plentiful for a while, but Harry's self-destructive habits continued, plus a new one he'd acquired: an eye for pretty young women. When Avis discovered a barmaid's photo in Harry's wallet, inscribed "to Harry with love," she whacked him so hard on the head with a heavy hairbrush that she nearly killed him.

She never forgot this betrayal, but she did forgive him—at any rate, enough to become pregnant by him again. On May 29, 1903, she gave birth to a healthy baby boy whom they named Leslie Townes Hope, but who is known the world over today as "Just plain Bob (keep the troops laughing) Hope."

With five siblings competing for their mother's attention, and another, Sydney, arriving in 1905, one would think Leslie Townes might have suffered from an identity problem when he was growing up. But not Leslie.

As a toddler, he was already showing signs of becoming an

entertainer. According to his older brother Jack, now deceased, Leslie took to mimicking other members of the family when he was only four. His impersonations were so on the mark that he kept his great-great Aunt Polly, who was 102, in stitches whenever he was taken to her house for a visit. As payment for his performance she would give him a cookie. "Not much, but at least I didn't have to give my agent ten percent of it," Hope would later quip, although he doesn't reveal much about himself during those formative years. "Most of what I know was told to me by my older brother, Ivor," he says.

Ivor recalled that Grandpa Hope, James, would put four-year-old Leslie on a table and have him dance or sing or play a tune on a comb. He also taught him to recite "The Burial of Sir John Moore," a favorite poem of declaiming youngsters in turn-of-the-century England.

Hope's father, however, was more interested in teaching his sons the manly art of self-defense. At least once a week he would take his boys down to the cellar and give them boxing lessons. Harry would crouch down to their height, stick his chin out and say, "Hit it!" Young Leslie's punch wasn't very lethal at age four, but the lessons had such an impact on him that after the family had moved to the States, he took up professional boxing for a brief time.

Harry neglected to give his sons swimming lessons, however. This oversight nearly cost Leslie his life one summer when the Hopes were at Herne Bay, a popular watering place on the seashore.

Having a natural curiosity even then, little Leslie wandered away from the group, probably in search of bathing beauties. When his absence was noticed, everyone in the family panicked except Ivor. He found Leslie submerged under a pier, pulled him onto the beach, and wrung water out of his lungs until he started breathing regularly again.

The world of comedy, not to mention Hope's brothers—all of whom wound up making a good income with him after he became famous—owe a great debt to Ivor for saving Leslie from drowning.

2

In the best of times it wasn't easy to raise a family of seven on a stonemason's income. But after the Boer War ended in 1902, England found itself in the depths of a terrible depression. Quarries were shut down, there were soup lines for the unemployed poor, and Harry found it impossible to get stone-cutting work in Eltham.

A year after Leslie's birth, Harry moved the family to Weston, the resort town where he'd grown up. Avis approved the move, because it took Harry away from the temptation of the barmaid in the photograph.

But the move didn't help him get gainful employment. To supplement the family income, Avis obtained a job as cashier in a tea shop. She often dragged Leslie along with her since there was no one at home to baby sit him. To augment her cashier's salary, she sometimes did house cleaning jobs for local families.

When Harry fractured his ankle and was unable to work for several months, Ivor and Jim obtained jobs cleaning out stables in a local dairy. They also sold newspapers on streetcorners in the mornings and early evenings as well.

To maintain family morale, Avis would play the spinet and sing Welsh songs in the evenings. She gave Leslie, who was fast becoming her favorite, singing lessons. In nice weather, on

Sundays and holidays, she took her boys on picnics or to the boardwalk to watch the magicians, sword swallowers and puppet shows. This early exposure to carnival life may have whetted little Leslie's appetite for show business.

Unfortunately, the financial picture didn't improve for Harry. He soon grew dissatisfied with Weston's lack of opportunities and moved his family to Bristol.

There he struggled, trying to make ends meet, until the spring of 1906, when he received a letter from his older brother, Frank, a master plumber, who'd migrated to America—more specifically, to Cleveland, Ohio—several years earlier, along with his younger brother, Fred. The letter spoke glowingly of opportunities in the building trades in America, even for stonecutters, and suggested Harry come to check it out himself.

A move of such magnitude can be fairly traumatic on the family members left behind, so naturally there was discussion, pro and con. Pro won out, with Avis reluctantly consenting to let Harry go over alone to establish himself in the land of opportunity.

The goodbyes were long and tearful. Avis suffered a severe depression after Harry sailed away. But she perked up when she received her first letter from Harry extolling the virtues of America and enclosing a small check from his earnings.

In the spring of 1908, Harry finally sent for Avis and their six kids, who were forced to cross the Atlantic in two crowded steerage cabins directly over their ship's drive shaft. Even so Avis wouldn't have been able to scrape together enough money for the passage if she hadn't cut down on house fuel the previous winter, and sold her precious spinet and grandfather's clock.

After a fourteen-day voyage, the ship was due to land at Ellis Island in New York Harbor. Before it docked, the immigrant travelers had to line up on deck to be vaccinated.

"I was only two away from getting the scratch," Hope recalled in his 1954 autobiography *Have Tux, Will Travel* (written with Pete Martin), "when I decided I didn't like the idea and bolted.

I headed a keystone cop chase around the deck with everyone after me. They finally cornered me and scraped me with the scalpel."

That was Hope's introduction to America. And it's been a comedy bit ever since.

3

Walter Bunker, former president of Young & Rubicam, the advertising agency that launched Bob Hope's hit radio show for Pepsodent toothpaste in 1938, told me recently, "I'm very fond of Hope—he's a lovely man. He'll give you his time, and maybe even his blood, but try to get a buck out of him, and he'll fight you every inch of the way."

When he was working on his film career at Paramount, and doing his weekly radio show as well, Hope's radio writing staff was expected to be on call twenty-four-hours a day. In addition to writing his radio show, the writers would, for no extra money have to punch up his movie scripts, write material for his stage appearances, and give him one-liners for his charity affairs.

"You could be asleep at two in the morning," recalls Seaman Jacobs, veteran Hope writer, "when suddenly the phone would ring and it would be Hope calling from, say, a hotel in South Bend, where he'd be doing a dinner for the Notre Dame football team and faculty. 'I need two football jokes, and a Catholic Priest joke,' he'd say, 'and get them to me by nine tomorrow morning, South Bend time.' And you'd be expected to stay up the rest of the night thinking up jokes to submit to Hope in the morning. If you refused, you'd be off the show come next option time."

When Sherwood Schwartz, the writer-creator of *Gilligan's*

Island and *The Brady Bunch*, graduated from the University of Southern California in 1939, he landed a job as a gag writer on the *Bob Hope Pepsodent Show* for fifty bucks a week.

The work was hard, and the hours long and irregular. At least once-a-week after the show's preview, there'd be a late-night rewriting session, conducted by Hope in the show's offices in the Bank of America building on Hollywood Boulevard. It wouldn't end until Hope managed to squeeze the last bellylaugh out of his writing staff, which was usually around three in the morning. At that point Hope would turn to Schwartz, because he was the junior writer of the group, hand him thirty-five cents, and order him to run across the street to the Pig n' Whistle restaurant to buy him a pineapple ice cream sundae. "When I brought it back to him," remembers Schwartz, "he'd sit down at his desk and start eating it, while I and the rest of us looked on hungrily. It never occurred to him to treat us to some ice cream too."

Norman Panama and the late Mel Frank worked on Hope's first radio show for about a year after they graduated from Northwestern University in the mid-forties. They were earning seventy-five dollars a week for the team, and happy to be getting it. But after a year of grinding out jokes for America's top-rated comedian, Panama and Frank received offers of five-hundred-a-week from the *Phil Baker Show*.

Feeling they owed Hope some loyalty for giving them their first break in the big time, Panama and Frank went to him and said they'd stay with him if he would match Baker's offer.

"Hope didn't believe Baker offered us that," recalls Panama, "so he picked up the phone and called Baker right in front of us, to find out whether we were lying or not. When he found out we were telling the truth, he shrugged and said, 'Okay, boys, take it. I don't want to stand in your way.'

My sometime-collaborator, Robert Fisher, and I once sold Hope an idea for a film. Our agent got us fifty thousand dollars to write the screenplay, with the last ten thousand of it being withheld until we wrote a second draft or polished whatever work Hope thought the script required.

After we'd turned in the screenplay we heard from Hope's movie agent, Doc Shurr. He said that Hope liked the script just the way it was. Whereupon we asked for the remaining ten thousand dollars due us.

"Sure, boys. No problem."

No problem to him. But when Shurr got back to us a day later, he told us that Hope didn't want to give us the ten thousand dollars because "you didn't do the rewrite."

It was Hope's decision that a rewrite wasn't necessary. We reminded him of this fact. But Hope still refused to give us the rest of our money. As a result, our agent had to contact Hope's lawyer, Martin Gang, and explain to him that Hope wasn't living up to the terms of the contract.

It was a struggle but eventually we got our money.

Several years after that, when Hope was getting a great deal of publicity for his Christmas trips to Vietnam to entertain our servicemen, *Time* magazine ran a story listing some of the top tycoons in America, with the amount of their wealth next to their names.

Mark Taper, the Los Angeles banker and philanthropist was listed at $200 million.

Bob Hope topped him with $500 million.

When Lester White, one of Hope's regular writers, saw the *Time* article, he went to his boss and said, "Bob, if you've got five hundred million, why are you so cheap with your writers?"

Hope frowned and snapped, "That article's got it all wrong. I'm not sure I'm worth even four hundred million."

✿ ✿ ✿ ✿

Call it greed or insecurity (a much overused word that many performers from Jolson and Cantor to Groucho Marx to Cary Grant have used to explain their cheap ways), Hope's need to get the last dollar out of every deal and sock it away or buy more California real estate, can be attributed, at least in small part, to his childhood. Not that he ever went without a meal or didn't have adequate shelter or warm clothing. Still, there were trials to be endured that possibly left a mark (probably a dollar sign) on the young Bob Hope's psyche.

Sailing in the steerage cabin from Liverpool to New York, having to wear two suits of underwear and two suits of clothing at the same time as they disembarked at Ellis Island because Avis didn't have the money to buy enough suitcases for the large group, must have had an impact on such a young boy. Riding from New York City to Cleveland on an immigrant train that wasn't much better than a cattle car—no restrooms, no heat, no diner—stayed vivid in his memory too. Whenever the boys had to relieve themselves, the conductor would tell them to "Hold it!" until they reached the next station. At this point everyone would scramble off the train to try to get to the lavatory first. Then they had to grab what food they could find and/or afford at the cigar counter, and quickly make a mad dash for the train again as it started to chug its way out of the station.

After long, uncomfortable travel, Avis and her sons arrived at Erie Station on the outskirts of Cleveland. There they were met by Harry, looking dapper in a pin-striped suit. With him were his two brothers, Frank and Fred. Since Harry hadn't taken a place of his own yet, the arrangement was that he, Avis and the four youngest boys would stay with Frank and Louisa in the small apartment over Frank's plumbing shop, while Ivor and Jim would be put up at Fred and Alice's apartment down the street.

For their first night in Cleveland, Aunt Louisa had prepared a sumptuous meal for Harry, Avis and all her nephews. Following two days of near-starvation rations on the journey, Leslie and his brothers went through her meal like locusts.

After a few days of living under her in-laws' roof, Avis couldn't endure the crowded conditions and despite a lack of funds, went out and rented a one-family house with three bedrooms and one bath, near Euclid Avenue and 105th Street. The rent was $18.50 a month, which came near to breaking them, since the stonecutting job market, wasn't much better for Harry in Cleveland than it had been in England.

The United States in the winter of 1908–09 was having its

worst depression in fifty years, and a financial panic set in that spring that nearly sent Harry and Avis back to England, "where at least we could starve to death with friends," quips Hope today.

In addition, the weather that winter was more severe than any of them could remember having to endure in England.

Harry persevered, however. He formed a partnership with another stonecutter, and the two made a bid on a Cleveland high school building contract. Their low bid got them the job. Unfortunately it was too low. They lost money on the job, dissipating what little savings Harry had accumulated.

To compensate for this setback, Avis moved the family to a larger house, with a higher rent, at 1925 East 105th Street. On the face of it, this bit of extravagance would seem to be a wrong move at the wrong time. But Avis had a plan to make the extra expenditure pay for itself—she took in boarders. This gave the Hopes a monthly income, in addition to extra living space.

The larger quarters became a necessity by the winter of 1909, when Avis gave birth to still another son, George Percy. That made seven sons altogether, but George enjoyed the distinction of being the first of the brood to be born a United States citizen. The rest of the family had to wait to become Americans until later in the year, when Harry became eligible for naturalization. When Harry swore allegiance to the U.S., his family automatically became citizens.

There was, however, little time or money for celebrating such a milestone. With Harry out of work, or drunk so much of the time, the burden of keeping the family in necessities fell on Avis's strong shoulders.

Avis ironed, sewed, cooked, kept the house spotless, made clothes for the boys, and traveled miles by streetcar to find food markets with the best bargains. And every Saturday night, she lined up the kids in the kitchen and gave each of them a bath in a galvanized iron tub. She took them in the order of their behavior for the week. The best behaved got to go first and enjoy the cleanest water. Hope recalls not being eligible for a tub of clean water until he was thirteen.

With her ability to scrimp, Avis eventually saved enough money to buy a secondhand upright piano so her favorite son, Leslie could resume music lessons. By the time he was eight, Leslie, who had a good ear for music as well as an excellent soprano voice, was singing in the school's glee club and also in their church choir.

Meanwhile, her other sons weren't exactly idle. The two oldest brothers, Jim and Ivor, held down regular jobs after school, while Fred, Jack, Sid and Leslie (when he wasn't in the choir) sold newspapers on the corner of 105th Street and Euclid. Each boy stood at a different corner. Leslie chose the southwest corner, because the Southwest Grocery Store was on it and it stayed open long enough for him to duck inside and warm his hands around the potbellied Ben Franklin stove on wintry afternoons.

One of his regular customers was an old man, with a wrinkled leathery face and heavily veined gnarled hands, who came by late every afternoon in a black Peerless limousine driven by a chauffeur. Usually he'd roll down the window of the back seat, hand Leslie the exact change—two cents—for a copy of the *Cleveland Press*, and drive on. But one evening he handed Leslie a dime, and Leslie, unfortunately, didn't have change. Which he told the old man, hoping he'd say, "That's all right, son, keep the change." Instead the old man just stared at Leslie with hand extended palm up until Leslie got the message and told him he'd go and get change, which he did at the grocery store. While he was gone, however, he lost two customers who bought their papers from another newsboy. When Leslie returned with the change and dropped it in the old man's outstretched palm, he looked at the youngster and said, "Young man, let me give you some advice. If you want to be a success in business, trust nobody, never give credit, and always keep change in your hand. That way you won't lose customers."

"Sure," young Leslie told a companion as the man drove away. "If he hadn't been so stingy and let me keep the change, I wouldn't have lost any customers."

As Leslie stood there shaking his head, the grocer came out

and said to him, "Know who that man was? That was John D. Rockefeller!"

Although it's doubtful if Leslie knew that Rockefeller was the richest man in America at the time, it's apparent from how he's conducted his business affairs that he embraced John D.'s advice about not trusting anyone.

Leslie was street smart, but he never was crazy about school. His favorite subjects were music and physical education in which he excelled at foot racing. But on his first day of grade school he was forced to develop his boxing skills as well, because the other children started picking on him and kidding him about the name of Leslie and his British accent. As soon as they heard his name was Leslie Hope, they switched it to "Hope-Les" which quickly became just plain Hopeless.

They also teased him about the clothes his mother made him wear to school—an Eton jacket and a stiff white turned-down collar. Between his name and his outfit, Leslie was always scrapping to defend his honor. That first semester he came home with quite a few bloody noses and a gap where his two front teeth should have been before his peers learned that he was pretty handy with his fists and to stop teasing him.

When he was in his early teens and beginning to have theatrical ambitions, Avis took Leslie to Keith's 105th Street in Cleveland to see Frank Fay, vaudeville's top monologist, who was reputed to be making $2,500 a week.

A monologist didn't do anything but stand on the apron of the stage and tell stories. It didn't look as if it took much talent, but here looks were deceptive. Halfway through Fay's performance, Avis turned to Leslie and said in a voice loud enough for the entire audience to hear, "He's not half as good as you are."

Embarrassed, Leslie shushed her, and sank farther into his seat to make himself inconspicuous.

In the summer of 1915, when Hope was only twelve, Charlie Chaplin contests were all the rage throughout America. Every youngster with a streak of ham in him was blacking his upper lip, putting on his father's derby, grabbing his grandfather's cane and imitating the famous Chaplin walk.

Leslie could do a pretty good imitation of Chaplin, too, and one Sunday afternoon his older brothers took him to Luna Park located in a shoddy section of Cleveland, to enter him in a Chaplin contest.

To everyone's surprise except Leslie's, he walked off with first prize and with enough prize money to buy his mother a new stove.

It was an encouraging sign to the family that Leslie was showing talent for some business, even if it was only show business, because by the time he was sixteen he wasn't setting the world on fire doing anything else.

At school he barely made passing grades, and in his part-time work after school he never was satisfied, and jumped from job-to-job like a honey bee in a field of clover.

Nothing about work excited him.

What he enjoyed was hanging around the Alhambra Billiard Parlor, after work with his pal Whitey Jennings, and taking on all customers with a cue. Three-cushion billiards was Leslie's speciality, and his speciality was hustling the suckers who came in.

Often he did his hustling in collaboration with Whitey and two other chums, Johnny Gibbons and Charlie Cooley, two talented but unemployed vaudevillians who were accomplished tap dancers.

When a potential sucker came in to the Alhambra, Les, acting as the shill, would pretend he didn't know a cue ball from a corner pocket. Then the sucker, egged on by Gibbons and Cooley, would challenge Leslie to a game of three-cushion billiards, and of course we know who won.

Leslie became so skillful at separating suckers from their bankrolls, that people who frequented the Alhambra at the time were still talking and writing about it years later. In 1974 a writer for the *Cleveland Plain Dealer* remembered Leslie in his daily column:

> I shilled for a guy I ran around with. He was missing most of one
> arm but boy could he shoot pool! He'd cradle the cue in the

stump of his bad arm. One day we suckered this kid named Hope into a game and he trimmed us both. He pocketed the money, grinned and said, "You guys don't even know how to shill properly." They say he's a millionaire today.

And he is. But he didn't accumulate his millions with a pool cue. Nor did he intend to. As soon as he could legally quit school—and he did at the age of sixteen—he made up his mind that show business was going to be his bag. He knew he had talent. After all, hadn't he already won a Chaplin contest? And he was sure he could act; otherwise he couldn't have been such a successful shill in the pool room. Moreover, he was learning how to dance from Johnny Gibbons and in his spare time he was singing in a quartet outside Pete Schmidt's Beer Garden. Schmidt wasn't paying him, but on their way out, the drunks would tip Leslie and the other members of the quartet.

But the road to Broadway and Hollywood was long and bumpy. Along the way Leslie took a detour to try his hand at boxing.

Ever since Leslie had taken boxing lessons from his dad in the cellar of their house in England, he'd harbored secret dreams of becoming a professional fighter. This manifested itself during his billiard hustling days. Before going to work at the Alhambra, he and his pals would spend the early part of the afternoon at Charlie Marotta's Athletic Club on 79th Street. There they'd work out, jumping rope and throwing their hardest jabs at the punching bag.

One day Whitey surprised Leslie by telling him that he had entered the featherweight division of the Ohio State amateur matches, under the name of Packy West. Why Packy? Well, explained Whitey, there was a legendary fighter around in those days who fought under the name of Packy McFarland.

Not to be outdone, Leslie, who had just turned sixteen and weighed 128 pounds, entered the boxing tournament in the lightweight division (to his misfortune, he just missed making the featherweight class by three pounds). Not being very inventive when it came to choosing a ring name—even then he needed writers—Les decided to call himself Packy East.

Surprisingly Packy East won his first bout by a knockout. But he had to do it by surprising his opponent with a belt to the jaw when the latter had turned away from the ring to get some instructions from his corner.

He managed to box his way into the semifinals.

The semifinal bout was to take place not at Marotta's Gym, but at Moose Hall, a professional fight arena in downtown Cleveland.

Leslie was feeling sanguine about his fighting career so far, and for several days swaggered up and down Euclid Avenue for the benefit of the girls he knew.

But his world fell apart when he learned from an article in the *Cleveland Plain Dealer* that his next opponent would be Happy Walsh—a tough thug who got his name because he smiled whenever he was slugged. Nothing upset this fellow—fists, knives, clubs, guns—and certainly not a callow youth who was skinny as a toothpick, probably had a glass jaw and had absolutely no experience.

Just seeing Happy Walsh's picture in the paper sent a chill up and down Packy East's spine. He later quipped that by the night of the fight his knees were knocking against each other so hard he sounded like a marimba band. He practically had to be carried into the ring by his handlers.

Because he was quick on his feet from all those dancing lessons and foot races, Packy was able to elude his stronger opponent for the first round. He managed this by bobbing and weaving and relying on some fancy footwork as he retreated from Happy without once trying to lay a glove on him. Encouraged, he threw a strong right at Happy soon after the bell rang for the second round. The blow landed on Happy's chin—which Happy didn't like. He smiled at Packy, then put him away for good, with a blow that Packy never saw coming.

Packy's corner man threw a bucket of water on his fighter to revive him, then carried him half conscious out of the ring.

As Hope recalls, "Packy East was the only fighter in Cleveland's history who was carried both ways: in and out of the ring."

When Packy finally regained consciousness, he changed his name back to Leslie, and kept it Leslie until a theater manager several years later urged him to change it to Bob, "because it looked better on a marquee."

4

Leslie Townes Hope was seventeen years old, but a pretty worldly seventeen. He dropped out of East High School in his sophomore year in 1920, and set his sights on a show business career. He was braced to live the same hardship-ridden life so commonplace among struggling vaudevillians of his day.

In spite of the fact that East High School's most famous dropout could do an acceptable buck-and-wing, and had a quick wit, Les Hope had no immediate prospects of a job in show business when he forsook the cap and gown for greasepaint and Haney plates.

Consequently he was forced to accept work as a butcher's helper from his Uncle Fred, who was the proprietor of a meat stand in Cleveland's Grand Central Market, a long streetcar ride away from his parent's home on Euclid Avenue.

It's hard to picture the Hope we now know working in a butcher shop and getting blood stains on his neatly manicured hands. Evidently he wasn't too fond of the idea, either. Aware that his escape route from a life of drudgery eviscerating chickens and carrying beef carcasses from the delivery trucks to the meat stand lay along the road to show business, Les used much of his meager earnings to take tap dancing lessons in his spare time from a black entertainer named King Rastus Brown.

He practiced his dancing skills on a wooden platform above Uncle Fred's meat stall during his work day.

Customers were amused by Les's spirited performances, especially when he started adding singing and mimicry to his ad-lib act. Uncle Fred was more exasperated than amused and would probably have fired Les had he not been his nephew.

Another benefit of working for Uncle Fred was that the market was close to Halle's Department Store in downtown Cleveland, where Mildred Rosequist, Hope's first serious heart-throb, worked as a saleslady in the cosmetics department and doubled as a fashion model. As Hope remembered Mildred in *Have Tux, Will Travel*, "she was tall, blond, willowy, graceful and a slick dancer." But what really attracted her to him was that he thought she was a better dancer than Irene Castle, who, with her partner Vernon, were the Astaire and Rogers of their day.

Les met Mildred at a party at a neighbor's house and fell for her immediately. But though she was attracted to him too—he was tall and skinny and would have been handsome were it not for his ski-jump snoot—she was turned off by his indifferent behavior the night they met. Early on, Les became bored with small talk, and went with several male guests into the kitchen to shoot craps. Annoyed, Mildred walked out of the party in a huff, and went home—alone.

But Les knew a good thing when he saw it—especially if it wore a skirt. He dropped in to Halle's during his lunch hour and flirted with Mildred over the cosmetics counter. He made her laugh with his flip banter. "Did anyone ever tell you you had gorgeous eyes?" he would say, ogling her rather assertive bust, or, "Why don't we get married during your lunch break?"

Eventually she was charmed by his brash ways, and the two started going together steadily—so steadily that Les took an extra job at the Cleveland Illuminating Company as a lineman in order to earn enough money to buy Mildred an engagement ring. According to his biographer, William Faith, Hope presented the ring to her in front of his second favorite hangout at Doan's Corners, Hoffman's Ice Cream Parlor. Mildred took one look at the ring and wisecracked, "Does a magnifying glass come with it?" Les was hurt, and ducked inside Hoffman's to drown his disappointment in a root beer on the rocks. Guilt ridden, Mildred followed him into the ice cream parlor, apologized and accepted the ring.

Though the ring was as much as he could afford, and Hope was far from the multimillionaire he is today, being chintzy with a girlfriend established a pattern that he has stuck to all his ninety years.

Les made up for the tiny ring by sneaking meat out of Uncle Fred's butcher shop and taking it to Mildred at her house whenever they had a late date to practice their dance routines together. Mildred had only faint aspirations of a life in show business, but being stuck on Les, she went along with his desires in order to be near him. She would cook a dinner of stolen meat for the two of them after work, and then when the rest of her family had gone to bed, she would wheel the phonograph into the kitchen where they would practice their dance steps on the linoleum.

Aware that they would have to improve their dance act if they were to become any kind of a threat to the Castles, Les and Mildred (with the help of some of her earnings) began taking lessons from another vaudeville hoofer named Johnny Root, who taught at Sojack's Dance Academy.

With Root's help, Les and Mildred worked up a dance act that was admittedly an imitation of the Castles. They weren't as adept as the Castles, but the act was good enough, with Root's help, to get them their first professional engagement—a three night stint for the Social Club in the Brotherhood of Locomotive Engineers Building.

Their performances went over all right until the last show of the third night, when Les, drunk with success, started doing the buck-and-wing extra-fancy, throwing in a lot of intricate steps that Mildred couldn't keep up with. Exhausted and irritable from working all day at Halle's and dancing all night for the Locomotive Engineers, Mildred lost her cool and stopped dancing in the middle of the routine. Bursting into tears, she announced to the audience that she was too tired to continue and ran off the stage. Les was sore as hell, but covered her unprofessional behavior smoothly by picking out a little old lady in the front row and saying, "See, Ma, you never should have made her do the dishes tonight."

That ad-lib, which was probably Les's first in front of a paying audience, got a laugh from everyone but Mildred.

Following their "success" came a number of other small-time engagements at movie and vaudeville houses in and around greater Cleveland for the two spatting dancers and lovers. The way Hope recalls it, they were getting about eight dollars a performance, which he and Mildred would split. But the way Mildred told it in an interview in the late 1970s, Hope never gave her a nickel for being his partner. "He lied to me and said we were just doing benefits."

It was naive of Mildred to take Hope's word for it. But the one thing she was wise about, and this may have been her mother speaking, was that she refused to go on the road with Les when he got his first out-of-town booking. According to Mildred's mother, "No daughter of mine will ever go unchaperoned on the road with an actor." It was clear to her that Hope was the lecherous type even in his teens. "So she hid Mildred until she was sure I was out of town," remembers Hope.

That put an end to their professional relationship. Their emotional attachment was to remain visible for several years.

As a result, Hope had to seek a partner to replace Mildred. To keep his love life separate from his work, Les decided on a male dance partner this time—a talented kid named Lloyd "Lefty" Durbin whom he had met at Sojack's dancing classes. Durbin was clever, and the two worked up a soft-shoe routine that they combined with some eccentric dances played for humor.

After a mildly successful tryout at a Luna Park amateur contest, in August of 1924, and another appearance in an amateur contest at a vaudeville house in their own neighborhood, the new dance team of Durbin & Hope caught the attention of Norman Kendall, a local booking agent. He was impressed with their act and got them a booking at the Bandbox Theater in Cleveland, which was looking for cheap talent for a revue they were presenting that featured the former movie star Fatty Arbuckle. The fat comedian was trying to make a comeback after his film career collapsed after his involvement in a messy scandal with an underage girl.

In the revue, Durbin & Hope did a soft-shoe and buck-and-wing routine, then sang "Sweet Georgia Brown." For their wow finish they did an Egyptian number wearing brown derbies in front of some papier mâché pyramids. For the blackout they pretended to be dipping into the Nile River with their derbies to bring up drinking water. The gag was that they poured real water out of the derbies when they finally turned them over at the finish of their act. It was a wild routine, and according to Hope, "It got a boff."

Arbuckle was amused by the young duo's antics, and introduced them to Fred Hurley, who produced "tab" shows—miniature musicals about an hour long. Hurley put the boys in one of his productions called *Hurley's Jolly Follies*.

A tab show was one grade up from burlesque, and not quite as smutty. It was filled with music, lots of girls, and comedy sketches with blackouts. It couldn't have been better training for a young man who didn't know that someday he'd be Bob "fill-in-your-own-description" Hope.

The *Jolly Follies* opened in East Palestine, Ohio, then toured the south and the midwest and part of the eastern seaboard. The troupe traveled by bus, the audiences were tough, and the living conditions tougher.

Hope got forty dollars a week for his half of the partnership, and sent twenty of it home to his mother. Whenever the *Jolly Follies* was in the vicinity of Cleveland, Les would drop in on Mildred, and also visit his family. Not particularly impressed with his career, the family was hoping he'd soon tire of the stage, return to Cleveland, take a regular job and settle down, perhaps with Mildred. Dreamer that she was, Mildred was looking forward to the same thing. Unfortunately she failed to reckon with Hope's wandering eye.

One of the girls in the *Jolly Follies* was a Morgantown, West Virginia, lass named Kathleen O'Shea. If that name conjures up visions of a green-eyed, auburn-haired Irish beauty who was irresistible to the opposite sex, you are absolutely correct. Les Hope fell for her the moment he laid eyes on her, and immediately relegated Mildred to the back burner.

In those ancient and Puritanical times, having a relationship with a girl you weren't married to was more difficult than getting booked at New York's famous Palace. But the rules didn't apply to actors and actresses, who were considered to have few, if any, morals.

To illustrate the difficulties of bedding down a female who wasn't a hooker or your wife, Hope recalls an incident that took place one night in a hotel in Bedford, Illinois. Hope came down with a bad chest cold, and Kathleen suggested that he come up to her hotel room after the show. She offered to give him some salve to rub his chest. Eager not to pass up an opportunity like that—who knew what a handful of Vicks salve could lead to?—Hope turned up in Kathleen's room promptly at the appointed time, shut the door, removed his shirt, and was just accepting the salve when a loud peremptory knock shattered the tranquillity of Nurse Kathleen's attempts to be a second Florence Nightingale.

The topless Hope opened the door and found himself eyeball-to-eyeball with the hotel manager, who had murder in his gaze and God-knows-what in his hands, which were behind his back.

"What's the number of your room?" he asked.

"Two twelve," replied Les.

"What number is this?" asked the manager.

"Three twenty-four."

"Get downstairs," ordered the manager.

"You've got me wrong," pleaded Les. "I just—"

But the manager was not about to listen to any explanations. He pulled a hand containing a revolver from behind his back and pointed it at Les. "Get downstairs," he repeated.

Not one to argue with the muzzle of a gun, Hope grabbed his shirt and the jar of salve, and retreated to his own room, where he had to rub the salve on his chest himself.

The *Jolly Follies* lasted a year, and Hurley followed that with *Hurley's Smiling Eyes*. There was not much smiling in the company, however, when Lefty Durbin, Les's partner, collapsed on stage one night in Huntington, West Virginia.

The other members of the cast thought it was ptomaine poisoning, because the food in most of the greasy spoon joints along the Gus Sun Vaudeville Circuit was pretty awful. "The only way you could be sure of not getting poisoned in those dumps was to order something that had been untouched by human hands," recalled the late Groucho Marx when speaking of his vaudeville experiences. "More specifically, a coconut, a hardboiled egg or a banana."

Unfortunately, Lefty Durbin's illness turned out to be a great deal more life-threatening than ptomaine poisoning. When Lefty started coughing up blood, the local doctor suspected TB, which he wasn't equipped to treat. As a result, Hope volunteered to take Lefty back to Cleveland by train.

When they arrived there, he put Lefty in the hands of a doctor, who examined him. Lefty was then checked into the Cleveland Hospital, where he died.

A much saddened Hope rejoined the show in Parkersburg, West Virginia. The manager told him that he'd hired a new partner for the act. Durbin's replacement was a pink-cheeked Ohio boy named George Byrne. Byrne was a smooth dancer and had a likable personality. He and Les hit it off immediately. They became such buddies that several years later Byrne's sister married Hope's kid brother, George.

As a dance act, Hope & Byrne were better than Durbin & Hope. Consequently, Hurley was pleased to find a spot for them in the 1925 edition of *Hurley's Smiling Eyes*. But Hope was becoming restless. He was tired of being just a hoofer. He wanted to try his hand at comedy, so he dreamed up a blackface act for the two of them. The act went over all right, but Hope didn't like having to remove the burnt cork after each performance. It took too long, and interfered with his girl chasing.

Consequently they skipped the blackface, but stuck with

comedy, gradually doing more and more of it between their dance routines.

Their material was corny. Hope couldn't afford the stable of fourteen writers he later would employ, or even one, for that matter, on the hundred dollars a week he and Byrne were paid by Hurley. Hope and Byrne had to make it up themselves, with the result that George S. Kaufman, Al Boasberg, and the other great comedy writers of their time had nothing to fear.

Sample Joke:
(Byrne walked across the stage with his suitcase, set it down, then stepped over it.)

HOPE: How are you?
BYRNE: Just getting over the grippe.

Second Sample:
(Byrne would walk across the stage with a woman's dress on a hanger.)

HOPE: Where are you going with that dress?
BYRNE: Downtown to get this filled.

That'll give you an idea of the kind of material they were doing, and why a lady, who reviewed them for the *Cincinnati Enquirer*, remembered years later:

"Hope was a swell guy. We all thought he was like most of the amateurs, who believe they'll make the grade. We all hoped he would, but I doubt if any of us thought he would make it any more than he already had. I do remember he couldn't be trusted much with 'bits'."

Certainly his girlfriends couldn't trust him—a condition that hasn't changed much over the years. Although he was closely involved with Kathleen, he kept stringing Mildred Rosequist along.

Whenever Les was between engagements, he would bring Byrne home—along with his dirty laundry—and the two of them would avail themselves of Avis's room and board until they got another booking. When they weren't eating his mother's home cooking, they'd rehearse dance routines and comedy bits in the living room.

Juggling two women, even though they lived in separate towns, wasn't easy. Mildred learned about Les's romance with Kathleen probably from his younger brother, George, whom he had foolishly taken into his confidence about the "beautiful Irish doll" he was working with in the show. He never expected George to blab to Mildred.

Whenever Les and Mildred would be sitting on her front porch smooching, she would grill him about his other girl. Les, of course, would deny having anything more than a professional interest in Kathleen, and would pacify Mildred by taking her dancing after they'd finished necking.

In 1926, Kathleen left the show to open a dress shop in her hometown. Between the money she had saved and the meager amount Les contributed, she went into business for herself.

Being separated from Kathleen made things difficult, but Les remained faithful to her for a while. Whenever he was home in Cleveland, he managed to sneak away from Mildred in the Model-T Ford he borrowed from a friend and make the five-hour drive to Morgantown, West Virginia. This, of course, ate into the time Mildred expected him to spend with her. When she discovered his duplicity, she ended the romance, much to Avis and Harry's disappointment.

In the middle of 1926, Hope and Byrne decided they didn't have much of a future doing "tab" shows, so they left Hurley and found an agent in Detroit named Ted Snow. He booked them into the State Theater at $225 a week. This was the first real money Les had ever earned, and he was on a cloud during that engagement.

The reviews were as good as the money: "Very clever soft shoe dancers," said the *Detroit Free Press*. "Hope and Byrne, two young men in grotesque costumes, with their eccentric dancing, won the big applause Sunday."

As a result, Ted Snow was able to book them into a number

of smaller theaters in Detroit, and then back into the State, where they were billed as HOPE & BYRNE—DANCING DEMONS. It also proclaimed, "Back by demand," which was an absolute lie, but acceptable theater license.

After Detroit they played the Stanley Theater in Pittsburgh. There, the act went over so well that the boys immediately, but prematurely, started dreaming of the Big Time—New York City. Before New York, they spent a fortune on publicity photographs by the well-known show biz photographer, Maurice Seymour, whose studio was in Chicago. They bought new costumes for the act: Eton jackets and big white collars, high hats and white tipped black canes. To top off their new look, they bought an expensive theatrical trunk to replace the battered one they were using which was held together by rope.

Then it was on to the Big Apple, where they checked into the Lincoln Hotel, on Eighth Avenue, only one block from Times Square. Once settled in their new digs, they went to B.F. Keith's booking office to drop off their new photographs and their most favorable clippings.

The Keith office, which handled such vaudeville giants as the Marx Brothers, Eddie Cantor, W.C. Fields and Will Rogers, wasn't exactly bowled over by what the two "dancing demons" had to show them. But they did give the pair some audition bookings—actually tryouts—in second, third and fourth rate vaudeville houses, at close to starvation wages. The serendipity was that agents did come out to scout the performers.

Abe Lastfogel, of the powerful William Morris Agency, was impressed. He booked Hope & Byrne into what was known in those days as a "deuce spot" in a William Morris package on the Keith Circuit. It was an important circuit, and because it gave birth to a lot of great talent, did exceptionally well at the box offices around the nation.

Hope & Byrne played six months in most of the larger cities except Manhattan—Philadelphia, Washington, Baltimore, Reading, Youngstown, Pittsburgh, York, and Providence, Rhode Island. They did four shows a day when they were with Keith. It was hard work but excellent seasoning for the two.

By the time they reached Reading, Pennsylvania, the team received what's known in show business lingo as a "money review" from the local critic.

> Hope & Byrne have untamed feet; they just behave as if they have no control whatsoever, but of course their control is perfect. The boys are versatile dancers, with humor crowded into every step.

It may have been a "money" review to them, but when Hope asked the producer for a raise, using the Reading review to strengthen his claim that he and George deserved more, he was laughed at.

Undaunted, the two cocky vaudevillians bid Mr. Keith good-bye and took the next train for New York City, where they checked into the Somerset in the Times Square area.

The Somerset was the kind of theatrical hotel that would carry performers if they were down on their luck. Hope recalls that "George and I hadn't been reduced to cuffing it yet. With the reverses we'd had in the past, [we] had learned to save our money for the time when nothing was coming in."

In addition, they were sure they would have no problems getting more bookings, as there seemed to be a lot of work around. But if there was, they weren't getting any of it during the first few weeks of the summer of 1927.

Hope talked about going back to pool-room hustling in order to sustain himself. Then he and Byrne received a call from a choreographer named Earl Lindsay who wanted to audition them for a forthcoming Broadway revue called *Sidewalks of New York*.

A Charles Dillingham production, *Sidewalks* had words and music by Eddie Dowling and Jimmy Hanley. It starred Dowling's wife, Ray Dooley, who had scored a smashing success in the *Ziegfeld Follies* the previous year. Filling out the cast was the comedy team of Smith & Dale, Jim Thornton, an old-time vaudeville monologist, and a young tap dancer named Ruby

Keeler whose name was being linked to superstar Al Jolson in the Broadway columns.

Hope & Byrne were signed for specialty dancing and small speaking roles that shrank to virtually nothing as rehearsals progressed and the inevitable tightening of the book by its creators took place. Finally the pair was relegated to being little more than chorus boys in the production.

Ruby Keeler, who later was a neighbor of Hope's in Palm Springs, remembered Bob Hope's contribution to the show, but said there isn't a great deal to remember. According to Keeler, "Hope and his partner were nice gentlemen, who were fair dancers. Bob wasn't particularly funny, but then I don't think he tried to be. . . . They were an act that would go on after the curtain came down, not at the end of the show, but between scenes to give them time backstage to change the scenery and do costume changes."

This left Hope with plenty of free time to indulge in one of his favorite pastimes—skirtchasing, though Keeler categorically stated, "He never chased me." Which in itself is surprising, considering that she was one of the comeliest actresses on the Broadway scene. Hope may have been aware, however, that Keeler was Al Jolson's girl, and decided to keep hands off. Besides there were plenty of other girls around.

During rehearsals, Hope fell in love with an aspiring actress named Barbara Sykes. Barbara lived at the Princeton, another theatrical hotel. Hope solidified the relationship by moving into the Princeton himself.

After four weeks of rehearsals, *Sidewalks of New York* opened for its tryout at the Garrick Theater in Philadelphia, in September 1927. For their four-week stay in Philly, Hope, Byrne and a two other male members of the cast rented an apartment at the Maidstone Apartments, near Walnut and 10th.

The show received fair reviews, but it was too long and needed tightening. During this doctoring, Hope & Byrne's contribution was whittled down to the point where it barely paid them to put on makeup.

In addition, Hope missed Barbara. He wired her to come and

stay with him and "keep house" in his apartment. She wired back that she would be on the six o'clock train. However, she neglected to say which afternoon.

After a week of dutifully going to the station to meet the six o'clock train from New York, and finding no Barbara Sykes on it, Hope wired her again. She wired back apologies, and promised to be on the next one. She showed up as promised and Hope was happy again.

In Barbara's honor, Hope's pals in the show threw a party for her that night at the Maidstone after the performance. It was wild, with a lot of bathtub gin and rotgut whiskey, and considerable noise. The management refrained from breaking up the soiree until a few of the chorus boys from the show turned up as drag queens. Then the police were called.

When the blue-coated gentlemen burst in flailing billy clubs and blowing their whistles, everyone scattered. Hope and Barbara took refuge in one double bed, in his half of the apartment he shared with Byrne and the others. Fortunately, Hope and Barbara's bed was behind a sliding door that cut the apartment in two and insured them a modicum of privacy for their last night together.

"The Last Night" because, while they lay in each other's arms, Barbara confessed that the reason she hadn't shown up in Philadelphia earlier was because after Les departed New York, she fell in love with a piano player who lived at the Princeton. She'd been reluctant to be away from him. At the same time she didn't have the heart to tell Hope.

Swallowing his disappointment, Les walked her to the train station the following noon. That was the end of Barbara, but only the beginning of Bob Hope's checkered sex life, which took a bizarre turn after she jilted him.

Years later, Hope himself, in a moment of rare candor about his personal life, which he hardly ever discusses, shocked a roomful of his writing staff by telling them about a one-night stand he'd had back in his vaudeville days with the premier drag queen of the time.

According to Hope, he was lying in bed alone in his

Philadelphia hotel room when this absolutely gorgeous chick, who was actually a man in woman's clothing, poked his/her head into the room and purred enticingly, "Leslie?"

"Yes, honey. What do you want?"

"I want to suck your cock."

Hope took one look at the drag queen's long gold tresses, dimpled cheeks, fluttering eyelids and sexy curves, then said to himself, "Why not?" and invited the transvestite in.

"At least four of us heard Bob tell us that, and we were absolutely stunned," recalls one of Hope's former writers who happened to be in the room when his boss made his confession but who wishes to remain anonymous. "We just couldn't believe our ears or understand why this man, Mr. U.S.A. himself, would admit to us that he'd had a homosexual affair. After all, we weren't exactly his fishing buddies. But he did and we all heard it. The only thing he didn't tell us was whether or not he enjoyed it."

5

After a four-week run in Philadelphia, and a one week stand in Atlantic City, *Sidewalks of New York* opened on Broadway in October 1927 to rave reviews. Hope & Byrne were barely mentioned. During the out-of-town tryout, their parts had been condensed to an opening bit. They then disappeared from the stage until the curtain calls two hours later.

One reviewer wrote, "Ray Dooley has something, Ruby Keeler has something, and Bob Hope has something too, but you won't notice it if you sit back about five rows."

After eight weeks, the management let Hope & Byrne go, in order to save their salaries. Their Broadway debut, which they had hoped would skyrocket them to fame, had been a fizzle. What's worse, their vaudeville career seemed to be in the garbage pail as well, since they had foolishly kissed off the Keith circuit. You didn't do that to E.F. Albee, who ran the Keith circuit and was considered the czar of vaudeville. As far as Albee was concerned, Hope & Byrne no longer existed. Added to the negatives was the growing appeal of radio, and that new gimmick, talking pictures. Both were killing vaudeville. Only the big stars could be assured of work.

An agent named Milt Lewis got them a second spot on an eight-act vaudeville bill that was a showcase theater where booking agents scouted fresh talent. Because the bill was top-heavy with dance acts, Hope decided to shrink their hoofing routine and add more jokes.

Their choice of material was unfortunate.

Sample:
HOPE: Where do bugs go in the wintertime?
BYRNE: Search me.

Hope invited Johnny Hyde of the Morris Office to come uptown to see them. But Hyde, who later discovered Marilyn Monroe, sent word that he wasn't interested. When Hope asked why, Hyde replied, "Because I've heard about your act. You ought to quit the business."

Desperate, but not defeated, Hope wired Mike Shea, a booker he knew in Cleveland, to get him and Byrne work. "Anything!" Shea wired back that he could book them for three days at Newcastle, Pennsylvania, for fifty dollars for the team for the engagement. They would be the third act on the split-week bill that had only three acts.

Before they went on to do their first show at Newcastle, the manager asked Hope, "When you finish your act, would you mind announcing the show that's going to play here next week"

Hope agreed, and when he and Byrne finished their routine, to mild applause, they danced off the stage and into the wings. Then Hope sidled back out onto the stage, in the effeminate way he remembered Frank Fay made his entrance, and said, "Ladies and gentlemen, next week there's going to be a good show here." (MILD LAUGH) "Marshall Walker is going to be here with his Big Time Revue. Marshall is a Scotchman. I know that, because when he got married, he held the ceremony in his backyard, so his chickens could get the rice."

That joke got a tremendous laugh, so Hope added another Scotch joke at the next performance. "That got a laugh, too," recalled Hope, "so for the next show I added two more. The manager came back and said, 'Hey, that's good. Keep it up.' So the next night when I came out to announce Marshall Walker's coming show, I discovered I was doing four or five minutes.

After the show, the orchestra leader took me aside and said, 'You two guys are doing the wrong kind of material. Your double act with dancing and those corny jokes have nothing. Mr. Hope, you ought to be a master of ceremonies by yourself.'"

As difficult as it was to break up an act after all the travail he and George had been through, Hope was inclined to agree with the musician. The laughs he received doing his solo announcement confirmed his hunch that he could be successful alone, something he'd been telling himself for some time.

While he was agonizing over how to broach the subject to his partner, Byrne saved him the trouble.

"I know what you're thinking," Byrne said. "I don't blame you. I'm going back to Columbus to start a dancing school."

Relieved to be let off the hook so painlessly, Hope phoned his friendly booking agent in Cleveland, Mike Shea, and told him he wanted to do a single.

"What kind of a single?" asked Shea.

"Singing . . . dancing . . . talking . . . and working in blackface."

To this day Hope isn't sure why he threw in blackface, except possibly because the top blackface artist of them all, Al Jolson, was hot at the time. At any rate, Shea got him a booking playing a different theater every night in Cleveland. Delighted, Hope went out and bought all the Jolson accouterments: a big red bow tie, white cotton gloves, a box of cigars and a small derby.

He threw in a bunch of blackface jokes, some of which he'd stolen from other acts he'd seen, and some of which he'd created himself. For an encore he added a song and dance routine.

During this engagement he lived at home with his family, and fattened up on Avis's cooking. One night he missed the streetcar he normally took to the theater, and consequently didn't have time to put on the cork for his blackface routine. So he just ran out on the stage with the derby and the cigar, and his face as pale as the Paleface he later played in the Paramount picture of the same name. He was surprised when his jokes went over better without the black makeup.

As he danced off the stage, Mike Shea was waiting for him in the wings. Hope thought Shea would be annoyed with him for screwing up his act, but Shea surprised him.

"Don't ever put that cork on your puss again," said Shea. "Your face is funny enough the way it is."

****

Actually Hope, at twenty-four, was neither funny-looking nor handsome. But with his slightly protruding jaw and overexaggerated pug nose, his face was just enough off-center to keep audiences from taking him seriously as a leading man, no matter how sexy he imagined himself. Everything about his face, from sandy hair to his defiant chin and mischievous brown eyes was perfect fodder for the eager caricaturist.

No one around Cleveland was knocking at his door to do his caricature, however, or even to give him a job doing his single act. So after breaking in his new act in Cleveland, he decided to try his luck in Chicago.

Chicago was the hub of the entertainment business in the midwest, but its audiences weren't quite as choosy or sophisticated as the ones in New York City. In the Windy City, reasoned Hope, he'd have a better chance of getting work as a master of ceremonies in one of the many vaudeville houses that had been converted to motion picture theatres, where between films there were a few live acts, usually tied together by a bouncy emcee. It seemed right up Hope's alley, so he moved into a cheap theatrical hotel around Dearborn Street and made the rounds of the booking agents.

It was January 1928. May came and he was still "at liberty," behind in his hotel rent, and owing the local greasy-spoon joint nearly two hundred bucks for coffee, doughnuts and snacks.

Hope had a chance meeting with an old pool hall pal from Cleveland, Charlie Cooley.

When Cooley asked him how he was doing, Hope was just desperate enough to tell him the truth, in spite of the fact that he felt he had found his niche being an emcee. Feeling sorry for his old buddy, who seemed to have lost all his spirit, Cooley escorted him inside the Woods Building and upstairs to a small office that was the domain of Charlie Hogan, a sandy-haired, freckle-faced Irishman, not much taller than Mickey Rooney, and the head of National Playhouses, Inc.

Cooley had enough clout to tell Hogan, "This guy's a great emcee. I want you to get him a job."

It so happened that Hogan had a spot for Hope. "How would you like to play the West Englewood Theater on Decoration Day?" he asked. "It pays twenty-five bucks for three shows."

To a fellow who'd just had his credit cut off at the coffee shop, twenty-five dollars seemed a God-sent windfall.

Hope's new act went over so well at the Englewood that as he skipped off the stage after the third show, the manager approached him and said, "You open at the Stratford Sunday."

"How come?" asked Hope, totally surprised.

"Charlie Hogan called me," explained the manager. "I told him you were okay so he told me to tell you he's putting you in as master of ceremonies at the Stratford."

The Stratford was a popular local vaudeville house, and Hope was delighted with the assignment until he discovered that the emcee who had worked there before him had been such a local favorite that he'd been held over for two years. He had an engaging personality, and audiences couldn't get enough of him. Unfortunately all that acclaim went to his head, so when he became difficult to work with the management decided to let him go. Following his dismissal, a number of other emcees had been hired to fill his shoes, but the Stratford audiences resented them and were extremely hostile—sometimes to the point of throwing tomatoes—with the result that nobody else endured.

To please an already hostile audience with his string of tired jokes would be harder than getting laughs from the lions in the Roman Coliseum. But Leslie had no choice. He'd do his stuff and hope for the best.

His opening Scotch joke about the farmer who got married in his backyard paid off with a respectable laugh, so he followed that with a couple of other tightwad jokes. But the one that really fractured the audience was the one he told about his grandfather, "Robert Casanova Hope. He was a sort of a Casanova of the Gay Nineties . . . he had a notch in his cane for every women he'd made love to. That's what killed him— one day he leaned on his cane."

Hope was beginning to learn, even then, that sex and sexist jokes, usually paid off.

On the bill with Hope at the Stratford was a strange pointy eared, elfin-like little fellow named Barney Dean. He wasn't much of a dancer, but according to his pals, he had a good sense of humor, and the booking agents liked to have him around, because he made them laugh.

When the first show was over, Hogan called Dean and asked how Hope had done. Dean raved about him. "You'll be hearing from this kid. I guarantee it."

Dean was a good prognosticator. Hope stayed at the Stratford for six months, replacing the first emcee in the hearts of the theater regulars. His salary went from twenty-five dollars a day to three hundred a week.

"It was like having a job in a mint with toting privileges," wrote Hope in *Have Tux, Will Travel.*

❖ ❖ ❖ ❖

Because the Stratford engagement proved to be a turning point in Hope's career, everytime he played an engagement in the Chicago area after he became successful, he saw to it that Charlie Hogan received a five percent commission. This arrangement continued until Hogan died, in the early seventies.

In addition to being a financial success for the longest period in his life, Hope acquired Barney Dean as a friend as a result of the Stratford run.

Many years later, after Hope became an international star and a fixture at Paramount Pictures, and vaudeville was dead, there were no bookings around for guys like Barney Dean. Hope insisted that the front office at Paramount hire Dean as a film writer for five hundred dollars a week. Dean couldn't write any better than he could dance, but he turned out to be the ideal Court Jester for Hope and Crosby when they were doing the "Road" pictures. He performed invaluable services for them, but particularly for Hope. Besides keeping Hope company on the set between takes, and making him laugh, he was not afraid to come up to Hope and tell him that he thought the material he was doing "stank," if indeed it really did stink, and Hope would actually take it from him. Dean also acted as Hope's "beard" when the comedian wanted to go out to dinner or to a movie with a girl who wasn't his wife.

During his successful run at the Stratford, Cupid's arrow once again pierced Hope's romantic heart. His new flame was Grace Louise Troxell, a raven-haired Chicago native with a doll-like face and model's trim figure. Grace Louise wanted to be an actress, but worked as a secretary to keep food on the table and to pay the rent. Hope found her sitting behind a desk in a booking agent's office.

It was nearly love at first sight.

After Grace Louise moved into his small, southside apartment, she campaigned to get Hope to include her in his act. Easy to get along with, especially if the girl filled a size 34 brassiere, Hope agreed to make her a foil for him in the new act he planned to take on the road following his Stratford engagement.

Believing Hope had played the Stratford long enough and needed a change to broaden his appeal and give him more seasoning, Charlie Hogan wangled him some bookings on the Keith-Western Time, this was a junior Orpheum Circuit a notch below its senior counterpart. And since Hope was weary of being an emcee, and Grace Louise was eager to show her stuff in front of an audience, he decided to take on a partner once again.

As a result, he threw together an act for him and Grace Louise. In it, he utilized many of his monologue jokes, and stole a few from other comedians he had worked with on various vaudeville bills. What he came up with was a routine very popular in those days called a "Dumb Dora" act. It was the kind of routine George Burns & Gracie Allen did, with Grace Louise playing Gracie and Hope playing her straight man.

GRACE LOUISE: (walking out on stage with a little paper bag in her hand) How do you do?
HOPE: What do you have in that little bag?
GRACE LOUISE: Mustard.
HOPE: What's the idea?
GRACE LOUISE: You never can tell when you'll meet a ham.

Their jokes became even more sophisticated as the audience warmed up to them.

HOPE: Where have you been?
GRACE LOUISE: I just came back from the doctor.
HOPE: And how are you?
GRACE LOUISE: The doctor said I'd have to go to the mountains for my kidneys.
HOPE: That's too bad.
GRACE LOUISE: Yes, I didn't even know they were up there.

Hope and Grace Louise opened in St. Paul, Minnesota, where they were a moderate hit. They moved on to South Bend, Indiana, home of Notre Dame.

As he always did, Hope made his entrance wearing a brown derby and smoking a big cigar. To his surprise, his entrance was greeted by a huge roar of applause. And his first joke got one of the biggest laughs he'd ever received. Hope didn't know what he was doing that warranted such a big response until learning that Notre Dame was a Catholic college, and that Al Smith, a notorious Catholic machine politician from New York, was running for President that year against Herbert Hoover. A brown derby and a cigar were Al Smith's trademarks.

Following South Bend, Hope and Grace Louise played Sioux City, Peoria, Bloomington, all to appreciative audiences. By the time they reached Fort Worth, Hope was on "next to closing," which was the featured spot on every vaudeville bill, and reserved for the top act. But at the first show in Fort Worth, Hope laid an ostrich-sized egg. He was so furious that when he left the stage and hurried into the wings, he told the theater manager, "Get me a ticket back to the U.S.A. I'm quitting."

Later, while Hope was sitting dejectedly in his dressing room when a man named Bob O'Donnell knocked and came in.

"What seems to be the matter, Fancy Pants?" he asked the comedian.

"My act's not for foreigners," complained Hope.

"It might be if you'd give them a chance to hear what you're saying," suggested O'Donnell.

"What are you talking about?"

"You're talking too fast for Texans. These people down here aren't in a hurry. They aren't going anywhere. They came in here to enjoy themselves. It's summertime, and it's hot. Let them understand you. Why make it a contest to keep up with you. Relax a little, and you'll be all right."

Hope thought it was pretty nervy of this square from Texas to be giving him advice on how to play comedy, and had no intention of slowing down. But then someone tipped him off that O'Donnell was the head of the International Vaudeville Circuit, and knew what he was talking about. Consequently Hope slowed down his fast patter just a few beats, and to his surprise, found that he was getting laughs, even from those tough Texans in the ten-gallon hats.

While experimenting with his delivery speed, Hope accidentally discovered something else that worked: his method of not waiting for the laugh at the end of a punch line but proceeding right onto the first words of the next joke. By then he'll usually be interrupted by the laughs and stop. But if the audience still doesn't get it, he can almost be certain of pulling a laugh out of them by stopping on his own, and then adding: "Take your time. I've got all night." Or else just stare them down into laughter.

Fort Worth audiences liked the act and when he and Grace Louise moved their routine to Dallas they were a solid hit. Without telling Hope about it, O'Donnell wired the Keith office in New York and told them that they ought to catch his new act.

When Hope got back to New York City, Keith spokesman Lee Stewart suggested that he do his tryout stint at the Jefferson, on 14th Street. Hope was leery of the Jefferson; it was a dumpy theater, and its audiences were boisterous. It was the kind of audience where you needed a catcher's mask if they didn't like you, and Hope didn't own a catcher's mask and had no intention of buying one. He told Stewart to book him into a decent uptown theater or he wasn't interested.

He couldn't afford to be as independent as he sounded, but there was another vaudeville circuit called the Publix Circuit that had shown interest in booking him.

His independence paid off. Lee Stewart came back to him and said he'd booked him at Proctor's 54th Street. Proctor's was a barn-like theater that also showed movies. Occasionally movie stars made personal appearances there to promote their latest films.

Hope didn't know anything about Proctor's when he was making the arrangements with Lee Stewart to play there. But he knew enough to ask who would be on the bill before him.

"Leatrice Joy," replied Stewart. "She's doing a personal appearance."

At the time Leatrice Joy was a movie star married to leading man John Gilbert. The couple was having marital problems, which made headlines almost daily.

"What's the money?" Hope asked.

"Very little," said Stewart.

"The littler the better," said Hope.

"You kidding?"

"No, I don't want any money. I just want your office to see my act."

Stewart was astounded. Who ever heard of an actor wanting to work for nothing? He didn't argue the point.

Arriving at Proctor's stage door the afternoon he was to play his first performance there, Hope asked the doorman, "How's the audience here?"

"The toughest in the city," he replied.

Hope broke into a cold sweat, as he waited in the wings watching Leatrice Joy doing her thing. He realized his was going to be a make-or-break performance insofar as his career was concerned. So while he waited in the wings, he tried to think of a show-stopper that he could use as his entrance line.

One came to him even as Leatrice Joy took her bows. The orchestra went into Hope's entrance music. Skipping out onto the stage with his derby cocked jauntily to one side on his head, he gazed down at a lady in the first row and said, "No, lady, I am not John Gilbert!"

The line stopped the show, and from that moment on everything he said got huge laughs. He took several curtain calls before the audience would let him go. And as he pranced off the stage to thunderous applause, he was greeted in the wings by an agent from the William Morris office. The agent informed him that Abe Lastfogel, president of William Morris, would like to offer him a representation contract. Lastfogel would like him to come downtown to his office after the next show and sign with the Morris office.

Feeling somewhat cocky after his hit performance, Hope told the agent that if Abe Lastfogel wanted to sign him, he should bring the contract to the theater.

"Mr. Lastfogel wouldn't consider that," said the agent. "Don't you know he's the top agent in the business?"

"I thought he was the shortest," quipped Hope, having heard Lastfogel was only five-feet tall.

Cracking jokes about Lastfogel's size was a no-no in the business and likely to keep you from ever being handled by the agency, if it ever got back to him. But with the applause from his last show still ringing in his ears, Hope wasn't worried.

As it turned out, Hope didn't need an agent. After the second show the Keith office offered him a three-year contract at $400 a week. Businessman that he was turning out to be, Hope got his price up to $450 before shaking hands on the deal.

But though the money was excellent, and a three-year guarantee of employment, more than he had ever hoped for, the important carrot in the deal was that the Keith office controlled New York's famed Palace Theater on Broadway. If you weren't with Keith, your chances of playing the Palace were zero. And since the Palace was the plum of all vaudeville bookings, it was every ham's dream to play there.

6

Although there would be other lean years before Bob Hope became a major star, the Keith deal started him on his elevator ride to the top.

Hope's first weekly paycheck under the new contract was handed him closing night after he and Grace Louise played the Albee in downtown Brooklyn. When he looked at the $450 check in his hand, he realized for the first time it was not a dream. He'd taken John D. Rockefeller's advice about not trusting anybody and now he was on his way.

Out of his new income he sent fifty dollars a week home to his mother, raised Grace Louise's salary from fifty dollars a week to one hundred. He kept the balance for himself.

One of the first things he wanted was a new expensive car. He was torn between a Packard and a Pierce Arrow, the one with those sleek headlights growing out of the front fenders. He was standing on the sidewalk outside the Pierce Arrow showroom, with his ample nose pressed against the plate glass window, trying to make up his mind whether or not to take the plunge, when Al Lloyd, a former theatrical agent who'd become an insurance salesman, sidled up to him.

When Lloyd heard that Hope was considering springing for a fancy new car, he made a pitch for Hope to put the $250 he was going to use for a down payment into an insurance policy instead. "In this business you're going to have to put something away for your old age," Lloyd advised him.

Hope wasn't sure it would be much fun driving around on an insurance policy, but he eventually acquiesced to Lloyd's sound advice and put the money into an annuity. He's been putting his money away for his old age ever since, and while it's unlikely he'll ever have a need for any more annuities now that he's over ninety, with approximately $400 million in assets, he's never been able to kick the habit.

After a successful engagement at the Albee, Hope and Grace Louise, who was unbilled in the act because she was just his stooge, were booked into Proctor's 54th Street again, the first week of November 1929. There an unfortunate thing occurred. His act not only got a good review from *Variety*, the week of November 5, but Grace Louise's performance was singled out for special mention.

> Strongest is interlude in which Hope feeds for unbilled girl, latter of the sap type and clever at handling comedy lines. . . . Next to closing here, and had no trouble handling spot.

The special kudos Grace Louise received caused her to corner her live-in boyfriend and employer, Mr. Hope, and demand the chance to do a single spot by herself, or else she would quit the act.

Miffed that the girl he said he loved and vice versa was giving him ultimatums when she should be thrilled just to be working with him, Hope immediately wired Mildred Rosequist, asking her to replace Grace Louise in the act. She could start the following week when he'd play Cleveland. As a bonus, he also asked her to marry him.

To his shock, Mildred wired back that she was engaged to someone else, and not interested in him or the work. Hope had no choice but to make up with Grace Louise, who was not so difficult to make up with since she'd been fearful that he was calling her bluff.

In Cleveland, Hope introduced Grace Louise as his fiancée to his family.

This marked the first time Hope had played his hometown since becoming a hit in vaudeville. All of the family attended his opening matinee performance, except Avis and Harry. Avis felt that her presence might add to her son's nervousness and ruin his performance. Hope's father, Harry, who was in one of his sober periods, was employed out-of-town doing the ornamental stonework on a courthouse.

Clevelanders were happy to see a local boy make good, and the *Cleveland Press* gave the act a rave review. So much so that Avis was able to shake off her stage fright by the next day's matinee. She sat in the first row applauding every sound that came from her son's mouth. While he was taking his bows, she beamed and announced to the strangers in the neighboring seats that her boy was lots better than Frank Fay.

That was the good news. The bad news came at the celebration at the house that night. His older brother Jim took him aside and told him that Avis was suffering from cervical cancer. So far, she'd refused exploratory surgery.

Whether or not his news had any bearing on Hope's decision to buy his parents a new house now that he was in the chips has never been made clear. It's probable that he wanted Avis to live out her years in a better home than the shabbily furnished one she and Harry were currently renting.

Consequently he talked his brothers into contributing toward a purchase of a house for the old folks.

Though the country was still reeling from the previous month's stock market crash, Hope's older brothers, Ivor, Fred and Jim, all seemed to be unaffected by the Depression. Fred's butcher shop was still turning a modest profit, Ivor was doing well in metal products, and Jim was a supervisor for the Cleveland Power Company.

Hope, with his customary luck in real estate, had picked a good time to buy his parents a house. Because of the market crash, real estate values were plummeting all over the city, especially in the exclusive Cleveland Heights area.

Hope opted to do his house-hunting in Cleveland Heights, and spent all his free time seeking the right place for Avis and Harry. He finally found a three-bedroom house at 3323 Yorkshire Road, which he picked up, furniture and all, for $6,500.

Hope kept the purchase a surprise from Avis, however, until the day he was to leave town. Then he walked into his mother's room and announced that he was throwing out all her old furniture.

Avis protested that the furniture they had was good enough to last her and Harry until the end of their days. But Hope insisted. The furniture had to go. Then he and his brothers put her in the family car and drove her to the new place.

When she saw the house, and was told that it belonged to her, Avis was stunned. Her sons helped her move, and the only things Hope allowed her to keep from the old place were her sewing machine, her upright piano, and of course Harry.

❖❖❖❖

In those days, the other important vaudeville circuit beside Keith was the Orpheum. The Keith Circuit extended only as far west as Chicago, but if you were a hit on the Keith you were automatically a candidate for the Orpheum, which included such Canadian cities as Winnipeg, Calgary and Vancouver. From there you worked your way down the Pacific coast to Seattle, Portland, San Francisco, Los Angeles and San Diego, and then last to New York City by way of Salt Lake City, Denver, Omaha, Kansas City, and St. Louis.

After Cleveland, Hope and company headed west, and while he didn't lay any eggs along the Orpheum Circuit, some of the critics were lukewarm about his material. Until then, Hope had never employed a writer. He was content to rely on his own wit and creativity at artfully lifting and switching other comics' material. What helped him overcome his lack of first-class writing skill was an ingratiating personality and his slick, sassy way of delivering a one-liner. Even today his delivery and his willingness to kid himself have helped him overcome material that he has become stuck with when his highly priced writers have failed him.

But in 1930 he wasn't a big enough star to get by on his name alone. If he expected to entertain sophisticated audiences at venues like New York's Palace theater, which he had yet to come near except when he was taking a stroll down Broadway, he wouldn't be able to surfeit them with second-hand jokes including the "groaners" he'd come up with on his own.

In New York, Hope hired gagman Al Boasberg to write fresh material for him. Boasberg, a gargantuan man, loved to eat, hated exercise and got most of his inspiration while sitting in a bathtub of hot water. He was one of the all-time top comedy writers. Before he died of a heart attack (no wonder) in the mid-thirties, he had written jokes for Burns and Allen, Jack Benny, Eddie Cantor, the Marx Brothers and many others. When Benny was at the height of his radio career he used to pay Boasberg one thousand dollars for a single joke. Boasberg originated the Burns and Allen "Dumb Dora" routine but he didn't really enjoy them as an act. He once told Groucho Marx that he had invented a radio.

"We already have radio," Groucho reminded him.

"Yeah, but this one's different," said Boasberg. "It's special."

"What's so special about it?" asked Groucho.

"It has a Burns and Allen eliminator on it. No matter how hard you try, you can't tune in Burns and Allen."

Boasberg was as irreverent as he was funny, and he couldn't be pushed to create comedy when he wasn't in the mood. Once, while working for MGM's Irving Thalberg, who'd hired him to write some material, Boasberg was several days behind in turning in a scene for the Marx Brothers' forthcoming film, *A Night at the Opera.*

When Thalberg pressed him, he finished the scene, then cut each line on the page into individual strips and tacked them to the ceiling. He called Thalberg to come to his office and pick up the scene. When Thalberg arrived, Boasberg pointed to the ceiling, which was covered with strips of paper.

If he'd been tall enough, Thalberg would have hit the ceiling. As it was, he just became apoplectic and called for a ladder.

Hope didn't have a formal writing agreement with Boasberg. But when Boasberg, whose home was in New York, thought of a funny piece of business or a witty line, he'd jot it down on a piece of paper and mail it to Hope in whatever town Hope was playing.

When Hope was in New York the two would meet at Lum Fong's Chinese Restaurant until the early morning hours sharpening lines, rewriting bits while the owner poured tea for them and wished they'd go home so he could close the joint.

Eventually Boasberg came up with a revue format for Hope, who wanted to go on the road with something new. The revue was called *Antics of 1930*, and it had a *Hellzapoppin* flavor to it, though it was years ahead of Olsen and Johnson. This included plants in the audience heckling Hope during his monologue, talking through his routines in loud voices as if there was nothing taking place on the stage. Bob would talk back to the audience and insulting them, and do take-offs on current vaudeville personalities, like Rudy Vallee. There was even a little political satire.

One of the jokes resulting from Hope and Boasberg's Lum Fong sessions was so successful that it was soon being stolen by other comedians working around New York. Hope would come out on the stage and say to the audience, "I was standing out in the lobby when a lady came up to me and asked if I could tell her where she could find the restroom. So I told her it was just around the corner, and she said, 'Don't give me that Herbert Hoover talk—I'm in a hurry to go.'"

According to Hope, "that line got one of the biggest laughs I ever got in vaudeville."

With Boasberg's help, Hope's monologue became sharper. "It's very exciting at my hotel . . ." began Hope. "The other day a lady guest came down to the lobby and demanded to see the manager . . . she said, 'Something terrible is happening. There's a bat in my room.' And the desk clerk said, 'Don't get excited, Lady. We'll send up a ball. . . .' Another guest walked into the lobby and asked, 'Is there a Katz in the hotel?' And the clerk told him, 'No, there's no Katz here.' And the guest said, 'Well, if one comes in, send him up . . . the mice are eating my shoes . . .'"

In addition to improving Hope's material, Boasberg was responsible for getting him his first Hollywood screen test. Convinced that Hope had the makings of a popular screen star, Boasberg told Bill Perlberg, an agent with the William Morris Hollywood office, to look at Hope's act.

When Hope and Grace Louise played the Hill Street Theater in Los Angeles two weeks later, he received a call from Perlberg asking, "Would you like to make a movie test?"

Hope acted as if he couldn't be more disinterested. "I'll try to work it in," he said, "though I was planning to play some golf this week."

"Forget the golf," said Perlberg. "Get out to the Pathé lot next Thursday. I'll set up a test for you."

At Pathé, Hope was surprised that there was no script for him and Grace Louise to perform. "Just do your vaudeville act," he was told, "and we'll film it."

When the cameras rolled, Hope went into his monologue. Then he and Grace Louise did their Dumb Dora routine. According to Hope, the stagehands and camera crew laughed, "I went away convinced I'd soon be bigger than Charlie Chaplin."

On a high from such sanguine thoughts, Hope and Grace Louise took their first Sunday off and drove down to Agua Caliente, south of the border. There he lost six hundred dollars at the gaming tables. He wasn't very upset because he was certain that with his screen test in the can, it would only be a matter of time before every studio in Hollywood would be after him to sign a contract.

Consternation set in, however, when Hope returned to his hotel and found no messages. Unable to endure the suspense, he took the initiative and phoned Perlberg.

"When do I see the test?" Hope asked.

"Do you really want to see it?" responded the agent.

"Of course," replied Hope.

"Well, go out to Pathé tomorrow, and they'll show it to you."

"What'd *you* think of it?" asked Hope, apprehensive by now.

"Go and see it," suggested Perlberg, artfully dodging the question.

It was not "Hail the Conquering Hero" when Hope walked onto the Pathé lot. Not only weren't there any "hails," but he couldn't find someone willing to escort him to a projection room.

Finally Hope persuaded a janitor to lead him to Projection Room C, where he and Grace Louise sat in the dark and waited for the new Charlie Chaplin to strut his stuff on the screen.

A little way into the screen test, Hope could understand why everyone from the policeman at the gate to William Perlberg was treating him like a pariah. After seeing his puss projected on the screen, he knew he would have been smarter to stay in Caliente and become a jockey at their crooked horse-racing track.

"I'd never seen anything so awful," Hope once told Steve Allen. "My nose came on the screen twenty minutes before I did. I couldn't wait to get out of the screening room. I wanted to run all the way to Salt Lake, our next booking, and clasp vaudeville to my bosom."

7

On the way back to New York along the Orpheum Circuit, Hope decided to spend more time on golf. He figured the game was one way he could get his mind off the giant omelette he had laid at Pathé.

Seeing other performers come down into the hotel lobby every morning toting golf bags full of clubs made him want to take a whack at becoming another Bobby Jones, the world's most famous golfer. He followed them out to the public course in Salt Lake and hit a bucket of balls. Encouraged by his success on the practice tee, he played eighteen holes with rented clubs. Then he bought his own set, and started taking lessons from whoever was the home pro in whatever town he happened to be playing.

By the time he arrived back in New York, he had already broken 100. He's never become a scratch shooter—his lowest handicap has been nine, but he's been a slave to the game ever since, and one of its enthusiastic boosters.

Although business on the road had been good, in spite of the deepening depression, it ate at Hope's insides that he hadn't yet played the Palace. He brought the subject up to Lee Stewart one day when the two were lunching at Lindy's.

Stewart assured him it was only a question of time before he'd be trodding the hallowed boards at the Palace. Meanwhile, he advised Hope to return to the road. He'd get new booking for him.

While waiting, Hope returned to Cleveland to visit his mother. Avis said she was worried about her youngest son, George. He was flunking school, but he seemed to show some interest in acting. Could Bob, she asked, get his kid brother a job in the theater?

Hope wasn't impressed with his brother's acting ability, but he saw a way he could please his mother and at the same time save some money in salaries for his act. He'd use George as one of the stooges he planted in the audience, and pay him only half of what he was paying the current stooge. He knew George was in no position to argue about salary. So George became a member of his cast for their next engagement at New York's Coliseum Theater. It was another movie house that featured vaudeville. Hope was all set to fracture the midtown Manhattan audiences, and therefore impress the Keith boys enough that they'd be on their knees, begging him to play the Palace.

Unfortunately, on the bill with him at the Coliseum was the movie, *All Quiet on the Western Front*, starring Lew Ayres. Not only was the film a huge hit, but it had a terribly downbeat ending: the hero was killed by a sniper's bullet while reaching for a butterfly over a barbed wire fence, seconds before the armistice was to be declared.

Unaware of the deadly impact that scene had on the audience—most of the people were reduced to tears—Hope skipped out in front of the footlights to do his monologue. Through no fault of his own, except the bad timing, Hope's monologue was a dud. There wasn't a snicker. It was quieter than on the Western Front after the armistice.

Hope was so annoyed that he went to Lee Stewart and told him he wanted to quit the engagement. But Stewart warned him that if he ever did that, not only would he never play the Palace, but he'd be banned from vaudeville forever.

Hope reluctantly finished out the week, altering his opening monologue to accommodate the conditions. Then he, Grace Louise and George left for another crack at the Orpheum

Circuit. They finished the tour playing the Cleveland Palace in February. Although Bob was happy to see his mother, he was startled at how thin and sickly-looking she had become. That was depressing enough, but the weather was cold and bleak, the theater business was just so-so because of the Depression and the competition from movies, and Louise was going around acting as if she were already Mrs. Bob Hope.

Suddenly, the picture brightened. While he was sitting in his dressing room, removing his makeup, the door opened and in walked Lee Stewart, with the news that Hope was booked into the Palace for two weeks, starting the following Monday.

It was the opportunity he'd been waiting for. Now that it was here, or nearly here, Hope was visibly scared. Years later, in an interview with *Silver Screen Magazine*, Stewart recalled: "Before the close of his Cleveland run, Bob was on the verge of a breakdown. I've never seen him so nervous. But in spite of his nervousness, his brain was clicking. He knew he was going into fast company, and that he was following the best in the business."

His nervousness was even more understandable when he discovered who was on the bill with him. Actress and comedienne Bea Lillie was the headliner, and Hope was billed in the second spot. Also on the bill was singer Vivian Segal, fresh from Hollywood, as well as Harry Hirschfield, the popular humorist and cartoonist.

It was the second holdover week for Bea Lillie, and consequently the critics didn't pay much attention to the new acts that joined the lineup. Most of the press comments about Hope's *Antics of 1931* were lukewarm, but the one that galled him the most was one written by Jerry Wald, In the *New York Graphic*. Wald would later become an important Hollywood writer and producer as well as the prototype for Sammy Glick in Budd Schulberg's devastating portrait of filmland, *What Makes Sammy Run?*

"They say," wrote Wald, "that Bob Hope is the sensation of the midwest. If that's so, why doesn't he go back there?"

Hope was clearly disappointed. Only the Palace's Celebrity Night on Sunday saved him from complete obscurity.

Celebrity Nights were usually sellout events, with many of the stars of Broadway shows turning up to do their thing for their peers, who didn't get an opportunity to catch other shows during the week because they, too, were on the stage, in their own shows. (Legit houses were dark on Sunday night.) Fortunately, the manager of the Palace, Elmer Rogers, asked Hope if he would do the Celebrity Night honors and be emcee. A number of superstars had promised to be there, including Eddie Cantor, Ken Murray, Ted Healy, and Al Jolson.

The mere thought of being on the same stage with those people made Hope jittery. But he braved it out, and then got lucky, when he and comedians Ken Murray and Ted Healy got into an ad-lib exchange.

It began when Ken Murray got out of his seat in the fifth row, ran down the aisle, climbed over the brass railing into the orchestra pit. Using the lap of the trombone player, he clambered onto the stage.

Reaching Hope, he said, "I'd like to tell a joke."

"I've already heard it," quipped Hope.

This got a roar from the audience, and loosened them up to the extent that they began to laugh at every syllable Hope uttered.

In short, Celebrity Night at the Palace made Hope a celebrity—of sorts.

Although Hope's two-week gig at the Palace could hardly be termed a smashing success, enough people saw him and laughed at him as a straight emcee that he was soon given a second opportunity to conquer Broadway—this time in a legit show.

Moreover, Hope's vaudeville salary on the Keith Circuit, which he played regularly until the spring of 1932, shot up to nearly a thousand dollars a week as a result of his exposure at the Palace. When you realize that most social historians consider 1932 to be the darkest year of the Great Depression, one thousand dollars a week was a great comfort to the former newsboy from Cleveland. He was beginning to get some very encouraging reviews from the media as well. On September 4, 1931, the *Chicago Sun* said:

> Equipped with the sort of engaging personality that could put over any material, Hope has the practiced trouper's idea of timing his humorous sallies, emphasizing them with mugging and pauses so that they never miss.

In March of 1932, *Variety's* review of Hope's act noted his ability to hold an audience.

> Just a so-so lineup on tap here this week, with Bob Hope playing the role of lifesaver. It took this funster to finally wake them up to a degree. After he got under way he had them howling at his comedic reactions and great comedy material. Hope is a pippin performer, and ad-libbing helps tremendously to get many extra laughs from the supporting company, and the musicians in the pit, as well as the audience.

In 1932, Hope played the Palace Theater in New York with his *Antics of 1932.*

That spring a producing group, consisting of Bobby Connelly, Norman Anthony, Lou Gensler and Russell Patterson planned a musical revue for the fall entitled *Ballyhoo of 1932.* The show got its inspiration from the very popular but smarmy magazine of the time, *Ballyhoo,* which featured burlesque versions of advertising, photographs of leggy, skimpily dressed girls, and off-color cartoons and jokes. The show had a revue format, and slated to be in its cast were some of the biggest purveyors of comedy in the business: Willie and Eugene Howard, Lulu McConnell and Vera Marsh. The cast would include dancers Paul and Grace Hartman, plus a plentiful supply of beautiful chorus girls.

Billy Grady, Al Jolson's manager, suggested to Gensler that he add Bob Hope to the cast. He brought the producers over to the Palace and after catching Hope's act they decided to sign him.

The salary was less than he was earning in vaudeville—only

six hundred a week—but noticing the lineup of beautiful chorus girls, Hope decided to swallow the cut. Moreover, the Keith Circuit was gracious about granting Hope a leave of absence to perform in *Ballyhoo*. They figured he'd be an even more valuable name to them after he'd appeared in a Broadway show.

Ballyhoo rehearsed all summer, and opened in Atlantic City in August of 1932, in the Nixon Theater on the Steel Pier.

Opening night was a shambles, with everything going wrong, from the electrical system breaking down to the chorus girls not being ready for their opening number while the orchestra had to play the overture over and over to stall for time. Finally the audience got restless and started clapping their hands in unison. Added to everyone's discomfort the theater actually went dark for a minute as a result of an electric short-circuit. At that moment, Lee Shubert, one of the investors, started to worry that the audience would panic, so he buttonholed Hope and told him to go out on the stage and entertain so the people wouldn't get frightened while the stagehands worked to get the lights back on.

Hope told Shubert he was afraid a premature appearance would spoil his regular entrance later in the show. "Don't be so hard to work with," Shubert chastised the young comic. "Get out there and do your thing."

Since Shubert was such a power in the theater world, Hope reluctantly agreed.

Skipping out onto the stage under just a dim work light, Hope led off with, "Ladies and gentlemen, this is the first time I've ever been on before the acrobats. But seriously, folks, we're doing a new number tonight, and we rehearsed late. Things aren't quite set up, so please be patient."

Hope stayed there ad-libbing for six minutes. The spot was such a success that Shubert suggested that he open the show that way every night.

Hope said he would if he could throw in a few other funny bits as well, which the producers agreed to. One of the bits that brought down the house came as he was telling a joke during his monologue and was interrupted by a vendor strolling down the aisle, carrying a basket and calling out, "Peanuts . . . Popcorn . . . Crackerjacks."

"Just a minute," Hope yelled down to him. "What's the idea of selling peanuts and popcorn during my act?"

"I have to do this to make a living," replied the vendor. "I only make a hundred dollars a week."

Hope jumped down into the aisle, and said, "How much did you say you make doing this?"

"A hundred a week."

"Give me that basket," said Hope, grabbing the basket. "You get up there on the stage."

Ballyhoo opened at the 44th Street Theater in Manhattan on September 7, 1932. Notices were lukewarm, but because of the big names in the show, it managed a sixteen-week run. Aside from Hope and his antics, there were Willie and Eugene Howard, favorites with the New York audiences. People never tired of their burlesque kidding of the Quartet from *Rigoletto*, which they performed with two buxom female singers in low-cut gowns. The laughs came from the way Willie Howard spent most of the number leering down the cavernous cleavage of the buxom wench standing beside him.

Although the show wasn't a hit, Hope had his first taste of radio performing during its run on Broadway. Twice during the sixteen weeks, he was invited to make appearances on the Thursday evening *Rudy Vallee Fleischmann Yeast Hour*, one of the most popular radio programs of the time. It had millions of listeners, and was considered a very important showcase for performers.

Hope enjoyed working with Vallee, but couldn't quite get used to performing comedy without an audience. As he later recalled, "It seemed strange talking into a microphone instead of playing in front of real live people, though some of the people I played to in vaudeville weren't always alive either, now that I think of it."

Ballyhoo's closing was a disappointment to Hope, but he still had his vaudeville career to pursue. More specifically, an offer to emcee the bill at the Capitol Theater in New York for two weeks, starting December 2, 1932.

Sharing billing with Hope (billed as "Star of *Ballyhoo*") was a rising young crooner from Gonzaga University in Washington State named Harry Lillis Crosby, better known to the world at large as just plain Bing. Crosby, who had recently become a big star thanks to Paramount's *The Big Broadcast*, had come east to host a radio show for Chesterfield Cigarettes that was to start in January, and his brother/manager Everett got him an interim booking at the Capitol.

The Capitol engagement was Crosby's first appearance in the Big Apple, though he was no stranger to Hope at the time they appeared together. They'd met before at the Friar's Club, and seemed to like each other.

Tired of merely singing, Crosby suggested to Hope that they work out a comedy routine they could do together—something with humorous banter of the kind that later made them such a popular duo in the "Road" pictures.

In the routines they worked out, they kept insulting each other. Audiences loved it.

Reviewing the show at the Capitol, the *New York Times* wrote:

> Bing Crosby pours out his heart to the strains of several sentimental ditties. Bob Hope pops in and out of the show as master of ceremonies, bringing with him some amusing chatter on the political situation.

Following his stand at the Capitol, Hope's personal life becomes a bit of a mystery.

Hope has always maintained, in every puff piece about him, and in every autobiography and authorized biography that he's approved, that he's only been married once in his life, and that's to the former Dolores Reade. Hope claims to have wed Dolores in Erie, Pennsylvania, on February 19, 1934, after just a two-month whirlwind romance. He also claims that he was in such a love-sick fog at the time that he can't remember why they chose Erie, Pennsylvania.

According to the marriage bureau in Erie, there is no record of Bob Hope marrying Dolores there on February 19, 1934, or on any other date. However, according to documents he did marry his former vaudeville partner and live-in girlfriend, Grace Louise Troxell, in Erie, Pennsylvania, on January 25, 1933, more than a year before the time he claims to have married Dolores there.

On the marriage certificate (shown in the illustration), Hope gave his name as Leslie T. Hope, occupation "salesman," and his home, 3323 Yorkshire Road, Cleveland, Ohio. Grace Louise gave her occupation as "secretary" and her home address as 642 West 64th Street, Chicago, Illinois.

Since Hope wasn't yet the kind of name whose marriage the press would have been much interested in covering, and since he also could have used all the publicity he could get to further his career, there seems to be little reason for all that secrecy.

Nonetheless, the marriage ceremony was kept completely under wraps. It was performed in a small office by an alderman named Eugene P. Alberstadt, and witnessed by William M. Dill, "Clerk of the Orphans Court."

Inasmuch as nobody in the Hope camp is willing to discuss it, what happened to the comedian's marriage to Grace Louise after that is not known, though apparently they were still together in July 1934, for she appeared with him in his act at Loew's State, according to a small blurb in the New York *Herald Tribune*.

What *is* known is that after Hope and Grace Louise were divorced (it must be assumed they were divorced, for the date and place of their legal split is also shrouded), Grace Louise returned to Chicago, where she married David Halper, a prominent Chicago gambler and bookmaker whose customers were mostly show people. Being one of those customers, comedian Milton Berle can attest to this part of the story. He was a friend of Hope's in those far-off vaudeville days, and knew Grace Louise as well, but only as Hope's vaudeville partner and not his wife. In an interview with me, Berle expressed surprise when I informed him that Hope and Grace Louise had been married.

Sometime after her marriage to Halper, Grace Louise gave birth to a daughter who is now about sixty and who lives in West Hollywood, California. And here's another interesting fact: this daughter whom supposedly Halper fathered, has received a monthly support check from the Hopes for years.

I confirmed this with William Faith, who did publicity for Bob Hope in the sixties and who later wrote an authorized book about him. And though he doesn't mention it in his Hope biography, Faith tells me he was aware of Hope's first marriage at the time of the writing; also he knew of Grace Louise's subsequent marriage to Halper and the birth of her child, but was forced to suppress the information in exchange for Hope's cooperation in giving him access to some of his business files and personal papers.

✿ ✿ ✿ ✿

In the spring of 1933, following his marriage to Grace Louise, Hope got another shot at playing the Palace. The Palace had fallen on hard times by then, and was no longer able to attract the top names of the period. Most of them either had gone to Hollywood or were appearing in legitimate shows. But what was bad for the Palace was good for Hope. For his appearance there led to another rung up the show business ladder.

During Hope's latest Palace engagement, Broadway producer Max Gordon dropped into a matinee one day to check out the talent. More specifically, he was trying to find an actor to fill the role of Huckleberry Haines in his forthcoming Broadway musical production, *Roberta* (or *Gowns By Roberta*, as it was called until it opened), with music and lyrics by Otto Harbach and Jerome Kern.

The show was about a college fullback who inherits his aging Aunt Roberta's fashionable dress salon in Paris. When he takes over the business, he falls in love with the chief designer who turns out to be a Russian princess. The fullback's best pal is a fast-talking orchestra leader named Huckleberry Haines.

By the time Gordon caught Hope at the Palace, all the major roles had been cast except for Haines. Singing star Fay Templeton had been lured out of retirement to play the aging Madame Roberta; George Murphy had been hired as the fullback, but because he didn't physically look the part he was replaced early in the rehearsals by booming baritone Ray Middleton, and was given the smaller part of Haines's manager. Tamara, a popular Russian chanteuse on New York's nightclub circuit, was hired to play the Russian princess. Also in the cast, but playing bit parts were Sydney Greenstreet, Imogene Coca and a young juvenile named Fred MacMurray. In the pit was an unknown drummer, Gene Krupa, who was taking nightly lessons in reading music from the trombonist in the orchestra, Glenn Miller.

After seeing Hope, Gordon felt that he was a perfect Huckleberry Haines, and went directly to Jerome Kern and Otto Harbach with the news of his find.

Somewhat square and snobbish, the two composers were reluctant to hire what they called "a cheap vaudevillian." They wanted a higher class of actor since this was Broadway "the-atuh." But Gordon persisted. He talked Kern and Harbach into at least catching the young comedian's Palace act, so they could judge for themselves.

Hope's routine that matinee was centered around his monologue. Every time he told a joke, a stooge in the balcony would yell out, "You think that's funny? Let me tell you the one about the two Irishmen who . . . " etc., etc.

With his snappy rejoinders, Hope was a smash that afternoon, and needless to say, was hired to play Huck Haines in *Roberta*.

Although he enjoyed listening to the Kern–Harbach score during rehearsals, Hope wasn't too satisfied with the lines Harbach's book provided him with. He didn't think they were funny enough, but every time he suggested a joke to replace one of them, Harbach or the director would put him down. So he suffered silently. He hated to deliver lines that he was sure weren't going to get laughs.

He was right about his lines. Many of them just lay there on the opening night of the tryout run in Philadelphia. The entire production, in fact, didn't get enthusiastic reviews either, which is ironic because *Roberta* went on to become a smashing hit. It has since become a classic, having twice been made into major Hollywood films, once starring Fred Astaire, and much later staged twice by Hope for television.

It's likely, however, that its Jerome Kern-Otto Harbach score which included the standard "Smoke Gets in Your Eyes" had more to do with making it a hit than its libretto.

Roberta seemed like anything but a hit in Philadelphia. This prompted Max Gordon to send for Hassard Short, the New York director, to doctor the show, then being directed by Jerome Kern himself. He did so, restaging the numbers and rewriting the book, which the Philadelphia critics felt was too serious and melodramatic for a musical comedy.

There was a scene, for example, in which the Russian princess is confessing to Huck Haines that she loves her football player, but the romance isn't going anywhere. This was a buildup to the "Smoke Gets in Your Eyes" number. Tamara led into it by telling Hope, "There's an old Russian proverb, 'When your heart's on fire, smoke gets in your eyes'." Since he felt the scene was getting too serious, Hope wanted to add, "We have a proverb in America too. 'Love is like hash. You have to have confidence in it to enjoy it'."

Harbach thought the line was too flippant and out of character. It wasn't the proper cue for his beautiful ballad. So he insisted that Hope forget the idea.

However, when the scene didn't seem to be working during the Philadelphia tryout, Hope took Jerome Kern aside and told him that he thought some humor might help the scene, and that he knew how to fix it.

"Really?" said Kern. "How?"

"Put this line in," and Hope told him the hash joke.

Kern smiled and said, "Why not?"

Hope put the hash line in the show that night, and it got one of the biggest laughs of his Broadway career.

Needless to say, the joke remained in the show for the duration of its run.

The show received mixed reviews when it opened on Broadway at the New Amsterdam Theater in November of 1933. However Hope's portrayal of Huck Haines was singled out for special mention by New York's two most powerful critics, Brooks Atkinson of the *Times* and Percy Hammond of the *Herald-Tribune*.

Atkinson wrote, "The humors of *Roberta* are no great shakes, and most of them are smugly [sic] declaimed by Bob Hope, who insists on being the life of the party and who would be more amusing if he were Fred Allen."

Percy Hammond added to Hope's scrapbook of good reviews by writing, "Mr. Bob Hope is a quizzical cut-up. He's an airy sort of chap who says things like, 'Long dresses don't bother me, I have a good memory,' and 'Love is like hash; you have to have confidence in it to enjoy it.'"

Encouraged by the success of those two lines, Hope tried to slip more of the same kind of material into Harbach's book.

"He'd met a fellow around Broadway named Billy Reade, who'd hang around the stage door to sell him one liners for ten and twenty bucks a crack," recalls television producer William Harbach, Otto's son. "Then Bob would stop in the middle of a scene during a performance to turn to the audience and try out one of the jokes he'd bought. Corny jokes like 'Did you hear about the farmer's daughter who wouldn't go to bed with the traveling salesman? . . . Well, you won't because it hasn't happened,' or something like that. Well, this was a book show, and my father would hit the ceiling every time Hope would try to throw in one of these vaudeville jokes that had nothing to do with the plot. But Hope wouldn't stop until my father finally had Billy Reade barred from the theater, and banned from hanging around the stage door."

Roberta ran from November 18, 1933 through July 14, 1934, and while Max Gordon was somewhat disappointed in the overall reviews and the moderate length of its run—twice he had to ask the cast to take cuts in their salaries—*Roberta* managed to make stars of Bob Hope and Fred MacMurray. Fred MacMurray's stardom didn't even wait until the show closed.

During the show's Broadway stand, MacMurray was spotted by a Paramount Pictures scout and offered a screen test in Hollywood. Paramount was looking for a new leading man to appear opposite Claudette Colbert.

When MacMurray told Hope about the offer, all Hope could think of was what happened to him at Pathé. He figured they'd kick MacMurray's brains out on the coast. Hollywood wasn't for a nice guy like MacMurray. But MacMurray was not to be deterred. He took a leave of absence from the show to make the test in Hollywood, and never came back.

Four months later, when Hope was walking down Broadway, he looked up at the Paramount Theater marquee and did a big take. In glittering letters were the words:

CLAUDETTE COLBERT IN "THE GILDED LILY"
with
Fred MacMurray

MacMurray conquered Hollywood on his first try, but Bob Hope had to wait several more years for his own stardom.

8

With his success in *Roberta*, thirty-year-old Bob Hope had everything he needed to make him happy: a comfortable three-room apartment on Central Park West, a Scottie dog named Huck, a brand new Pierce Arrow, and a chauffeur to drive it.

What he no longer had was a wife. Sometime between July and December of 1933, Grace Louise left him and obtained a divorce—either in Juarez, Mexico, or Reno or Las Vegas or possibly even Chicago.

At any rate, Hope was back leading the carefree bachelor life, but as Christmas 1933 approached, he was beginning to get the holiday blues, not only because his mother Avis was terminally ill with cancer, but also because he was without a steady girl. At least according to his *Roberta* pal, dancer George Murphy, who decided to do something about the situation and introduce him to Dolores Reade, a singer who was working at the Club Richman, a nightclub on West 56th Street.

On the night of December 21, Murphy and his wife, Julie, invited Hope to join them for a drink at The Vogue after the show. The Vogue was an "in" spot of the period and it attracted celebrities, mainly because of the high caliber of the talent it featured. Bea Lillie had initially made it famous, and was rumored to be one of the club's owners.

Also in the Murphy party was Bobby Maxwell, a musician, who was dating Dolores at the time. Nevertheless, Hope was drawn to Dolores the moment he laid eyes on her as she stood at the mike, singing a Libby Holman-type torch song. It was her only appearance at this club. Dolores was in her mid-twenties, tall with a shapely figure, a good voice and a sultry way of putting over a number. Moreover, she wasn't the ordinary bimbo type of chorine he was used to romancing; Dolores had class, and that appealed to him.

Dolores wound up her set with "It's Only a Paper Moon" and "Did You Ever See a Dream Walking?" then strolled over to the Murphys' table, where she was introduced to Bob. After that Murphy suggested that they all go dancing at the Ha Ha Club.

After ordering a round of drinks, the Murphys headed for the dance floor. Bobby Maxwell excused himself to go to the men's room, and never came back. This left Hope alone at the table with Dolores, who, after some snappy small talk, asked him if he'd care to dance, since he hadn't asked her.

"No, I don't like to dance," he replied. "I do enough of that in my business."

From that, Dolores assumed he was a chorus boy in *Roberta*, so she didn't press the issue. "Then," she later recalled, "George and Julie came back to the table, and George asked me to dance. George was a beautiful dancer, and we had danced around the floor just once and I was enjoying myself, when Bob cut in, saying, 'I changed my mind.' I was so astonished that for the first time I took a good look at him. I saw a very young, and very serious fellow. Then and there I knew I liked him."

Bob knew he liked her too, and before the evening was over, he invited her to see him in *Roberta*. Since she was singing nightly at The Club Richman, she chose the Wednesday matinee performance on December 27.

Ordinarily, Hope wouldn't allow a week to pass without attempting to make another date with a woman he found attractive. But his mother's illness had taken a turn for the worse, and knowing this would probably be the last Christmas he could be with her, he spent the holiday in Cleveland at her bedside. He tried to cheer her up with jokes and anecdotes about his show business experiences.

Avis's weight dropped to seventy-six pounds and she was too weak to get out of bed. But she wasn't too weak not to smile at her son's one-liners.

Realizing there was little he could do to help her—it was just a matter of time, according to her doctor—and knowing she was in the capable hands of the private nurse he hired, Hope returned to New York the day after Christmas.

He resumed his courtship of Dolores. He was disappointed when she didn't come backstage to see him in his dressing room after she attended the matinee of *Roberta*. He couldn't understand it. He waited two days, and when he still hadn't heard from her, he dropped in on her at The Club Richman one night after his own show.

"What happened?" he asked, after she had sat down at the table with him.

"I didn't know you had such a big part in the show," she explained somewhat sheepishly. "I thought you were just a chorus boy. When I saw you had the second lead I felt so embarrassed that I didn't know better, that I was ashamed to look you in the face. And I'm still embarrassed."

He assured her that was nothing to be embarrassed about. "I'm just glad the reason you didn't come back wasn't because you thought I'm a lousy actor." That broke the ice, and he invited her to join him on New Year's Eve.

"I work that night," she replied.

"So do I," he said. "But let's do something after."

Whatever they did after, for the first two weeks in January, their romance heated up to the point that Dolores's mother, Theresa Kelly DiFina, a strict Catholic, voiced her disapproval of her daughter's choice in men. Theresa was the kind of mother who didn't believe that any of the men Dolores or her sister Mildred brought home were good enough. And this "chorus boy" from *Roberta*, who wasn't even Catholic, was no exception. Consequently Mother Theresa couldn't have been more pleased when Dolores got booked into the Embassy Club in

Miami for a four-week engagement, with an option for another four, beginning January 14. She was convinced that a vacation from this "wisecracker" from *Roberta* would probably cool Dolores's ardor.

Absence only succeeded in making their hearts grow fonder. Hope was on the long-distance phone with Dolores frequently and on one of these calls he proposed marriage.

Dolores was delighted. She offered to break her contract at the Embassy Club and return to New York immediately to marry him.

They were in the throes of trying to decide exactly when to tie the knot, when Hope received word from Cleveland that his mother had died on Sunday, January 22.

Hope went to Cleveland for the funeral (which he paid for), then returned to New York, saddened and depressed. In need of a sympathetic shoulder to cry on, he phoned Dolores in Florida to ask her to quit the Embassy Club and take the next train home.

She returned to New York on February 13. It should have been smooth sailing to the altar from that moment on. But in every good romantic drama there's usually some kind of a hitch—boy meets girl, boy loses girl, boy gets girl. In this case two major problems stood in the way of the young lovers: (1) Dolores mother still opposed the nuptials on the grounds that Hope wasn't good enough, and (2) one of the New York gossip columnists alluded in print to another woman—presumably Grace Louise—in the comedian's life.

Dolores was able to overcome her mother's objections by telling her it was none of her business whom she married, but the item in the gossip column was quite another thing, and she sulked for several days after reading it. With his gift of gab, Hope was able to persuade her that the other lady was no longer in his life.

It's at this point where the official story strays from the facts and fiction takes over.

Not only is there no record of the Hopes getting married in Erie, Pennsylvania, on February 19, 1934, as pointed out earlier, but the following story appeared in the New York *Herald-Tribune* on August 4, 1934:

BOB HOPE TO WED MISS READE

Bob Hope, who played a comedy lead in *Roberta* last season, and Miss Dolores Reade, a nightclub singer, announced their engagement yesterday. They will be married about Thanksgiving. Both are appearing in the stage show at the Capitol Theater. Mr. Hope also has appeared in *Ballyhoo of 1932* and in vaudeville.

As of now, half-a-century or so later, there's no denying that Hope and Dolores are actually married. And if they're not they've been getting away with murder on their joint tax returns for years. But when and where they actually tied the knot is a secret that very few people besides the combatants know. Milton Berle knows, for he was there to witness the ceremony, along with several other invited guests from the show business fraternity, including the late Fred MacMurray, the late George Murphy and his wife, and Ritchie Craig, a Broadway vaudevillian who contributed jokes and comedy routines to Hope's act. And although the whole thing is a little hazy in Berle's mind today, he seems to remember that the nuptials took place in a Catholic church, somewhere in Manhattan, in either the fall of 1934 or the spring of 1935.

One thing Berle knows for sure: he would not have gone to Erie, Pennsylvania, to see the Pope married.

"Anyone who would go to Erie for any reason, let alone to get married, would have to be crazy," states Berle with a flick of his cigar ash. "And I'm not crazy, although I've been married enough times for people to think I am."

9

Ever since he caught Bob Hope's act at the Capitol and the Palace, Broadway agent Louis Shurr had been after Hope to let him represent the comedian for a film career.

Known simply as "Doc" to the Times Square crowd, because on several occasions he had been able to doctor and salvage some sinking Broadway shows, Shurr had an impressive list of clients including Bert Lahr, Victor Moore, Lou Holtz, Billy Gaxton, Ken Murray and George Murphy. Shurr was a short, rather unattractive, dark-haired bachelor with the angular face of a lizard. This didn't limit his success, and he was able to attract the most beautiful showgirls in town to squire to restaurants and theater openings (and often to his apartment afterward). Part of his appeal to the ladies was that he owned a mink coat that he loaned to his date-of-the-night for Broadway openings. It was just for the night. The coat was repossessed as soon as the evening was over.

A nice man, Shurr was convinced that Bob Hope had a future in Hollywood. Hope wasn't. He'd been sour on the movie business ever since his fiasco at Pathé. He showed little enthusiasm when Shurr told him that he would try to get him the part of Huckleberry Haines in the film version of *Roberta*.

Hope gave him the go-ahead, but wasn't surprised when RKO cast Fred Astaire in the role. It further confirmed his belief that Hollywood wasn't for him and vice versa. It was the beginning of a beautiful relationship between him and Shurr, however, which lasted until Doc's death in Hollywood in the sixties.

In passing I should mention that one thing that made Hope and Shurr so compatible was their mutual love of women, and Shurr's ability to procure girls for his friend when Hope was in the mood for some extramarital stimulation.

✿ ✿ ✿

Nor was Louis Shurr discouraged by RKO's rejection of Hope for the Huck Haines part. Shurr succeeded in getting him a shot at a featured role in a Jack Oakie film at Paramount. However, the studio demanded a screen test of Hope before the front office would sign him to a picture deal. And the only reason Hope agreed to another test was because it would be shot at a studio in Astoria, Long Island.

Hope didn't believe he came off any better in the Paramount test than he had at Pathé, so he was surprised when he was offered the role.

"The problem was," recalls Al Melnick, Louis Shurr's West Coast partner, "they offered Bob $2,500 for four weeks work. When I told them that he was making $1,750 a week on Broadway, they weren't impressed. They wouldn't match it so Bob turned them down."

Soon after that Educational Pictures in Astoria made an offer for Hope to appear in a musical short with Leah Ray called *Going Spanish*. If they liked the end result, they would offer him a deal to appear in five more short subjects. *The* comedy gimmick in *Going Spanish* was simplistic: after the two of them accidentally ate some Mexican jumping beans, they would jump around nonstop.

It was a miserable attempt in comedy. After sitting through it in a theater on Broadway, Hope bumped into columnist Walter Winchell on the sidewalk.

"How'd you like your film debut?" asked Winchell.

Hope made a face, and replied, "When they catch Dillinger they're going to make him sit through it twice."

Winchell thought that such a funny remark, he made it the lead item in his next morning's syndicated column. Jack Skirball, who ran Educational Pictures, was not amused. He phoned "Doc" Shurr and yelled, "We're having enough trouble selling that guy without him knocking the picture! He's fired!"

Shurr warned Hope against such a loose-cannon mouth but Hope didn't care. He was still gainfully employed in *Roberta* on Broadway. In addition, Warner Brothers cast him in a shortened Vitaphone version of Cole Porter's 1929 Broadway musical, *Fifty Million Frenchmen*. This was scheduled to be filmed at the Eastern Studio, on Avenue "M," in Brooklyn.

This turkey was retitled *Paree, Paree* and though it was anything but an Oscar contender, Hope did manage to curb his mischievous tongue this time after viewing the film at a screening for studio executives. They apparently thought enough of it to pick up his option for five more Vitaphone comedy shorts, also to be filmed in Flatbush during the next two years.

✿✿✿✿

Radio was showing an interest. In June, Hope had another guest slot on the *Rudy Vallee Fleischmann Yeast Hour*. Reviewing this appearance, *Variety* said Hope's jokes were "aged," but that his delivery was modern and that he "wore well" because of "his self-joshing."

The problem of his material playing second fiddle to his delivery of jokes is something that has plagued Hope all the way from small-time vaudeville to superstardom. That he's been able to overcome mediocre material is a tribute to the man's comedy genius and personality.

When Max Gordon posted the closing notice of *Roberta* in July 1934, Hope was confident that Shurr would get him another Broadway show. In the meantime, he'd return to vaudeville where he now commanded a healthy four-figure salary. Dolores would add beauty and class to his act.

The tour lasted ten weeks. It might have toured the entire country if "Doc" Shurr hadn't phoned Hope to say that Harry Richman wanted Hope for his new Broadway musical, *Say When*.

Richman was a song-and-dance headliner, but he also delivered a few jokes. He was known for his elegance—he worked in tails and top hat and carried a silver-handled onyx cane which he used as a prop when he danced. He'd been a big star in vaudeville but his career was on the wane, as was vaudeville itself. When he got together with librettist Jack McGowan and composer Ray Henderson to produce *Say When*, it was in an effort to jump-start his stalled career.

Richman gambled fifty thousand dollars of his own money in the venture, and persuaded notorious mobster Charles "Lucky" Luciano—known to insiders as "Charlie Lucky"—to put up the rest.

The plot was nonsensical. It involved two radio entertainers (Hope and Richman) who fall in love with a rich banker's two daughters on a transatlantic liner. The banker (Taylor Holmes) objects to his daughters marrying into show business, until the characters played by Hope and Richman discover that the old man has a floozy-type blond on the side. With this knowledge they blackmail him into giving his consent.

Also in the cast in a small part was one Harry Gurgesen from Brooklyn, later to become Prince Mike Romanoff of restaurant fame. (In the show, he was billed rather pretentiously as Prince Michael Romanoff.) Gurgesen wasn't much of a performer, but after hours he amused everyone when he passed himself off as an expatriate prince who'd fled to America after the Russian Revolution.

Despite the presence of Richman and Hope, *Say When* was doomed from the moment the curtain rose. The score by Ray Henderson and Ted Koehler was mediocre and the book by Jack McGowan didn't gel. Hope had most of the laugh lines, which Richman tried to change, since he was the star. But the tampering didn't help, and Hope's ad-libbing during the dull spots wasn't enough to hold the book together, as he discovered during the show's Boston tryout.

Hope had another problem while *Say When* was in Boston. In order not to be home alone in New York, Dolores had accepted a booking to do a straight singing act at Loew's State in Boston at the same time her husband was playing there.

Dolores didn't have enough confidence in herself to do a single; moreover, she didn't know how to stage her own act.

Hope was unable to attend her first show at 11:00 A.M. She was doing five shows a day. While she sang to a half-empty house, Hope was lolling around in his hotel bed after a late-night rehearsal. A little later he received a frantic call from a tearful Dolores. "They didn't like me," she sobbed. "The band is too loud and everything is wrong."

Hope dressed and rushed over to Loew's State in time to catch her second show. He recognized the problem immediately. Her act lacked showmanship. Dolores just walked onto the stage and sang.

Hope made some obvious suggestions to the manager: first, tone down the orchestra, so it didn't overpower her delicate voice. Second, give her more dramatic lighting.

These improvements seemed to pull her act together, and Dolores survived the rest of the booking. But Dolores didn't like doing a single. So when Bob accepted other Broadway roles without her after *Say When* closed after only a sixteen-week run on Broadway, Dolores was content to retire from show business and put all her energy into making a nice home for Bob in their Central Park West apartment.

✿✿✿✿

Hope was offered another shot at radio. He'd have to audition, but if the sponsor, Bromo Seltzer, liked him, said the ad agency, he would be the emcee for a radio show featuring Jane Froman and James Melton, with Al Goodman's band supplying the music.

Hope was concerned that the material he'd been using in his

vaudeville act was stale. When he confessed his fears to Harry Richman, who was thinking of retiring, the entertainer drove Hope to his upstate mansion and gave him access to his joke file. It was a mother lode of great material.

For two days before the audition, Hope culled the best of the jokes from Richman's file, and put together an audition monologue that really paid off. The Bromo Seltzer people were delighted, and signed Hope.

The show premiered on January 4, 1935 with a studio audience in attendance. *Variety*'s review of the opening show was discouraging, but it stopped short of panning Hope. It said he was "intermittently very funny, but that he relied too much on mugging, which could not be seen by the radio audience." The paper felt that "better material was required" and signed off with, "Hope is easy to take, but hard to remember."

With the help of writers Lester White and Fred Molina, Hope improved his monologues for subsequent shows. In one instance he did a parody of a society editor doing a rapid-fire Walter Winchell-like delivery:

"Flash . . . Newport, Rhode Island . . . Box of matches goes off in Reginald Dipster's hip pocket . . . Not permanent . . . just a flash in the pants . . ."

After discarding that format, Hope decided to try another boy-girl routine like the one he'd been doing with Louise in his vaudeville act. The only trouble was, Louise was about to quit the act, because she and Hope were splitting up, and she wanted to return to Chicago. So it became necessary to replace her with another girl.

"That's how I entered Bob Hope's life in the spring of 1935," Patricia Wilder reports from her home in Manhattan today.

At the time, Patricia was a sixteen-year-old blond with an attractive figure and a thick southern accent. "I was in New York, having run away from mah home in Macon, Georgia, for the second time. Mah uncle, Fred Ryan, and I were having lunch one day at Dinty Moore's on 46th Street—that's where a lot of theatah people hung out. While we were eating, a young man came over to our table—I later found out he was from

Louis Shurr's office—and asked me if I would like to be in the movies. I answered that I would like it very much, but mah uncle tried to put the kibosh on his offer by saying, 'You leave her alone. She's going back to Georgia on the next Greyhound.' The guy slipped me his card and whispered to me that if I changed mah mind to call him. . . . Later, mah uncle put me in a cab with instructions to the driver to take me to the Greyhound Bus Station. As soon as we pulled away from the curb, I told the driver to take me to Louis Shurr's office, which was just off Broadway, instead.

"When I got there, Louis introduced himself and took me into his office. He asked me mah name and everything else about me. I told him that mah name was Patricia Wilder, but that everyone called me 'Honey Chile.' Then Hope walked in, very perky and dressed like a successful actor. He was between performances at the Capitol Theater on Broadway. Louis introduced us, and I could tell from the way Bob Hope looked me over that he liked me.

"He smiled and said, 'Do you want to go on the stage?' and I said, 'Sure.' Then he told Louis to take me to the Capitol to catch his show. He did.

"Anyway, Bob said to me after the show, 'Do you think you can do it?' and I said, 'Sure,' even though I'd never been on the stage in my life. So his writers wrote me into the show."

After "Honey Chile" learned her part, Hope tested her in his vaudeville act before using her on the Bromo Seltzer radio show.

He needn't have worried about "Honey Chile." Nothing threw or embarrassed her. She was completely uninhibited from the moment when she walked out on the stage at the Capitol, thrust her magnificent chest out in Hope's direction, and asked, in her thick spoon-bread accent, "Pardon me, Mistah Hope, does the Greyhound bus stop heah?"

Instead of looking at Hope, she stared out into the audience, which broke everybody up. She was an instant hit.

Consequently, Lester White and Fred Molina wrote some

Dumb-Dora routines for Hope and "Honey Chile" to perform on the *Bromo Seltzer Intimate Hour*.

By today's standards, the comic routines weren't great, but "Honey Chile" had a way of getting a laugh with the dumbest jokes because of her exaggerated Southern accent, and the way she swung her nubile sixteen-year-old body around to emphasize a point.

Sample:

HOPE: You know, Honey Chile, there are a lot of comedians on the air. Why did you pick me as your partner?

HONEY CHILE: 'Cause ah had a fight with mah folks and ah want to do something to disgrace 'em.

HOPE: Uh-huh. Well, you picked the right partner.

HONEY CHILE: You know, Mr. Hope, ah've got two brothers at home that ah'm sure would be a big hit on the radio.

HOPE: What's their names?

HONEY CHILE: The oldest is Ed.

HOPE: What's the young one's name?

HONEY CHILE: Ed.

HOPE: Two boys in one family by the name of Ed?

HONEY CHILE: Yes, Father always said that two Eds were better than one.

In spite of the fact that radio audiences seemed to like Hope's new Southern belle foil, "Honey Chile" arrived too late to save the show. Its Hooper ratings remained low, and the Bromo Seltzer show was canceled after its April 5 broadcast.

Disappointed but not discouraged, the irrepressible Hope spent the summer playing the big Loew's movie houses, with "Honey Chile" as his foil and Dolores as his vocalist.

Whenever his act played close to New York, Hope was tapped on the shoulder by Sam Sax, boss of Vitaphone Comedy Shorts, to fulfill his commitment with them to appear in five more two-reelers.

Hope wasn't crazy about this because it meant he had to get up at six in the morning to be at the studio all made-up, by the time the cameras started rolling at eight. This was hard for him after having to work late at the theater doing his vaudeville act. He was used to sleeping until noon. However, he did manage to complete three more shorts: *The Old Gray Mayor, Watch the Birdie,* and *Double Exposure* before getting a shot at another Broadway production, *Ziegfeld Follies of 1936.* The Shuberts and Florenz Ziegfeld's widow, Billie Burke, produced this one together. Rehearsals began in the fall of 1935. Hope had the leading male comedy role.

Fannie Brice was the major star (it was her fifteenth and last Broadway show), but the rest of the cast wasn't bad, either: Gertrude Niesen, Josephine Baker, Eve Arden, Judy Canova, Cherry and June Preisser, Hugh O'Connell, the Nicholas Brothers and Stan Kavanagh, plus a bevy of gorgeous showgirls. Edgar Bergen and Charlie McCarthy and Ken Murray were also signed to appear but were dropped before the show opened.

Two unknowns at the time, Vincente Minnelli and George Balanchine, were hired to design the sets and choreograph the ballet numbers respectively. (Robert Alton staged the modern dances.)

The show had music by Vernon Duke and Ira Gershwin, and special material by Ogden Nash, Dave Freedman and Billy Rose.

The *Follies* promised to be the glitziest production Hope had yet appeared in on Broadway. And indeed it was a marvelous showcase for him. There was no way you could overlook him in this show. He was in and out of every scene, doing comedy bits and musical numbers with Fannie Brice, Gertrude Niesen and Eve Arden.

At the time Eve Arden was an unknown, although she'd appeared in *New Faces of 1935.* However she wouldn't be for long, because she was big, beautiful and redheaded. She and Hope did a duet with what turned out to be the showstopping number, "I Can't Get Started With You," which featured Eve in a gorgeous evening gown, and Bob in a tux trying to seduce her on a street-corner. Each time Hope sang a few bars of the song to Eve, she would walk away; completely indifferent. Then he'd catch up with her, and lean over her shoulder and breath deeply. But she didn't return his passion.

The number didn't seem to be working, and the doorman at the Winter Garden Theater suggested to Hope, "When you lean over her shoulder panting like that, have her look back at you and say, 'What's the matter? Have you been running?'"

Hope integrated that line in the scene, and Arden got a big laugh with it.

For the blackout of the sketch, Eve finally succumbed to his entreaties and let him embrace her ardently. At that point he straightened up, adjusted his cuffs and said, "That's all I wanted to know. Well, good night." And walked away as the scene went to BLACK.

✧✧✧✧

While the *Follies* was in rehearsal in November, Hope was hired for another radio series, *The Atlantic White Flash Program*. It starred the popular tenor Frank Parker, but the sponsor thought it needed a comic to liven things up. The sponsor favored Hope over a number of other comics because as the star of the forthcoming *Follies*, he could give the program additional publicity. But the sponsor was also interested in hiring "Honey Chile" Wilder, who had become known around New York as Hope's delicious Southern belle. And the only way the show could get "Honey Chile" was to hire Hope, too.

Hope was pleased at the opportunity to work with "Honey Chile" again. For not only was he attracted to her physically, but he loved to do comedy with her.

It's long been believed in Hollywood and Manhattan that Hope and "Honey Chile" were lovers. But "Honey Chile" denies there was anything more to their relationship than a deep attraction to one another. And the most she'll admit to today is, "Rumors get started. How I don't know. We just did cute things together. He loved me . . . he still loves me. And I love him. And I love his wife, maybe better than I do him."

Whatever the truth of their relationship is, there's no denying that Hope was disappointed when "Honey Chile" told him in December of 1935, that her new agent was Zeppo Marx, the fourth Marx Brother, who dropped out of the act after he, Groucho, Chico and Harpo made their fifth film. He had signed her to a movie contract at RKO. She would be moving West to Hollywood immediately. Zeppo told her she'd have a part in a Fred Astaire movie.

❈ ❈ ❈ ❈

Following its Boston and Philadelphia tryouts, *Ziegfeld Follies* opened on January 30, 1936, at the Winter Garden, and as predicted was a hit. The critics were particularly enthusiastic about Fannie Brice and Gertrude Niesen, Eve Arden and Bob Hope. And they were happy about the fact that a *Follies* was on the boards again and in fine fettle after several Broadway seasons without a Ziegfeld extravaganza after Flo's death.

With the success of the *Follies*, Hope was able to settle down to the less nomad-like existence of a Broadway star, with a healthy income. He could sleep late and enjoy a leisurely noontime breakfast with Dolores. He could scan *Variety* and the *New York Times* to hunt for his name in print.

Ever since he first saw his name in lights, Hope believed in the power of good publicity, and has always had two and sometimes as many as five publicity men on his payroll.

After breakfast and a few phone calls to his PR men, Hope would then either work out at Harold Reilly's gym or play golf at Bayside, Long Island, usually with Freddy DeCordova. DeCordova was stage manager of the *Follies* and went on to become a film director and eventually the producer of Johnny Carson's *Tonight Show*. DeCordova soon would become a brunch regular with the Hopes.

Despite her innate shyness, Dolores Hope gradually became an accomplished Broadway hostess. She loved to entertain. She threw bridge parties for her friends and Bob's, and did a lot of charitable work for her Catholic parish. She still does. Often she offered Bob advice about his career, and perhaps criticized a line or a comedy bit that she considered too off-color. Hope had a tendency to rely on blue material, a habit which cost him several radio sponsors who considered hiring him during his early days on the air.

One thing Dolores wanted more than a career or great wealth was to have a family. That wasn't to be. No matter how diligently she and Hope tried, Dolores couldn't get pregnant. And Hope tried hard, frequently dashing out of the theater in a hurry after a night's performance, with the announcement, "I have to get home to Dolores to start a family."

According to Hope's younger brother, George, who died of cancer in 1969, it definitely wasn't Bob who couldn't have children.

"I became very friendly with George at Paramount after Hope brought him out from Cleveland to work for him as a writer because he wasn't able to make a living in Ohio," states Robert Slatzer, author of a very revealing biography of Bing Crosby called *The Hollow Man*. Slatzer was a publicist at Paramount during the height of the "Road" pictures. "And it was George who told me, around the time Bob and Dolores started adopting all those kids, that Bob had once remarked to him that it wasn't *his* fault that Dolores couldn't get pregnant—it was hers. Bob knew that, because of all the girls he had to fend off during his vaudeville days who accused him of being the father of their children. Bob confessed to George that he'd had so many fingers pointed at me over the years saying, 'You're the father!' that he became gun shy. Since then he'd been very careful to take the proper precautions when he played around, said George."

Dolores has never given the reason why, other than to say she "couldn't," but the late Lillian Kramer, who with her husband Nathan Kramer owned New York's Edison Hotel—where many actors, including the Hopes, stayed during their vaudeville travels—told a friend of the author that Dolores once confessed to her that she'd had an abortion before marrying Hope. The doctor had botched the job and in the process permanently damaged her reproductive organs.

It was a startling admission from one who professes to be a

strict Catholic, but Lillian, who was close to the Hopes, had no reason to make up such a story.

Even more startling was a proposal Dolores made to her good friend Rita Canzoneri, wife of lightweight boxing champion (1933–35) Tony Canzoneri. The Hopes and the Canzoneris were neighbors on Central Park West, and the two couples became friendly. Frequently, when Hope was working late at the Winter Garden, Dolores would visit Rita Canzoneri in her apartment.

After Rita gave birth to a baby girl named Denise in the spring of 1936, and brought the infant home from the hospital, Dolores dropped in one night to bring her a baby gift. Toward the end of their visit, most of which she had spent admiring the new baby Dolores turned and said, "Rita, why don't you give me your baby?"

"Are you kidding?" exclaimed Rita.

"No, I'm not kidding," explained Dolores sadly. "You see I can't have a baby. You can have all you want."

10

Although *Ziegfeld Follies of 1936* was a critical and popular hit, it didn't enjoy as lengthy a run on Broadway as was expected. Due to Fannie Brice's illness—she suffered from acute arthritis and a terrible depression resulting from her troubled marriage to legendary showman Billy Rose—its producers announced late in the spring that they would shut down for a vacation during the summer and would reopen in the fall after their star regained her health.

True to their promise, the producers did open the show again that fall, but without Bob Hope. He turned down the Shubert's offer to sign with the *Follies* for the run of the show, because of other offers.

For one thing, Mitch Leisen, a Hollywood director, and Harlan Thompson, a producer, had seen Hope in the *Follies* and wanted him to do his stuff in a revue-type movie Paramount intended to produce to be called *The Big Broadcast of 1936*. For a number of reasons, the picture wasn't released until two years later when, of course, it became *The Big Broadcast of 1938*.

Before the *Follies* shut down for the summer, Louis Shurr had persuaded producer Vinton Freedley to costar Hope with Jimmy Durante and Ethel Merman in a vehicle that would finally be called *Red, Hot and Blue*. Howard Lindsay and

Russel Crouse, who authored some of the biggest hits on Broadway, were signed to write the book, and Cole Porter agreed to provide the words and music.

Red, Hot and Blue was to go into rehearsals late that summer, and open on Broadway at the Alvin Theater in October 1936. With so much talent involved in the production, it seemed a good candidate for box-office success.

But like many "sure things" intended for Broadway, there was many a slip twixt the cup and the hit. With so many temperamental people involved, *Red, Hot and Blue* was a troubled production from the start, beginning with the billing of its stars. Neither Merman nor Durante was willing to accept second billing to the other, and it was a stand-off until Cole Porter finally came up with a compromise suggestion that satisfied them both. They would criss-cross their names like this:

There were also problems with the Lindsay and Crouse book, which was cumbersome and artificial. To top it off the producer wasn't entirely happy with Porter's score, either, which included *It's De Lovely*, that has since become a standard. At one point in the rehearsals Porter became so annoyed with Vinton Freedley picking on his score and demanding new songs that he walked away from the show while it was trying out in Boston. But after the show moved on to New Haven for an additional tryout and the critics panned the music, Porter returned to Boston and labored to improve his score.

Writer Larry Gelbart, who began his career forty-five years ago working for Hope in radio, has since written the books for *A Funny Thing Happened on the Way to the Forum* and *City of Angels*. He also wrote the pilot for the TV series *M*A*S*H*. Years ago he made a remark about troubled musicals apropos of what *Red, Hot and Blue* was going through. The remark became a show business classic. During World War II, someone asked Gelbart what should be done with Hitler if they captured him. Gelbart replied, "Send him on the road with a musical."

Hope was enjoying the experience, however. In addition to having a good part and getting plenty of laughs whenever he opened his mouth, he was working alongside Jimmy Durante for the first time. Schnozzola was a kick to work with and a constant surprise.

At one point in the show Hope and Durante did a sketch in which they portrayed two duck hunters. When they aimed their shotguns into the flies of the theater and pulled the triggers, creating a loud blast, several ducks fell to the stage. The blackout gag was that when they didn't pull the trigger, a duck fell at their feet anyway.

According to Hope, he and Durante rehearsed this sketch until it was letter perfect. But on opening night in Boston Durante's memory seemingly went blank. Befuddled, he stared into the orchestra pit, then came back to Hope, stuttering as he tried to pull his lines out of the air. He then walked over to the wings and said in a loud voice to the prompter, "Trow me da book."

The audience roared. When the same thing happened at the next performance, Hope realized that Durante had deliberately "forgotten" his lines to squeeze out an extra laugh for himself.

Hope wasn't averse to doing a little fooling around himself in order to get a laugh from a not-very-deserving line. Other members of the cast including Merman were thankful he had such a quick wit but were worried he'd overdo his ad-libbing.

In a newspaper interview, an indignant Merman complained to a reporter, "Bob would almost rather kid me and break me up and get the chorus girls on the stage to laughing than he would to make the audience laugh."

But despite his unprofessional ways, Hope couldn't be stopped, and audiences appreciated his attempts to wring humor out of lines that weren't very humorous. The critics commented on this after *Red, Hot and Blue* opened on October 29, 1936.

Walter Winchell said of Hope, "He's a clever comedian when the material is better than it is at the Alvin." However, John Mason Brown wrote, "Hope as a comedian is a cultivated taste, which I must admit I have never been able to cultivate."

John Anderson of the evening *Journal-American* found, "Mr. Hope, is, as usual, urbane, sleek and nimble of accent. He knows a poor joke when he hides it, and he can outstare most of them."

Critics aside, Bob Hope was becoming a genuine Broadway star, with a four-figure salary.

Red, Hot and Blue struggled through the winter months and ended its New York run in May of 1937. Broadway still suffered from the Great Depression. Without smash reviews, and even with a galaxy of stars, you were dead. And a six months run, with only mixed reviews, was about as much as a producer could hope for.

Nevertheless, there was a belief among the producers, its creators and the cast that *Red, Hot and Blue* would do well on tour, and especially in Chicago where Jimmy Durante was a huge favorite.

Durante fans in the Windy City didn't buy tickets, however, and so, after only two weeks, *Red, Hot and Blue* gave up the ghost.

It didn't seem a particularly good year for Hope. His father Harry had died just weeks before *Red, Hot and Blue* did. He was sixty-six. According to Hope, Harry had been pining away for his deceased wife for the past three years, and never adjusted to living alone.

More cheerful news for Hope was that radio and Hollywood continued to beckon. He got a call from Louis Shurr telling him that the Woodbury Soap Company wanted him to emcee a radio show it was sponsoring. It would feature the orchestra of Shep Fields and his Rippling Rhythm and was to be called *The Rippling Rhythm Revue*.

The job was for thirteen weeks over at NBC, with an option for another thirteen if the show got picked up by the sponsor.

With Lester White and Fred Molina again churning out

material for him, Hope performed valiantly for Woodbury Soap. The critical reception (which then weighed very little in radio) was only so-so, but audiences again took a liking to Bob Hope's impudent banter. And, according to *Variety*, "Bob Hope added enough fresh chatter and gags to the show to give the entire broadcast a lift."

While Hope was keeping Woodbury Soap afloat in the ethereal bathtub, *The Big Broadcast* was ready to shoot and Hope was told to report to Hollywood. The reason it took so long for Paramount to set the deal was because the studio wanted Jack Benny for the part Hope got. It waited for Benny to say "Yes" but Jack had bigger fish to fry so the studio had to settle for Hope.

Matters became complicated when Woodbury picked up the *Rippling Rhythm Revue* option for another thirteen weeks. Since the radio show emanated from New York, and Hope couldn't be on both coasts at once, his new radio agent, Jimmy Saphier, worked out a deal whereby Hope could do his monologue for Woodbury by long distance from an NBC studio in Hollywood.

Hope wasn't being completely disloyal to Louis Shurr by going with Saphier for radio. But Shurr was pure Broadway and didn't have an "in" or an interest in advertising moguls at the big agencies. Saphier did.

"All I know is," remembers Al Melnick, Shurr's longtime partner, "Jimmy Saphier was suddenly in there ahead of us getting radio deals for Bob with the account executives without Louis and me knowing about it, and suddenly we found ourselves locked out completely. Well, not completely. Bob paid us a token commission on his radio show."

Hope stayed with Shurr for his movie deals, but he did sign with Saphier for a year, and when that contract expired they entered into a handshake agreement that lasted until the end of Saphier's life.

So it was on to Hollywood for Hope, Dolores and their two scotties.

Hope still had a large chip on his shoulder, when he, Dolores, and their two dogs clambered off the Super Chief in Pasadena on Thursday, September 9, 1937.

Al Melnick, who headed Louis Shurr's West Coast office, met the three of them at the train station. Recalls Melnick today, "Hope's eyes took in the palm trees, the peaceful setting, the warm sunshine and the mountains in the background. Then he took a deep breath and said, 'I like it here. But if they don't like me, fuck 'em! I've got a hundred thousand bucks in the bank."

11

Bob Hope wasn't alone among the transplanted Broadwayites to express contempt for Hollywood in those days. Just about anyone who'd originally made a mark in the legitimate theater, either as a writer, director, performer or novelist, looked down on Hollywood as a place of uncultured money-making heathens. Its product was considered mostly trash, turned out by uneducated former junk dealers, song-pluggers and glove makers. More specifically, Louis B. Mayer, Harry Cohn and Sam Goldwyn. The last couldn't speak straight English but his publicity-man generated malaprops were internationally famous.

Wisecracks about Hollywood proliferated daily and were brought back to New York by novelists and playwrights who'd been lured West by the prospect of easy money but who failed to make it as screenwriters. These put-downs of Hollywood made entertaining dinner conversation in dining rooms from Park Avenue to the Hamptons.

✾ ✾ ✾ ✾

"Hollywood's a great place to live if you're an orange."—Fred Allen

"No matter how hot it gets in Hollywood during the day, there's never anything to do at night."—Dorothy Parker

Advised that he ought to work in Hollywood because the streets were "paved with gold," George Kaufman, who'd long resisted the temptation, retorted, "You mean you have to bend down to pick it up?"

At thirty-four, Bob Hope was still spry enough to bend down and pick up more than his share of the gold no matter how unpleasant were his past memories of the town. Twenty thousand dollars a picture (for approximately ten weeks work), which Louis Shurr had wangled for him, along with a seven-year option arrangement, was not to be spit at.

Though he wasn't to report to Paramount until the following Monday, Hope was already champing at the bit to get started just hours after he and Dolores checked into the posh Beverly Wilshire Hotel at the foot of Rodeo Drive catty-cornered from the Beverly Hills Brown Derby Restaurant.

Not waiting to unpack, he kissed Dolores good-bye and told her to entertain herself while he visited the Paramount Studios on Melrose Avenue, to see if he was needed for anything. Once on the famous lot, he checked in with Harlan Thompson, the producer of *The Big Broadcast*, and met staff members. After the amenities were over, Thompson showed Hope his dressing room, then took him down to the music department, where a rinky dinky rehearsal pianist played and sang a new song that staff composers Leo Robin and Ralph Rainger had just finished for him to sing with Shirley Ross in the picture, "Thanks for the Memory." Although Hope had no way of knowing it at the time, it was to become his trademark for the rest of his life.

The Big Broadcast of 1938, written, or rather slapped-together, by Ken Englund, Walter De Leon and Francis Martin, was kind of a "Grand Hotel" on a transatlantic liner. Rather, two oceanliners. The plot involved a transatlantic race between a pair of steamships, the S.S. Gigantic and the S.S. Colossal. There was an all-star cast to make up for the sparse story line: W.C. Fields as the ship's sacroiliac-troubled captain, Bob Hope as an emcee of shipboard entertainment, and Martha Raye, Dorothy Lamour, Shirley Ross, Ben Blue, Leif Erickson,

Patricia "Honey Chile" Wilder, Kirsten Flagstad and Tito Guizar.

Hope remarked, "*Variety* is offering a ten thousand dollar reward to anyone who can tell them the plot of the film after seeing it."

The character that Hope played had been married three times, and in one of those great movie coincidences, all three ex-wives just happened to turn up on the voyage with him. This set up a scene in which Bob and Shirley, his most recent wife, engage in a bittersweet exchange about their defunct marriage and cap it off by singing "Thanks for the Memory" in duet.

It was not the most promising place in a story to position a musical number. How was one to write a tender song about two people who had a failed marriage and were now both involved with other mates and/or lovers?

"It was an almost impossible assignment," lyricist Leo Robin told publisher Lyle Stuart. "Several other songwriters had already struck out. When the studio head turned to Ralph and me, we were really challenged. After learning from the other songwriters' mistakes, we managed to come up with a bitter-sweet song that accepted the reality yet left you with the feeling that there was a large residue of nostalgia and a strong mutual affection between the two people."

According to Dorothy Lamour, who had been a successful café singer with a society band in Manhattan before signing with Paramount, the director Mitchell Leisen played her the score first in order to get her valued opinion of it. She told him the score was okay, but that "Thanks for the Memory" had the makings of a hit.

He told her that the tune had been written expressly for Hope and Ross, but if Lamour liked it that much he'd take it away from them and arrange to have her sing it as a solo. But Lamour said "no" to that. Not only would it involve major rewriting of the script and the lyrics, but she liked Hope too much to do that to him. She'd known the Hopes socially when all three were living and working in Manhattan, and she liked them.

"I wouldn't steal it away from Bob," replied Lamour. "I want him to sing it."

Hope was excited about "Thanks for the Memory", but when he brought a recording of it back to Dolores, she said, "I don't think it's so hot."

"What's wrong with it?"

"You were supposed to have a solo in the picture."

"Well, I'm not doing a solo. I just have this duet with Shirley," he explained.

"I still don't think it's much."

"Well, I think it's terrific," replied Bob. "And I'm going to do it."

✸✸✸✸

"Thanks for the Memory," of course, became the most important song in his life. Hope doesn't blame Dolores for misjudging it. "She's only human," he says today.

Around Times Square the Hopes were celebrities of the stage and radio. But in Hollywood, as Dolores discovered that afternoon at the beauty parlor, hardly anyone had heard of Bob Hope. When she tried to make an appointment to have her hair done where "everyone who was anybody" went, she was told that all the girls were busy.

"But I'm Mrs. Bob Hope," protested Dolores.

"Who?"

"Mrs. Bob Hope," declared Dolores. "You've heard of my husband. He's one of Broadway's biggest stars. He's on radio too. Listen in this Sunday night."

Hope, however, refused to be affected by her gloom. He was on a "high," as he always was, and is, when he's doing what he loves best—actively entertaining in front of an audience or preparing his next appearance.

A gagman named Wilkie Mahoney, who wrote jokes for a high class publication called *Captain Billy's Whiz Bang*, had been hired to write a monologue for Hope's NBC radio broadcast, which was shoehorned into his filming schedule.

Hope worked with Mahoney on his monologue all day

Saturday, fine-tuning the jokes. And he spent the Sunday afternoon of the broadcast at NBC working with the engineer whose responsibility it would be to cut Bob's insert spot into the *Woodbury Soap Rippling Rhythm Revue*, which was originating in New York City.

All went smoothly until four in the afternoon when Hope asked Walter Bunker, the NBC executive assigned to oversee his spot, what time the audience would be admitted.

"When I told Bob we weren't planning to have an audience for such a short spot, Bob was very upset," recalls Bunker from his Pebble Beach, California, home today.

"But I'm dead without an audience," Hope protested. "I need people to bounce laughs off. Otherwise my jokes will lie there like dead fish!"

"Too late," Bunker told him. "Where are we going to find an audience now?"

Hope thought it over a minute, then said, "I saw a lineup of people outside Studio A. Let's lasso them."

"They're for the *Edgar Bergen-Charlie McCarthy Show*," Bunker informed him.

"What time is that on?" asked Hope, nursing an idea.

"It's on from five-thirty to six."

"Good. I'll go have a talk with him."

Hope knew the famous ventriloquist from his *Ziegfeld Follies* days. (Bergen had originally been in the *Follies* cast but was let go before it opened because the show had been top-heavy with comedians.)

Hope waited in the wings for Bergen to finish his rehearsal, then buttonholed him on the way to his dressing room. He explained the situation. "Can I borrow your audience, Ed, when you're finished?" asked Hope.

"Why not?" replied the ventriloquist.

Bunker agreed it was a workable idea and instructed the ushers to set up ropes leading from Studio A's exit doors to Studio B, where Hope would do his monologue. The audience was surprised when they found themselves being led into another studio instead of to the exit.

A few of them started to walk up the aisles toward the doors when Hope pleaded with them to stick around a few minutes. "I'm Bob Hope," he introduced himself, "and I'm going to be doing a monologue that's going to be cut into a show in New York that's called *The Rippling Rhythm Revue*. It's a funny show, and I think you'll enjoy it. If you don't, we'll give you your money back."

Since they hadn't paid anything to get in, that got a laugh.

The insert spot was a success, and Woodbury Soap was so pleased, they gave Bunker permission to use an audience every week.

And just so people wouldn't be disappointed at having to sit through a mini radio program, Hope did a warm-up spot and then an afterpiece as well. The audience got a full thirty minutes.

✿ ✿ ✿ ✿

In those days, no matter how big a star you were on Broadway, or how many hit shows you were in, if you didn't have a caricature of yourself on the wall of the Brown Derby on Vine Street, you were "nobody." And if you walked out of the Derby and were approached by a dirty-faced autograph hound, who took one look at you and turned away complaining "Aw, he's nobody!" you either had to have an awfully thick hide or be ready to hop the next Super-Chief for New York.

Hope had a thick hide, of course. Otherwise he wouldn't have survived all those years in small-time vaudeville. But he was not prepared to have his nose insulted by makeup artist Wally Westmore when he reported to the studio that Monday morning.

After studying Hope from all angles, Westmore suggested that he consider having a nose job when he finished his first film. "I can take care of your problem with some makeup now," Westmore informed him, "but—"

"What problem?" interrupted Hope. "I've gotten along with this schnoz for years."

"The stage is different," said Westmore. "The people aren't

108

right on top of you. But in screen close-ups, any little flaw in your features is magnified."

Remembering his first screen test, Hope couldn't deny that his nose wasn't his best feature. He actually considered Westmore's suggestion when he returned to the hotel that night and talked it over with Dolores.

Dolores may have been wrong about "Thanks for the Memory," but she was on the mark when she told Bob that she liked his nose just the way it was. "They're trying to turn you into a leading man," she pointed out. "Your nose is perfect for getting laughs."

Hope kept the nose he was born with, despite some pressure to do otherwise by Paramount's president Y. Frank Freeman and the other top executives.

Tips from director Mitch Leisen proved helpful to Hope in the inchoate days of his filmmaking. One involved his timing: on the stage, Hope was used to waiting for the laugh after a line before going on. But you couldn't do that when you were playing a scene in front of the cameras, because you could never be sure where the audience would laugh, if at all. Pausing at the end of a one-liner was a difficult habit to shake after all those years on the boards. After several days of having Leisen shout "cut" when he caught the comic reverting to his stage timing, Hope got the message and stopped doing it.

Another trick he picked up from Leisen was to act with his "eyes." Just before Hope's big "Thanks for the Memory" scene with Shirley Ross, Leisen took him to Lucy's, an Italian restaurant opposite the studio on Melrose Avenue, and over spaghetti and meatballs said, "I'm not going to tell you how to act, Bob. You've been around the theater long enough to know what it's all about. And if I didn't think you could act, I wouldn't have hired you after I saw you in *Follies*. But I want to give you one tip that I believe will be very helpful. In movies, particularly in close-ups, emotions come through your eyes. Before you say a line, think about its meaning. Whatever the emotion you want to express—happiness, sadness or fear—it'll show up in your eyes. You can't have happy eyes and a sad face. It won't work."

Hope learned his lesson well. You can actually see the mischief in his eyes when he's about to say something amusing in one of his movies. If it's a line he doesn't have any faith in, his expressive eyes will often show uncertainty.

Despite the movie acting lessons learned, and the fact that the studio bosses were pleased after he'd finished shooting the "Thanks for the Memory" scene with Shirley Ross—the technicians and other people sitting around the set actually burst into applause—Hope still had an identity problem before *The Big Broadcast of 1938* was released.

Paramount had many major stars under contract at the time: In fact, on the 24-sheet billboard of the film, Hope's name was buried fifth below the title (W.C. Fields had sole star billing).

Hope was about to tell Louis Shurr to find another Broadway role for him when he was informed by Al Melnick that studio executives liked what they'd seen of the rough cut of *The Big Broadcast* and would pick up his option for another year. Moreover, said Melnick, they were putting him in *College Swing* opposite Martha Raye in a role originally intended for Jack Oakie. George Burns and Gracie Allen were the stars.

Hope was delighted to be replacing Oakie, who was already a film star, even though he discovered that the reason Oakie wouldn't take the role was because of its minuscule size.

A quick perusal of the script convinced Hope that Jack Oakie had good reason to turn the part down. You needed a magnifying glass to the role.

Hope was still on friendly terms with Lew Gensler, who was producing the film. Gensler, if you remember, had been one of the producers on the short-lived Broadway show, *Ballyhoo of 1932*, in which Hope had been featured. When that show folded, Gensler and his backers still owed Hope about eight hundred dollars in back salary, which they didn't have and so didn't pay.

Hope didn't make an issue of it, for which Gensler was grateful. But now Hope figured he had a marker on Gensler who could redeem it by enlarging his part in *College Swing*. Gensler agreed, and ordered a rewrite of the script.

The revised script met Hope's approval. It included a Frank Loesser-Burton Lane song titled "How'd Ya Like to Love Me?" which Hope would sing with Martha Raye. It was the studio heads' hope that this number would duplicate the success of "Thanks for the Memory" and do as much for the picture as the latter did for *The Big Broadcast*. Unfortunately, the chemistry wasn't there, and *College Swing* was just another star-packed vehicle that was quickly forgotten.

When he wasn't making a film, Hope tried to keep his name in the public eye in every way possible. He participated in photo opportunities with other stars. He encouraged interviews for the movie magazines. He accepted all benefit appearance requests. He showed up in the Winner's Circle at Bing Crosby's racetrack at Del Mar to hand out trophies to the winning horses, and to clown around with der Bingle. And he even played a much publicized charity golf match with Crosby at Lakeside for the alleged championship of the motion picture colony. The loser of the match would have to work for one day as an extra in his opponent's next picture.

Also in the match was Broadway columnist Ed Sullivan. This guaranteed built-in national publicity.

✿ ✿ ✿ ✿

When *College Swing* was a wrap, Hope felt let down. He was lost among all those stars at Paramount. Although Paramount scheduled him for a third picture, he was depressed about his progress in the film business.

Dolores suggested they move back to New York. She was tired of living in a rented home, with somebody else's furniture. By now they'd moved from the Beverly Wilshire Hotel to a leased house in North Hollywood that belonged to Clark Gable's second wife, Rhea.

Two things happened that turned Hope's career around. Shortly before Christmas, agent Jimmy Saphier got Hope a chance to do two guest spots on *Your Hollywood Parade*, a coast-to-coast variety radio show sponsored by Lucky Strike cigarettes. The show's regulars were Dick Powell and Rosemary Lane.

Albert Lasker, who headed the Lord and Thomas ad agency, was a Hope fan from earlier and promised him a permanent spot on the show if the audiences liked his two appearances. The first was scheduled for December 29.

Hope's two guest shots pleased not only the audience in the great wasteland, but more important, Albert Lasker. Lasker, in fact, was so impressed that he wanted Hope to replace Dick Powell as emcee. Powell was a popular crooner, but not a laugh-getter. However, he had an iron-clad contract.

So Hope had to be satisfied with the comedy spot for the run of the show. *Your Hollywood Parade* might have made it had it featured more Hope and less Powell, but it didn't and so it went on the air for the last time on March 23, 1938.

Notwithstanding, March turned out to be a good month for Bob Hope, for that was the month that *The Big Broadcast of 1938* was given national release.

The reviews were mixed, but the one by Frank Nugent in *The New York Times* was downright vicious.

> *The Big Broadcast of 1938* should have claimed partial if not complete disability and gone off the air while it was still in the rehearsal stage. The hodge podge revue being offered at the Paramount is all loose ends and tatters, not too good at its best and downright bad at its worst. And by demonstrating that not even William Claude Fields is invariably comic, it has shattered our fondest illusion . . .

Nugent did add, however, "Mr. Hope and Shirley Ross acquit themselves commendably, meanwhile, of 'Thanks for the Memory.'"

Nugent's critique was hardly the kind of thing to promote big box office, and Hope might have been boarding the next train for New York had it not been for a column in the *New York Journal American* that Damon Runyon devoted to the Hope-Shirley Ross number of "Thanks for the Memory."

Hope's favorite line in the column, and one he'll never forget because of the boost it gave his career was: "What a delivery, what a song, what an audience reception!"

And what a plug for Bob Hope.

If there's one single incident in Bob Hope's career that made the difference between him being just another comic and the world famous icon he is, it would have to be the Damon Runyon paean to him and his ability to put a number over in an otherwise mediocre picture. Without that, Paramount might not have picked up his option and put him in yet another unmemorable comedy, *Give Me a Sailor*, in which he costarred again with Martha Raye.

In the next two years, Hope's movie career began to take off. He had more clout around the studio and was given a second dressing room bungalow right next to the first. The first was furnished as an office and he used it to hold script conferences or meetings with his manager-brother Jack, or his agents, or his radio writers. It's also where he got into costume and was made up.

"But the second dressing room was strictly for entertaining his women," declares Robert Slatzer. "This one was luxurious—a set decorator's dream—down-filled couches, a coffee table, a pullman kitchen, a bar, and a daybed. It also had a back door, especially built for Bob so that his women could come in and out without being noticed, and also depart in a hurry if need be. That's where Bob did a lot of his hanky-panky."

12

Hope may have had a "star" dressing room, but he was still annoyed with Paramount for putting him in such turkeys as *The Big Broadcast, College Swing* and *Give Me a Sailor,* despite his increasingly better billing from fifth to fourth to second. If roles in lame vehicles like the one he just finished with Martha Raye (their third in a row together) were going to be all he could expect from the Hollywood oligarchy, what was laughingly called his motion picture career would soon, in his opinion, grind to a halt, and he'd join the growing ranks of stage stars who couldn't make it in films.

Ironically, it took radio to separate him from that flock.

Jimmy Saphier heard that Pepsodent toothpaste, who for nine years had sponsored *The Amos 'n Andy Show,* was thinking of replacing the two radio blackface comedians with something new. *Amos 'n Andy* were still immensely popular with fans, but the fans weren't buying enough toothpaste.

Saphier had an inside track with Tom MacAvity, who headed the West Coast operation of Lord & Thomas, which had the Pepsodent account.

Recalls Al Melnick: "The first thing I knew, Saphier was negotiating a radio deal behind our backs for Bob with Edward Lasker, who headed the agency in the East."

The deal Saphier was trying to get Hope called for a six-year contract to begin in September 1938, at $3,000 a show and progressing, with increments, to $5,000 by 1944.

The money was fine but what was holding up the deal was Hope's insistence on having full production control. Albert was willing to give it to him, but Eddie, who was top man, balked at the idea of signing him to a long-term contract at all because (a) Hope had a reputation for doing risqué material and being stubborn about censoring himself, and (b) he thought his character was too brash to appeal to radio audiences.

Saphier spoke to Hope about Eddie Lasker's concerns, and got his client's assurances that he'd behave and also try to develop a more sympathetic character. This seemed to satisfy Eddie Lasker, who finally signed Hope to the six-year deal that gave Pepsodent annual options.

Hope's radio show for Pepsodent was slotted into NBC's impressive Tuesday night comedy lineup, starting September 28, between two powerhouse programs which almost guaranteed a healthy rating.

Fibber McGee and Molly	6:30 to 7:00 P.M.
Bob Hope	7:00 to 7:30 P.M.
Red Skelton	7:30 to 8:00 P.M.

These were Pacific Time. On the East Coast, of course, the show was heard three hours later.

Not one to sit around, and having finished his contractual commitments to Paramount until they either did or didn't pick up his next option, Hope accepted an offer from Edwin Lester to recreate his role of Huckleberry Haines in the Los Angeles Civic Light Opera's West Coast premier of *Roberta*. The show was set to run for two and a half weeks, beginning June 6, at the prestigious Philharmonic Auditorium on Pershing Square.

In those days the Philharmonic Auditorium was to L.A. what Carnegie Hall is to New York, the home of L.A.'s symphony orchestra and of concerts by such world famous artists as Sergei

Rachmaninoff, Jascha Heifetz and Andrés Segovia. It was a class house, and more than the money, Hope was eager to show his Hollywood friends how good he could be when he wasn't bogged down by a tired movie script.

The production featured a bright new sexy actress, Carole Landis, playing the part of Sophie. The score included several new Jerome Kern songs written expressly for the engagement. Good reviews in the local papers kept the seats in the Philharmonic filled for the entire two and a half weeks.

Hope's appearance in *Roberta* had the effect of showing the Paramount bosses that Hope could get along very nicely without Hollywood.

Studio head Y. Frank Freeman phoned Louis Shurr the morning after the opening and told him that Paramount was picking up his client's option, and that Hope should plan to return to work at the studio as soon as *Roberta* closed on June 21.

To capitalize on the success of "Thanks for the Memory"—a recording of Hope and Ross's duet was selling well—Paramount now intended to reteam the pair in a feature film conveniently titled *Thanks for the Memory*. The film also introduced the hit song "Two Sleepy People." The script was an adaptation of a play called *Up Pops the Devil*. Shurr, of course, was delighted, as he was getting only a five percent commission on Hope's Pepsodent deal. However, Shurr informed Freeman, there would have to be a slight delay before Hope returned to the studio because while Paramount had been making up its mind whether or not to pick up his option, he'd accepted an offer from the Loew's circuit to play a live summer tour, beginning at Loew's State in Manhattan.

For this gig Hope brought along the former child star, Jackie Coogan, as his foil and drafted Dolores for the singing chores.

Variety's review of the show (June 29, 1938) saved most of its praise for Bob Hope and his mastery as an emcee, but was impressed with his attractive vocalist as well.

An especially pleasant and rich torcheroo is projected by Dolores Reade (Mrs. Hope) who knows how. Tone quality is individual. Diction good, too.

Interestingly, Hope was already starting to use "Thanks for the Memory" as his theme song.

For a show closer, Hope returns to paraphrase "Thanks for the Memory" to celebrate, half-facetious, half-nostalgic, the forgotten delights of vaudeville. Kidding or not, there's a heart tug in that routine for anybody who dotes upon the theater and rues its sorry defeat at the hands of mechanization. Hope, with the typical coloration of a true trouper, would probably swap Pepsodent, his new sponsor, for the old Palace any day.

Hope's vaudeville training had taught him a valuable lesson—that a little sentimentality mixed in with comedy never hurt. In fact, it's probably one of the reasons for his longevity as a performer, and why he's so widely liked by the public.

More than just an opportunity to be back on the boards again, the trip East along the Loew's circuit gave Bob and Dolores a chance to close their Manhattan apartment, relinquish their lease in mid-July, and ship their belongings to North Hollywood, where they had already rented another house, this one from Walter Lantz (creator and producer of "Woody Woodpecker" cartoons). The house was on Navajo Street, in the Toluca Lake section of the valley, the section where the Hopes live today, though in more lavish surroundings.

It was a convenient area, not only close to Warner Brothers, Universal and the Columbia Pictures ranch, but also handy to Lakeside Country Club, where Crosby was a member and Hope would become one.

Lakeside is one of the most racially exclusive country clubs in Southern California. Wasps are welcome. Jews, Blacks and other racial and religious minorities, once barred, now have only token representation. Over the years Hope and Crosby were criticized for being members of this racially-biased playground.

But in the days when Hope and Crosby joined Lakeside, nobody gave much thought to such things, except the people who weren't allowed to join. At any rate, Hope has never let Lakeside's racial policies bother him. He's still a member. Crosby, eventually dropped out to join the more liberal Bel Air Country Club.

Because of Toluca Lake's proximity to the Warner lot many stars under contract to that studio were neighbors of the Hopes: Bing Crosby, W.C. Fields, Mary Astor, Ruby Keeler, Jimmy Cagney, Humphrey Bogart, Ozzie and Harriet Nelson, Brod Crawford and Forrest Tucker.

Between his next film and preparation for his September radio debut, Hope didn't have much time to socialize with his glitzy neighbors. He had a capacity and a great love for work. If he had a choice between sitting with his writers preparing next week's script in an all-night session or spending leisure time with Dolores, he'd opt for being with the writers.

When everyone else would be exhausted, he could recharge his batteries by taking a five minute catnap, then be ready to go again.

Shirley Ross once told a newspaper interview, "Bob is shrewd. I don't think there's anybody in Hollywood his equal at weighing the possibilities of a joke. And I don't know anyone with such a terrific capacity for work and play at the same time. No matter how hard we're working, nothing interferes with his love of fun."

To allow himself a little more time for fun, Hope persuaded older brother Jack to come to the Coast as his assistant. Hope knew that Jack hadn't been happy in the meat market business, and would rather have been a songwriter. Realizing he'd have a better chance to fulfill his dreams in Hollywood than in Akron, Jack eagerly accepted his increasingly famous brother's offer.

According to NBC executive Walter Bunker, Hope made Jack the producer of the Pepsodent show. "Jack was a very sweet guy and didn't have to answer to anyone but Hope. But Bob was actually the producer and Jack his assistant."

Now that he was the star of his own radio program, and fully responsible for what went into it, Hope had a major decision to make: what would be the show's format, and what kind of a character should he play?

Before settling on anything, Hope carefully analyzed his competition, in order to see what made other comics tick: Fred Allen played a curmudgeon who commented on the times through the mouths of a cast of eccentric characters whom he interviewed in "Allen's Alley"—Titus Moody, a Down East farmer; Senator Claghorn, a blowhard Senator; and Mrs. Nussbaum, a yenta. Jack Benny relied on his miser character, giving all the insult lines to his radio "family."

Red Skelton had his own cast of funny characters, all played by him: the Mean Widdle Kid, punch-drunk Cauliflower McPugg, and country bumpkin, Clem Kadiddlehopper. Rudy Vallee played a pompous fool who thought he was God's gift to women. Edgar Bergen played foil to wooden dummies Charlie McCarthy and Mortimer Snerd. And Fibber McGee and Molly played a homespun couple who couldn't keep their closet straight, with the result that an avalanche of junk cascaded down on them every time they opened the closet door.

With the help of Wilkie Mahoney, Hope devised a simple format that's not much of a departure from the kind of show he does today.

The show would open with a musical number by Skinnay Ennis and his orchestra. It would be followed by Hope's monologue, and then some witty banter with his cast. This would consist of Bill Goodwin, a top announcer who was very good at delivering comedy lines; bulgy-eyed Jerry Colonna, whom Hope met during the filming of *College Swing*, and thought would make a better foil for him than a girl (Colonna became a lifelong pal); a singing group called Six Hits and A Miss; a girl singer—young Judy Garland first, then Gloria Jean, Frances Langford and Doris Day, among others, and a weekly guest star who'd either do a musical number or a sketch with Hope and the cast, or both.

The one ingredient Hope felt he needed to insure his success on radio was a monologue filled with topical gags. He wanted his jokes to be as up-to-date as the day's news.

As he explained in a book he wrote with Mel Shavelson, "I decided that would give *The Pepsodent Show* an immediacy that I find missing today when so many shows are taped weeks in advance. And we had no canned laughter then to cover the clinkers. You had to be good, or else."

Another problem: weekly radio ate up material like a hungry tiger. In vaudeville you could use the same sketch for a year and sometimes for many years, because the audience was different in every town. But in radio, you played to the same audience week after week, and so you had to come up with new material week after week.

To be fresh and topical for the thirty-nine-weeks of the radio season meant hiring a platoon of writers. Those who served Hope had to be on call twenty-four hours a day. Since there was still massive unemployment in America in 1938, it wasn't that difficult to find talented young men, just out of college, who were willing to give up their lives for fifty or seventy-five dollars a week (and perhaps even a hundred if Hope picked up their option). Unlike Jack Benny who relied on just two writers, Ed Beloin and Bill Morrow, whom he paid handsomely, Hope believed there was safety in numbers. For the two-thousand-a-week Benny paid his two writers Hope could hire twenty writers. And instead of having two writers collaborating on one script, he'd have ten writers turning out ten scripts. When their individual work was completed, they'd all gather and each writer would read his material aloud to the group. "If he could get laughs from the other writers, I knew his material was good," recalled Hope.

In short, he pitted them against one another, creating a competitiveness which kept them from becoming lazy. Every time a particular line got a laugh at the reading, Hope would make a note of it. Then, when all the readings were finished, he culled the best from each script and put the funniest lines into a master script. However, the writer wasn't allowed to keep the material that Hope didn't use. Contractually, all of it belonged to Hope. He'd gather the overage and put it in his files for future use.

In the early days his joke files were of modest proportions; just two steel filing cabinets in his garage. Today they occupy a two-thousand-square-foot fireproof vault on his Toluca Lake estate.

Hope's "slave-labor" contracts were drawn up by the late show business attorney, Martin Gang. His office represented Hope for several decades. Provisions included an option clause for the next radio season that Hope didn't have to exercise until eight weeks after the current season had ended. That meant that a writer who was borderline wouldn't have much chance to get another job if Hope waited until the last moment before letting him go. For, by then, all the jobs on other shows were filled.

Hope, of course, wasn't the only comic to take advantage of his writers. Edgar Bergen was just as chintzy, and so was Rudy Vallee. Hope actually had an excuse to be tight that first Pepsodent season. His weekly budget for the entire show was only $3,000, and out of that Hope had to pay his own salary, and also the cast's. Every nickel saved went into his own pocket.

Hope had a sadistic streak when it came to the treatment of his writing staff. On payday for the writers, Hope would gather the group at the bottom of his staircase that led up to the second story of his house where his office was. Then he'd come out of his office with their paychecks, and while standing on the landing above them, he'd fold the checks into paper airplanes and sail them down to the first floor, making them scramble for their money.

Hope kids about that today, claiming he did it only because they'd been chained to their typewriters all week and needed the exercise. But the writers I know who got their paychecks sailed down to them didn't think it funny and felt Hope enjoyed making them grovel for their hard-earned money.

Since there were more unemployed aspiring radio writers than there were jobs, most were willing to suffer humiliation in order to get a foot in the door of show business. As a result, Hope wound up with a very talented group of writers on the first Pepsodent season: Wilkie Mahoney, Al Schwartz, Milt

Josefsberg, Mel Shavelson, Jack Houston, Carl Manning, and Bob Phillips.

Later on in the season he also added Al Schwartz's brother, Sherwood Schwartz, to the group, along with Norman Panama and Mel Frank and Norman Sullivan. Sherwood Schwartz is known today as the creator of *The Brady Bunch* and *Gilligan's Island*, and Norman Panama and Mel Frank, wrote many of Hope and Crosby's best "Road" pictures. Later the pair developed into a successful writing-producing-directing team.

Milt Josefsberg went on to become one of Jack Benny's top writers and Mel Shavelson, with his future partner Jack Rose, developed and wrote Danny Thomas's long-running TV series, *Make Room for Daddy*. He also wrote and produced one of Hope's better films, *The Seven Little Foys*.

Because of the popularity of "Thanks for the Memory," Hope used that song as his introduction at all of his benefits and personal appearances. He decided to use it as his theme on the Pepsodent program as well.

History was in the making when Bob Hope went on the air for Pepsodent for the first time that Tuesday evening in September. But for that show, the Bob Hope phenomenon might never have happened.

He didn't break into any new territory when he stepped to the microphone for the first time for Pepsodent on September 27, 1938 and said, "How do you do, ladies and gentlemen. This is Bob Hope, telling you that if you don't brush your teeth with Pepsodent it'll soon be Bob 'unemployed' Hope . . . Well, here we are with a brand new sponsor, a brand new cast, and ready to tell some jokes. I'm very happy to be back on the air again. I've been very busy all summer working on a few projects . . . what do they want all those ditches for, anyway? . . . But I'm happy. We have a nice cast on the program that consists of. . . ."

Bill Goodwin, the announcer, then interjected with:

"Connie Bennett, Jerry Colonna, Skinnay Ennis and his Orchestra, and Six Hits and A Miss."

Hope then cut in with, "Thank you, Bill. That was our announcer, ladies and gentlemen, known as Bill 'Teeth' Goodwin. Show them your teeth Bill. . . . That's enough. Two more payments and they're his."

Hope did seven minutes of monologue, followed by a number by the Skinnay Ennis orchestra, then a commercial by Bill Goodwin.

After that was a "three-spot" involving Hope and Constance Bennett and Bill Goodwin. This segued into a sketch about a girl's baseball team. The payoff joke in that sketch had Bill Goodwin saying, "Look at that woman going round and round without stopping at home. Who is it?"

HOPE: "Oh, that's Mrs. Roosevelt."

(Eleanor Roosevelt was the "legs" for crippled Franklin D. and was always on the move.)

Another musical number. Another commercial. A sketch between Hope and Jerry Colonna, followed by Colonna singing a comedy version of "The Road to Mandalay."

Hope's comment after listening to Colonna sing: "I know I have a lot of enemies, but who sent you here?"

For his signoff, Hope sang a parody of "Thanks for the Memory," which went like this:

> *Thanks for the memory,*
> *Of this our opening spot*
> *Oh! I practically forgot*
> *You'll love the show next Tuesday*
> *There's a scene where I get shot . . .*
> *You'll like that so much*
> *Etc., etc.*

The Hope show was a huge hit but to illustrate in what low esteem radio was held by the people in a town largely devoted to movie-making, neither of Hollywood's trades, *The Hollywood Reporter* or *Daily Variety*, carried a review of Hope's initial program for Pepsodent. There was a one-line mention of it in somebody's column in *Daily Variety*, which wasn't particularly encouraging: "None of the opinions of the new Hope show seemed to jibe."

Hope and his sponsors were pleased, however, that his show was accepted favorably by the people who counted most—the radio audience—and in the coming weeks Hope worked hard to maintain the quality of his opening show. The fame of his guest stars helped insure good ratings: Madeleine Carroll, Shirley Ross, Groucho Marx, Joan Bennett, Pat O'Brien, Rosalind Russell, Paulette Goddard, and a seventeen-year-old Judy Garland. Garland's appearance was so successful, in fact, and she worked so well with Hope that he hired her to be the show's regular vocalist for the following season.

Hope fine-tuned his own character, mining big laughs by playing either the dumb wiseguy or the brave coward character of the "Road" pictures, and, always, of course, the leering womanizer.

"He still had a tendency to go overboard on the sexy innuendoes," recalls NBC executive Walter Bunker, who was in the control room in the early days of *The Pepsodent Show*. "During rehearsals the NBC continuity acceptance guy [censor] would say to Hope, 'You can't use that word.' And Hope would snap back, 'I'm going to use it anyway.' The continuity guy would then tell him, 'If you do, we're going to bloop you if you do it on the air.' So I was told to bloop him if he tried to use a dirty word. I was at the controls, and this was live radio, don't forget. So when he went to say the word, 'I'd bloop him right out, and cut him back in again right after.' That was my first real contact with Hope, and I think he was surprised that we'd dare do that. But radio listeners weren't like audiences today. They were easily shocked by anything slightly risqué, and you could lose 'em easily. Anyway, that happened a few times the first few weeks of the show. But finally, Hope gave up. He said to me, "Okay, if I can't use a word, from now on I won't."

He learned his lesson well. And the lesson was simply: one off-color line in an otherwise socko routine can cause your entire audience to tune in another station. In those ancient times, radios audiences would not accept blue material.

By the end of the first radio season, *The Bob Hope Pepsodent*

Show was in fourth place behind Jack Benny, Fred Allen and Edgar Bergen.

Naturally Lord & Thomas picked up Hope's option for another season.

The Bob Hope juggernaut was on its way.

13

With the success of *The Pepsodent Show*, Bob Hope now had two careers to juggle: radio and films.

To the ordinary mortal, working as a film actor five and sometimes six days a week, and simultaneously having to prepare, rehearse and perform live in a coast-to-coast radio show, with a few benefit performances squeezed in between, would seem like quite a burden. But Bob Hope isn't, and never was, an ordinary mortal.

Having dual careers wasn't just a challenge; it was his life blood. The man was incapable of slowing down.

For example, after giving him a thorough physical, his personal physician Doctor Tom Hearn once advised the comedian to take a rest, or risk a heart attack or a stroke. According to the doctor, Hope's vital signs were showing signs of overwork. "I want you to back off from work completely. Take no phone calls, do no benefits, in fact, do nothing at all for two whole weeks."

Frightened by such a grim prognosis, Hope chartered a fishing boat out of Seattle, and took along a couple of his best buddies, including orchestra leader Phil Harris.

But three days later Hope was back in Hollywood, more heavily involved in the rat race than ever. Hearing of his patient's return, Hearn phoned Hope in a scolding tone, "I thought I told you two weeks. Why are you back so soon?"

"Fish don't applaud!" answered Hope.

It wasn't just the applause he needed. Work gave him the opportunity to escape from home. Despite his devout "Republicanism" and his espousing of "family values," Hope is no family man. In fact, according to Jan King, who worked as his secretary and confidante for over two decades before he unceremoniously dumped her, Hope is no adoring husband or father, either. "He's a lecher who had women stashed away all over town. Part of my job was to help him conceal his secret harem from Dolores."

* * * *

Believing that the surest way to keep her husband close to home would be to tie him down to a family, Dolores started planting the bug in Bob's ear, as soon as she realized she couldn't have children of her own. They ought to adopt a baby. She'd already checked around with some of their friends, like George and Gracie Burns, who'd already gone the adoption route, and had been told that the most reliable place to get a child was at a place called "The Cradle" in Evanston, Illinois, just outside of Chicago.

The Cradle was run by a lady named Florence Walrath, who, according to the Burns, was the person to contact if the Hopes were truly serious about adopting a baby. Dolores was serious; Bob was on the fence about it. Anything to tie him down to home and hearth he looked upon with suspicion. Eventually he acquiesced to Dolores's entreaties and told her to contact Mrs. Walrath.

Dolores's first conversation with her by long-distance phone wasn't encouraging. "First the two of you need to come here for an interview," said Mrs. Walrath. "And then if you pass our examination for prospective parents, there'll probably be a long waiting period. At the moment all the babies from expectant mothers that are up for adoption have already been spoken for."

Since there were no babies available, the Hopes decided to

postpone the interview until the prospects were more promising.

Though Dolores was disappointed, Bob had little time to share her disappointment. He had his Pepsodent radio show for the 1938–39 season to complete; his last program wouldn't be until June, and this was only February. Simultaneously Paramount put him in two more movies: *Never Say Die*, based on a creaky play by William Post, in which he again costarred with Martha Raye, and a second called *Some Like It Hot*, based on an old Gene Fowler-Ben Hecht play called *The Great Magoo*, opposite Shirley Ross for a third time.

Neither made film history, but they helped to continue to establish Hope's star potential, which, fortunately for him, the brass at Paramount wasn't too nearsighted or dimwitted to notice.

Because of his public acceptance not only on radio but also in mediocre to bad films, Paramount decided to costar Hope with Paulette Goddard in *The Cat and the Canary*. In this vehicle, based on a play by John Willard and directed by Elliot Nugent, Hope played Wally Hampton, a mystery novel buff who gets involved in a crime involving a will and a creepy house in a swamp. It was the first role in which Hope was able to take advantage of an innate talent—his ability to portray comedically the "brave coward" who's never at a loss for self-deprecatory wisecracks while winding up as the film's hero who gets the girl.

Hope loved the script as well as the idea of costarring with sexpot Goddard. ("You call this work?" he asks, as he glances down at her cleavage.)

The Cat and the Canary went before the cameras in April 1939 and was completed in May.

His last show for Pepsodent that season was on June 20. To no one's surprise, the sponsor picked up its option for another thirty-nine weeks.

Delighted to be a success in two important entertainment mediums, Hope surprised Dolores by announcing that he was going to take her to Europe, and more specifically Paris, where she'd always wanted to go.

Dolores was pleased that her husband would actually take time off. But when she discovered he planned to accept a few vaudeville engagements on the way East, she insisted that while in Chicago, they take a side trip to Evanston, Illinois, to be interviewed by Florence Walrath about their adoption plans.

The vaudeville tour was a success, the first of many to feature the mustachioed Jerry Colonna. During the radio season, Colonna had become a favorite among Hope's radio fans. Some of his lines, such as "Greetings, Gates, let's operate!" and "Who's Yuhudi?" had become national catch phrases.

Bob and Dolores's interview with Florence Walrath was a success. Before they'd met face to face, Mrs. Walrath had shown some reluctance to handing over one of her infants to a Hollywood couple. Hollywood couples were not especially noted for having stable, long-lasting marriages. But Mrs. Walrath decided the Hopes were a good bet to stay together.

Perhaps this is where the giant cover-up of Bob Hope's first marriage to Grace Louise Troxell got its start. For if Florence Walrath had known of Hope's short-lived union with his former vaudeville partner, it's possible she might have reconsidered their request for a child.

Bob hoped it would be a boy; Dolores was willing to take a baby of either sex.

Mrs. Walrath just smiled, and said, "We'll see . . . we'll see."

＊＊＊＊

Chicago was the home of Ray Smith, who owned the Pepsodent Company. He was pleased with the way the radio show was selling his toothpaste. On Hope's last day in the Windy City, Smith invited the Hopes and advertising mogul Albert Lasker for a cruise around Lake Michigan on his two-hundred-foot-yacht.

As they boarded the yacht from the launch that took them out to meet Smith, Lasker turned to Hope and said, "I just want you to remember one thing, Bob. Amos and Andy built this boat."

With a twinkle in his eyes, Hope shot back, "When I finish with Pepsodent, Smith'll be using this yacht for a dinghy."

130

Smith was a gracious host. He plied his guests with everything from golden Russian caviar to the finest champagne. At evening's end, when he was walking them to the gangway, he presented Hope with round-trip tickets for deluxe suites on the S.S. *Normandie*, which would take them to Europe, and on the *Queen Mary* for the return voyage. Also in the envelope with the tickets was a $2,500 letter of credit on a London bank.

Ocean travel in those days was a luxury reserved for the rich and famous. The S.S. *Normandie* was the largest and most luxurious of the French transatlantic liners. The Hopes were minor celebrities compared with some of the other names when they sailed for Europe on the Wednesday following his successful stand at New York's Paramount Theater. The passenger list included such box office lummaries as Charles Boyer, Norma Shearer, Madeleine Carroll, George Raft, Roland Young, Edward G. Robinson, and Ben and Bébe Lyons. Not of the Hollywood establishment but also on board was Henry Morganthau Jr., then FDR's Secretary of the Treasury.

In Europe, Bob and Dolores visited London for a week, shopping on Bond Street by day, and attending West End theaters in the evenings.

During their second week in Great Britain, Bob drove Dolores out to see his birthplace at 44 Craighton Road in Eltham, a short distance from London. They also spent a night in Hitchin, where they hosted a party for Grandfather James, who was celebrating his birthday.

In a private room at the Hitchin Inn, where the clan gathered, Hope stood up and delivered a short monologue, which drew few laughs. His comedy went over the heads of his less-sophisticated English relatives. But keeping in mind the old saw that a "prophet is without honor in his own country" Hope didn't allow this to bother him.

He and Dolores got a kick out of the merrymakings when 96-year-old Grandfather James stood up at the end of the evening and said, "Now I'll show you folks something." Then he danced a lively jig that had everyone in hysterics.

✿✿✿✿

The Hopes planned to sail on the Queen Mary in the middle of September, but with war clouds looming, they had their booking moved back to August 30.

The ship was crowded with Americans fearing the outbreak of war.

Always the optimist, Hope believed there was nothing to fear but fear itself. However, three days after the Queen Mary sailed, England and France declared war on Germany.

Many passengers on board the unarmed luxury liner were fearful they would be the first victims of a German U-boat attack. To take their minds off the war, Hope agreed, at the suggestion of the captain, to entertain that night in the main salon. He spent the afternoon writing a timely monologue.

"When I got on board," he opened, "the steward told me that if anything happens, it'll be women and children first. But the captain said in your case, you can have your choice."

That was greeted by a roar, which got the evening off to a fast start. Hope then segued into his regular vaudeville act, and ended with a parody of "Thanks for the Memory," which he had written that afternoon.

> *Thanks for the memory,*
> *Of this great ocean trip,*
> *On England's finest ship,*
> *Though they packed 'em to the rafters*
> *They never made a slip.*
> *Ah! Thank you so much.*

> *Thanks for the memory,*
> *Some folks slept on the floor,*
> *Some in the corridor,*
> *But I was more exclusive,*
> *My room had "Gents" above the door*
> *Ah! Thank you so much.*

By the time Hope finished his act, the passengers were more lighthearted, and the captain was so delighted with his closing number that he had a copy of it printed for each passenger.

When the *Queen Mary* docked in Manhattan two days later, Hope told his publicity man, Mack Millar, to deliver a copy of the parody to *Variety*. There, it was used as a boxed item on the front page of their next edition.

World War II was less than three days old, but already the amazing Bob Hope had learned to capitalize on it.

14

Turmoil in Europe, perhaps, but the period between Great Britain and France's declaration of war against the Nazis and the U.S. involvement following the Japanese bombing of Pearl Harbor was a time when everything good seemed to come together for Bob Hope's skyrocketing career.

The *Pepsodent Show*, with seventeen-year-old Judy Garland, fresh from her success in *The Wizard of Oz*, doing the vocals and doubling in comedy sketches with Hope, was a contender for the number one spot in the ratings by the end of the 1939–40 season. The show was strengthened by the addition to its cast of two zany female characters named Brenda and Cobina (played by Elvia Allman and Blanche Stewart) who did a weekly takeoff on the reigning debutantes of the day, Brenda Frazier and Cobina Wright, Jr. With these two laugh-getters, plus the Hope regulars, *The Pepsodent Show* had radio audiences roaring in their rocking chairs every Tuesday night.

In addition to his cast of regulars, Hope tried to use "Honey Chile" Wilder whenever there was a spot for her.

Hope's friendship with "Honey Chile" started up again after he and Dolores moved to Hollywood. By then her movie career had fizzled out—she never got the Astaire film she'd been promised—and she was "at liberty" a good deal of the time.

"Honey Chile" and Hollywood just weren't meant for each

other. "After being totally ignored by the studio after they signed me, I was finally put in a picture with opera star Lily Pons," remembers "Honey Chile." "It was called *I Dream Too Much*. But three weeks into the shooting, Pan Berman, [RKO's] head of production, got mad at me and replaced me with an unknown bit player named Lucille Ball."

When RKO dropped her, "Honey Chile" became just one of hundreds of pretty women desperate for a break in Hollywood. Competition was tough, and the people in a position to help were ruthless.

For example, "Honey Chile's" agent, Zeppo Marx, said to her one day, "Hey, would you go to bed with John Ford if he'd give you a part in one of his pictures?"

"I looked at him and said, 'You're my agent. YOU go to bed with him.'"

Ambitious as she was, "Honey Chile" refused to be part of that scene. As a result, even with Hope's help, she didn't get very far in films.

There is a legend that Hope and "Honey Chile" once had a falling out about something, and after that, she refused to have anything to do with him for weeks. Upset by this, Hope allegedly sent her a check for two hundred dollars to make amends.

When I questioned "Honey Chile" about this, she told me, "The whole story is a lie. I don't know where it got started. First of all, Bob wouldn't send his mother two hundred dollars if she was dying of cancer. And secondly, I never needed his two hundred dollars." (Actually, Hope took good care of his mother when she was ill with cancer. Nonetheless, "Honey Chile" was well aware of his cheapness.)

❋ ❋ ❋ ❋

The Cat and the Canary opened November 1939, and Frank Nugent's wrote in *The New York Times*,

Streamlined, screamlined and played to the hilt for comedy, [it] is more hair-brained than hair-raising, which is as it should be.

Panels slide as menacingly as ever; Paulette Goddard's screams would part a traffic snarl in Times Square; the lights dim and an eerie wail rises when the hopeful legatees assemble in the manse in the bayous for the reading of Uncle Cyrus's will. Over them all broods Bob Hope, with a chin for a forehead and a gag line for every occasion.

Some of his lines are good ("I'm so scared even my goose pimples have goose pimples") and some are bad ("Let's drink scotch and make wry faces"), but good and bad profit alike from the drollery of Mr. Hope's comic style. It is a style so perfidious we think it should be exposed for the fraud it is. Mr. Hope's little trick is to deliver his jests timidly, forlornly, with the air of a man who sees no good in them. When they are terrible, as frequently they are, he can retreat in good order, with an "I told you so" expression. When they click, he can cut a little caper and pretend he is surprised and delighted too. It's not cricket, but it is fun . . .

The reviews were good in the *New York Herald Tribune* and the *Motion Picture Herald* as well, but the compliment that pleased Hope the most came from no less an expert on comedy than Charlie Chaplin, who, at the time, was married to Paulette Goddard.

Bumping into Hope at the racetrack one afternoon while *The Cat and the Canary* was still in production, Chaplin said to him, "Young man, I've been watching you in the rushes every night. I want you to know that you are one of the best timers of comedy I have ever seen."

****

Hope and Crosby appeared together at charity benefits, where they had sophisticated audiences rolling in the aisles at their never-ending, good-natured mutual insults. Paramount's production chief, William LeBaron, considered starring the two of them together in a film.

The studio owned a property called *The Road to Mandalay*, about two vagabond entertainers on the lam in the South Pacific. It had been shelved because Paramount didn't know how to cast it. It was written by two first-rate comedy writers of the period, Frank Butler and Don Hartman (who later became studio head). Fred MacMurray and Jack Oakie had turned it down. LeBaron had considered starring the team of George Burns and Gracie Allen in it, with a third personality, Bing Crosby, supplying the crooning. That, however, would have required a major rewrite, with no guarantee that it would work.

The idea of teaming Hope and Crosby plus Dorothy Lamour in a sarong to supply the sex appeal was pure inspiration.

Hope and Crosby both liked the idea. It seemed to have all the ingredients for a hit: Music, a colorful South Pacific background, Crosby's songs, Hope's jokes and Lamour as a beautiful Polynesian girl.

"However," recalls Dorothy Lamour from her San Fernando Valley home today, "I must admit that none of us ever imagined the picture would be as successful as it turned out to be."

While Hartman and Butler were occupied fine-tuning *The Road to Mandalay* into a Crosby-Hope-Lamour vehicle, "Rapid Robert," as Crosby referred to him, had plenty to keep him busy. In addition to his weekly radio show and personal appearances, Hope had a home life, to which he had to pay some attention, if only for publicity stills.

In the fall of 1939 the Hopes received word from Mrs. Walrath that she had a baby for them to adopt. The infant was a girl, but if Hope would accept her, she was theirs.

Dolores made the trip to Evanston to pick up their first child, whom they named Linda Theresa—after Dolores's mother.

Meanwhile Victor Schertzinger, one of Hollywood's better directors of musicals, had been given the assignment to direct *Road to Singapore* when it went into production in January 1940. (The title had been changed from *The Road to Mandalay* because studio executives felt that Singapore was a more treacherous-sounding place.)

Schertzinger had little experience working with free-wheeling types like Hope and Crosby. To these two, no pieces of business were too sacred to change.

In his autobiography, *Call Me Lucky*, Crosby remembered that when he and Hope began to take liberties with the script's dialogue, Schertzinger kept stealing bewildered glances at his script to try to figure out where the new lines were coming from.

Dorothy Lamour, being the pro who always stuck religiously to her lines, was even more bewildered than Schertzinger when she would play a scene with Hope and Crosby and fail to recognize any of her cues.

"When it was time for my first scene with them, the assistant director called 'Action' and then their ad-libs started flying in every direction," remembers Lamour. "I waited for cues that never came. Finally, in exasperation, I asked the guys, 'Please, when can I get my line in?' At that point they stopped dead and broke up laughing."

The writers of the script were not amused by the boys' antics, especially when they ambled onto the set one day and Hope greeted them with, "Hey, boys, if you recognize any of your lines yell 'bingo!'"

Their noses bent, Hartman and Butler rushed off to complain about the rape of their script to Bill LeBaron. But that got them nowhere, for LeBaron and the other studio executives were pleased with what they were seeing in the rushes at the end of each day's shooting, and didn't dare come down hard on Hope and Crosby for fear it would inhibit their free-wheeling style of comedy.

Up-and-coming Anthony Quinn, who played the heavy in *Road to Singapore* recalls two incidents.

"I remember once, Bing was supposed to take a swing at me in a scene and hit me hard on the chin. He wasn't supposed to actually hit me, but somehow he mistimed his swing during the take and landed a pretty hard blow to my jaw. I just stood there and looked at him, but didn't go down. Suddenly Hope turned to him and cracked, 'You can't hit very hard, can you, Bing?'

"In another scene, I was dancing with Dottie in a big production number. There must have been a hundred extras in the scene as well as Bing and Bob. I was supposed to be holding Dottie very close to me in the dance. Now Dottie is a very tough broad. Suddenly she put her hands on my shoulders and shoved me away fiercely, which wasn't in the script. This brought Victor Schertzinger, the director, to his feet. 'What's wrong, honey?' he yelled out. 'Why'd you do that?'

"'I can't dance with him,' screamed Dottie. 'The son of a bitch has got a hard-on!'

"The silence was deafening. Suddenly Bing yelled out, 'You should be happy you can give someone a hard-one, Dottie!'

"Everyone on the set roared, except Dottie."

The writers, director, and Dottie Lamour may not have appreciated Hope and Crosby's horseplay on the set, but without it *Road to Singapore* might have been just another forgotten film.

****

Hope was given the honor of acting as emcee at the Motion Picture Academy's Oscar presentation night.

It was held at the Ambassador Hotel's Coconut Grove on February 29, 1940, and broadcast over an NBC national radio hookup. *Gone With the Wind* garnered a record-breaking eight Oscars that night, plus the Irving Thalberg Award for its producer, David O. Selznick. As he handed Selznick his award, Hope quipped, "What a wonderful thing, this benefit for David Selznick."

This supposedly off-the-cuff line brought down the house, though it was anything but ad-lib. In those days names of the winners were known well in advance of presentation time, giving Hope and his army of writers ample opportunity to prepare his gags for the affair.

Emceeing the Oscars was a first for Hope, but it marked the last time the names of the winners would be known in advance. After twelve years, the board of directors wisely decided to keep secret the names of the winners until the awards ceremony.

****

Road to Singapore wasn't planned as the start of a series, but when it became clear to Paramount studio bosses that it was a box-office winner, they sent their story mavens back to their script files to hunt for another in-house screenplay that could be quickly converted into a Hope-Crosby-Lamour road vehicle.

They found their treasure between the covers of a shelved screenplay called *Find Colonel Fawcett*, by Sy Bartlett. It was a takeoff on the Stanley–Livingston yarn, and it had possibilities for a "Road" picture, so Butler and Hartman were assigned to rewrite it to fit Hope, Crosby and Lamour.

The vamped concoction was titled *Road to Zanzibar*, and was scheduled to go into production the following fall.

Paramount was getting its money's worth out of Bob Hope. Between *Singapore* and *Zanzibar*, producer Arthur Hornblow reteamed Hope and Paulette Goddard in a follow-up to *The Cat and the Canary* called *The Ghost Breakers*. The plot of this film is that Paulette Goddard inherits a castle on the West Indies and finds herself up to her neck in ghosts, zombies, buried treasure, and Bob Hope, whom she hides in a steamer truck because he's on the lam from a murder he's been accused of committing but, of course, didn't.

While Hope was filming *The Ghost Breakers* that spring, he was diligently plugging *Road to Singapore* on his radio show every Tuesday night, by doing funny sketches about it.

As soon as his new film with Paulette Goddard was completed, Hope took his radio program on the road for the final five broadcasts of the season so that he could do vaudeville shows at the local movie houses.

Hope had now turned into such a superstar name that halfway through his tour, for which he was guaranteed $12,500 weekly, and fifty percent of everything taken in over $50,000, the show broke attendance records. While he was doing five-shows-a-day in Chicago, the box-office lines were so long, stretching completely around the block, that the theater could not accommodate everyone who wanted to see Bob Hope & Company. To accommodate his eager fans—not to mention reap the most from his percentage of the box-office deal—Hope agreed to do seven shows a day. The two extra shows were squeezed in by cutting the newsreel, the cartoon and the coming attractions. This upped the gross to $73,000 a week, with Hope's share coming to twenty grand.

Since his touring income amounted to more per week than he was earning at Paramount, Hope felt that he was worth at least $50,000 a picture, not just the $20,000 he'd been getting.

Louis Shurr and Al Melnick, who, after flying to the Windy City and seeing the lines around the block at the Chicago Theater, agreed with Hope. The problem was Hope still had four pictures to go under the terms of his contract, and Paramount certainly wasn't likely to agree to a change.

Shurr had an idea. He'd met producer Sam Goldwyn in Philadelphia a few weeks before, and at that meeting Goldwyn had said to him, "You have to get Bob Hope for me for a picture. I saw him at the Academy Awards—he's vonderful!"

Shurr replied. "He's signed exclusively with Paramount."

"You can do it," Sam told him. "I just borrowed Gary Cooper for *The Westerner*. Get them to do me another favor."

When Shurr returned to the coast, he and Melnick asked the bosses at Paramount, if Hope could do an outside picture. Surprisingly, they agreed.

Then Shurr phoned Goldwyn and said, "Good news, Sam. Paramount okayed the deal."

"Great!" Goldwyn exclaimed. "I want to be fair with Bob. I don't want to take advantage of him. I'll pay him exactly what Paramount pays him."

"That," snapped Shurr, "is not the idea."

"Vell, vot is the idea?" asked Goldwyn, pretending to be surprised.

"One hundred grand," said Shurr.

Hearing that astronomical (for those days) amount Goldwyn sputtered and ranted and finally told the Shurr office to forget it. Which everyone did, until that fall, when Paramount asked Hope to emcee the premiere of *The Westerner*, which was to be staged simultaneously at two movie houses in Texas—one in Dallas and the other in Fort Worth.

Hope was scheduled to make eight appearances in Texas— four in each city.

Prior to his last show at the Will Rogers Coliseum in Fort Worth, Hope bumped into Goldwyn in the wings, just before going on the stage.

"My boy," said Goldwyn, "I am still hoping we can make a deal. But your agents want too much."

Hope said he would discuss it with him later. In the back of his mind an idea was brewing. As part of the show, Gary Cooper and a number of actors from *The Westerner* were to troop across the stage single file along with Goldwyn and be introduced by Hope to the audience. When it was Goldwyn's turn, Hope said,

"And now I want to introduce one of the truly great men in our business, Mr. Sam Goldwyn."

After acknowledging the applause, Goldwyn told the audience, "I haven't made a comedy since Eddie Cantor left me. I never found a comedian who I thought could do as well—until now. I finally found one in Bob Hope." He turned to Hope and asked, "How about it, Bob?"

Feeling he had the producer just where he wanted him, Hope said, "Okay, Sam, let's talk money."

Flustered, Goldwyn replied, "Not now, Bob."

"Yes, right now," insisted Hope. "Let's just lie down here on the stage and talk deal until we arrive at something." He grabbed Goldwyn by his coat lapels and pulled him down to the floor of the stage, along with the mike. "I want a hundred grand," grinned Hope.

"Too much," snapped Goldwyn. "I only pay Cooper—"

"Who cares what you pay that drugstore cowboy?" cracked Hope.

The audience ate up this routine. And Goldwyn, the ham that he was, played right along with it. Finally they compromised at $75,000.

The result was a picture that didn't get made until 1942 called *They Got Me Covered*. A spoof on espionage, the film, which costarred Dorothy Lamour, was written by Harry Kurnitz and produced by Goldwyn for RKO. It wasn't a great picture, but Hope was such a strong box-office draw that it didn't matter.

To Hope, the important thing was money and the more of it the better.

The Goldwyn deal enabled Shurr to negotiate Hope's price up to $75,000 a picture at Paramount. That, combined with what he was making as the star of *The Pepsodent Radio Show*, put Hope's income for the year 1940 at the half-a-million mark. This was really impressive for the time.

With her husband earning that kind of loot, Dolores decided it was time for them to buy a house. In the fall of 1940 they received word from Mrs. Walrath, from The Cradle, that she had another baby waiting in the wings for them. This one was a boy.

That decided the housing issue. Soon after Dolores returned from Evanston with their newest prize, whom they christened Anthony, she and Bob searched for new digs to shelter their growing family.

They settled on a white-brick, fifteen-room English farmhouse style abode, on Moorpark Street, in Toluca Lake, which they bought for $28,000.

Just a drive and a five-iron shot away from the Crosby estate in the same area, the Hopes' new residence had everything to make it the complete movie star's home, except a swimming pool. But more water wasn't something they needed after spending their first California rainy season in the house. They could just about go swimming in their living room, according to Al Melnick, one of Hope's agents at the time.

"The house was in bad shape," recalls Melnick. "Among other things, it needed a new roof. I remember going out there to bring Bob some contracts one rainy day and finding the living and dining rooms filled with pails of water on the floor, and more dripping down into them. Water was everywhere you looked. Eventually Bob remodeled the place and then bought all the property surrounding them until he finally had nine acres altogether."

❊ ❊ ❊ ❊

Over the years Hope turned the property into a business and living compound, which today includes his and Dolores's separate living quarters, another building to house his nine secretaries and joke files, and a one-hole golf course for the master to hone his golf swing on when he doesn't have time to run over to nearby Lakeside.

Surrounding the estate is a high wall, softened by beautiful shrubbery, and a gated entrance with twenty-four-hour security guards to log visitors—as well as family members—in and out.

By the end of 1940, *The Pepsodent Show* was giving the rest of the comedians on the air a real run for their money, despite the loss of its star vocalist, Judy Garland.

Judy was a favorite of Hope's, for not only could she sing well, but she clowned around with him, both on and off the air.

For a novelty, a performer's departure from the Hope show had nothing to do with a disagreement about salary. Judy left when her contract ran out because she was told to do so by her boss at MGM, the powerful Louis B. Mayer, who feared the competition of radio, as he would later fear TV. He discouraged anyone in his stable of stars from performing in any entertainment medium that the public could get for free. He had another, darker reason for taking Garland away from the Hope show: he had a lech for the teenage star and was jealous of her relationship with Hope.

Though it was a disappointment to Hope, Judy's departure made not one iota of difference to the show's ratings. For the 1940–41 radio season (and a number of seasons thereafter) Frances Langford took on the singing chores.

By year's end, *The Pepsodent Show* still trailed Jack Benny by a couple of points in the Hooper ratings, but *Radio Daily* named Bob Hope the "top comedian of the nation," based on a poll of radio critics. Which was pretty good consolation.

15

As 1941 dawned, Bob Hope didn't believe that the United States would become involved in World War II. As far as Hope was concerned, it was show business as usual. For the second February in a row, he was asked to emcee the Academy Awards. FDR opened the show with a six-minute radio address from Washington extolling Hollywood for its contribution to national defense, and for boosting American patriotism and morale. He also praised the citizens of Tinseltown for helping to raise money for the Red Cross, Franco-British War Relief, Greek War Relief, and his own favorite cause, the March of Dimes.

That got the Awards dinner off to a somber start, but from the moment Hope took over the mike, the mood changed. Glancing over at a tableful of Oscars that were to be given out that night, Hope quipped, in sly reference to David Selznick's *Gone With the Wind* sweep of the year before, "I see David brought them back!"

When the laughter abated, he wisecracked to a table of Paramount executives, "They just loaned me to Sam Goldwyn for a picture—it's sort of a lend-louse bill." (This was a switch on the lend-lease agreement the United States had with England.)

Hope had the room in the palm of his hand by the time he ended his opening remarks with, "I see Paramount has a table,

MGM has a table, Warner Brothers has a table, and 20th Century-Fox has a table. Monogram has a stool." (Monogram was a comparatively small studio.)

Although *Road to Singapore* was ignored, and rightfully so, by the Academy voters, the members surprised Hope that evening by giving him a special award, a silver plaque, for "achievement in humanities and for his unselfish services to the Motion Picture industry."

This was one of the first of numerous plaques, scrolls, medals, silver cups, and gold trophies that would be awarded to Hope over the years. But this one, coming as a total surprise, stunned him almost beyond words. "I don't feel a bit funny," he admitted as he stared numbly at the silver plaque in his hands. "How am I going to get this thing in my scrap book? I'll have to build a whole new room for it."

He had no way of knowing how prophetic that line turned out to be. In the years that followed, he received so many awards for his philanthropic efforts that he and Dolores actually added on an entire wing to their playroom of their Toluca Lake house to accommodate all the silver, gold, and bronze hardware he has accumulated.

According to Hope's longtime secretary-companion Jan King, her boss was never satisfied with the hundreds of trophies and awards. He pressed his press agents to lobby for more. "They even approached various congressmen to get him medals and honorary degrees," reveals Jan. At last count Hope has been awarded forty-four doctorates, plus a host of civic awards, keys to cities and numerous citations.

＊＊＊＊

It was a busy spring for Bob Hope. He was filming *Caught in the Draft*, a spoof of Army life, when *Road to Zanzibar* was released in March of 1941. This second of his "Road" pictures, was a huge improvement over its predecessor, and received uniformly good reviews.

The producers and writers of *Zanzibar* had learned some invaluable lessons from their first experience working with Hope and Crosby. First of all, don't let the romance get too serious or in the way of the story. And second, Crosby was better when he was the schemer and Hope the victim. Ergo, Crosby should be the lover who wins the girl, and Hope, his partner who gets the nervous laughs and winds up with no girl.

Howard Barnes of the *New York Herald Tribune* was in the vanguard of pleased reviewers: "*The Road to Zanzibar* is nonsense, but it is nonsense of the most delightful sort," he wrote.

With reviews generating healthy ticket sales, Paramount didn't waste time capitalizing on Bob Hope's pull at the box office. By the time *Road to Zanzibar* was in release, studio bosses were encouraging him to get started on another picture, his third with Paulette Goddard. This one was called *Nothing But the Truth,* and it was based on a creaky Broadway farce about a stockbroker who bets a friend $10,000 he can go twenty-four hours without telling a lie, and, of course, is put to the supreme test before it is over.

Hope and Goddard, plus a witty script by Ken Englund and Don Hartman, and slick direction by Elliot Nugent, seemed to be just the box office ordered for audiences anxious to get their minds off the approaching war.

Though an audience pleaser, *Nothing But the Truth* was not the kind of movie fare hard-boiled critics generally go for. But even the nation's most respected critic, Bosley Crowther, of *The New York Times,* found it hard to find fault with this comedy in his review.

Honesty may be a policy of which the screen cannot always boast, but Paramount has certainly turned it to advantage—and to further elevation of Bob Hope—in *Nothing But the Truth,* . . . For here is and ancient farce comedy, already seen twice in films, which derives from an idea so obvious that it no longer supports a parlor game. Yet Paramount, plus director Elliot Nugent, plus the ever entangled Mr. Hope, kick it around so blithely and with such candid application of hokum, that you can't help but find it amusing.

Hope's radio program was giving the public plenty of escapist entertainment too. And was about to add yet another ingredient to the mix—an ingredient that would not only further cement his hold on the comedy-loving American public as their favorite comedian, but also make him the darling of all our uniformed boys in service.

After a script session with his writers at NBC in Hollywood one afternoon in early spring, Hope exited through the "Artists Entrance" and was heading for his Cadillac when Al Capstaff, one of Pepsodent's watchdogs on the show, hailed him from across the parking lot, and shouted, "Hey, Bob, can I have a word with you?"

Hope stopped and waited.

"We've got a great idea! How would you like to take the program out of the studio one week and do your broadcast from one of the Army bases around here? The Air Corps guys down at March Field would love to have you."

"What for?" asked Hope. "Why drag the whole show down there? We're doing all right without leaving the studio."

Not yet the superpatriot, Hope was resisting the idea of traveling away from the studio on a Tuesday afternoon when he and Bing could be playing golf at Lakeside.

"Pepsodent wants you to do it," said Capstaff. "They think it'll be good publicity."

"Why doesn't the Air Force come up here?" asked Hope.

"All two thousand of them?" exclaimed Capstaff. "That's a little impractical."

Hope considered the possibilities of playing in front of a captive audience of that size. From past experience, he knew that it was always easier to get laughs from a large audience than a small one. Not only that, but playing for servicemen opened the door for more topical jokes of the kind he liked to do—jokes about the government and the draft and army life. Too, he saw an opportunity at the camps to publicize *Caught in the Draft*.

"Okay," he told Capstaff. "You arrange it."

Little did he realize that this change of venue from Sunset and Vine to March Field would alter his life.

The following Tuesday found Hope, his radio cast, including Bill Goodwin, Jerry Colonna, Vera Vague, and his new vocalist, Frances Langford, plus Skinnay Ennis's band and a half-a-dozen broadcasting technicians, traveling seventy miles by bus to Riverside's March Field.

The date was May 6, 1941, and Bob Hope says he will never forget the wildly enthusiastic greeting he and his radio family got from the GIs when their bus pulled through the gate. But once the broadcast began, Hope got tremendous laughs from the sea of homesick, entertainment-starved faces that seemed to stretch all the way from the apron of the stage to the horizon, he had to ask himself, "Where have these people been all my life?"

Hope's opening monologue again contained the phrase that became his trademark: "Good evening ladies and gentlemen, this is Bob 'March Field' Hope telling all the aviators, while we can't advise you on how to protect your chutes, there's nothing like Pepsodent to protect your tooths."

As Hope remembers the moment, "The laughter was so loud I looked down to see if my pants had fallen. I mean, there must have been something funnier going on than that joke. There wasn't."

As much as the GIs ate up Hope's material, they also loved Frances Langford's singing and the sexy interplay between her and Hope. That was another lesson Hope learned that night about entertaining sex-hungry servicemen. Jokes were important, but beautiful girls for him to fool around with on stage were what brought out the wolf whistles. Beautiful girls were a main ingredient for success at the Army camps.

※ ※ ※ ※

Despite the warm reception at March Field, Hope hadn't planned on broadcasting from Army bases in the future. And so for the following Tuesday night's broadcast, *The Pepsodent Show* again did business at the same old stand on the corner of Sunset and Vine. To Hope's disappointment, the civilian audience in Studio A was not the pushover the soldiers had been. You couldn't, for example, get laughs by merely mentioning the name of a particularly tough lieutenant and alluding to the fact that when the war was over *he'd* be returning to his civilian profession of being a janitor or street cleaner, and former privates would have the cushy jobs.

As he stood before the mike and waited for laughs, Hope found himself yearning for that pushover audience at March Field. Never had he felt such a strong urge to entertain our fighting men in khaki. Never had he felt so patriotic.

The following week, Hope did his Pepsodent broadcast from the San Diego Naval Base, one of the largest in the U.S. The jokes were about the same caliber as the ones that fractured them at March Field but more slanted toward life on the briny.

"Good evening, ladies and gentlemen, this is Bob 'San Diego Naval Base' Hope, saying it's no fun being a gob. How about those seamen's uniforms? Thirteen buttons on the pants instead of a zipper! Imagine trying to get your pants on when the General Quarters alarm sounds. A whole battleship can be caught with its pants down!"

Hope and his writers had much to learn about Navy customs and Navy language. And they learned the hard way that first show at the San Diego Naval Base.

At one point in the program, Vera Vague, who played a frustrated old maid, was supposed to say to a sailor who'd just made a pass at her, "If you get fresh with me I'm going to go to the head of the Navy. He's a dear friend of mine."

Barbara Allen, a.k.a. Vera, only got to the word "head" before the place exploded into laughter—so loud that it stopped the show. The rest of her line was never heard.

Hope and cast just stood dumbly on the stage, waiting for the audience to settle down. They tried to figure out what exactly the audience was laughing at. They didn't know "head" was the seaman's word for toilet.

Later Frances Langford was forced to cut the song *You Go to My Head* from a medley she planned to sing at another naval base.

Hope had stolen the thunder from other radio comedians by being the first to do his broadcasts from the service camps. His patriotism was a bonanza for the show. Ratings climbed to the top by year's end. The sponsor told Hope, "We'll pay for anywhere you want to take the show."

That was the beginning of seven years of playing service camps. And while other comedians did entertain the troops, none did it for that long a stretch, or so unremittently, or traveled so far. Which is why, in the minds of many ex-servicemen, Hope's the one who comes to mind when the question is asked, "Who's America's favorite comedian?"

16

It took the Second World War to make Bob Hope the icon that he is.

Hitler's barbarians were storming the gates of Stalingrad. Allied shipping losses by German U-boats in the Atlantic mounted daily. Japan was threatening to dominate the entire Pacific Rim. American troops were everywhere and Bob Hope's career was picking up impetus.

He finished his most successful radio season in the spring of 1941, playing service camps up and down the California coast. He found the audiences at the bases so to his liking that he previewed his newest picture, *Caught in the Draft* at the army's Camp Callan. Identifying with the problems of a draftee, Hope style, the GIs were wildly enthusiastic about what they saw on the screen, as were civilian audiences when the film was released in June.

With its positive reviews and Bob Hope's talent for self-promotion, *Caught in the Draft* took off at the box office and was Paramount's biggest grosser of 1941. This so impressed *Time* magazine that with its glowing review of the film, it also published a profile of Hope.

Bob Hope has made twelve pictures to date (three of them this year), has five more lined up and waiting. He is on NBC air every week for Pepsodent. If people grow weary of Hope's stylized impudence, it will be largely due to the star's appealing avarice.

Physically, Bob Hope's biggest asset is his chin, a granite abutment fit to warm the heart of any quarry-bound sculptor. However, he rarely leads with it. Around the Paramount lot he is known as a "hard man with a dollar."

This affinity for cash reveals itself in many small ways. On Hollywood's Lakeside Golf Club, where he customarily spends Sundays, he lays his bets with the guile of a shill operating a shell game. This procedure, plus his capacity for shooting fanatical golf in the 70s, nets him a pretty penny. But not from Bing Crosby. The crooner has bested him so often that Hope calls him Trader Horn.

Crosby also introduced Hope to the delights of horse racing. On their first day at the track together the jut-jawed comedian ran wild. Placing $2 here, $2 there, he ran up a sizable wad of folding money. But when one of his entries finished out of the money he decided that horse gambling was too uncertain for pleasure.

The reference to Hope's cheapness angered Bing Crosby. The crooner felt impelled to come to Hope's defense. In one of the few instances that he's been known to write a letter, Bing addressed *Time*'s letter column saying,

My friend Bob Hope is anything but cheap. He does an average of two benefits a week. His price for a personal appearance would be about $10,000, so he gives away $20,000 every week of his life. Is that cheap?

Editors usually get the last word, and this exchange was no exception. "*Time* agrees with Bing," wrote the magazine in response. "However, Bob Hope, from time to time has been known to put undue pressure on a nickel."

✸✸✸✸

Nowhere has this reality been more in evidence than in Hope's dealings with writers. Even after *The Pepsodent Show*'s initial success, Hope was loathe to give his writers anything near what other radio writers were being paid.

While needling Hope for his penchant for penny-pinching, *Time* did acknowledge that he had one of the sharpest business minds in the entertainment world and that he had an unerring instinct for marketing and promotion. Hope's agent, the late Jimmy Saphier, once remarked, "If Bob hadn't become an actor, he could have been the head of General Motors."

Hope demonstrated this on his next trip to New York, when he and Pepsodent's advertising executives met to discuss a national promotion stunt that would put their toothpaste into the top sales bracket.

The Pepsodent people were thinking along the lines of a contest. Hope had a different suggestion. How about a tongue-in-cheek autobiography of himself? The sponsor could give away copies as premiums.

Lord & Thomas, the Pepsodent ad agency, was excited by the idea. Pepsodent would pay printing costs. Paramount would promote it by getting its stars to be photographed reading copies.

At publication time, Lord & Thomas arranged a mock literary tea at Manhattan's Stork Club for the press.

The price of the book would be ten cents and a box top from a package of Pepsodent. On a ten cent book, Hope wouldn't realize much in the way of royalties, but he would retain the rights to the book.

While Hope's gnomes were hunched over their Underwoods that summer pounding out Hope's gag-filled "autobiography," the master was on the Paramount lot filming *Louisiana Purchase*, based on the Morrie Ryskind Broadway musical of the same name with a score by Irving Berlin. A political satire, centered around the life of Louisiana political boss Huey Long, *Louisiana Purchase* enjoyed only a brief run on Broadway, but as a Bob Hope vehicle it was considerably more successful.

Hope's book was titled *They Got Me Covered* and, on September 23, 1941, the comedian's literary career was launched.

Hope plugged his book on the opening show of the 1941–42

season by doing a comedy sketch kidding the publishing business. The next day he attended the Stork Club reception in New York, where he autographed copies and exchanged witticisms with other celebrities—Milton Berle, Ethel Merman, and Al Jolson, to name a few. Broadway columnists Walter Winchell and Ed Sullivan were also on hand to give Hope's first literary effort a proper send-off.

As books go, *They Got Me Covered* wasn't much. It was more of a pamphlet, ninety-six pages of gags and pictures of Hope in vaudeville, Hope on the golf course by himself and with other celebrities, Hope with other Paramount stars—all neatly packaged between soft covers. But as a biography it contained little information. The only reference to "marriage" was a picture of him and Dolores posing together ten years earlier.

In Hollywood he began filming his newest comedy, *My Favorite Blonde* with the beautiful Madeleine Carroll. The picture was a spy spoof, written by his two former writers, Norman Panama and Mel Frank.

Hope always claimed that he commissioned Panama and Frank to write *My Favorite Blonde* specifically for him and Madeleine Carroll. "That's not true," recalls Panama today. "After a season with Phil Baker, Mel and I were unemployed. Since we weren't doing anything, we decided to sit down and try our luck writing a movie comedy, maybe for Hope. We constructed our spy-story after Alfred Hitchcock's *The 39 Steps* and by the time we finished, we had a hundred-and-twenty-five page treatment. Paramount bought it from us, for Hope, for $7,500. They thought we were too inexperienced to be trusted with writing the screenplay, so they gave that assignment to Frank Butler and Don Hartman. We had a good agent, however, and he got us a term contract at Paramount as a result."

My Favorite Blonde turned out to be one of the better Hope pictures. It was a tremendous box-office success and Panama and Frank went on to write the screenplays for a number of the "Road" pictures over the next few years, as well as Hope's later success, *The Facts of Life*, with Lucille Ball. The latter was not only a money-maker, but is now considered to be an all-time comedy classic.

Throughout the fall season Hope promoted *They Got Me Covered* on his Pepsodent show. With 23 million weekly listeners, the first printing of two million copies was completely sold out, or rather, given out, almost as soon as it rolled off the presses. This made publishing history for Hope was one of the first to use radio to tell the world he'd written a book. He's been doing it ever since, with the result that his books have sold in the millions.

Hope was asked by the Chamber of Commerce to ride a horse down Hollywood Boulevard in their annual Santa Claus parade on the evening of December 6, 1941. Hope agreed but with one proviso. He wanted the slowest, most worn-out looking nag in the stable. The parade committee was puzzled by the demand. They wanted to sit him on a more thoroughbred-like animal—something befitting an important star's bottom. However, they acceded to his request and, the night of the parade, were as amused by what they saw as were the huge throngs that lined both sides of Hollywood Boulevard.

Leading the parade were two of Hope's minions carrying a large placard reading "Bing Crosby's fastest racehorse." And right behind them came Bob Hope, trotting along on the swayed back of what looked like "the Old Grey Mare, who ain't what she used to be."

Exhausted from the long horseback ride in the parade, and all the autographs he'd had to sign at the end of it, Hope slept until eleven o'clock the following morning—December 7th.

While he was drinking his coffee, he was amused to see, on the front page of the *Los Angeles Times*, a photograph of himself astride his steed in the Santa Claus parade the night before. He remembered that he was also to be the subject of a profile in *This Week* magazine, the paper's Sunday supplement. He turned to the feature article, and was pleased by the coverage until he got to a couple of paragraphs near the end that delved a little too accurately into his finances. According to the piece, Hope's overall income in 1940 from radio, movies and personal appearances was $464,161.78. Out of that he had paid a total of $142,047.66 in taxes. The writer projected that Hope's income for 1941 would be even higher—probably around $575,000.

He was disturbed. He felt that kind of information set him and his two children up as possible kidnapping targets. Hope has never boasted about his worth, for when those figures are made public, it just makes it more difficult for him to justify the niggardly wages he pays his employees, or to refuse people who ask for loans.

But on the morning of December 7, 1941, Hope didn't have much time to grouse. No sooner had he scanned the profile on himself than Dolores came running into his bedroom to tell him that she'd just heard on the radio that Japanese planes had bombed Pearl Harbor in Hawaii.

"Sunday night we held our regular preview," recalls Hope. "We were all too shocked to cancel it."

There were empty seats in Studio A. Those were the seats normally reserved for men in uniform. They'd all been called back to their bases the moment the bombing news had been announced.

Laughs in the studio were fewer, people in the audience, in fact, people all over Southern California, were pretty jittery. They didn't know whether to expect a Japanese invasion of Santa Monica or an announcement from Orson Welles saying it was all a big joke.

It was no joke.

For the first time in Bob Hope's radio career, *The Pepsodent Show* didn't go on as usual Tuesday, December 9, at seven P.M. Hope had been preempted by the President of the United States.

Application for Marriage License

No. 138

Statement of Male:

Full name and surname .... Leslie T. Hope .... Color, White.

Relationship of parties making this application, if any either by blood or marriage .... none

Occupation .... Salesman .... Birthplace .... London, England

Residence .... 3323 Yorkshire Road, Cleveland, Ohio

Age .... 39 .... years. Previous marriage or marriages .... no .... Date of death or divorce of former wife or wives

.... x .... Is applicant afflicted with any transmissible disease? .... no

Name and surname of Father .... William H. Hope .... of Mother .... Avis Hope

Maiden Name of Mother .... Townes .... Residence of Father .... Cleveland, Ohio

of Mother .... Cleveland, Ohio .... Color of Father, White. Of Mother, White. Occupation of Father

.... Mason .... of Mother .... Housewife .... Birthplace of Father .... London, England

Of Mother .... Cardiff, Wales .... Is applicant an imbecile, epileptic, of unsound mind, or under guardianship as a person of unsound mind, or under the influence of intoxicating liquor or narcotic drug? .... no .... Has applicant, within five years been an inmate of any county asylum or home for indigent persons? .... no .... Is applicant physically able to support a family? .... yes

Statement of Female:

Full name and surname .... Grace L. Troxell .... Color, White.

Relationship of parties making this application, if any either by blood or marriage .... none

Occupation .... Secretary .... Birthplace .... Chicago, Illinois

Residence .... 642 West 64th St., Chicago, Illinois

Age .... 21 .... years. Previous marriage or marriages .... no .... Date of death of divorce of former husband or husbands

.... x .... Is applicant afflicted with any transmissible disease? .... no

Name and surname of Father .... Edward L. Troxell .... of Mother .... Mary Troxell

Maiden Name of Mother .... McGinnes .... Residence of Father .... Chicago, Illinois

of Mother .... Dec'd. .... Color of Father, White. Of Mother, White. Occupation of Father

Engineer .... of Mother .... x .... Birthplace of Father .... Chicago, Illinois

Of Mother .... Chicago, Ill. .... Is applicant an imbecile, epileptic, of unsound mind, or under guardianship as a person of unsound mind, or under the influence of intoxicating liquor or narcotic drug? .... no

Commonwealth of Pennsylvania
County of Erie } ss.

We, the undersigned, in accordance with the statements herein contained, the facts set forth wherein we and each of us do solemnly swear are true and correct to the best of our knowledge and belief, do hereby make application to the Clerk of the Orphans' Court of Erie County, Pennsylvania, for license to marry.

Signature of Applicant, Male: *Leslie T. Hope*

Signature of Applicant, Female: *Grace L. Troxell*

Sworn and subscribed before me this

.... 25th .... day of .... January .... A. D. 193 3

William M. Gill

License issued .... 25th .... day of .... January .... A. D. 193 3 .... 2nd Asst., ... Clerk of the Orphans' Court

Duplicate returned 27th day of January .... A. D. 193 3

Married .... 25th .... day of .... January .... A. D. 193 3

At .... Erie, Pa.

By .... Eugene P. Alberstadt

A/ Minister, Justice of the Peace, Alderman.

Hope's marriage license when he married dancing partner Grace L. Troxell in Erie, Pennsylvania on January 25, 1933. Hope denies he married Ms. Troxell, claiming he only took out the license, but the ceremony actually took place, a fact sworn to on this document (see lower left-hand corner) by the performing justice of the peace, Eugene P. Alberstadt.

Hope in his Cadillac, with Dolores at the front door of their Toluca Lake house—
early fifties. PHOTO BY GENE LESTER

The Hope family.
From left to right:
Bob, Dolores,
Linda, Tony, Nora,
and Kelly. PHOTO BY
GENE LESTER

Bing Crosby, Bob Hope, Jerry Lewis, and Dean Martin, in 1953.

Groucho Marx and Hope looking over a box of chocolates—late forties.

PHOTO BY GENE LESTER

Hope, Dinah Shore, and Vice President Henry Wallace washing dishes at the Hollywood Canteen during World War II. PHOTO BY GENE LESTER

Top left: Hollywood bond tour celebrities in Philadelphia. Front row, left to right: Charles Boyer, Pat O'Brien, Frank McHugh, Jimmy Cagney, Virginia Grey, and Bob Hope. PHOTO BY GENE LESTER

Above: Hope and Dolores' mother, Theresa Kelly Defina. PHOTO BY GENE LESTER

Below: Hope clowning around with columnist Hedda Hopper on her front lawn. PHOTO BY GENE LESTER

Left to right: Stan Laurel, Oliver Hardy, Charlotte Greenwood, Jerry Colonna, and Hope, dining at Bookbinders in Philadelphia on one of Victory Caravan's stops. PHOTO BY GENE LESTER

Fred MacMurray, Rita Hayworth, and Hope accepting awards from Hollywood photographers for being the most cooperative celebrities. PHOTO BY GENE LESTER

Hope and Crosby, on one of the rare occasions when Bing allowed himself to be photographed without his toupee. Hope was guesting on Crosby's CBS radio show. PHOTO BY GENE LESTER

Dean Martin and Natalie Wood with Hope on the Bob Hope TV Show, 1959.

Eleanor Roosevelt invited the celebrities from the Hollywood Caravan to the White House, where they assembled on the back lawn for this photo. PHOTO BY GENE LESTER

Left to right: gag writer Chuck Stewart; Jerry Briskin, assistant to agent Jimmy Saphier, who's standing in center; gag writer Norm Sullivan; and Bob Hope. PHOTO BY GENE LESTER

17

It's a lucky thing for the war effort that Bob Hope, who'd be thirty-nine years old on May 29, 1942, was too old for the draft. He was physically fit, and a versatile enough athlete to learn how to shoot a rifle as well as he could handle a five-iron, but there was no doubt in anybody's mind that he'd be more valuable to Uncle Sam entertaining homesick GIs, and helping to lift civilian morale by continuing to make movies and doing his weekly radio broadcasts.

Hope must have felt so too. While other overage show business luminaries were displaying their patriotism by scrambling for ill-deserved officers' commissions and trying to land cushy jobs in the Motion Picture Signal Corps, where they'd be permanently stationed on the Fox Western Avenue lot in Los Angeles, Old Ski Snoot in his spare time was raising money for War Relief and the Red Cross by participating in a series of golf exhibitions across the country with Bing Crosby, helping to sell War Bonds.

In other words, Hope was doing what he could do best—make people laugh and forget the war for a few minutes.

His first broadcast after Pearl Harbor began with a serious note reflecting the somber mood of the times.

"Good evening, ladies and gentlemen, this is Bob Hope, and I just want to take a moment to say that last Tuesday night at this time, I was sitting out there with you listening to our President as he asked all Americans to stand together in this emergency. We feel that in times like these, more than ever before, we need a moment of relaxation . . . all of us in this studio feel that if we can bring into your homes a little laughter each Tuesday night, we are helping to do our part."

Even the sponsor's commercial was tinted with patriotism.

"Every hour of work that is lost through illness pushes victory just a little further away . . . avoid wet feet, drafts, and watch your throat because that's where illness often starts. Gargle with Pepsodent Antiseptic regularly."

Only the devious mind of an ad agency man could have come up with such a foxy way of plugging the product while simultaneously exhorting the listener to take care not to sabotage the war effort by catching a cold.

The war was fertile ground for jokes that worked particularly well for Hope. The main staple of his comedy was topicality. He thrived on jokes about blackouts, and food, rubber and other shortages . . . "Well, Los Angeles had its first blackout the other night. Every electric light in the city went out. I saw one guy standing in the street and laughing like anything. I asked, 'What are you so happy about?' And he said, 'At last I'm not alone. Look—this month nobody paid their electric bills.'"

On shortages:

"And the shortage of everything is worrying me. This morning when the bank sent back my check it was marked, 'Insufficient rubber.'"

On bomb shelters:

"I'm tired, I've been digging a bomb shelter under my cellar, but I can't quit now. The tunnel almost reaches Hedy Lamarr's house." (The actress was a sex-symbol of the time.)

****

Because of the austerity, Hope didn't get to emcee the Oscars in February. No one did. At first, the Motion Picture Academy considered calling off the ceremony altogether—not only because of the war and blackouts, but because Carole Lombard, one of Hollywood's top stars and the wife of Clark Gable, had been killed in an airplane accident on January 16 while returning from a bond-selling tour.

Finally, after much discussion, the Academy decided to go ahead with the Oscars, but under modified conditions. Formal attire was out, the ceremony was labeled a "dinner" rather than a banquet, and there were no searchlight beams criss-crossing the skies above the Biltmore Hotel the night of February 26, 1942.

Without the Oscar show, however, Hope had plenty to keep him busy. Between his December 12 broadcast and the following April, he assiduously continued to play the army camps but confined appearances to those around Southern California, because, soon after the first of the year, he and Crosby would make another movie, *Road to Morocco.*

Don Hartman and David Butler concocted the script. According to many, they had come up with the funniest of the series yet. In this one, the boys are stranded in Morocco. Where Crosby sells Hope into slavery to pay their dinner check. Hope winds up the prisoner of a beautiful princess, played of course, by Dorothy Lamour, who happens to be the property of a very mean Sheik, portrayed by Anthony Quinn.

In the end Crosby saves Hope from Quinn, and as his reward wins Dorothy Lamour.

The picture was directed by David Butler, who not only had a way of getting the most out of Hope and Crosby. He also had a habit of letting the cameras keep rolling even though something untoward happened in the scene that would've caused another director to shout apoplectically "Cut!"

In one scene, for example, Hope was to be kissed on the back of the neck by a slobbering camel, believing the lips belonged to Crosby. The camel performed but encored by spitting in Hope's face. This wasn't in the script and so surprised Hope that he staggered backwards with a look of shock on his face.

Everyone on the set, except Hope, doubled up with laughter. It was so unexpectedly funny that Butler kept the scene in the picture in the final cut.

On another occasion Hope and Crosby were supposed to be chased down a narrow alley by a thundering herd of wild horses. There was no exit from the alley except at the far end. The horses weren't supposed to be turned loose until Hope and Crosby were near enough to the end of the alley to be able to escape before being trampled. But the assistant director made a mistake and released the horses when Butler yelled, "Action—roll 'em!"

The two understandably terrified stars were nearly run down as they dashed madly toward the exit. Realizing they couldn't outrun the horses, each found safety in his own way. Crosby dropped into an open manhole. Hope leaned flat against the wall of a building as the thundering herd brushed by him.

Hope and Crosby were more than a bit annoyed at how narrowly they'd escaped serious injury, but the expressions of real fear on their faces made the scene so believable and comic that the assistant director's goof was worth their wrath, in Butler's opinion. He shouted, "Great shot, print it," and it remained in the film.

There were times, however, in working with the two stars, that even Butler wasn't able to have his own way. And even with Hope siding with him against Crosby.

"In one picture," recalls Hope, "Bing and I were to do a scene where both of us were in a double bed. But when Bing came to bed he was still wearing his hat, a fedora. So I said to him, 'Bingo, nobody comes to bed wearing a hat. How about removing it?' He refused. Evidently he didn't have his toupeé on and he was too lazy to put it on. Then Butler asked him to remove his hat. And when he still wouldn't do it, Butler sent for three executives from the front office and explained the problem to them. One of them was Y. Frank Freeman, the head of the studio. Freeman said he'd handle it, and went over to Bing who was in bed with his hat on and said, 'Mr. Crosby, is everything all right? Are you happy with the picture?' And Bing nodded, 'yes, everything was fine.' So Freeman turned to Butler, barked, 'Okay, roll 'em,' and walked away. They were scared to death to say anything to Bing to upset him, so we ended up shooting the scene with Bing's hat on, and I covered it with some joke like, 'Do you always get your nightcaps from Stetson?'"

        ❋❋❋❋

While Hope and Crosby were facing their "Road" problems in a fictional Morocco, the United States was having larger real troubles in the Pacific and on the western front.

To help morale, the Hollywood establishment got into the spirit of things by forming the Victory Committee, which was a coalition of all the guilds—actors, writers, directors and producers—whose purpose was to lend support to the USO, the Hollywood Canteen, and to sell War Bonds. Out of this was born the idea of the Victory Caravan, a trainload of stars criss-crossing the nation and putting on shows in various cities to sell bonds.

The Victory Caravan consisted of nine Southern Pacific railroad cars, including a diner and a lounge car, complete with full bar. Each star would have his or her own compartment, and all the luxuries a first-class train could provide.

The train would go from Union Station in Los Angeles straight to Washington, D.C., where its occupants would be given a gala reception on the White House lawn, hosted by the First Lady herself, Eleanor Roosevelt. They would put on a three-hour show the following night in Constitution Hall, then get back aboard the Victory Caravan train, which would then whistle-stop its way across and up and down the country, stopping at all the major cities to sell War Bonds, and raise money for War Relief.

Riding the Victory train were Cary Grant, Joan Bennett, Joan Blondell, Groucho Marx, James Cagney, Desi Arnaz, Pat O'Brien, Charlotte Greenwood, Merle Oberon, Charles Boyer, Olivia de Havilland, Spencer Tracy, Irene Dunne, and Betty Grable. There was an impressive roster of writing talent as well, to write special material as needed: playwrights George Kaufman, Moss Hart, Jerome Chodorov, Howard Lindsay, and

Russel Crouse. Songwriters on the tour were Jerome Kern, Johnny Mercer, Frank Loesser, and Arthur Schwartz. Hope would emcee, and Crosby would croon and play comedy sketches with him.

Being something of a loner, Crosby didn't join the Caravan until it pulled into the La Salle Street train station in Chicago on its way east. And because of commitments on the West Coast, Hope didn't show up until the Caravan arrived in Washington, D.C., on April 29, 1942.

To the average movie fan, being locked up in a train for four days with some of the most famous names in Hollywood would be the answer to his or her wildest fantasy. But to the stars themselves it was no novelty, or any great pleasure, to have to be in the constant company of so many of one's peers.

As Bob Hope once said about that particular train ride, "When you were sitting around with super-egos like Cary Grant, Spencer Tracy, Charles Boyer and Jimmy Cagney, you were lucky if you could mention your own pictures once every half-hour."

On the second day, the train's cooling system broke down while it was crossing the desert. The stars began to get on each other's nerves.

Fortunately there were plenty of girls along to ease the tension. In addition to the female stars, there were a number of pretty young starlets on board, including Frances Gifford, Elyse Knox, Juanita Stark, Arlene Whalen, Alma Carroll, Fay McKenzie and Marie (The Body) MacDonald.

The men and women in the cast were assigned compartments in separate sections of the train. This didn't mean there wasn't any comingling, but it made the trip look legitimate enough to quell the complaints of the spouses of the stars who were forced to stay behind in Hollywood.

Groucho Marx remembered the screen's great lover, Charles Boyer, taking him aside, and asking him very quietly, "Groucho, can't you get me a girl? Everyone else has one."

This incident always amused my father, who told me, in a

chortling tone, after he returned home, "Imagine the screen's greatest lover couldn't find a girl, among all that muff, to go to bed with him! It was pathetic!"

One of the busiest womanizers on the trip was super-agent Charlie Feldman, who had wangled a spot on the train ostensibly to look after the interests of some of the stars he handled. According to Fay McKenzie, "Joan Bennett and Joan Blondell were both nuts about him, and vice versa. He was also a big drinker. One night he got so drunk he wound up in his own bed!"

***

A mob of screaming fans greeted the Victory Caravan's train as it pulled into Washington four days after it left Southern California.

Groucho, sans cigar and greasepaint black mustache, was in the vanguard of the important stars alighting from the train. To his disappointment—or was it chagrin?—the fans surrounded the other stars, asking for their autographs, but Groucho was left standing by himself. No one recognized him without his stage makeup, so he went around to the rear of the train, leaped aboard, dashed into his compartment, slapped on his makeup, lit a cigar, and then descended again to the station platform. He was mobbed by autograph hounds and Marx Brothers fans in general. This was the incident responsible for his growing a real mustache. Despite his claim that he enjoyed anonymity, he actually couldn't stand being ignored while the fans were yelling "Where's Bob Hope?"

***

Hope arrived in Washington, just in time to join the others at Eleanor Roosevelt reception on the White House lawn. While Groucho was standing next to Mrs. Roosevelt, the Marine Band struck up a spirited medley of Sousa marches. After hearing a few bars from the very loud brass band, my father turned to her and quipped, "Mrs. Roosevelt, now I know why you travel so much."

Hope was no match for Groucho when it came to ad-libs. Notwithstanding, Hope was a huge success on radio and in the movies, while Groucho's career in 1942 was on the wane. Groucho envied Hope's success and never overlooked an opportunity to disparage him as a comedian. This was never more noticeable than during the all-night rehearsal of the show at Constitution Hall under the direction of Mark Sandrich. While Sandrich was struggling to coordinate all the various personalities into one cohesive show by curtain-time the next night, Groucho, who didn't have a staff of writers along with him as Hope did, kept grousing about the skimpiness and quality of his material.

"What's wrong?" Sandrich asked Groucho at one point. "You don't see Hope complaining."

"It's all right for guys like Hope," retorted Groucho. "He has seventeen guys writing his jokes for him. But I've got to worry about my own material."

"Hope only has six writers," Sandrich corrected him. "And the only reason he has them along is because he's also doing his radio show while we're on the road."

"Only six writers!" retorted Groucho. "Why for Hope that's practically ad-libbing."

Groucho felt justified in complaining about his material, or lack of it, because when Herb Golden reviewed the three hour star-filled extravaganza for *Daily Variety* on April 30, he labeled the show "Bob Hope's Victory Caravan."

The critic wasn't too enthusiastic about the show in its entirety, but about Bob Hope's contribution he had no reservations. As long as Hope was on the stage, the show had zest and lift. With his departure, it dropped to various levels of mediocrity.

✦✦✦✦

After Washington, the Victory Caravan show played to packed houses in Madison Square Garden in New York City, the Boston Garden, and various civic auditoriums in Philadelphia,

Cleveland, Detroit, Chicago, Milwaukee, St. Louis, St. Paul, Minneapolis, Des Moines, Houston, and Dallas.

In addition to his work in the Caravan, and keeping the cast energized between performances with his wisecracking, Hope made Tuesday departures from the tour to do his radio broadcasts (usually in Army camps) and perform in golf benefits with Crosby.

As often as he could, Hope returned to the Caravan train at night to sleep and enjoy the camaraderie of the other stars. Hope particularly enjoyed singing barbershop quartets with Crosby, Groucho and whomever else they could dig up to sing bass.

"One night we were in a restaurant," remembers Groucho, "and the three of us started singing barbershop style again. But we needed a fourth to make it a quartet. So Bing went from table to table trying to recruit a bass. Everyone turned him down. I've often thought how ironic it was that the most famous singer in the world had to lower himself by pleading with customers to sing along with him. Perhaps they didn't recognize him—without his toupeé."

Sherwood Schwartz, one of Hope's writers along on the trip, says he'll never forget an incident that happened one night while everyone, including Hope and Crosby, was in the lounge car reminiscing about vaudeville experiences. Soon the phone in the lounge car rang.

"Hello?" said the porter who picked up the receiver. He suddenly got a puzzled expression, then asked, "Bing who?"

Crosby, who was no slouch himself when it came to hoisting the bottle, finally became so fed up with Pat O'Brien's carousing on the trip that he suddenly snarled, "Listen, Pat, you've got to stop acting like Father Flanagan all day and Sherman Billingsley at night." (Flanagan ran Boys Town and Billingsley, a former bootlegger, owned the Stork Club.)

By the time the Caravan arrived in Minneapolis, the travelers were so sick of life in those cramped train compartments that Hope and Crosby rented several floors of the Nordic Hotel for the cast and other members of the troupe to enjoy a night's sleep in a real bed.

In keeping with the propriety of the times, it was arranged that the men and women would sleep on different floors. Gene Lester, the official photographer for the Caravan, and the only Hollywood lensman privileged to go along and document backstage life on the tour, remembers Bing saying to Bob, after they were settled in their rooms at the Nordic, "Let's call up Mike Caruso and have him send enough girls over here to take care of all the guys."

Minneapolis was a wide-open town in those days, and Caruso was in control of all the whorehouses.

Lester doesn't remember seeing any of the girls, but he does recall that "every corridor on the floor where the male stars were staying had MPs guarding the entrances and exits so that none of the guys would be disturbed that night while they were playing around."

Groucho, who was a bit of a prude, didn't take on any of the ladies of the evening, but he did recall that "there was plenty of screwing on the trip."

"While we were playing Dallas," adds Lester, "Hope had two girls flown in from Houston. I was sitting with him in his compartment when these two good-looking young chicks arrived."

"These are my cousins from Houston," a poker-faced Hope explained to Lester.

Lester took a long look at the two stacked babes, then said, "Hi, Cousins," and diplomatically walked out.

"I remember," says Sherwood Schwartz, "there were always five or six pretty young girls hanging around in the corridors outside Hope's room—sort of like today's 'groupies.' Since I was a virgin, I was pretty envious of all the action he seemed to be getting."

* * * *

The Victory Caravan did its last performance in Houston, after which the stars resumed their own careers. It was one of the few times that anyone can remember that any of those giant show business names worked for nothing.

Uncle Sam was the real winner, for the Caravan, during its tour, sold nearly one billion dollars worth of War Bonds.

18

While the Caravan's cast was headed for home, Hope took off on a four week tour of military bases and army hospitals around the country, doing sixty-five shows before returning to Hollywood. There he begin filming the picture he negotiated for with Sam Goldwyn.

Hope's agent, Al Melnick, had even bettered the deal by getting him a $100,000 guarantee for the film, plus a percentage of the profits. This made Hope one of the highest-paid film actors in Hollywood.

Goldwyn probably wouldn't have come up with that kind of money if Hope's latest picture, *My Favorite Blonde*, hadn't smashed all previous box-office records at New York's Paramount Theater during its four-week run there in May 1942.

Harry Kurnitz, who wrote the *Thin Man* film series for MGM, was hired by Goldwyn to pen the script. In it, Hope played a foreign correspondent stationed in Moscow who was fired by his news agency for having overlooked a certain story—the Nazi invasion of Russia. His excuse: "I was busy at the time."

It was a typical comedy-melodrama, and Hope had no peer when it came to that kind of a part. Dorothy Lamour played his fiancée, and helped him win his job back by exposing a couple of Nazi saboteurs.

It was one of those scripts that didn't suggest a natural title, but Goldwyn, with his usual guile, took care of that. When he heard that the distribution of Hope's comic autobiography, *They Got Me Covered*, was three million copies, he gave his picture the same title.

It was a meaningless title in the context of the plot. As a matter of fact, the film didn't have a very strong story, but that didn't bother the fans who flocked to see it.

❋ ❋ ❋ ❋

While Hope was shooting *They Got Me Covered* in the summer of 1942, Lyle Morain, a former stand-in for him and now an Army sergeant, visited him on the set one afternoon. He asked the comic if he would consider taking his camp show to the Alaskan Army bases where some of his buddies were stationed. "They're desperate for entertainment up there," he told Hope.

Until then Hope had confined his troop entertaining chores to bases within the U.S. borders. However, after checking with comedian Joe E. Brown and ventriloquist Edgar Bergen who'd already played Alaska, Bob asked his producer-brother, Jack Hope, to advise the War Department that he was available to play igloo-land as soon as he did his last broadcast for Pepsodent before the summer hiatus.

The War Department was delighted, and immediately arranged for Hope and Company to entertain troops in Alaska and the Aleutian Islands.

Hope drafted Frances Langford, Jerry Colonna and Tony Romano, a guitar player from San Francisco, to handle the musical chores, since Hope's regular orchestra leader, Skinnay Ennis, and his whole band had already gone into the service and were stationed at the site of the Santa Anita Racetrack. (Santa Anita had been converted into an Army base instead of "a rest home for Bing Crosby's horses," to borrow a joke from Old Ski Nose's own memories.)

A slight hitch arose in Hope's travel plans when the Goldwyn picture ran a few weeks over schedule and didn't finish filming until September 5. This left only seventeen days before Hope was to kick off the new radio season for Pepsodent, on September 22.

Undaunted, Hope devised a schedule that seemed manageable. He would leave for Alaska on Tuesday the eighth. That would give him ten days up north to entertain the troops before flying back to Seattle where NBC had arranged for him to do his opening broadcast of the fall season.

Hope flew out of Lockheed Airport in Burbank—L.A.'s only major airport at the time—on an Army transport, refueling in Seattle, then flying north along the bleak Canadian and Alaskan coasts until reaching Fairbanks.

There Hope and his company ate dinner that night at the local officer's club with Special Services Captain Don Adler, and the men who would be their pilots, Captain Marvin Seltzer and Bob Gates, as they hopped from one bleak Army outpost to another in a stripped-down version of a DC-3, beginning early the next morning.

Hope was advised to enjoy these last few moments of comfort in their Fairbanks bivouac because the outposts where they would be doing their shows would be fairly austere. Their living quarters would be Spartan-like, and the quonset huts where they would put on the entertainment cold and drafty and jam-packed with soldiers.

For ten days the group hopped by plane from one small frozen outpost to another. The temperatures dipped below zero, but their audiences were warm.

In Anchorage, Hope met General Buckner, who told him, "What we're suffering mostly from up here, Bob, is cabin fever. Some of the boys have been stuck in these God-forsaken outposts for more than a year . . . with old books, old newspapers and magazines, old movies and stale relationships. You have no idea what you're doing to uplift their morale."

"Well I've got some old jokes to go with their old books and magazines," responded Hope.

His jokes, old or not, were well appreciated. Sample:

"This is our first trip up north and the Army is really taking care of us. They gave us a plane that was flown by a four-star general . . . General Pershing . . . I knew it was an old plane when I saw the pilot sitting beside me wearing goggles and a scarf."

Another joke that never failed to get a laugh: "You heard about the airman who was making his first parachute drop? His lieutenant told him which cord to pull and told him when he hit the ground there'd be a station wagon waiting to drive him back to the base. The airman jumped out of the plane, but when he pulled the cord nothing happened. As he plummeted towards the ground he said, 'And I'll bet the station wagon won't be there, either.'"

The flyers enjoyed Frances Langford, the first American girl they'd seen in months. When she sang a sentimental love song such as "My Buddy" or Berlin's "What'll I Do?" it wasn't unusual for some of the pilots to shed tears. Seeing a pretty girl and hearing her languid voice brought back visions of home that jokes couldn't do.

Hope was able to get his cast back to Seattle in time to launch his first Pepsodent broadcast of the new season on September 22. Following which he and his cast hit the quonset hut circuit in Alaska for another five days, then doubled back to Seattle for the second Pepsodent broadcast of the season, before returning to Hollywood.

Despite close calls in the frozen north, Hope was determined to tour again as soon as possible. As he later wrote, "How could I stay safely home in the U.S. putting on shows when all those casualty reports . . . were in the daily newspapers. There was something wrong about sending boys overseas to their possible deaths while the entertainers were working at Sunset and Vine and eating dinner at the Brown Derby. You had to go overseas, where the danger was, to be truly appreciated. And I was determined to be appreciated, even if it killed me."

19

Having made up his mind to risk his life along with the rest of the fighting men, as soon as he returned to Hollywood, Hope volunteered to tour the European Theater of Operations for the United Service Organization, which would become known as the USO.

Before that, however, Hope had to spend the balance of 1942 and part of 1943 fulfilling his obligations in the States.

When he'd returned from Alaska, Paramount announced a new picture for him, *Let's Face It*, based on the long-running Broadway musical of the same title. It was written by Dorothy and Herbert Fields with a musical score by Cole Porter, and starred Danny Kaye and Eve Arden.

Hope, stimulated from entertaining troops, asked the studio for a couple of months delay. He wanted to return with his unit to Alaska to play some of the camps he had missed the first time around. At least this was the reason Hope gave for refusing to report to work on the Paramount lot on the day they had announced they would begin shooting.

The strategic reason for his stalling was that he wanted Paramount to match the same $100,000 a picture he received from Goldwyn.

While Hope's agents, Louis Shurr and Al Melnick, were trying to convince Paramount's money lords that the comedian was worth every penny of $100,000, based on the grosses of *Road to Morocco*, Hope spent November and December doing his radio broadcasts from Army camps in Colorado, Oklahoma, Missouri, Iowa, Ohio and Indiana. When he returned from that tour, his radio show had topped Jack Benny's in the ratings, and Paramount finally cried "uncle" and agreed to pay him $100,000 a film.

In January and February of 1943, Hope filmed *Let's Face It*. This farce about Army life contained topical jokes about rationing and assorted shortages in wartime USA.

Hope had the role that Danny Kaye played on Broadway, but minus the tongue-twisting patter songs that only Kaye could bring off and which wasn't Hope's forte. The part had been retailored by scriptwriter Harry Tugend to fit Hope's style. Hope was teamed with up-and-coming Betty Hutton, the brassy blonde whose frenetic style complemented his rapid-fire comedy. Eve Arden of his Broadway days was also in the cast along with ZaSu Pitts.

He had no time for camp shows during this period, but he did take an afternoon off in February to immortalize his hands and nose imprints in cement in the forecourt of the Grauman's Chinese Theater in Hollywood. Aside from winning an Oscar, being asked to put one's footprints, handprints or any other anatomical prints, in the entrance to the Chinese Theater was about as big a tribute as an entertainer could be paid.

A crowd of fans and city officials was on hand to watch the ceremony, and Hope's ad-libs didn't disappoint them.

After he dipped his nose in the wet cement, he quipped, "If this hardens I won't be able to blow it for months."

❈ ❈ ❈ ❈

To no one's surprise, Hope was asked to emcee the 1943 Academy Awards. *Mrs. Miniver* won the Best Picture Oscar, with Jimmy Cagney coming up with the statuette for his portrayal of George M. Cohan in *Yankee Doodle Dandy* and Greer Garson winning for Best Actress in the title role of *Mrs. Miniver*.

In keeping with wartime austerity and metal shortages, the

usual bronze-filled, gold-plated Oscars were supplanted by ones made out of plaster (to be replaced by the real thing at war's end). It was also the last time the Academy Awards were handed out at a relatively small industry banquet. With the world at war and many people around the world facing deprivation, it seemed insensitive to continue presenting awards at elegant dinner parties. So Oscar moved into a theater the next year and it never returned to its former rubber-chicken-with-green-peas-under-glass banquet days.

Several of Hollywood's brightest stars, including Marine private Tyrone Power and Air Corps private Alan Ladd, turned up in uniform at the 1943 Awards bash, which had a distinctly patriotic flavor from start to finish.

For the show finale, Power and Ladd unfurled a huge industry flag that carried the names of 27,677 film workers who were already in uniform.

✵ ✵ ✵ ✵

As much as Hope was doing for the war effort, he never could quite overcome a sense of discomfort because he wasn't in uniform himself, especially when people in the news media started questioning whether helping GI morale was as patriotic as putting one's life on the line. Inevitably, when Hope was playing an Army camp or doing a Command Performance broadcast over Armed Forces Radio in front of a GI audience, some wise guy in uniform would jump to his feet and yell out, "Why the hell aren't you in the service, Hope?"

Hope had a standard answer for those occasions. "I was classified Four-Z, meaning 'coward.'"

It was suggested that both Hope and Crosby be offered commissions as lieutenant commanders in the Navy, but FDR had vetoed the idea. "I want these two to play for *all* the services," he told the War Department. "Not just the Navy."

✵ ✵ ✵ ✵

At age forty, with a left eye that was prone to hemorrhaging, Hope didn't stand a chance of being drafted (nor did he have any reason to feel guilty about his civilian status). Notwithstanding, if he had volunteered for Army duty, or if, through his influence and name he had been able to pass the Navy physical, he most likely would have been assigned to Special Services, where his assignment would have been to entertain the troops anyway. So what difference would it make if he were telling jokes in or out of uniform?

Hope embarked on another camp show tour in the States, this one taking in service camps in Arizona, Texas, Louisiana, Florida, Georgia, Virginia and Ohio. It lasted ten weeks, and he was able to continue broadcasting his weekly show on Tuesday nights, while entertaining at Army camps and Navy facilities between radio shows.

Hope worked at such a feverish pace that Dolores and his friends worried about his health. He told them he wasn't worried—he came from strong stock. But whether he was traveling or telling jokes in front of a bunch of GIs, the one thing that saved him was that he could catnap in a plane or in the back seat of a car or on a bus traveling over pothole-filled roads, and awake as refreshed as if he had been reposing in his own king-sized bed in his home in Toluca Lake.

By now Dolores was becoming used to his long absences. Between her devotion to the Catholic church—she attended mass every day—and her war work for the American Women's Voluntary Services she was able to keep from worrying about her peripatetic husband, except at night when she was home alone, or with her mother who had moved in with the Hopes. Dolores expressed the wish that Hope would "drop into the house occasionally" so that Linda and Tony could get to know their father. She seemed to accept the fact that her husband was a rover by nature. "The first year we were married I saw so little of Bob that I wasn't sure we'd make a go of it," she once confided in an interview for one of the women's magazines. "I've gotten accustomed to his being away. I couldn't imagine life being any different."

Never was Bob Hope more hyper than during his tour of the Southern camps with Frances Langford and the mustachioed

Jerry Colonna. His old pal from vaudeville, Barney Dean, was a source of constant amusement to Hope (and often acted as his beard). Dean, out of a job, joined Hope on his Southern tour to be his valet and "gofer."

According to Dean, who has since gone to that Great Vaudeville House in the Sky, traveling with Hope to Army camps "was a great experience, and a mad one. In the first place, there were never less than three telephones in our room, and all of them rang at the same time, every second of the day and night. And people . . . people . . . people all trying to get to him for money or for some cause. Bob didn't seem to mind. He thinks he's superman. He does practically all the work himself. He never gets tired. He made me weak just watching him."

Dean never ceased to marvel at Hope's inexhaustible supply of energy and never tired of telling friends the story of the night the four of them arrived in Atlanta. They'd spent five grueling days and nights on the road playing Army camps. Hope was to do his Pepsodent show from Atlanta the following night.

Exhausted Langford and Colonna were both looking forward to a decent night's sleep before rehearsing the radio show.

Hope and Dean said goodnight to them and retired to their hotel suite. The comedian had just stretched out on the bed when the telephone rang. Dean answered it and was surprised to find himself on the line with Mike Dennis, a Paramount wardrobe boy who'd been drafted and who was stationed in the small town of Albany, near Savannah. As soon as Hope got the gist of the conversation—could he put on a show for Mike's GI buddies—he grabbed the extension phone. "Hi, Mike, this is Bob. You want a show? Sure, we can come over; just tell me where it is. We'll be there. We'll leave right now."

Hope wasn't deterred when he heard from Mike that the camp was a hundred miles away from Atlanta, but Colonna and Frances Langford were. They refused to go along, claiming they needed some rest. Hope hopped in a car anyway with Barney Dean and drove to the camp in Albany. There he did a show, with Dean acting as his stooge, for Mike Dennis and the hundred soldiers in his battery.

As someone once said, Hope would put on a show for a cigar store Indian, just to be performing.

✾✾✾✾

Next on Hope's schedule was an overseas trip to entertain in the European Theater.

One member of Hope's staff who wouldn't be going along with the comedian on the trip was writer Sherwood Schwartz.

Schwartz, who was making $75 a week from Hope, stayed with *The Pepsodent Show* until he was drafted into the Army in 1943. The Army assigned him to Armed Forces Radio in Manhattan, writing jokes for the overseas broadcasts to the troops (these, incidentally, were transcribed, not direct broadcasts).

"In, 1943," remembers Schwartz, "I read where Hope was doing a *Pepsodent Show* from New York and that he was rehearsing in an NBC studio there. So I found out what studio he was working in, then went over to Schrafft's on Madison Avenue and picked up a pineapple sundae, which they put in a paper carton for me, so I could take it over to the Hope show at NBC.

"I got there in the middle of his rehearsal, and waited until they were taking a break. Then I sneaked up behind Hope and without telling him who I was, I said, 'Here's your sundae, Mr. Hope' and put it in his hand. Without turning around, and without missing a beat, Hope took the sundae from me, and snapped, 'What kept you so long, kid?' "

✾✾✾✾

No matter how generous he was with his time and despite his generosity to his parents, Hope never got over his innate cheapness. "If you went to his house to work on a script, he'd never offer you anything to eat, even if it was mealtime," relates Hal Goodman, who wrote for Hope for two radio seasons after the war. "I was working with him in his house once. When it got to be lunchtime, he said, 'Come with me, I want to talk to you,' and he walked me into his kitchen and ordered a meal from his butler. But he never even asked me if I wanted a cup of coffee. I'm not bashful, so I just said to the butler, 'And I'll have some eggs and bacon.' Hope gave me a long look, but of course couldn't very well say 'No,' so I got fed."

Hope hasn't changed much with the passage of time, or the growth of his bank account. Melinda Manos, who acted as his correspondence and scheduling secretary from 1987 to 1989, but resigned because he wouldn't raise her salary, remembers two writers coming to see him about a job one afternoon around the "Happy Hour."

When Hope asked them if they would like anything to drink, they each asked for a beer.

Hope relayed their order to his butler, who returned with one bottle of beer and two glasses on a tray.

* * * *

After finishing his radio show of the season for Pepsodent in 1943 Hope remained in his suite at the Waldorf-Astoria with Dolores to await his flying orders. Three days before the flight, Hope fell ill as a reaction to the typhoid and tetanus shots the Army insisted he have before going into a war zone, and had to crawl into bed. He felt he'd never be able to recover in time for the flight, even if he were carried aboard the plane on a stretcher.

But when word finally came from the USO that he was to be at PanAm's LaGuardia Marine Terminal at one in the morning on June 25, he was able to pull himself together.

Dolores accompanied him to the gate, where she hugged and kissed him and cautioned him to be careful. Hope knew that there was no point in his being careful if the pilot wasn't. But he didn't want to worry Dolores too, so he assured her that he would be all right, then kissed her and headed for the boarding area, with some trepidation.

Hope was a seasoned air traveler. Even before flying was safe, he was one of the first celebrities to opt for air travel over long, dull, cross-country train rides. With his hectic schedule he didn't have time to travel any other way. And he was constantly assuring friends and relatives who worried about him that flying was actually safer than driving on the Los Angeles freeway.

Months before, another PanAm Clipper had been shot down by the Germans near Lisbon, Portugal. Ironically, one of the passengers killed in that crash was Tamara, the beautiful Russian actress. She'd co-starred with Hope in *Roberta* and sang the Jerome Kern song "Smoke Gets in Your Eyes" to Hope in one of the few serious love scenes of his acting career.

Hope was luckier than Tamara. His plane arrived in the British Isles without incident.

20

In the next decade, Hope would fly more than a million miles. He'd play before nearly one million servicemen at some four hundred camps, naval stations and military hospitals in every part of the world.

As a result Hope became known as the "GI's guy," an American folk figure.

Time magazine recognized what a legend Hope had already become by age forty when they put his picture on the front cover of their September 20, 1943 issue and published a glowing account of his wartime experiences of the previous summer.

For fighting men this grimmest of wars is in one small way also the gayest. Never before have the folks who entertained the boys been so numerous or so notable; never have they worked so hard, traveled so far, risked so much . . . From the ranks of show business have sprung heroes and even martyrs. But so far, only one legend.

That legend is Bob Hope. It sprang up quickly, telepathically among U.S. servicemen in Britain this summer, traveling faster than even whirlwind Hope himself, then flew ahead of him to North Africa and Sicily, growing larger as it went.

Like most legends, it represents measurable qualities in a

kind of mystical blend. Hope was funny, treating hoards of soldiers to roars of laughter. He was friendly—ate with servicemen, drank with them, read their doggerel, listened to their songs. He was indefatigable, running himself ragged with five, six, seven shows a day. He was figurative—the straight link to home, the radio voice that filled the living room and that in foreign parts called up his image. Hence boys whom Hope might entertain for an hour awaited him for weeks. And when he came, anonymous guys who had no other recognition felt personally remembered.

❈❈❈❈

"Last night I slept in a barracks," he would tell the servicemen. "You know what a barracks is . . . a crap game with a roof . . . A discharge—that's a little piece of paper that changes a lieutenant's name from 'Sir' to 'Stinky'. . . . Soldiers are real strong. I walked into the barracks with a blond on one arm, a brunette on the other. Ten minutes later, no blond, no brunette, no arms."

Hope's most memorable exchange with a wounded GI in a hospital ward was not written by a gagman. In fact, Hope didn't even get to snap the punch line. It was delivered by a young GI who had both legs up in traction.

When Hope stopped at his bed, he asked the lieutenant who was showing him through the ward, "What's wrong with this youngster?"

"This is Joe," replied the lieutenant. "He's the bad boy of the company . . . a real fuck-up. Can't even cross the street without getting hit by an Army truck—that's how he broke his legs, trying to go AWOL."

Hope looked down at him and said, "What's with you, Joe?"

Joe looked at Hope and asked, "Mr. Hope, did you ever give blood to the Red Cross?"

Hope said he had.

"Then," countered the young man with a huge grin, "I must have gotten your blood."

21

Returning to Hollywood and the same old motion picture grind was something of a letdown after what Bob Hope had been through all summer. Not that he wasn't happy to drop into his home in Toluca Lake and say hello to Dolores and the kids again, and have a breakfast of bacon and *real* eggs for a change. But after a few days on the home front, he found that he actually missed the excitement of flying through flak-filled skies or being awakened by air raid sirens at three in the morning and having to duck into a bomb shelter with Frances Langford, still in her nightie, on his arm. The Bob Hope legend was firmly established.

The decompression period took longer than Hope could have imagined. He had trouble adjusting to life as just a radio and movie star. As he himself put it, "I have gotten hooked on fear, the real thing, not the sort you felt when a joke didn't play or a movie got panned."

He had been hyped on danger, real danger, and he was looking forward to doing it all over again.

Within a week after he returned home, Hope was at the Pasadena Civic Auditorium doing his first Pepsodent broadcast of the season. After that he planned to go out on the camp show circuit again.

Bing Crosby was Hope's guest on his first broadcast, so there was no shortage of insult jokes.

"Welcome home, Ski Snoot. My . . . my, look at you. No more pot tummy. How'd you manage that?"

"I didn't," retorted Hope. "During an air raid it went around back to hide."

The jokes were light, familiar and usually managed to poke fun at Hope's feigned cowardice. But what touched the hearts of his listeners more was his pitch at the end of the show to remind everyone that war was hell, and still going on:

> Well, folks, during the summer we popped in on your sons overseas. We ate Army chow and jumped into ditches with him when the junkers came over. We saw the shadow of pain and tragedy on his face, and we've seen the bellylaughs chase the shadows away. We came home and found that all some people are talking about is the high cost of living, and what a pain in the you-know-what rationing is. Maybe they ought to figure the high cost of dying on that beachhead at Salerno . . .

That tag to his show brought smiles, combined with a few tears, to his listeners. When Jack Goodman, editor-in-chief of Simon & Schuster, heard the broadcast, he immediately offered Hope a contract to produce a book based on his wartime experiences, but with "a light, humorous touch."

Hope figured "Why not?" He quickly found out he was no writer. For a few nights Hope fooled around with an opening chapter to present to Goodman so the contract could become a reality. But when it became clear to him that he would need professional help, he contacted Carroll Carroll, at J. Walter Thompson's advertising agency, and offered him the job of ghosting the book.

Carroll was head writer on Crosby's *Kraft Music Hall* radio show and had contributed dialogue and ideas for comedy routines to a few of the "Road" pictures, so he was familiar with Hope's style.

Hope had taken notes on his camp show experiences ever since he started doing them. He had jotted down his ideas on everything from the inside of matchbook covers to Claridge Hotel envelopes and even on toilet paper if he happened to get an idea while on the toilet.

He stuffed all these loose scraps of paper into a large brown envelope, and gave them to Carroll.

Carroll asked Hope if he had any title suggestions.

"*I Never Left Home,*" replied Hope.

"Why that?" asked Carroll.

"Because," answered Hope, "everywhere I went, I met people from places I knew or had played vaudeville or had lived. And I kept running into people I knew who were now in uniform. So it was like I never left home."

Carroll's nights were free to work on an opening sample chapter. For a comedy writer, his concept of an opening was quite serious, but it got the desired effect:

I saw your sons and your husbands, your brothers and your sweethearts. I saw how they worked, played, fought and lived. I saw some of them dying. I saw more courage, more good humor in the face of discomfort, more love in an era of hate, and more devotion to duty than could exist under tyranny. I saw American minds, American skill, and American strength breaking the backbone of evil.

And I came back to find people exalting over the thousand plane raids over Germany . . . and saying how wonderful they are! Those people never watched the face of a pilot as he read a bulletin board and saw his buddy marked up missing . . .

I didn't see very much. And God knows, I didn't do any fighting. But I had a worm's eye view of what war is.

Dying is sometimes easier than living through it. This is not a book about the serious side of the war. That isn't my field. All, I want you to know is, I did see your sons and daughters in the uniforms of the United States of America . . . fighting for the United States of America.

I could ask for no more.

Hope liked Carroll's beginning and sent it to Jack Goodman, who gave it his swift approval and Hope a contract: the advance against royalties was $500. Hope turned the $500 check over to Carroll, with the understanding that there would be no further compensation for his labors. The royalties, if there were any, would go to the National War Fund. This was okay with Carroll, who had a large income and could afford to work for nothing.

From then until the first of the year, Hope and Carroll met one evening each week in Hope's Toluca Lake home. They discussed ideas for new chapters and went over what had already been written. Hope's secretary, Jane Brown, took down everything discussed in shorthand, then transcribed it. As Carroll finished a chapter, he'd bring it to Hope, and the two would rewrite and refine. Hope also gave copies to his gagmen to punch up with jokes. Carroll would take what he liked of these and fit them into the script.

The book was ready by mid-December and Hope sent it off to Goodman, who loved it and scheduled it for spring publication.

While Carroll was writing *I Never Left Home*, Hope left home quite a few times to play more Army camps, mostly ones in California, but occasionally straying as far away as the Las Vegas Gunnery School in Nevada.

Hope had time for this because there was a delay in getting his and Crosby's *Road to Utopia* in front of the cameras.

The delay was caused by script trouble. This was the first of "Road" picture that had not been assigned to Don Hartman and Frank Butler, but rather to the young writing team of Norman Panama and Mel Frank, who were responsible for the original story of *My Favorite Blonde*.

Having worked on the Hope radio show for a full season, the team certainly knew how to write for him, but whenever you have three people in a film, each of whom considers himself the star, there are bound to be disagreements over how the parts should be written. So before there could be a final draft, there were endless story conferences, plenty of conflict, and extensive rewriting.

"The problem," Norman Panama told me recently, "was not that there was anything wrong with the script, but all three of the stars, Hope, Crosby and Lamour, had become such big names by then that they had to be catered to individually and their egos constantly fed.

"Crosby was being talked about as an Oscar contender for his acting in *Going My Way*, and Hope, as *Time* magazine wrote, was 'first in the hearts of our servicemen.' Dottie wasn't quite as big as the other two, but still, you couldn't just hand her a script either and say 'Do it!' even though, contractually, none of them had script approval. "In order to get them to do *Utopia*, and stop their nit-picking, Mel and I had to go to each of them individually. We told the plot to Crosby, but made it sound like it was *his* picture. Then we told it to Bob, but from *his* point of view, so he thought it was *his* picture. Once we got their approval, it was no problem selling the idea to Lamour. She knew she had to go along with it, or Paramount would replace her."

Ultimately, *Utopia*, which was about two stranded vaudevillians prospecting for gold in the Yukon, contained some of the wildest, most-hazardous-to-perform comedy sequences of all the "Road" series.

In one sequence, Bob and Bing had to climb a rope up the side of a glacier and the rope was to break. They were using a fairly high wall, and mattresses were always put at the bottom of it in scenes like that, just in case. Unfortunately, when the rope did break, someone had moved the mattresses and Bing threw his back out when Bob landed on top of him. Bing's back trouble started with that accident.

In another sequence, Hope and Crosby had to work with a "tame" grizzly bear. The trainer assured them that the bear was well-mannered and no danger.

The scene called for the bear to wander into a mountain cabin looking for Hope and Crosby. To escape, they hid under a bear rug. The bear sniffed his way through the cabin, finally plodding across the rug, with them under it.

Hope and Crosby were leery about this scene, but agreed to try.

"Just don't come out from under the rug until I chain him up again," cautioned the trainer.

Unfortunately, the bear didn't do what the script called for it to do. Instead of walking over the rug, the bear planted himself on top of it and stood menacingly, sniffing at the strange lumps underneath. Hope and Crosby were scared to death when the bear started to snarl and paw at the rug with its huge sharp claws. The trainer managed to recapture and chain up the animal before it could maul the two stars.

"I told you there was nothing to worry about," said the trainer as the two crawled out from under the rug.

Nothing to worry about? The next day the bear went berserk and tore the arm off his trainer.

After that narrow escape Hope and Crosby welcomed an invitation to play in a charity golf match when they were scheduled to shoot a musical sequence with Lamour.

Pretending they didn't know they'd had a "call" for the next day, the two played hookey in order to compete in the golf exhibition. But nobody bothered to tell Lamour, who was supposed to sing "Personality" to Bing and Bob, while dressed in a sexy, extremely tight-fitting evening gown.

"I had to be corseted and practically poured into the dress," recalls Lamour. "The elaborate hairstyle and makeup also took about two hours, so that for me to be on the set by nine o'clock, which was the director's 'call,' I had to arrive at the studio by six. But make it I did. I was on the set by nine and on my leaning board [a kind of recliner for actresses whose very tight gowns prevented them from sitting down]. I waited from nine until noon for Bing and Bob to show up.

"Nobody seemed to know what had become of them, or could locate them. So I went back to my dressing room, got out of the tight dress and had a light lunch. After that, I put the dress back on and returned to the set, where there were about fifty extras waiting around too. I waited until about four-thirty, at which time Gary Cooper ambled onto the set and asked what was going on. When I recounted my tale of woe to him, he said, 'Dottie, you shouldn't let those guys take advantage of you. Why don't you just give them a taste of their own medicine? Go back to your dressing room, take off your costume and makeup and go the hell home.'

"It wasn't my style, but Gary insisted I had to teach the boys a lesson. He took my arm and escorted me back to my dressing room. As soon as I had taken everything off, the phone rang and it was the assistant director informing me that Bob and Bing had arrived and the front office wanted to know why I wasn't on the set. I told them why and said I was too tired to begin working at five in the afternoon.

"That was all right with Bing and Bob. They didn't feel like working after the golf match, either. But they never pulled a stunt like that on me again . . . From that moment on, though, they always insisted on calling me 'that temperamental Lamour woman who stormed off the set.'"

Utopia was one of Hope's favorite "Road" pictures—perhaps because it contained one of his favorite funny lines, when he and Bing entered a tough saloon in the Yukon, bellied up to the bar and ordered a drink. Since they were masquerading as two famous tough guys, Bing ordered "a couple of fingers of rot-gut," but Bob requested a glass of lemonade. When Douglass Dumbrille, who played the villain, did a double-take and glowered at him suspiciously, Hope hastily added, "in a dirty glass."

Hope also liked *Utopia* because, in it, *he* and not Crosby got the girl. It was a first. This happened, because when Bing, Bob and Dottie were running across an ice floe, trying to escape the bad guys, a crevice opened, leaving Hope and Lamour on one and side and Crosby stranded on the other along with the villains. Assuming Crosby had been killed, Hope and Lamour married.

The final sequence takes place thirty years later, when an aging Crosby pays a call on the long-married Hope and Lamour. Just then, in walks their son, the spitting image of Crosby. It was a daring touch for those days, and the censors probably wouldn't have passed it, if Bob hadn't softened it by shrugging his shoulders and saying to the audience, "We adopted."

Utopia's ending may have been a case of art imitating life. At the height of their popularity as a team, and while they were still close friends, Hope and Crosby used to trade girlfriends. Not girls they were serious about, but the bimbo, one-night-stand types that were so common on studio lots or around broadcasting studios. If, for example, Crosby found a girl he thought was particularly good in bed, he'd introduce her to Hope and vice-versa.

One time in the late forties, while Crosby was recuperating in the hospital from an appendectomy, he had a sexy nurse who gave him what he later described to Hope as the "greatest blow job of my life. You ought to try her, Bob."

Hope wrote down her name and the floor she was on, and the next day had his personal physician, Tom Hearn, check him into St. John's Hospital on the pretense that his nerves were shattered and that he needed a rest. He insisted on having the same room and the same nurse that the Groaner had. What he got was anything but a rest.

Road to Utopia finished shooting in March 1944, but wasn't released until February 1946. This because, according to Paramount, the studio had a film backlog.

❀❀❀❀

Hope felt run-down when he finished *Utopia.* He had a cold that he couldn't shake, and an infection in his left ear that caused him a lot of pain. Tom Hearn, Hope's doctor in Toluca Lake, told him that the best way to recover was to stay in bed. But rest rarely figured in Hope's busy itinerary. Not only had he agreed to do his Pepsodent broadcast from Brookley Field, Alabama, on Tuesday night, February 29, but he had scheduled his March 7 broadcast from an officer's training camp in Florida. Four days after that, on March 11, he was to emcee the annual Gridiron Dinner in Washington, which was a roast of the capital's political figures, put on by the National Press Corps.

FDR was to be the guest of honor at the dinner, and Hope was looking forward to meeting and performing for him. During Hope's travels he had already met Winston Churchill, Dwight

Eisenhower and Eleanor Roosevelt, but he'd never been face to face with President Roosevelt.

To restore his health, Hope reluctantly followed his doctor's advice and didn't keep the Brookley Field engagement. Instead he delivered his monologue for the show by remote from NBC in Hollywood. The rest of the Pepsodent program was broadcast from the East.

His health improved from the rest, and he was able to do the March 7 show in Florida.

That Saturday, the day of the Gridiron Dinner, he flew to Brookley Field to play golf with General Mollison, who had been disappointed when Hope didn't show up for the February 29 broadcast. But the golf game never came off, because the area, in fact, the entire East Coast, had been hit by severe thunder and lightning storms. No commercial planes were flying, and it looked as if Hope would miss the Gridiron event until Gen. "Hap" Arnold came to the rescue and sent an Army plane for him with instructions to the pilot to get Hope to Washington in time for the dinner at any cost.

General Arnold or not, Hope was still an hour late arriving at the dinner, and as a result, Ed (*Duffy's Tavern*) Gardner had to replace him as emcee. By the time Hope arrived, Gracie Fields had already sung, Fritz Kreisler had already played "The Flight of the Bumble Bee" on his Stradivarius, Elsie Janis had done her comedy bit, and was followed by a trained seal act that captivated the audience. These were tough acts to follow, but Hope, who went on last, was up to the challenge. He had a whole bag of political jokes aimed at the President's chief nemesis in the Senate, Alben Barkley, Eleanor's newspaper column, and the Roosevelt's lovable Scottie, Fala.

> Good evening, Mr. President and distinguished guests. I'm delighted to be here . . . I've always wanted to be invited to one of these dinners . . . and my invitation was a long time coming . . . I thought it had been vetoed by Barkley . . . perhaps I shouldn't mention Alben here . . . it's too much like talking about Frank Sinatra to Bing Crosby . . .

By then the President was roaring with laughter, and probably would have been rolling on the floor, except he was confined to his wheelchair. Hope went on:

"Trying to find a room in Washington is like trying to find "My Day" [Eleanor's column] in the *Chicago Tribune* [a violently anti-FDR newspaper] . . . and did you know . . . speaking of the *Chicago Tribune* . . . that Fala was housebroken on that paper?

Hope was the hit of the evening, and received the ultimate of compliments, when several of the newspaper columnists who attended wrote the next day that "someone had finally come along to fill the shoes of the late political humorist pundit, Will Rogers."

Although Hope hadn't quite shaken his cold by the night of the Gridiron Dinner, his glowing reviews, plus the fact that he'd finally been able to meet President Roosevelt, buoyed his spirits and speeded his recovery. He was then not only able to fill out the rest of the month doing his regular Pepsodent broadcasts, but to honor his camp show commitments as well—in Florida, the Caribbean and Arizona.

Following that, he took a few days of rest in Palm Springs before reporting to the Goldwyn studio to do a second picture on loan-out.

Another fish-out-of-water yarn, the film, concocted by Don Hartman, Melville Shavelson and Everett Freeman, from an adaptation by Allen Boretz and Curtis Kenyon from a story by Sy Bartlett (you talk Hope and you're talking a battery of writers), was originally titled *Sylvester the Great*, but was released under the title *The Princess and the Pirate*, a swashbuckling costume spoof, in which Hope played a cowardly "between gigs" actor-magician who had bravery thrust upon him.

This was one of the beautiful Virginia Mayo's first featured roles, and although her acting left something to be desired, her bountiful bosom, in a tight sixteenth-century bodice, with a lot of cleavage showing, was found not wanting. Crosby also did a gag walk-on at the film's fade-out.

Wrote *New York Times* critic Bosley Crowther: "Hope can literally keep a film alive, even when his retinue of writers rather obviously and languidly despair."

❋ ❋ ❋ ❋

Hope didn't make another film for a year.

With all the volunteer work he'd been doing to entertain troops and with the amount of taxes the government was taking out of his paychecks, he suddenly found himself cash poor. In spite of an income of a million or so a year, what he was left with, after deducting his business and living expenses, were a number of annuities and some real estate in the San Fernando Valley. He was paying large property taxes, but not realizing any income.

Hope's lawyer, Martin Gang, told him that the only way he could retain more of his earnings was to form his own production company, and make movies in partnership with Paramount. While that's a common practice among today's stars in today's film business, it was almost unheard of in the forties. One of the few who was doing it was James Cagney.

Hope invited Y. Frank Freeman, the head of Paramount, to lunch at Perinos, L.A.'s most elegant restaurant. This was a few weeks before he was scheduled to appear in the studio's all-star *Duffy's Tavern*, based on the popular radio show.

After the usual small talk, Hope startled Freeman by announcing that he wanted to form his own production company.

Freeman asked, "Why do you want to do that?"

"So I can hang on to a little of my money," replied Hope. "I also want to have more to control of the movies I make."

"It can't be done," Freeman told him.

"That's what you say," countered Hope.

"Forget the whole idea," Freeman said, "and tell me what you think of the script of *Duffy's Tavern?*"

"I haven't read it, and I refuse to think about it until I get my own production company."

"In that case, we'll have to suspend you," threatened the studio chief.

"Then you'll have to suspend me," answered Hope. "In the meantime I'll just go on doing my radio show and entertaining the GIs."

Freeman thought Hope was bluffing when the rebuffed comedian stood up and left the table, and the studio chief had to pick up the tab. But Hope didn't show up on the Paramount lot the day *Duffy's Tavern* was to begin shooting and was immediately put on suspension. He ended up being the only star on Paramount's glittering roster *not* to be in the film, which wasn't too good anyway.

Meanwhile, the first two hundred thousand copies of *I Never Left Home* had been distributed by Simon & Schuster. One hundred thousand of them were in hardback, and sold for two dollars each, the then standard price of a book; the other hundred thousand more were in paperback and shipped out to the GIs.

Reviews were enthusiastic. Hope's following was so large that by September the book had sold a half-a-million copies, and would go on to sell another million by the following year. Since then, all of Bob Hope's books, despite glaring omissions of truth and accuracy, have been huge sellers.

One thing Bob Hope gingerly avoided in his own books is telling the truth about his life. Not only has he conveniently obliterated eliminated all traces of his first marriage to Grace Louise Troxell, but whenever he has been able to, he has used his money, power and influence to suppress episodes in his life which might lead fans to discover that he, like everyone else, has feet of clay.

In the late fifties, for example, the publisher of one of those scandal magazines that were so popular then had been tipped off by a newspaper reporter from Cleveland that Hope, as a teenager, had served a few days in jail for stealing a car,[1] but had been released after promising the judge that he'd turn over a new leaf.

[1] In her biography of Bob Hope, British author Pamela Trescott says the offense was for "stealing tennis equipment."

Not wanting to run the story until he checked it for accuracy, the publisher searched the records in the Cleveland Hall of Justice, but came up empty. Someone had removed the Bob Hope file.

"I still wanted to do the story," relates the publisher, "so I hit upon a way of doing it with Hope's cooperation. I called his brother Jack, who was his manager. I told him I'd like to run the story, but put a positive twist on the end of it by saying, in effect, 'See, even if you were a delinquent, you can still make something of yourself,' and I suggested that Hope could give his version of his arrest, thereby giving credence to it.

"Well, Jack said he'd to talk it over with Bob and get back to me. When he did, he said, 'Why don't you and your wife come down to Palm Springs as Bob's guests? You can play golf with Bob, have some fun together, and all that shit.' It was apparent that the story was true, and that they would try to talk me out of running it. So I told him I wasn't interested in socializing and just wanted to do the story.

"Well, the next thing I knew, Hope went to publisher Walter Annenberg, who called up my distributor to warn me to lay off, and if I didn't, he'd put my distributor out of business. Annenberg could do that because Hope would never again cooperate with any of the magazines my distributor handled—all the mags that were constantly running Hope's puff pieces.

"So I never saw proof of Hope getting into that kind of trouble as a kid, but I did see proof of the pressure a guy as powerful as Hope could put on the media if he wanted—in those days, that is. Only now is the truth beginning to leak out, and for the first time Bob Hope is no longer able to silence it."

✿ ✿ ✿ ✿

Hope's last Pepsodent show of the season was scheduled for Tuesday, June 6, 1944. This just happened to be D-Day, the day the allies crossed the English Channel to establish a beachhead on the shores of Normandy.

The invasion was the beginning of the end for Hitler's armies, but while it was happening it was no night for flip jokes. Many GIs would lose their lives before the day was out.

Having viewed the horrors of war, Hope realized there was too much on the line that evening of June 6 for him to be anything but serious. So he threw away most of his prepared script, and gave his audience a serious side of Hope most were unfamiliar with.

> You sat there and dawn began to sneak in, and you thought of the hundreds of thousands of kids you'd seen in camps the past two or three years . . . the kids who scream and whistle when they hear a gag and a song. And now you could see all of them again . . . in four thousand ships on the English Channel, tumbling out of thousands of planes over Normandy and the occupied coast . . . in countless landing barges crashing the Nazi gate and going on through to do a job that's the job of all of us. The sun came up and you sat there looking at that huge black headline, that one great bright word with the exclamation point, INVASION! The one word that the whole world has waited for, that all of us have worked for.
>
> We knew we'd wake up one morning and have to meet it face-to-face, the word in which America has invested everything these thirty long months . . . the effort of millions of Americans building planes and weapons . . . the shipyards and the men who took the stuff across . . . little kids buying War Stamps, and housewives straining bacon grease . . . farmers working round the clock . . . millions of young men sweating it out in camps, and fighting the battles that paved the way for this morning. Now the investment must pay—for this generation and all generations to come.

Hope had as many listeners that night as did any of Franklin Roosevelt's fireside chats.

✿ ✿ ✿ ✿

Sixteen days later, on June 22, Hope, Frances Langford, Jerry Colonna, Tony Romano, Barney Dean, and a pert young dancer named Patty Thomas took off in a C-54 to entertain the boys on the islands of the South Pacific that had been retaken by Douglas MacArthur's forces, and which had seen virtually no entertainment since the war in the Pacific had begun.

After flying first to Hawaii, and doing a show there for the boys at Hickham Field, they changed to a transport General MacArthur had lent them. The troupe spent the summer island hopping, under conditions that were miserable—hot, mosquito-filled sleeping quarters, and lousy chow.

They played Canton Island first, then Tarawa, then Kwajlean in the Marshall Islands, and on to Saipan. From there they went to Majuro, and then on to Bougainville. After exhaustion set in they decided to take a few days rest in Australia. They flew in a Catalina flying boat. When one of their motors conked out, the plane had to crash-land in the middle of a shallow river in Australia. They were rescued by natives and taken ashore to a small village, Laurieton, population six hundred.

So it shouldn't be a total loss, Hope and his crew did a show for the natives, too.

All told, Hope and his troupe traveled a total of 30,000 miles that summer, and did approximately 160 camp shows, before taking off from New Guinea in a military transport on September 13 for the long flight home across the Pacific. After fifty hours in the air, with a couple of stops for refueling, they finally landed at Lockheed Airport in Burbank, just a jokebook's throw from Hope's home in Toluca Lake.

Two days later, he was doing his first radio show of the new season at the Marine Air Station in Mojave, California.

He was still under suspension at Paramount, which meant he couldn't accept employment at any other film studio. There was nothing to keep him in Hollywood, except Dolores and the kids, so he was free to continue doing his radio broadcasts from Army and Navy and Air Force bases, and hospitals across the nation until the end of the year and through the following June of '45.

22

For Bob Hope, 1945 was a banner year.

It was for the rest of the world, too.

Bing Crosby won an Oscar for *Going My Way* and Hope personally presented him with the gold statuette at the 17th Annual Academy bash at Grauman's Chinese Theater in Hollywood.

In January *The Pepsodent Show* finally beat out Fibber McGee and Molly for top position in the Hooper ratings. As a reward, Lever Brothers gave Hope a new ten-year contract beginning at $10,000 a week and perks that, some said, brought his total radio income to something close to a million-a-year.

Later in 1945, Hope and Paramount made peace when the studio acquiesced to his demand that he be allowed to form his own company and make pictures in partnership with the studio.

Thus was born Hope Enterprises, which eventually would be the umbrella company that would handle not only his show business ventures, but his real estate and other investments as well.

On the worldwide scene there were some momentous events, too.

On April 12, Franklin Delano Roosevelt died in Warm Springs, Georgia, and Harry Truman became President.

Two weeks later, representatives of fifty nations met in San

Francisco to draw up the Constitution of the United Nations Organization.

On the 30th of April, Hitler and his mistress, Eva Braun, committed suicide in his bunker in Berlin. And on May 7, Admiral Friedberg and Gen. Joseph Jodl signed the unconditional surrender of Germany at Eisenhower's headquarters in a small schoolhouse in Rheims, France. The war in Europe was officially over at 23:01 the next night.

Though the guns in Europe were finally silenced, there was still an army of occupation to be entertained and would be for many years to come.

Hope kicked off the seventh War Loan drive on May 12 by putting on a three-hour show in Washington. Part of the entertainment was his regular thirty-minute radio broadcast for Pepsodent. The show brought in pledges of two-and-a-half million dollars for War Bonds.

That was gratifying, for it meant Hope's pull at the box office was as strong as ever. He got an even bigger thrill when an invitation arrived for him to perform the exact same show in the Gold Room at the White House for the new president and his family. And after the show Harry Truman personally escorted Hope and company on a tour of the White House, stopping in the music room to play a Chopin etude for them on his upright piano.

That was the beginning of Hope's relationships with American presidents. Democrat or Republican, it was all the same to him. Politically, though, he is a right-wing Republican.

During the radio season, Hope continued putting on exhibition golf matches with Bing Crosby and playing camps and Army hospitals.

Hope also accepted the USO's invitation to do a two-and-a-half-month tour in the European theater during his summer radio hiatus. His cast had changed slightly. Frances Langford had been given her own radio show that summer, so she was unavailable. But Hope was able to get Jerry Colonna and Patty Thomas again, singer Gale Robbins, plus humorist Roger Price and the comedian Jack Pepper to help out with the comedy sketches.

The troupe sailed on the *Queen Mary* at the end of June. Dolores, as usual, stayed behind to take care of the kids. Hope's crew arrived in London in time to do a show in Albert Hall on the Fourth of July in front of ten thousand screaming, appreciative GIs.

During the rest of the summer, the group entertained servicemen in Paris, Nice, Italy, Austria, Munich and Nuremberg.

Having saturated Europe with his one-liners, Hope was ready to do it again in the South Pacific.

There was no need.

On August 6, 1945, the first atomic bomb was dropped on Hiroshima, and three days later a second over Nagasaki. Altogether, 120,000 Japanese died in those two attacks.

On August 15 Japanese Emperor Hirohito agreed to a surrender. On September 2 it was made official with the signing of the surrender documents on the deck of the U.S.S. *Missouri* in Tokyo Harbor.

The need for troop entertainment was not over, but many of the biggest names were unwilling to sacrifice any more of their time and talent.

Bob Hope didn't feel that way. He was determined to do his radio program from camp shows as long as there was a need for it; also, GI audiences were easier to get laughs from than civilians.

Unhappily, his radio audience was becoming tired of service jokes. Letters came in to Hope's sponsors asking, "Why isn't Bob Hope doing shows for *us* now that the war is over?"

Hope stuck stubbornly to his guns. "As long as there are guys and gals still in service, they get the first call," he announced. "They need entertainment now more than ever. The days they spend waiting to get home, or the hours they spend lying on hospital beds, hoping to get well, are plenty tough, and a laugh won't hurt them.

23

There's no questioning Bob Hope's devotion to his adopted country or his sincerity about keeping the troops entertained. When pressed though, even his friends will grudgingly admit that his camp show trips were at least partly motivated by his need to get as far away from hearth and home as possible, so that it would be more convenient (and safer) to make love to his coterie of willing girlfriends.

In many cases the sole criterion for choosing an actress to take along with him on tour would be whether or not she was willing to have sex with him. If later she changed her mind or chose not to have understood the requirements set forth by whoever recruited her, there'd be no escaping Hope's wrath.

On the surface, and to those who don't know him intimately, Hope seems to have a very even disposition. But actually he's quick to lose his temper when he isn't getting his way or if someone displeases him.

One of the most persistent rumors about Hope's wartime entertaining was that once, while on a USO tour of the South Pacific, he became frustrated with a young actress who refused to sleep with him. With the cooperation of the local commanding officer, he left her stranded at a remote Army island outpost while he and the rest of his troupe flew off in their C-47 on the next leg of their junket. When the girl finally found her way back to Hollywood and told the head of the local USO chapter, her complaint was treated lightly.

First USO officials told her they'd look into it and get back to her. Then they said that Hope told them the actress had overslept, and missed the plane. "Next time set your alarm clock," they advised her.

I heard that story from two reliable sources: the late Rudy Vallee, who had his own entertainment unit in the South Pacific during World War II, and Bob Howard, a young writer who'd got his first show business job on the Hope radio show after he was discharged from service in 1946.

Howard, a buddy of mine, was excited. Hope had hired him for fifty-dollars-a-week—with the usual Simon Legree contract. But Howard soon became disillusioned. First, he hated Hope's habit of sailing the salary checks down to the writers from the top of his staircase humiliating writers by making them scramble for their weekly pay.

And second, he didn't like having to accompany Hope, in the comedian's car, out to the sticks the night of the broadcast.

Although the radio script was finished by broadcast day, and the show already had a preview under its belt, Hope still demanded that at least one of his writers drive out with him to the site of the broadcast, just in case there were last minute changes in the script, or he himself had a sudden idea for a new line.

The senior writers weren't crazy about this part of their job, and when they could they wiggled out of it with lame excuses. Since Howard was the junior writer, he was usually the one to get stuck.

The first time he was chosen, he thought it a great privilege. "Oh, boy, I must be Mr. Hope's favorite writer," he naively thought, contemplating a welcome raise in salary.

But after several such trips out to the tullies in Hope's car, Howard discovered the real reason no one else on the staff wanted to go along.

More often than not, Hope would meet and get friendly with

one of his female "groupies" at the show. If she appealed to him, and vice versa, he'd tell Howard to get lost after the show and he'd ride off with the girl to a motel. Howard would be left to his own devices to make his way back to Hollywood. Usually this meant hitchhiking and sometimes not arriving home until four in the morning.

"I remember one time," recalled Howard with a bittersweet smile, "I had just gotten home and fallen asleep after one of those horrible excursions. The phone rang. It was Hope. 'I hate to bother you, kid,' he said, 'but I'm doing a benefit tomorrow night for the UJA in Pittsburgh, and I need a couple of fresh bar mitzvah jokes before I leave from Burbank tomorrow morning at ten. Get on it right away. I want them by eight tomorrow morning.' "

✿ ✿ ✿ ✿

Walking was—and still is—another of Hope's favorite forms of recreation. Whether he's in Toluca Lake or Palm Springs or London, it's not unusual for him to get out of bed at two in the morning, put on his clothes, and take a stroll around the neighborhood.

When he was doing his radio broadcasts from outlying communities, he'd often use a break in a rehearsal to stroll around the town and see the sights. On one such occasion he was walking down a tree-lined sidewalk in a small southern California town, when a striking-looking young lady came dashing out of a house he was passing and thrust an autograph book into his hand for him to sign. After he put his signature in her book, she invited him into her house, saying, "I want to ball you, Mr. Hope, so I can tell all my friends."

It was an offer Hope couldn't refuse.

According to the story Hope told his writers, after he'd obliged the lady, her twin sister suddenly appeared in the doorway to the bedroom and exclaimed, "Now it's my turn!"

Hal Goodman, a talented writer Hope picked up after the war, could hardly contain his laughter when I asked him if it was true that the comedian fooled around. "Are you kidding? Hope had a girl in every city and small town and farming hamlet where we played. . . . Azusa . . . Cucamonga . . . you name it. Anyway, in this one town—I forget which one—but somewhere out in the sticks, he had a girl who complained to me, 'I can't put out for him anymore. He never gives me any money.'

"Well, that's Hope. He never gives anybody any money. He's one of the richest men in America, but he never gives anybody any money. He used to tell us writers, 'Crosby has more money than I have.' Well, Crosby never had as much money as Hope, because Hope worked at accumulating it. Crosby didn't.

"You know why he never played Vegas? Because he didn't want money per se. Like there was a time when he could have gotten two-hundred-thousand-a-week there. But he didn't want a check. He wanted them to buy his land in San Fernando Valley and give him land in Las Vegas in return. He wanted to trade up, and not pay taxes. The Vegas casino owners wouldn't go for that.

"He's made more money than anybody else in show business . . . all those trips to play for the boys . . . the government paid for transportation, accommodations, etc. Then he kept all the money that NBC gave him, so it didn't cost him anything, except the salaries of his cast . . . and he made a huge profit. No overhead, and he would end up with the special . . . the reruns, the film clips, the publicity and all the other perks.

"I met him toward the end of World War II. I was a lieutenant in the Army, stationed in Mannheim, Germany. He was doing a camp show there. . . . He had [world champion fighters] Joe Louis and Billy Conn in his cast. Anyway, he asked somebody in my regiment, 'Do you know anybody around here who writes?' And someone told him about me. That's how we met.

"After we got together, he asked, 'How would you like to write jokes for me . . . some boxing jokes for Louis and Conn?' So I wrote some material, which he liked. He asked me to look him up after I got out of the Army. 'I may have a job for you.'

"I thought it was bullshit, so I didn't. But his agent Jimmy Saphier somehow found me and sent me a contract, which was very nice, except it was sort of a jail sentence. If you went to the bathroom, he owned the material . . . if you thought of something in the middle of the night, he owned the material. And the contract was full of options. He had you, at his option, for five years. But he didn't have to notify you he was picking you up until four weeks into the next season, when it would be too late for you to get a job with another show.

"Aside from his cheapness, he could be stubborn as hell. I remember my first experience. . . . It was around Easter . . . in 1946. We were doing an Easter Parade routine. At the rehearsal for the preview, Hope put a joke in his monologue that went like this: 'The lady in the parade had so many flowers on her hat that two funerals followed her.' So after the rehearsal, I went up to Hope . . . now, mind you, I'm just a kid . . . and told him, 'That funeral joke is in very bad taste. Why don't you take it out? You don't need it. You have dozens more.'

"Well, Hope looked at me with a jaundiced eye, and snapped, 'What the fuck do you know, kid?' And he went ahead and did it, and it got a big laugh. But if he didn't want a joke to get a laugh, like something you'd fought to keep in, but he didn't believe in, he would deliver the lines badly, just to prove his point."

✤ ✤ ✤ ✤

There's no disputing the fact that Hope knows what kind of material works best for him. There was a slight dip in his radio ratings at the beginning of 1946 when his show fell a few points below Fibber McGee and Molly. Hope found this very disturbing.

Newspaper critics, and other professionals in the business, blamed his drop in popularity on the sameness of his material— that he was catering too much to GI tastes. They said that playing Army camps had made him lazy about trying anything new.

Hope answered his critics by admitting that perhaps the show could use a few changes, but that he was too busy to start monkeying around with his format in the middle of the current radio season.

Well, busy he certainly was.

In addition to his own radio show, he was making movies, doing guest shots for Tony Martin, Bob Crosby and other radio stars, recording transcriptions for Armed Forces Radio, participating in his usual heavy schedule of benefits around Hollywood, and taking on a theater personal appearance tour of twenty-nine cities in thirty-one days.

The tour became more or less a necessity after his accountant told him he owed $62,000 more in taxes than had been withheld from his paychecks by Paramount and NBC.

Admittedly an ambitious undertaking, the tour proved worth the extra effort.

In between all this, he managed to squeeze in four more pictures for Paramount—*Monsieur Beaucaire, My Favorite Brunette, Where There's Life,* and the all-star *Variety Girl* in a bit with Bing.

Not only did he star in these films, but under his new deal with Paramount he also wore the mantle of co-producer.

As he was quick to discover, having to produce and make decisions as well as act, could be a pain in the coccyx. Even though he and Paramount had employed one of his favorite writing teams—Panama and Frank—to come up with a new version of Valentino's oldie *Monsieur Beaucaire,* turning it into the swashbuckling spoof of a sixteenth-century Spanish barber, sent on a suicidal mission, there was script trouble from the start.

After reading the first draft, producer Paul Jones felt the script was much "too straight" and wanted to bring in Frank Tashlin to "punch it up." Feeling they were being unjustly let go, Panama and Frank complained to the Writers Guild, who sided with them in the dispute.

Hope disagreed with Jones about the script. He thought it just needed a few extra jokes, which his radio writers could come up with. Jones, however, felt it needed more than minor surgery. This impasse caused a long delay in getting the film before the cameras. Impatient to get going, Hope used his clout to persuade studio head Henry Ginsberg to go with the Panama and Frank script. This they eventually did, only to discover at the first preview that Jones might have been right. The audience didn't laugh very much.

Consequently Tashlin was hired to heighten the comedy with additional scenes that could be woven into the already completed film. This paid off. At the second preview, the picture played better, and actually received a rave review from *The New York Times*'s Bosley Crowther.

> It's a cinch the late Booth Tarkington would not have remotely recognized his *Monsieur Beaucaire* in the picture of that title which came to the Paramount [theater] yesterday. His yarn was a ruff and rapier romance, and the film is, well, call it straight burlesque. But considering that Mr. Tarkington was a fellow who liked a hearty jest, he would probably have howled at the picture, just the same as everyone will.

Hope's heavy schedule of filmmaking, while exhausting mentally and physically, did one thing. It kept Dolores's wandering husband close to home—at least for a while. This break in his traveling gave Hope the opportunity to get to know his children. When he had an eight o'clock studio call, he could have breakfast with them; if he didn't have to do a benefit, he could have dinner with the family; and on weekends, when he didn't have a golf date, he could romp in the backyard with the kids and Suds, their Scottie, and Red Sun, their Great Dane.

Being around home so much also gave him the opportunity to wheel and deal in San Fernando Valley real estate. By the late forties he had bought several of the estates adjoining his Toluca Lake residence. The new places were razed in order to give the main house more acres of yard space for the kids, and to accommodate a one-hole golf course for the Master.

In addition Hope started to accumulate acres of empty land

in the Valley, some for as little as ten dollars per. Eventually these parcels attained an asking price of $40,000 an acre.

To help his brother Jim, who was struggling in the real estate business, Hope bought a driving range across the street from Warner Brothers studio for $10,000. Years later he sold the range to NBC for $1 million as part of a contract renewal deal that saved him a small fortune in taxes. During the years he owned the property, he gave Dolores's brother the job of managing the driving range, which also turned a profit.

To Hope's credit, when he became successful, he kept his money-making ventures in the family, when possible.

For example, he gave younger brother George a gag-writing job on his pictures. He'd already made brother Jack his radio producer. He went into the wholesale meat distributing business with his Cleveland-based brother Fred, a butcher, and their partnership became highly profitable.

And he went into another partnership with eldest brother Ivor in a company they called Hope Metal Products. By 1946 this one was netting him an additional $100,000 a year.

✿ ✿ ✿ ✿

Sidney Hope, another younger brother of Bob, had elected to stay out of show business. He didn't make much money, but he and his wife Dorothy preferred the country life. Sid, a machinist in the small farming town of Ridgefield Corners, Ohio, had five kids, when he fell ill of cancer in mid 1946.

Hope was playing his touring show in Kansas City when he received word from brother Fred, informing him that Sidney was terminally ill and would probably not survive the summer.

Hope canceled two days performances to fly to Sid's side. And though he tried his hardest to convince his younger brother that he would lick "the big C," Sid knew better. His only request was that Hope would take care of Dorothy and the kids.

Later while back in Hollywood in the middle of filming *My Favorite Brunette*, with Dorothy Lamour, he received word that Sid had died.

Hope didn't even finish the "take" the director was trying to get. He halted production immediately, chartered a plane and flew all the remaining children of Harry and Avis's to Sid's funeral at Ridgefield Corners.

****

At the suggestion of her mother, Theresa, who had quit her sales job in the fur department at Franklin Simon's department store in Manhattan to move in with the Hopes in Toluca Lake, Dolores started thinking seriously of adopting more children. Like Theresa, Dolores hoped that a larger family would encourage Hope to settle down. And to stop running around with other women.

Gradually she started planting the notion with Hope that it would be nice to have another infant around to hug, squeeze and pinch. Although Hope preferred squeezing and pinching much bigger babies, he gave in to his wife's entreaties. Dolores immediately put the adoption wheels in motion by once again contacting Florence Walrath back at The Cradle in Evanston, Illinois. Walrath promised to find the Hopes a baby "very soon."

"Very soon" turned out to be the end of 1946.

Hope was touring with his show in the east, and Dolores was at home in Toluca Lake when Florence Walrath phoned her and told her the good news.

Dolores called Bob, who, on hearing Walrath had another baby for them, agreed to meet his wife at The Cradle in Evanston, the next day. There they were introduced to a two-month-old girl.

While Dolores was oohing and aahing over their latest acquisition, the nurse brought in a three-month-old boy who, she informed her, could also be theirs, if the Hopes would only say the word.

Dolores wasn't sure how Bob would feel about it. She's have to take it up with her husband, who'd already disappeared into Walrath's office to sign the adoption papers with The Cradle's attorney.

When Hope returned to Dolores's side, she timidly broached

the subject of the second child. Would Bob consider it? Hope grinned, and announced that he'd already signed for the boy.

A few weeks later there was a christening at St. Charles Church, on the corner of Moorpark and Lankersham, in North Hollywood, where Dolores prayed every morning. The girl was named Nora and the boy Kelly.

❄ ❄ ❄ ❄

A little earlier in the year, Hope had completed filming *My Favorite Brunette*. In order to give the ending some much-needed punch, the writers had written a cameo appearance for Bing Crosby into the script.

Hope, who had a financial interest in the film, thought the old Groaner would gladly do it for nothing as a favor to him. But Bing demanded a $25,000 payment, and Hope was forced to give it to him.

Bing donated this to his alma mater, Gonzaga University. It was a tax write-off for him and a very expensive (for those days) short piece of film footage for Hope.

Although they continued to work and do golf charity matches together, that was the beginning of the cooling off of their relationship.

❄ ❄ ❄ ❄

On September 26, 1946, Hope kicked off the ninth season of his *Pepsodent Show*. Singer Carol Richards had replaced Frances Langford and Desi Arnaz replaced Skinnay Ennis as the bandleader (and fractured-English stooge). Most columnists criticized it for being the "same old thing," but *The Hollywood Reporter* was the most vitriolic:

> Returning to NBC last night for the new season, Bob Hope was unable to overcome some of the worst material his show has ever been burdened with, and it's a safe bet that everybody connected with the offering will have heard from Charles Luckman at Lever Brothers by this time . . . If this weren't the Hope Show

216

and if it were coming on the air for the first time, no reviewer in his right mind could give it more than thirteen weeks . . .

Equally unenthused, Jack Gould of *The New York Times* wrote:

> Bob Hope opened his ninth season on the air last Tuesday in the noble tradition of Jake Shubert's *The Student Prince*
>   You could enjoy it if you had not heard it the first, second, third, fourth, fifth, sixth, seventh and eighth times.
>   It was all there in this order: Irium (2) Pallid Patter (3) Irium (4) Joke about Bing Crosby (5) Jerry Colonna arrives (6) Hope insults Colonna (7) Colonna screams (8) Irium (9) Vera Vague arrives (10) Hope insults Vera (11) Vera Shrieks (12) Irium.

For all his success and his many millions in the bank, Hope is land-rich and cash poor. He has never been one to suffer a bad review lightly. He's been known to have his PR man make a personal call to the editor of *Daily Variety*, after a pan of a Hope Special and chew out the offending editor.

At one period *Daily Variety* was taking such heat from the "Great One," that Tom Pryor, who was editor at the time, instituted a positive-only policy regarding Hope reviews for members of his critical staff.

"Any writer who wrote a negative review of a Hope Special would automatically have his story killed," reveals Tim Gray, a reporter on *Daily Variety* today. "Pryor had some sort of fixation with Hope. Our instructions were 'no negative reviews, period.'"

Jane Galbraith, who now writes for the entertainment section of the *Los Angeles Times*, told me that in 1987 she wrote a bad review of a Hope Special while with *Daily Variety*. "I wasn't being unfair," recalled Galbraith. "I merely said his show was unfunny and that Hope looked like a tired old man and he was so busy reading his 'idiot' cards that he couldn't look at the actress he was talking to. I didn't know Pryor's policy on this. But he was on vacation when I wrote it, and my review got into the paper by mistake. At the time we had 'monickers' in place of our real names at the end of every review. My monicker was BRIT.

"The day my review ran, I got this call from Frank Liberman, who was Hope's PR man, but who I didn't know from Adam. Anyway, he'd gotten my real name from Maggie the switchboard operator. So I picked up the phone and he asked if I was BRIT. I said yes, and he asked if I had written the review about Bob Hope. I said yes again, and he said, 'You know, Mr. Hope has been in this town for many years.' And I said, 'Yeah.' And he launched into a long dissertation on who Hope was and why he deserved better treatment. And I said, 'Yes, but I didn't like the show.' To make a long story short, Liberman made a special trip over to *Daily Variety* from the Valley to see me. And when he walked into my office, he said, 'My, you're an awfully pretty young lady for the way you write.' And I said, 'Well, uh, gee, thanks, but what can I do for you?' And he said, 'Well, Mr. Hope wanted me to come over here and meet you in person and tell you that he's very aware of the things written about him.' So I said, 'Fine.' I was very polite to him. "And then he went in and said 'Hello' to Tom, who'd come back from his vacation by then, and then Liberman left.

"Pryor read me the riot act, and said that Hope employed a lot of people and didn't deserve to be treated that way. He was good for the business. And I retorted, 'Well, 20th Century-Fox employs a lot more people, and you have no rules about panning their product if it isn't any good."

"Pryor just looked at me, but had no answer, except that immediately after that I was transferred to another department.

"Two days later I opened *Daily Variety*, and there was a full page ad taken out to glorify Hope's special. It quoted glowing reviews from publications I'd never heard of . . . publications like the *Chicago Sentinel* . . . the *St. Louis Times Herald* . . . the *Chicago News* . . . The *Miami Voice*. Suspicious, I went to the advertising section and looked into the origin of these quotes. It turned out the *Chicago News* didn't exist. Nor did Sam Schwartz. Hope or his publicity people had made up the whole thing.

"I was appalled."

❋❋❋❋

Smarting as the New York reviews were to a man who, not long before, had his face on the cover of *Time,* Hope enjoyed the last yak. His ratings were close to the top after the first broadcast of the season, and following that, Lever Brothers extended his contract, with a $2,500 a week raise, which was huge in 1946.

On October 1, the very day of the Jack Gould review, there was a headline in *The Hollywood Reporter* which read:

> *Throngs Cheer as Bob Hope*
> *Receives American Legion Medal*

Below it was a story that went on to report that on the previous day, in San Francisco, the American Legion presented Hope with their highest honor, the Distinguished Service Medal, for his "tireless entertaining of troops." When he accepted the medal, Hope was flanked on the stage by FBI chief J. Edgar Hoover, Secretary of State Cordell Hull, and draft director General Hershey. Acknowledging the award, Hope vowed to the audience of Legionnaires that he would not quit entertaining the troops "until every hospitalized kid" was on his feet again.

❋❋❋❋

Two weeks later he was summoned to Washington, where, before forty top military men, the Chiefs of Staff, and leading congressmen, he was given the Medal of Merit, the nation's highest civilian award. General Eisenhower personally pinned it on the lapel of Hope's immaculately tailored gray suit.

In the euphoria of that moment, with press photographers popping flashbulbs and newsreel cameramen grinding away, Hope couldn't have cared less what Jack Gould thought of his first radio show.

The story and his picture were on the first page of every newspaper in America for the whole world—but particularly Bing Crosby—to see.

24

For Bob Hope's radio career, 1947 turned out to be a watershed year.

Broadcasters had been experimenting with television for over a decade, but not until 1947 was it considered reliable enough to be tested commercially. The spectre of television had many radio stars nervous.

To produce a TV variety show of the kind Hope was used to doing on radio was considerably more costly. Sets had to be built and costumes made to replace the radio listeners' imaginations. Dialogue had to be committed to memory; you couldn't just read it off a script. And the gagmen had to know how to write visual comedy, not just jokes. All of this took more time and money than it did to throw together the average radio program.

In Hope's case, moreover, converting to TV would mean a sharp curtailment, if not the end, of his service camp appearances, for his sponsor, Lever Brothers, would in no way stand for the extra cost of transporting elaborate sets, cameras, lights, props, costumes, and everything else that goes with producing a television show.

A major show would have to be telecast from NBC's broadcasting studio in New York, and later, when the coaxial cable was in place, at Sunset and Vine in Hollywood.

Under pressure from Paramount Pictures, which owned KTLA, the first television station in Los Angeles, Hope agreed to emcee the inaugural telecast. Sponsored by Lincoln automobiles on January 22, 1947, it would be beamed to the very few homes in the area that had television sets—approximately three hundred. (Paradoxically, Paramount Pictures fought tooth and nail two years later to prevent Hope from going into television. They feared it would hurt his pictures at the box office.)

Appearing with Hope on the show were the producer Cecil B. DeMille, Dorothy Lamour, Jerry Colonna, William Bendix, William Demarest, Ann Rutherford, Peter Lind Hayes, and the Rhythmaires.

Hope opened with his traditional monologue:

This is Bob "First Commercial Television Broadcast" Hope, telling you gals who have tuned me in . . . and I want to make this emphatic . . . If my face isn't handsome and debonair, it isn't me. . . . It's the static. . . . Well, here I am on the air for Lincoln automobiles . . . but I find television is a little different than radio. . . . When I went on the air for Elgin, they gave me a watch. . . . When I went on the air for Silver Theater, they gave me a set of silver. . . . Tonight I'm on for Lincoln, and they gave me this [he holds up a Lincoln penny]. . . . If you don't get it, don't knock it . . . this is only an experimental program.

He got his usual quota of laughs but complained after the broadcast that there was too much heat from the lights needed to illuminate the set. "I don't know where you're going to find actors who will stand for this heat. We're all wringing wet."

In short, Hope wished that television would go away; he was quite content maintaining the status quo.

Even having to get up at seven in the morning to be on the Paramount set at nine was a more agreeable way of making a living. And he hated that—getting up early, that is. Having formed his sleeping habits in his vaudeville and Broadway days, when he worked until midnight and slept until noon, Hope did not enjoy getting out of bed in the morning before ten. As he confided to one of his secretaries, "I'm up at ten . . . awake by twelve . . . and brilliant by two."

Aside from his weekly radio broadcasts, Hope spent early 1947 filming his fifth "Road" picture with Crosby and Lamour, *The Road to Rio.*

Rio was made from the same mold as the other "Road" pictures. The only thing different was that Hope and Crosby each owned a third of it, and Paramount the remaining third. As partners, who would share the profits, if any, Hope and Crosby were aware that every minute wasted on the set would cost them money. As a result, there was less horsing around and trying to get laughs from the crew during the actual shooting of the film.

April seemed to be a month when the pixie in Hope decided to test network censors again—and not just with off-color material. In those days, one of network chief David Sarnoff's most inviolate Commandments was: THOU SHALT NOT MENTION THE NAME OF ANY OTHER NETWORK WHILE ON THE AIR FOR NBC. Another was: THOU SHALT NOT RIDICULE NBC EXECUTIVES OVER THE AIR.

The fireworks began with Fred Allen. Allen told a demeaning joke on his Sunday night show about a mythical NBC vice-president. ("He was in charge of making molehills out of mountains.")

Allen's remark abruptly got him cut off the air briefly and his nasal voiced was replaced by organ music.

Hope, who, like most comedians, disliked any kind of network interference, immediately came to Allen's defense. He told the trade papers, "'If Allen's gag had been in poor taste or blue, I could see it, but to kid a network executive . . .'"

So incensed was Hope that he started to make a joke about NBC on his next Tuesday night broadcast. "You know Las Vegas . . . it's the place where you can get tanned and faded at the same time. . . . Of course, Fred Allen can get faded any time . . ."

He, too, was faded before he could go any further.

That same evening Red Skelton also made a joke about the

Fred Allen incident, and his remarks too were bleeped from the airwaves.

Two weeks later Frank Sinatra was Hope's guest star on *The Pepsodent Show*. At one point in the dialogue Hope told Sinatra that he would be seeing him on his, Sinatra's, show the following night. He didn't get to mention CBS before the NBC censors cut him off the air again.

Irked that the network could be so touchy, Hope was determined to make an issue of it with Niles Trammel, the president of NBC. Hope threatened to utter more "no-no's" on the air. Trammel retreated by announcing to the trades that Fred Allen never should have been faded. In a face-saving statement, he jokingly went on to announce that he was making Allen, Hope and Skelton "honorary vice-presidents" of NBC.

Hope's penchant for keeping network censors on their toes was never more evident than on April 27, 1947, when he was one of a host of important guest stars, on a radio special that included Art Linkletter and Groucho Marx.

The event was a once a year, hour-long radio special, sponsored by the Walgreen Drugstore chain. It was prerecorded. In it, in a sketch with Groucho, Hope was running a radio station in the desert. Groucho arrived to try to sell him a mink coat.

The sketch was put together by Manny Manheim and Charlie Isaacs, two of radio's top comedy writers. They subsequently told me that it had barely started when it turned into a battle of off-color ad-libs between Groucho and Hope—some so off-color that much of the funniest material had to be edited out of the final transcription before it ever reached the radio listeners' ears. Only the studio audience got a chance to hear it.

The sketch began with Hope answering a knock on the radio station's door.

HOPE: Why, Groucho Marx! What are you doing out here in the desert?

GROUCHO: (ad-lib) Desert, hell! I've been sitting in the dressing room for forty minutes.

(BIG LAUGH)

HOPE: Seriously, Groucho.

GROUCHO: Seriously, I've been selling mink coats. Or selling mink coats seriously. . . . Now here's a beauty for only forty dollars.

HOPE: Mink coats for only forty dollars! How can you sell them so cheap?

GROUCHO: I have no overhead . . . I don't advertise . . . I don't pay rent. And I steal the coats.

HOPE: Groucho, I know you don't steal those coats. Where do you get 'em?

GROUCHO: Very simple. I trap them with my big musical trap. I walk out into the woods and play seductive music on my zither. The little animals hear the music . . . do a strip tease and take off their furs.

HOPE: (ad-lib) Did I ever tell you about the two vultures who were plucking each other?

GROUCHO: (ad-lib) Well, it's hard to do without two. (AUDIENCE GOES WILD AFTER HEARING GROUCHO'S DOUBLE ENTENDRE)

HOPE: (also ad-lib—to the technicians in the booth) You can start editing the record now, fellahs.

(BIG LAUGH)

Oh, would we be faded!

GROUCHO: That'll be the biggest crap game in history. (HOPE BREAKS UP WITH AUDIENCE, LOSES HIS PLACE) I think it's your turn.

HOPE: I think so.

GROUCHO: Or do you want to quit right now? (THROWS SCRIPT DOWN)

HOPE: (ad-lib) I'm never going to feed you another line again.

GROUCHO: (ad-lib) Did I ever tell you about the two vultures who were plucking each other?

HOPE: You know we have a hook-up with Lea Frances [Hollywood's notorious madame].

GROUCHO: I'd like nothing better than to be hooked up with Lea Frances.

HOPE: (back to the script) But, Groucho, I don't need a mink coat. I'm an etching man myself.

GROUCHO: (picking up his script from floor, blows something off it) You know this radio station has termites. You ought to send for an exterminator to get rid of them.

HOPE: If we don't get back into the script, Walgreen will get rid of *us*.

GROUCHO: Of course. . . . Give me your last line again.

HOPE: I don't need a mink coat . . . I'm an etching man myself.

GROUCHO: Well, if you wear one of my mink coats you'll be etching . . .

(BIG LAUGH)

Well, we can cut that too, I guess.

HOPE: No . . .

GROUCHO: I fear the girls will be too warm in my mink coats out here in the desert.

HOPE: I always find the girls are warm when you promise them the coats. Once they get it on they cool off.

GROUCHO: Not these coats, Bob. These coats are all hot.

HOPE: I get it.

GROUCHO: This is some radio station here. What watts?

HOPE: What . . . what . . . what?

GROUCHO: Now look . . . you're not going to suck me into an Abbott and Costello routine . . . with me playing Abbott. Now, why have you got this place hidden out in the desert? I started out here last night trying to find it and it was like looking for a needle in a haystack.

HOPE: Well, where did you stay last night?

GROUCHO: In a haystack.

HOPE: Was it comfortable?

GROUCHO: No, I kept sitting on the needle. I found out one thing . . . a needle always points north.

In these few minutes of matching wits with Groucho, Hope managed to get off one joke about fucking (plucking), which Groucho immediately picked up on to further compound the felony, and one about "Madame" Lea Frances. The two come-dians became so uninhibited during the rest of the sketch that they literally threw away their scripts and "winged" one of the funniest sketches never to be heard on the air.

Fortunately, the show was being transcribed to be broadcast later, so the technicians who edited it were able to save it from being a total loss.

Incidentally, this sketch was responsible for Groucho getting one of the biggest breaks in his professional life. In the studio audience that evening was John Guedel, creator and producer of the Art Linkletter's *People Are Funny* and several other successful audience participation programs. After the show, he introduced himself and said, "Groucho, I think I know why you've been a failure on radio up until now."

Immediately Groucho's back went up, for the word failure had always been anathema to him, especially when it was linked to his own career. "Yes?" snapped Groucho, as if daring him to come up with the reason.

"Yes." answered Guedel. "Up until now you've been re-stricted to doing script shows. What you do best, I'm convinced after tonight, is ad-lib. If I can come up with a show for you where you can use your ad-lib talent, would you be interested?"

"What have I got to lose?" replied Groucho. "I'm not doing anything."

The result was *You Bet Your Life*, which after two seasons on radio developed into an NBC network television show that lasted for twelve seasons.

Groucho was no paragon of good taste. Once he found himself in a situation where the bars of good taste were lowered, he tested them again and again. His estate has several reels of hilarious but unusable ad-libs of Groucho's which were cen-sored from *You Bet Your Life* over its twelve-year life. But Groucho rarely got into off-color repartee unless the other fellow started it.

Hope, on the other hand, enjoyed baiting the censors, and was aggressive about doing it.

Two memorable examples of Hope's incorrigible broadcast

behavior occurred around that same period. Once, when Dorothy Lamour was a guest on *The Pepsodent Show*, she and Hope were playing a sketch involving two lovers arranging a meeting place.

LAMOUR: I'll meet you in front of the pawn shop.
Hope was supposed to reply, "Okay." Instead:
HOPE: Okay, Dottie, and then you can kiss me under the balls.

He was instantly replaced by organ music that drowned out the next few lines.

In another sketch with Lamour, at about the time the Johnny Mercer song "Accentuate the Positive" was popular, Hope used a catch phrase from the song when Lamour, reading from a script, insulted him. She continued:

LAMOUR: Don't take me seriously, Bob. I was just pulling your leg.
HOPE (ad-libbing) Listen, Dottie, you can pull my right leg, and you can pull my left leg—but don't mess with Mr. In-Between.

Again organ music came up as the audience went into paroxysms of laughter. Of course the resulting publicity in the next day's papers didn't hurt the next week's listenership.

✦✦✦✦

It was ad-libs like those that made columnist Hedda Hopper, who was a bit of a prude, take Hope to task in her nationally syndicated column.

She misjudged Hope's fans. As a result, Hedda received an avalanche of mail and telegrams scolding her for chastising America's favorite comedian. Typical of those telegrams is this one from an ex-GI:

DEAR HEDDA. CANNOT UNDERSTAND YOUR BLAST AT HOPE MATERIAL. AS A GI I FEEL I REPRESENT THE FEELINGS OF MILLIONS OF AMERICAN BOYS WHOM

BOB HOPE HELPED DURING AND AFTER THE WAR WITH HIS GREAT WORK. IF HE IS OFF COLOR, SO IS THE RED, WHITE AND BLUE.

MARVIN HOWARD

As usual Hope brought his retinue of hangers-on to the transcribing session of the Walgreen Show. In addition to Barney Dean, there was Fred Williams, a former New Orleans newspaperman turned gag writer. For some reason no one could understand, Williams was Hope's favorite. It was Williams's job to supply Hope with fresh ad-libs during breaks in the rehearsal so he could top Groucho. It was Barney Dean's chore to act as gofer (go for this, go for that) and to protect Hope's other interests. "Other interests," in this case turned out to be two well-constructed young ladies—a blonde and a brunette.

Charlie Isaacs wasn't sure to whom they belonged when he first noticed them sitting in the front row in the empty studio during rehearsals. Being the friendly type, he sat in the seat next to them during a break, and struck up a conversation. "At that point," recalls Isaacs, "Barney Dean shot me a poisonous look, shook his head and said, 'Hands off, Charlie—they belong to the Boss!'"

✷✷✷✷

Despite complaints from the critics about his radio material being antique, Hope's *Pepsodent Show* wound up first in the ratings when the season ended in June 1947.

Since he had a six-week break in his schedule before he had to start work on *The Paleface*, Dolores decided to hurry Hope off on a South American vacation before he could make any other commitments.

Dolores decided on South America, because (1) they'd never been there, and (2) they'd been invited to be the house guests, in Montevideo, of a wealthy Argentinian named Albert Cernadas, who just happened to be the husband of Hope's former radio stooge and girlfriend, Patricia "Honey Chile" Wilder.

The Hopes took Linda and Tony along on the trip, together

with Freddy Miron, Hope's Cuban masseur, who would also act as their interpreter and baby-sitter when needed. Hope has to have his daily massage or he's not himself. He considers it such an important part of his general well-being, in fact, that whenever he was setting an out-of-town deal, he'd insist that a "first-class masseur" be thrown in as one of the perks.

"I remember making a deal for him once," recalls former William Morris agent Cy Marsh. "He said to me, 'The money's okay. Just be sure you get me the best hotel suite, the best masseur, and the best hooker in town.'"

❖❖❖❖

Whether it was a disappointment to Hope, we'll never know, but when he and Dolores arrived in Montevideo, they were met by the local Paramount representative. He drove them to the Cernadas' estate and told them that they would have it all to themselves. Cernadas had whisked "Honey Chile" away to Europe for a vacation.

Why he chose that particular time to go traveling is a mystery. Perhaps he was all too aware of "Honey Chile's" rumored past relationship with Hope, and was taking no chances.

During their South American sojourn, Hope and Dolores played golf, showed the children the sights, and generally lived it up in all the cities they visited—Buenos Aires, Santiago, Lima, Balboa. They ended their vacation in Cartagena, Colombia, before boarding a luxury cruise ship back to New York.

On the return voyage, Hope spent too many hours in his deck chair improving his tan and got a bad case of second-degree sunburn. He had to be taken off the Twentieth-Century Limited in Chicago. He'd been on his way back to the West Coast from New York. He was hospitalized for two days.

The Paleface had to be postponed for a week. The comedy western costarred Hope with Jane Russell, whose biggest claim to fame was her oversized bosom which first overwhelmed audiences in *The Outlaw*, the Howard Hughes movie about Billy the Kid.

Russell wasn't much of an actress, and the script wasn't much of a script, but *The Paleface* emerged as a smash hit. Hope played his usual role as a cowardly braggart. He was Painless Potter, a correspondence school dentist sent out to set up a practice in the West, while, incidentally, taming it.

The best part of the picture, apart from Jane Russell's cleavage, was the Livingston and Evans song, *Buttons and Bows*, which Hope sang to Russell and made into a hit. It won an Oscar for Best Song. It was the second of the songs introduced by Hope to win this honor. The first was *Thanks for the Memory*.

****

Having smoothed over his censorship difficulties with NBC's president Trammel, Hope found himself heading for a brand new confrontation in the fall of 1947—this time with Lever Brothers, his sponsor. He did his first broadcast of the season from the El Capitan Theater on Vine Street in Hollywood. The El Capitan, a former legit house, had been converted into a broadcasting studio for Hope, so that he would have more of an incentive to do his show from Hollywood.

Immediately after the broadcast Hope announced plans to take his show on the road again. Lever Brothers didn't cozy to this. Touring the show cost more than doing it from Hollywood.

****

Because of who he was, and all he had done for charity, the Friars Club threw a testimonial dinner for Hope on November 2, 1947, in its posh headquarters in Beverly Hills.

The usual celebrity members attended including comedians Jack Benny, George Jessel, Lou Holtz, Al Jolson, George Burns, Danny Kaye. Also invited was Bing Crosby, an officer in the club, who never attended meetings.

To be "roasted" by the Friars is considered a great honor, an acknowledgment of one's professional standing in show business.

Crosby was listed as a speaker, but the chair reserved for him on the dais remained empty all evening, and Hope was genuinely hurt at this slight from a man who, heretofore, he had considered a pal.

To a reporter who questioned him about his absence the next day, Bing snapped irritably, "My friendship for Bob doesn't depend on appearing at testimonials for him."

To a fellow member of the Friars he was even more flip. "I didn't attend because I wasn't hungry," he retorted.

If he wasn't hungry, what was he doing dining at Chasen's with a young actress the night of the Friars roast?

"Louis Shurr and I knew he wouldn't attend," recalls Al Melnick. "We pleaded with him in his dressing room at Paramount not to disappoint Bob. After two hours he remained steadfast in his refusal. And, yes, he did go to Chasen's with a girl that night."

He was, incidentally, married to Dixie at the time.

Bing's excuse that his "friendship with Bob didn't depend on him appearing at testimonials" was put to the test two weeks later, when he turned up at a testimonial dinner given by the music industry for song plugger, Tubby Garron, whom Bing knew only slightly.

If Bing's "no-show" was the ultimate put-down, an invitation for Hope and Dolores to attend the wedding of Princess Elizabeth and Phillip Mountbatten in London on November 20, 1947, was, metaphorically speaking, his crowning social achievement of the year.

The wedding invitation, plus one to do a Command Performance for the Royal Family at London's Odeon Theater in the country of his birthplace, was an opportunity Hope was eager to accept—this in spite of the fact that the Royal festivities were to take place in the midst of his radio season.

Hope figured a way around that; he would transcribe most of his radio program before leaving the States, and just do the monologue section of his show direct from London.

Being shortsighted, as most sponsors were, Lever Brothers refused to see the publicity potential in all of this, and threatened Hope with cancellation when the current season ended in June of 1948.

Hope remained adamant. He wanted to be able to continue traveling his radio show—and while NBC and Pepsodent eventually acquiesced over the issue of the London trip, Hope instructed his agent Jimmy Saphier to start informing the other networks that he would soon be "available."

Because he scheduled a radio show from Will Rogers's home town of Claremont, Oklahoma, and also a benefit for United Jewish Welfare in Philadelphia on his way to New York, where he and Dolores were to board the *Queen Mary*, Hope brought a small writing staff with him on the trip.

At first Hope planned to take only two writers—Larry Klein and Fred Williams. Jay Burton, his other writer, wanted to go, but when he asked Hope if he would take him Hope replied, "No, you're too Jewish for the Queen."

Feeling they would need a third writer, Klein finally persuaded Hope to change his mind about Burton, saying, "Listen, Bob, you're going to break Jay's heart if he doesn't get to go along."

Klein was just as Jewish as Burton. But Fred Williams not only was a gentile, but he was a known (even to Hope) anti-Semite who spouted off about the Jews every time he got drunk, which was frequently since he was an incurable alcoholic.

Not only did Hope tolerate Williams, "he loved this guy," maintained Jay Burton when I interviewed him in 1992. He surmised, "Williams must have reminded Bob of his father."

An example of this affection for Williams occurred during World War II when the writer was stationed at some remote Army camp in Texas. In order to get a pass, Williams told the commanding officer, "General, if you let me off this weekend, I'll get Bob Hope to bring his show down here."

Naturally the general agreed to this *quid pro quo* deal, and Williams got a forty-eight-hour pass. The only problem was, Williams, with his alcohol-besotted mind, forgot to tell Bob Hope about the deal. Weeks passed without any word from Hope, and every time the general asked Williams when Hope would be coming down, the writer kept giving him the stall. Finally the general became so impatient that he phoned Hope himself one day. Since Fort Fox in Texas was not on his Army camp itinerary, Hope expressed surprise that he was expected there.

"Who told you I was coming?" asked Hope.

"Private Williams."

"Fred Williams?" asked Hope.

"That's right. Private Fred Williams. I gave him a weekend pass to go to see you and arrange it."

In order to save his favorite writer from trouble, Hope set a date, and actually did play Williams's camp.

As soon as the war was over and he was out of the Army, Williams rejoined Hope's writing staff.

He was as eager as the other two writers to make the trip to the Royal wedding even if it meant he first had to attend the Jewish benefit at the Warwick Hotel in Philadelphia with Hope, Klein and Burton.

The dinner was held in the ballroom on the twenty-second floor of the hotel, according to Burton. As usual Hope had the audience rolling in the aisles.

After the performance, Burton was sitting around the piano, sipping a drink, when Williams, who was as "drunk as I'd ever seen him," came up to him and said in a loud voice,

"Jay, are you Jewish?"

"Only on my mother and father's side," quipped Burton, sensing disaster approaching.

"Well, I'm not too crazy about the Jews," announced Williams in a loud voice that nearly everyone in the crowded ballroom heard. A hush fell over the room. One of the guests was so angry he grabbed Williams by the lapels and tried to push him out of the twenty-second floor window. Before he could, however, Hope ran over and separated the two and said, "I'll take care of this guy. He didn't mean that. He's just drunk. He says anything when he's drunk."

Embarrassed, Hope led Williams out of the ballroom. "When Bob came back a few minutes later," recalled Burton, "I asked, 'What did you do with him?' And Hope grimaced and said, 'I locked him in a closet.'"

❀ ❀ ❀ ❀

During the November voyage to London on the *Queen Mary,*
the Atlantic was extremely rough. Everyone was seasick except
the purser. Feeling a little queasy himself, Hope asked the
purser how he managed to keep from heaving his dinner over
the side.

"I eat a tremendous meal," replied the purser. "Everything
from soup to Napoleons. Then I walk around the deck for about
an hour."

"It seemed like the wrong advice to me," said Jay Burton,
"but Hope tried it, and he wound up being the only one in our
party who didn't get seasick."

"Of course, I had my own problems. I had to share a cabin
with Fred Williams. He woke up one morning after a big night
and accused me of stealing his wallet. Very drunk, he had
dropped it over the side the previous night, together with his
passport. But sober, he didn't remember any of that, and said he
would report me to Hope, who would talk to the captain, who
would have me thrown in the brig. I don't know how I got out
of that. I think I bought him a bottle of scotch and told him to
go have a good time."

❀ ❀ ❀ ❀

Laurence Olivier and American film star Robert Montgomery were also to appear at the Command Performance. During
the afternoon prior to the performance, all the important stars
were backstage at the Odeon. They gathered there dressed in
tails and milled about nervously.

"All of a sudden I hear Fred Williams, drunk as a skunk, and
stumbling around in the wings, shouting, 'Bob Hope, movie
star . . . big goddamn movie star . . . son of a bitch,'" recalled Burton. "Embarrassed, Hope went over to him and said
in a low voice, 'Simmer down, Fred, the King and Queen are
out front.' 'Who gives a fuck?' said Williams. 'We broke from the
British Empire in 1776 and I'm glad as hell of it.'

"Well, Hope turned to me and said, 'Jay, get him out of here.'

So I dragged him out of the theater through the stage door and threw him into a Rolls-Royce that was waiting there and told the driver to take him to the nearest bar and leave him there.

"That was the last I saw of Williams until we were getting ready to leave London. He sobered up eventually, but not for long. Five years later while drunk, he fell off a moving train and was killed."

❋ ❋ ❋ ❋

Despite Williams' behavior, Hope's Command Performance was a huge success. The Associated Press reported that the Royal box "shook with laughter" over Hope's routine about how difficult it was for him to get tickets for the forthcoming nuptials and how far away he had to stand to watch "four white mice pulling a gold covered snuff box."

The proceeds from the Command Performance were to go to the Cinematograph Trade Benevolent Association, which was the equivalent of the Hollywood Motion Picture Relief Fund. After the performance Hope would meet the King and Queen and the rest of the Royal Family in the reception room at the theater and present Princess Margaret with a gold-embossed album containing photos of famous movie personalities of past and present, done up to resemble eight-by-ten sized-postage stamps.

"The album was heavy," Burton remembered, "so I was told to carry it until Hope needed it at the presentation ceremony. Before that I was wandering around backstage with this heavy album in my arms. The theater was immense and I got lost. Someone finally found me and said Hope needed the album immediately. Well, in my hurry to find Hope I got lost again and walked into the wrong room. I was shocked to see King George standing in front of a mirror putting his sash around his waist. I couldn't believe I was alone in the same room with the King, and for once in my life I was speechless. But as he looked at me, I figured I'd better say something, so I blurted out, 'Hi, King,' and ran into the corridor."

Burton finally located the reception room, where Hope was waiting to meet the Royal Family, and handed the album to him. Hope presented it to Princess Margaret. While Hope was thumbing through it, showing her what it contained, King George looked over Margaret's shoulder and said, "Look at him. He's hurrying to get to his own picture."

"Why not?" quipped Hope. "It's the prettiest."

"Is Bing's autograph there, too?" asked the King.

"Yes, but he doesn't write. He just makes three x's."

"Why three?" asked the King.

"He has a middle name, of course," Hope reminded him.

❖ ❖ ❖ ❖

The next morning Hope's exchange with King George made headlines in the London papers. By then Dolores was eager to take him back to Toluca Lake and the kids. He was tired and beginning to look peaked. He seemed willing, until he attended a reception at the American Embassy that night. There he had a long talk with Secretary of State George C. Marshall, who thanked Hope for all the good work he had done during the war entertaining troops. "It's just too bad," he went on, "that now that the war is over Hollywood seems to have forgotten we still have troops over here that need to be entertained."

That was all Hope had to hear.

The next thing Dolores knew, the Hope family was on a plane to West Germany. There he did shows in Frankfurt and Bremerhaven. Symptoms of exhaustion set in by the time he finished the Bremerhaven show. He lost his voice in the middle of the performance, and further shows, at Munich and Garmisch, had to be cancelled.

Hope, Dolores and the three writers flew back to London in time for Hope to do his Tuesday night radio broadcast, with his guest star, British comedian, Sid Fields.

By now Hope had heard repeatedly from Jimmy Saphier that Lever Brothers were fed up with his constant traveling. His agent told him that he'd better iron things out with his sponsor.

Hope was too edgy for a long, dull ocean voyage, so he put Dolores and the children on the *Queen Mary*, while he and his three writers flew to New York.

"We had to change planes in Shannon, Ireland," remembered Jay Burton. "While we were waiting for the plane that would take us across the Atlantic, Hope observed Eleanor Roosevelt leaning against her luggage. She was waiting for the same plane."

"Go tell Mrs. Roosevelt I'd like to meet her," Hope instructed Burton.

"Didn't you meet her on the Victory Caravan?" Burton pointed out.

"Yes, but there were so many stars there she probably doesn't remember."

"Why don't you walk over and greet her yourself?" asked Burton.

"That's not how you do it," said Hope. "Now do as I say."

So Burton went over to Mrs. Roosevelt and said, "I'm a writer for Bob Hope, and he wants to meet you. Would you mind?"

Mrs. Roosevelt smiled that big toothy smile of hers, and exclaimed, "Ohhhh Ooooooooo. Mr. Hope is one of the few comedians I don't mind meeting."

25

Bob Hope, despite his frantic schedule, was never too busy to squeeze in extramarital affairs. Still he maintained the public persona of a devoted husband.

In 1948 Bob Hope's "folk hero" legend was as untarnished as it had been at the height of his troop entertaining days during World War II.

On January 27, he was made Honorary Mayor of Palm Springs, his second home and the place where Dolores whisked him off to whenever there was a break in his schedule and she could prevail upon him to take a rest.

There were no duties connected with the job. He just had to spend a couple of months a year in his eight-room-with-swimming-pool desert retreat on El Alameda Street, play a few rounds of golf with his fellow desert rats, and occasionally turn up to crack a few jokes at local functions publicizing Palm Springs.

Hope spent the spring of 1948 between Toluca Lake and Palm Springs while he finished out what would be his final season on the air for Pepsodent. The show was still in the top five of both the Hooper and Crossley ratings.

There was no dearth of sponsors willing to pick up the Hope Show. Swan Soap, another Lever Brothers product, replaced Pepsodent after Jimmy Saphier assured them that the program would undergo a face-lift during the summer hiatus and would have an entire new look when it premiered in September.

Gone would be the Army camp jokes. Likewise Vera Vague and Jerry Colonna. Hope finally had to part with Frances Langford despite liking her, because she had a drinking problem. In place would be a brand new cast including Doris Day, the Les Brown Orchestra, comedian Hans Conried and Hy Averback, who'd do announcing chores and be Hope's foil.

In addition there'd be an entire new staff of writers—Larry Marks, Al Schwartz, Marv Fisher and Larry Gelbart. Gelbart was the son of a Beverly Hills barber who used to cut Danny Thomas's hair in Harry Rothschild's barber shop. Thomas gave him his first job after listening to the man who was cutting his hair rave about his son's writing talent. Gelbart *pere* was a good judge of material.

After doing time with Thomas, and three years with Hope, Larry Gelbart went on to become one of America's most successful comedy writers.

Hope had decided that four high-priced writers could serve him better than a baker's dozen at bargain prices.

"Larry Marks and I—we worked as a team—started out getting $750 a week apiece from Hope," states Gelbart today from his Beverly Hills mansion. "I never felt exploited or put upon by him. For example, he never called me in the middle of the night for jokes. He called Al Schwartz instead.

"I only remember one time that Bob got annoyed with me. It was when I pulled into his driveway in Toluca Lake in a brand new Cadillac convertible. Hope looked at it, and exclaimed, 'Hey, what the hell is this!' My Cadillac reflected what he was paying me. And it probably occurred to him that he was paying me too much.

"He was a funny man, though, and I laughed at him constantly. When you work with the average comedian you see him at his house in Beverly Hills or Bel Air and you discuss what kind of a show you're going to do with him. Then you go away and write it. And then you see him at the show. But with Hope you were with him a great deal because of the traveling you had to do. Almost every week he went to play some Army base or hospital. I went with him to Guam, Manila, Alaska, Tokyo and Hawaii. I went to London, and Berlin during the airlift. And I went to Korea with him before MacArthur landed at Inchon. He had Marilyn Maxwell with him on that one."

When I asked Gelbart how Hope was able to conceal his womanizing from the public, he replied, "Well I don't think any one of us ever asked to perpetuate the faithful husband myth, but I think people were loathe to puncture it. You figure the press has been looking the other way for years, so you say to yourself, 'Why should I be the one to blow the whistle on him?' Meanwhile he fooled around with anyone he could who was young and nubile who guest starred on the show."

Gelbart remembers a time when he was sitting in the back seat of Hope's limousine, between Hope and Dagmar, a statuesque, large-busted blonde who frequently guested on his program. Hope was sucking on something in his mouth, presumably a hard candy. Dagmar looked at him coyly, and said, "Don't be selfish, Bob. Share that with me."

Hope shook his head, "No," but when Dagmar insisted, he leaned across Gelbart and gave Dagmar a long succulent kiss on the lips. At the same time he spat the object that was in his mouth into her mouth. She swallowed it, almost gagging on it.

"What the hell was that?" she exclaimed.

Hope laughed and said, "A throat lozenge. I have a strep throat."

Another incident that is vivid in Gelbart's memory took place in Hope's office at Young & Rubicam in Hollywood. "Larry Marks and I had brought him a sketch for the show. We were supposed to read it to him. With him was a girl he was going to take down to Palm Springs as soon as we'd finished the meeting. I read the sketch to Hope, with the girl also sitting in on the meeting. When I had finished, she had more comments to make than Hope did. 'Wasn't that an old joke?' 'Haven't I heard that one about the movie producer before?' 'I think the ending could be stronger!' After she had finished giving her opinion, Hope, who had laughed at the sketch all the way through the reading, and who apparently liked it, was suddenly telling us that it needed work, and sent us out to do a rewrite. Larry and I were furious but we couldn't show it. After all, we were employees . . . and cowardly ones, I guess. So we picked up what was left of our pride and headed for the elevator. Larry was really steaming, because he was the older man of our team, and it was more demeaning for him than it was for me. As soon as we were out of earshot of Hope, he turned to me and said, 'The pushy broad! Do I tell her how to suck his cock?'"

* * * *

While the new writing staff spent the summer of 1948 restyling the Hope radio format, their boss was on the Paramount lot, filming his latest picture, *Sorrowful Jones*. This was a remake of the 1934 hit, *Little Miss Marker,* based on the Damon Runyon short story, that made a star out of five-year-old Shirley Temple.

In the new version, written by Edmund Hartman, Jack Rose and Mel Shavelson, the script was tailored to make Hope's role of Sorrowful Jones, the bookmaker, the leading character.

This challenge concerned him less than whether he'd be able to win back some of his lost radio listeners when he returned to the air September 15. Of equal concern to him was whether television posed a threat.

Hope was disturbed when he learned that Milton Berle would make his TV debut on *Texaco Star Theater*, on the same Tuesday night as Hope would premiere his own radio show. Worse, Berle would make Tuesday night his *regular* telecast night.

Texaco Star Theater, yet untried, had promise. It was an hour-long revue, with blackout sketches, a chorus line of pretty long-legged ladies, and Milton Berle opening the show with a monologue not unlike Hope's.

At the time there were fewer than a million television sets in the U.S. Most of those were on the eastern seaboard, but Uncle Miltie's first TV offering was enthusiastically received by both critics and watchers alike, and became television's first comedy hit.

With the success of *Texaco Star Theater*, people without sets either made arrangements to watch shows with their friends or bought TV's of their own.

Bob Hope could see Uncle Miltie's handwriting on the wall. There weren't enough sets in the hands of the American public yet to kill off radio entirely, so Hope knew he had a short reprieve. Then he'd have to make the leap into television.

Tackling the new medium was something to be considered seriously. As he cracked to a reporter who interviewed him about TV, "I'd better get into it soon, before Uncle Miltie uses up all my jokes."

Meanwhile he garnered a good review in *Hollywood Reporter* for his first radio show of the 1948–49 season,

> The boss is back in business again, with a new product, and a new way of selling it, and from now on the dialers will be getting a new kick out of the *Bob Hope Show*—a kick that has been missing a bit in the last couple of years.
>
> It was the old Hope who came on the air for Swan Soap last night, switching over to that Lever Brothers product after ten years with Pepsodent. There was as little similarity between this Hope show and the Hope show of yesteryear as there is between the two Lever products. Gone were the stereotyped stooges and the ancient jokes which depended on the Hope ability to carry them along. Instead there was a new crew at the mike with the head man, and a new crew serving at the typewriters.

It wasn't all strawberries and cream, however. Doris Day, in spite of being a band singer doing one-nighters for eight years wasn't comfortable at the mike. She didn't like it when Hope took his radio troupe on a frenzied swing of cities because she was afraid of flying. Nor was she thrilled with the sketch material provided by Hope's writers. At twenty-five and relatively inexperienced, she was doing sketches with a comedian of Hope's stature. Doris was pretty discerning about what was funny and what wasn't. In her autobiography she offers the following banter between herself and Hope as a sample of what she thought wasn't funny.

DORIS: I'm certainly surprised to see you here in Palm Springs at the Racquet Club, Bob. Are you a member?

HOPE: No, I used to be, but I was thrown out in disgrace . . . it was over gambling.

DORIS: You mean you were cheating at cards?

HOPE: No, they caught me playing ping-pong, with a loaded ping. . . . But I love staying here at the Racquet Club, Doris . . . I've been here four days now, and it hasn't cost me a penny.

DORIS: I don't see why you didn't register like the other celebrities do. . . . Look at Clark Gable. He's got a $75 suite. . . . Van Johnson has a cabana that cost $50 a day . . .

HOPE: What about it?

DORIS: Well, sooner or later they're going to find out that you're living under the kitchen window in a wigwam.

HOPE: I'm just trying to save a little money.

DORIS: I don't mind you saving money, but aren't you carrying it too far . . . painting your face with Mercurochrome and selling beaded moccasins?

Hope, on the other hand, was pleased with his new vocalist. He felt she was a top-level ballad singer plus having a natural gift for light comedy. He also liked her attitude; she didn't mind, for example, when he kidded her about her body during rehearsals. He used to call her Jut-Butt. He'd say, "You know, J.B., we could play a nice game of bridge on your ass."

Sometimes he'd forget himself and call her "J.B." on the radio broadcast, but only the band knew what the initials stood for.

But though Doris could sing like a nightingale, she was afraid to face an audience. Often she first had to stop off in the ladies room to throw up.

❖❖❖❖

That November Harry Truman surprised everyone by defeating Thomas E. Dewey in the presidential election despite polls that said Dewey was a shoo-in. Hope sent Truman a telegram that simply said, "UNPACK."

Truman was so amused that he preserved the telegram and put it under the glass top of his desk in the Oval Office.

It was a lively time for politics, and radio audiences were particularly receptive to political jokes. Hope kidded everything, from Tom Dewey's diminutive stature and Chaplinesque mustache (he called him "The Man on the Wedding Cake") to Truman's piano playing and his verbal duels with a *Washington Post* music critic who didn't think much of daughter Margaret's singing.

Truman enjoyed being the butt of Hope's jokes. He repaid Hope for the free publicity by extending an invitation to him, just before the Christmas holidays, to take a troupe of entertainers to West Germany to bring yuletide cheer to the GIs involved in the Berlin Airlift.

The actual invitation came from Stuart Symington, Secretary of the Air Force, with whom Hope had played a few rounds of golf at Burning Tree Country Club, just outside of Washington.

Hope agreed to the airlift assignment, provided he could do his radio show from Berlin at his regular Tuesday night time, which happened to fall on December 25 that year.

Symington said okay, and with so many important people involved and pulling strings, it was a piece of cake to get NBC and Lever Brothers also to agree to the Berlin broadcast. It was just a question of getting Armed Forces Radio and NBC to coordinate the technical part of broadcasting commercial radio for an American audience from across the Atlantic.

Hope wasted no time in throwing together a cast, including not just his radio performers but some well known national figures: Irving Berlin, Mr. Music himself, composer of *God Bless America*, among hundreds of other standards; columnist Elmer Davis; actress model Jinx Falkenberg; a dozen Radio City Music Hall Rockettes; and through the courtesy of the White House, Vice President Alben Barkley and Gen. Jimmy Doolittle.

Along with his celebrity guests were his radio cast: announcer Hy Averback, Hans Conried, comedienne Florence Halop, and guitarist Tony Romano. Doris Day begged off, claiming a movie commitment, but actually she was too frightened of flying to make the long air trip. In her place was Jane Harvey, who would handle the singing chores along with Dolores. The Hope children, Linda and Tony, stayed at home; so did Les Brown's orchestra since there wasn't room in Symington's Constellation to accommodate an entire twenty-seven piece band.

Needless to say, this entertainment unit was a big hit with the GIs everywhere Hope played.

* * * *

After a bumpy flight across the Atlantic, the Constellation landed in Burtonwood, England. This was home base for the shuttle planes being used in the airlift. No show had been scheduled for the boys running the Burtonwood field; it was supposed to be just a refueling stop. But when the base CO mentioned to Hope that his men could use a little cheering up too, Hope and company put on an impromptu show before taking off on the flight to Wiesbaden, West Germany.

Hope's radio broadcast was to emanate from Berlin on Christmas day. First they'd fly to three other locations where shows had been scheduled: Wiesbaden, Hamburg and Frankfurt.

Hope was told by Gen. Lucius Clay that because of bad weather, Symington's Constellation might not be able to make the flight into Berlin in time for the broadcast. Hope told him, "Then get me there any way you can."

Hope, Dolores and Hy Averback climbed into a smaller, uncomfortable air cargo plane. It was jammed to the bulkheads with crates of canned milk, flour and other food staples. It flew the two hour trip to Templehof Airdrome in the American sector of Berlin.

The flight was a rough one, for the plane had to hug the ground to stay out of the sights of Soviet antiaircraft guns. At one point, when their plane was darting in and out of low clouds, and dodging ack-ack fire, Hope lost his usual cool and broke into a sweat. As his face turned a deathly pallor, Hope turned to Averback and said, "Hy, have you seen my latest movie, *The Paleface*?"

"No, I haven't," replied Averback.

"Look," exclaimed Hope pointing to his own face, "you're seeing it now!"

The weather improved the next morning, allowing the Air Force to transport the rest of Hope's cast to Berlin. In spite of the enormous obstacles, the broadcast was heard in the U.S. at its usual time on Tuesday, Christmas night.

It was the greatest Christmas gift the isolated GIs could have asked for, short of a chance to wrap their arms around the twelve gorgeous long-legged Radio City Music Hall Rockettes Hope had brought along.

But the biggest winner of all was Bob Hope. His heroic journey through the dangerous air corridor to bring comfort and joy to lonely GIs at a time when he could easily have stayed home with his kids, garnered him millions of dollars of free media publicity throughout the world.

✿ ✿ ✿ ✿

When Hope's newest picture, *The Paleface* premiered in Manhattan on December 15, 1948. It didn't exactly bowl over the nation's most influential film critic, Bosley Crowther. Normally a Hope fan, Crowther did a complete switch when he reviewed the film:

> If the new Bob Hope picture, *The Paleface*, goes down in history books as a memorable item, it will not be because it stands forth as a triumph of comic art. Even with Mr. Hope in it, having great fun pretending to be an itinerant chicken-livered dentist in perilous Indian country in the old Wild West, this new picture is just a second string "road" show at best, conspicuously lacking the presence of Bing Crosby and Dorothy Lamour . . .
>
> Neither is it worthy of historical note because of the fact that it generously offers Jane Russell, star of *The Outlaw*, a chance to reform. Miss Russell, while blessed by nature with certain

well-advertised charms, appears to be lacking completely even a modest ability to act.

Despite Crowther's disapproval, *The Paleface* became Hope's biggest grossing film. It grossed an impressive $7 million, which was considered fantastic in 1949. Hollywood was suffering a severe post-World War II depression, and the studios were laying off hundreds of workers. There was a community-wide apprehension, reaching almost to the panic point about what television would do to the film industry.

The *Hollywood Reporter* wrote:

> Bob Hope and Paramount execs are tiffing on the question of television. Hope wants to do it. Paramount execs say "No." Hope feels the video medium wouldn't harm his popularity at the box office. Paramount execs feel it would. Showdown between Hope and Barney Balaban, Paramount topper, is imminent.

Despite his glib and endearing ways and boyish charm, there is another, quite different Bob Hope underneath the facade—a Bob Hope that those who know him intimately consider to be one of the busiest "cocksman" in Hollywood.

While Hope has always had a legitimate reason for taking his show on the road—either he had discovered a forgotten or overlooked group of GIs who needed entertaining or he needed the extra cash he'd make doing personal appearances to pay his tax bill on March 15—the strongest motivation behind most of his traveling seemed to be his need for extramarital affairs.

Hope was discreet about his outside love affairs. And he felt he could count on the people he paid—his writers, producers, agents, etc.—to keep their mouths shut about what they saw and heard.

It worked well but with exceptions. For example, during his tour of the East and Midwest in January and February of 1949, Charlie Lee, one of his writers, blew the whistle on him. Hope had booked actress Gloria DeHaven to do a radio broadcast with him from his home town of Cleveland. Evidently, the two had been having an affair before that, for the two of them checked into connecting rooms at the Carter Hotel.

For some reason Charlie Lee became disgruntled with Hope over some criticism of his writing, and after downing a number of martinis, he decided to get even with his boss.

"He called up Dolores and told her that Hope and DeHaven were shacked up," says Jan King, Hope's former appointments secretary.

It's obvious Hope never found out who snitched on him, because Lee was still with him when he went to Korea to entertain troops in 1950. Notwithstanding, Hope was in the proverbial doghouse as far as Dolores was concerned.

But Hope has always claimed, "I'm no angel," and Dolores, though extremely jealous, seemed resigned to reality. She knew that he wasn't going to change.

And she was right.

✿ ✿ ✿ ✿

Just a few weeks after the DeHaven episode, in the spring of 1949, Hope became involved with Texas-born movie starlet, the notorious Barbara Payton.

Like thousands of pretty young women, Payton had migrated to Hollywood in 1947 hoping to make her fortune in the movies. Physically, she seemed to have what it took. She was twenty-years-old, five-four, with a well-constructed figure, blonde hair and a saucy personality. Moreover she was willing to bed down with just about any man who asked her provided he could supply the required incentives—money or a shot at a film role. Casting directors and movie stars were her main targets.

Not long after her arrival in Hollywood, she wound up with a term contract at Universal-International for a couple of hundred dollars a week. By 1949 she slept her way up to a bit part in *Once More My Darling,* starring Robert Montgomery. In 1950, she became a contract player at Warners and had a small role in *Dallas,* a Gary Cooper western. In 1951, she had costarring roles in *Kiss Tomorrow Goodbye* with James Cagney and *Only the Valiant* with Gregory Peck. Most of her time though was spent posing for cheesecake publicity stills with visiting firemen and attending Hollywood premieres and parties on the arm of whatever contract player the studio wanted her to be seen with.

According to Payton, who gave this story out to *Confidential* magazine in 1956, her affair with Hope began when she was visiting her home town of Dallas in March of 1949.

Hope had just done a whirlwind tour of twenty-one American cities with his radio cast. He'd undertaken it because (a) he claimed he was in need of cash to pay his income taxes, and (b) he felt a personal appearance swing would bolster his radio ratings which had slipped slightly in the previous eighteen months. He was now in fifth place behind Fibber McGee and Molly, Edgar Bergen, Jack Benny, and Fred Allen.

He crowded in the twenty-one cities in fifteen days because in February he was to start shooting *Fancy Pants* at Paramount. But on his return to Hollywood, he was informed that *Fancy Pants* would be delayed because the script wasn't ready.

He asked Louis Shurr to book him on another tour, this one through the South.

In Dallas, Hope checked into the Baker Hotel and made arrangements to host a party in his suite the night of his arrival. As fate would have it, Barbara Payton was staying at the same hotel. In the lobby on the afternoon of the party, Payton ran into a friend of hers, millionaire oilman Bob Neal. Neal was the man who had persuaded Hope to come to Dallas to play in a charity golf match at his country club the next day. Neal invited Barbara to the party Hope was throwing that night in his suite.

Barbara was Hope's type: blond, with a curvaceous figure, a sense of humor, twenty-five years younger than the comedian, and willing, oh, so willing. Of course, he appealed to her. Not only was he America's number-one motion picture star, but he was attractive, fun to be with, and able to keep pace with her in the drinking department. Contrary to his public image, Hope was fond of alcohol in his younger days. At one time, according to his secretary Jan King, he had a bout with alcoholism. He won.

In Dallas, at their first meeting, there was immediate chemistry between Hope and Barbara. "As a result," recalled Payton, "we only knew each other a few hours before we knew each other as well as a boy and girl ever can."

The next morning, while breakfasting in bed in Hope's suite, Barbara told him that she wouldn't be able to accept his invitation to attend his golf match that afternoon, as she had an appointment in Houston around the time he'd be on the course. She left for Houston as soon as she put her clothes back on.

But where there's Hope and a pretty girl involved, there's always a way. After his golf match, Hope ducked his Texas cronies, his agent, and a couple of his stooges who usually traveled with him. He caught a plane to Houston and taxied to the Shamrock Hotel.

Shortly before dinnertime, Barbara received a call from Hope, who announced that he had flown all the way from Dallas to share another night of love with her. "Are you free?" he asked. How "free" she was is anybody's guess, though she always claimed that "Bob is one of the closest guys with a buck I've ever known."

Thus began an affair that lasted approximately six months, and saw action in a number of cities across the country.

Having a romance with Hope and keeping it out of the papers is not an easy thing to accomplish. Not only did Hope have to maintain the pretense of being faithful to Dolores, once he and his paramour de jour were back in Hollywood, but he was on the move so much that Payton spent a great deal of their romance packing and unpacking her bags. Their romance was something like mating an airline hostess with a railroad conductor. One or the other or both were always leaving home.

Hope and Payton were rarely out of each other's sight. When Bob would pack for a trip to New York, so would Barbara; if Hope had to be in Washington, D.C., so did Payton. In fact, she spent so much time flying around the country with the comedian that her studio, Universal-International, first warned her, then dropped her contract. Why she gave up a promising career in order to be with a man who was forever promising but never delivering was a puzzlement to Barbara's friends.

"Of course, when you're fooling around with a married man who's rich and famous and who seems to be hooked on your charms, you always think you're going to be the chosen one he'll leave his wife for," theorized one of Barbara's girlfriends.

Or perhaps she got a high from being in the company of a man who had his picture on the cover of *Time* and who could pick up the phone and call the President of the United States and actually be put through to him.

Certainly Barbara Payton didn't stick with Bob Hope because of his prowess as a lover. "Bob was the greatest that first night in Dallas, but once it became 'old hat' to him he was no longer such a tiger," Barbara told a reporter.

Perhaps he was too vain. Hope seldom passed a mirror, according to Payton, without taking an admiring glance at his profile.

However, he was always good for "a lot of laughs," Barbara confessed, and she got to see much of the country at his expense.

For example, when Hope traveled to New York the first week of June to attend the premiere of *Sorrowful Jones*, he checked into a spacious suite at the Waldorf-Astoria; he also registered Barbara in a single room adjoining his in order to accommodate the hotel's moral code. In those medieval times it was strictly a "no-no" for two unmarried people to share the same room in a prestigious hotel like the Waldorf.

But once he was in his own suite, Hope unlocked the connecting door, so that he and Barbara could practice recreational sex together.

✦✦✦✦

Sorrowful Jones, in which Hope was teamed for the first time with Lucille Ball, premiered on June 5, 1949, at the Paramount Theater on Broadway. Hope attended with Barbara—but she was on the arm of Hope's agent-manager-beard Louis Shurr. The audience gave the comedy an enthusiastic reception, and so did the critics. The *Daily News* rated it a three-star film, and the *Times*'s Bosley Crowther liked it too.

With business out of the way, Hope and Barbara spent the week gadding about the Big Apple, wining and dining in such "in" spots as The Little Club, 21, and El Morocco.

Meanwhile, back at the ranch in Toluca Lake, Dolores Hope, who had no idea of what was happening in Manhattan, was having a run-in with L.A. Law.

Los Angeles Times, June 8, 1949
POLICE END RAFFLE
AT BOB HOPE HOME

Church Benefit Discontinued on Lawns
Donated by Film and Radio Comedian and Wife

A benefit raffle on the grounds of Bob Hope's home in San Fernando Valley was halted by police, a vice squad officer reported yesterday.

Sgt. David McCoy said no arrests were made when Mrs. Hope said she hadn't known the raffle for such a purpose was illegal, but added the raffle would be discontinued.

The Sergeant said he visited the home Sunday when officers T.C. Myers and L.A. Weber phoned him they had been tipped gambling was in progress there.

McCoy said he found 1,200 to 1,500 persons on the grounds and that six paddle wheels had been in operation, with hams and bacon offered as prizes.

He said Mrs. Hope told him she had donated use of the grounds for the benefit of a monastery in Alhambra, and was in effect "only a guest" at the affair.

The vice squad confiscated the paddle wheels, which had netted some $2500 for the benefit. But Mrs. Hope was not arrested—probably because Bob Hope for the last five years had starred in the annual Police Benefit Show.

While Dolores was talking her way out of jail, her funnyman husband, after being shacked up for a week with sexy Barbara at the Waldorf, was ready to hit the road with her again. This time their destination was Washington, D.C., where he had agreed to play in another charity golf match before returning to the Paramount lot.

After Washington, Hope and Barbara hopped a sleeper plane back to Hollywood. This time it was Barbara who was the one on top, for gallant lover that he was, Hope gave his girlfriend the upper berth while he took the bottom one. Upper or lower, however, a narrow berth on a DC-6 was not a perfect place for sexual intercourse. Instead Hope spent the flight passing suggestive notes up to Barbara, such as "Get ready for the big scene."

Moments alone with Bob were rare. Barbara discovered Hope's swarm of writers, agents, managers and gofers. They made it easier for him to pretend that whomever he was romancing belonged to somebody else in his entourage. After *Sorrowful Jones*, Hope made *The Great Lover* with Rhonda Fleming.

Just before he started work on *Fancy Pants*, Hope set Barbara up in a furnished duplex apartment in Hollywood on Cheramoya Avenue, just north of Franklin. Barbara's new love nest was easily accessible to the king of the Paramount lot, for she was now just a short drive from Melrose Avenue where the studio stood just east of Gower. This made it easier for him to drop in for a matinee.

The two were very pleased with the place, except for one thing—the four-poster bed in Barbara's boudoir was too narrow for a man of Hope's size. He complained about it so constantly that Barbara got him to open his wallet long enough for her to go to Barker Brothers one afternoon and buy a king-sized bed.

Barbara had so many fond memories of the X-rated good times she and Bob had on the king-sized bed that she kept it as a souvenir and moved it to several other apartments long after Hope stopped paying her rent.

It was inevitable, of course, that the pair would break up sooner or later, because Hope was not only incapable of being true to his wife, he consistently cheated on his mistress as well.

But before he split with Barbara he dropped into the

Cheramoya duplex with regularity—sometimes staying for dinner, and occasionally, all night.

For some reason Hope didn't mind playing the role of the domesticated husband when he was in Barbara's company. He enjoyed her cooking as well as her embraces. And occasionally, if he was not too tired from his day at the studio, he'd put on a gingham apron and do the dishes for her and sweep the kitchen floor. He made her promise that she would never tell anyone about his domestic side, and that it would be a secret just between them.

But then hell hath no fury like a—well, you know the rest.

As the novelty of their torrid affair wore off, Hope behaved less like an ardent suitor and more like a bored husband—a tightfisted one, at that.

According to Barbara in the *Confidential* magazine confession, the only gift Hope ever gave her (other than the king-sized bed) was three jars of jam. To pry cash out of Bob Hope for living expenses, which she sorely needed after she lost her job at Universal, was almost impossible. When she needed cash she would make a sortie to Bob's movie set, where in loud tones before the entire company she demanded money. Hope didn't embarrass easily. "I never got more than a hundred dollars out of him at a time," she complained bitterly in 1956.

There was no rational justification for Hope to be pinching pennies in the summer of 1949.

Several months earlier, when Hope and Bing Crosby had been in Fort Worth, playing a charity golf match, they became friendly with Will Moncrief, an oil tycoon. Moncrief took a liking to both of them and after they returned to California he phoned and asked them to invest $50,000 each in some potentially oil-rich property in Scurry County in West Texas. He expressed the belief that the wells he planned to sink couldn't miss.

"My writing partner Larry Klein and I were in the office with Hope working on a radio script for him when Hope got the call from Moncrief," recalls Hal Goodman. "After Hope got off the phone, he turned to Klein, who like the rest of us writers on the show was making very little, and said, 'Would you like to get in on that, Larry? You just have to put up fifty grand.' Larry responded, 'Sorry, Bob, all my money's tied up in cash.'"

Hope wasn't very enthusiastic after the first drills hit nothing but salty water. He wanted to pull out. But Crosby was more of a gambler than Hope. He said he was willing to take another shot at it if Ski Nose would. So at Moncrief's request the two of them each put up another $50,000. This time it paid off. In mid-August, while Hope was shooting *Fancy Pants*, the drill struck a gusher capable of producing one hundred barrels an hour.

In 1954 Moncrief sold the property for $21 million to the Ponies Oil Company. Hope's share of sixteen percent brought him $3.6 million.

Around the time they went into the oil business, Hope and Crosby also invested in the Minute Maid frozen orange juice company. The two of them made a fortune out of that too.

So, between his radio salary, his film-acting income and his oil profits, Hope could well afford the upkeep on his mistress's duplex on Cheramoya Avenue.

However, it wasn't over money that he and Barbara had their first serious spat. It was over food. It happened in late August, as the result of an accident Hope had on the set of *Fancy Pants* with his costar, Lucille Ball.

Fancy Pants was a new filming of the Harry Leon Wilson novel, *Ruggles of Red Gap*, which Charlie Ruggles had starred in in the thirties. In this version, Hope played the part of a British actor stranded in the Wild West, who was forced to pose as an English butler in Lucille Ball's employ.

In one scene Lucy was trying to teach Hope how to ride a horse—not a real horse, but a wooden barrel contraption rigged to buck and roll like an unbroken bronco.

Hope had no wish to mount the frisky phony steed, but after he watched a stunt extra test it, he decided he was enough of an athlete to handle it. Unfortunately the phony horse proved as hard to ride as a real bronc, and Hope slipped off it and landed on his head knocking himself unconscious.

He suffered a mild concussion, and lay on his back, with his eyes glazed, seemingly paralyzed. When he didn't recover consciousness, the motionless Hope was put on a stretcher and rushed to Hollywood's nearby Presbyterian Hospital, while his personal physician, Tom Hearn, was summoned.

Before Hearn arrived, the hospital's staff doctor examined the comedian, and came up with a quick diagnosis that he might never be able to walk again. As it turned out, the paralysis was only temporary, caused by the shock of the fall and a severe back spasm. X-rays revealed that there were no broken bones, and by the time Doc Hearn arrived, his famous patient had opened his eyes and was cracking jokes.

However, Hope did have to spend a week in the hospital.

Because of the likelihood that she might encounter Dolores in Hope's hospital room, Barbara stayed away from her wounded swain's bedside, except for a few brief visits in the middle of the night when no members of his family were likely to be around.

But not wanting him to think she was losing interest, Barbara prepared a gourmet meal for Hope and had it sent to his hospital room at dinnertime. Not hearing from him by eight-o'clock, she became concerned, so taking a chance on his being alone, she went to his hospital room to see how he liked his meal. But instead of the appreciation she expected for her cooking, she found Hope gorging himself on a three-course meal which he'd had delivered by Romanoff's.

One word led to another, and pretty soon they were having a terrific argument, at the end of which Barbara stormed out.

The way Barbara remembered it, that was the end of their relationship. And it might well have been. But there is some evidence that their affair went on months longer.

❁ ❁ ❁ ❁

After completing *Fancy Pants*, Hope opened his new radio season at an Army camp in El Segundo, California, on September 20, 1949. His material was funny and fresh and applauded by the critics.

After El Segundo, Hope took his radio program to the Music

Hall in Houston, Texas. There was an audience warmup before his broadcast (as was the tradition in radio days) that featured a fashion show utilizing local Texas beauties. In the pre-show, Hope was to do a comedy skit with a showgirl he brought from Hollywood.

"I was one of the models in the fashion show," recalls Claudette Thornton, who lives today in Beverly Hills and is the wife of playwright Liam O'Brien. "I had just won the title of Miss Houston in a beauty contest the week before. While we were rehearsing the fashion show, before the audience was admitted, Louis Shurr came to the apron of the stage, looked at us girls and asked, 'Is there anyone here who can do a blackout sketch with Mr. Hope? We lost our regular actress just a few minutes ago.' Well, I'd never had any acting experience, but being young and I guess stupid, I raised my hand, and Louis Shurr picked me. While I was in the wings backstage waiting to rehearse my bit with Hope, I heard that I was replacing a girl named Barbara Payton. I'd never heard of her until that night, but the scuttlebutt was that she and Hope were lovers but that they'd had fought during the rehearsal and that she walked out on him and took a plane back to California. That's how I know about him and Barbara Payton.

"I don't remember what the skit was about, but I remember being told what to do and I did it. I got a big laugh. After the show, Louis Shurr came to me—I was only eighteen at the time—and asked me if I'd do the skit with Hope in Galveston, too. That was his next stop on the tour. I said I would, and I did, and after that Shurr asked me if I'd join Hope's personal appearance tour permanently. I said I couldn't . . . that I had to finish high school first. He told me, 'Well, you're very good, and Mr. Hope liked you a lot. If you come to the Coast, look me up and I'll get you a job.'

"After Galveston I heard they got another girl to do the bit I had done with Hope. Her name was Marilyn Maxwell."

After her split with Hope, Barbara Payton's downfall was swift, shocking and melodramatic.

Over the next five years she starred in the bottom-of-the-barrel *Bride of the Gorilla*, and a few equally forgettable films. Then she married Franchot Tone, one of Hollywood's handsomest leading men, then on his way down even though she was actually in love with another man—an ex-prizefighter-turned-actor named Tom Neal. He was the Mickey Rourke of his day. But her marriage to Tone was stormy. The two were hopeless alcoholics. She continued her relationship with Neal, and Tone found out about it. Eventually the names in this unfortunate triangle erupted on the front pages of nation's tabloids when Tone, extremely jealous, attacked Neal in a nightclub. Being no match for the ex-pug, Tone went down for the full count.

Payton and Tone divorced, and she started to drink so heavily that she could no longer get work in Hollywood, even as an extra. Following a long period of unemployment, she became a high-priced, and then a low-priced, hooker. As her dissipation increased, she lost her looks, and finally was turning tricks on Hollywood Boulevard for five bucks a throw. Desperate and feeling unwanted, she committed suicide in 1966, at the age of thirty-nine.

26

When Barbara Payton went out of Bob Hope's life for good, someone new was waiting in the wings. She was a blonde actress named Marilyn Maxwell.

In discussing the qualities he admired most in women, Hope once said, "For want of a better description, I call it 'dignified sex.' My wife has it, and so have Ingrid Bergman, Madeleine Carroll, and Rhonda Fleming.

"But I guess my top favorites are the fun girls, the ones who love to clown—among them, Dorothy Lamour, Marilyn Maxwell, Lucille Ball, Jane Russell. I like the ones who quip back. For this reason I'll always be glad to see 'Honey Chile' Wilder, a great girl who was once a radio actress with me and who is now the Princess Hohenlohe."

The long list of actresses he's been reported to have had affairs with includes Gloria DeHaven, Janis Paige, Joey Heatherton, and Joy Monroe. The one he was said to have been crazy about was Marilyn Maxwell.

She was born Marvel Maxwell in Clarinda, Iowa in 1921. She moved with her family to Fort Wayne, Indiana, a few years later. "I went to school with her at Central High in Fort Wayne," recalls author Sally Presley, "and the thing about her I remember the most was that she had a very pushy mother, one of those stage mothers like you read about."

She must have been pushy, because Marilyn began her professional stage career as a dancer when she was a child of eight, and was only seventeen when she became a vocalist with the Buddy Rogers and then the Ted Weems orchestras.

A movie scout saw her in 1942 and brought her to Hollywood where she was signed to a term contract by MGM. Believing it sounded more glamorous, the studio changed her first name from Marvel to Marilyn.

For the five years that followed Marilyn was given small roles in about a dozen undistinguished MGM films including *Stand By for Action, Swing Fever, Thousands Cheer, Lost in a Harem,* and *Summer Holiday.* In 1947, MGM decided not to extend her contract, and Marilyn free-lanced for several years in a handful of films when Bob Hope hired her for *The Lemon Drop Kid* in 1951.

Although Marilyn's name wasn't linked in print to Hope's until 1950, the pair met prior to that.

"I married her in 1944," recalls her first husband, actor John Conte, today, "and I'm sure, from what she told me that she had known Hope during the war . . . either around the Paramount lot or working with him at one of the Army camps."

Conte and Maxwell were divorced in 1946, and soon after that she and Frank Sinatra had an affair, while the singer was still married to his first wife, Nancy.

Nancy discovered what was going on—and in a most unusual way. She was taking driving lessons, and one afternoon took Frank's car out of the garage for a short spin so she could practice. For some reason she opened the glove compartment, and to her surprise and delight, found a gray velvet jeweler's box containing a gorgeous diamond bracelet.

Believing that Frank intended to surprise her with it for Christmas, she put it back in the glove compartment and didn't mention it to him.

But there was a bigger surprise for Nancy. She didn't see the bracelet again until the night of the New Year's Eve party at their house when Marilyn Maxwell, one of the guests, walked in the front door wearing the glittering diamond trinket on her arm.

Before Maxwell had a chance to take off her mink stole, Nancy threw her out of the house. The scene was replayed in the mini-series about Sinatra produced by his daughter Tina in 1992.

The Sinatras weren't divorced until 1950. But Frank must have continued to have a yen for Maxwell because he became extremely jealous of her when she became Hope's lover, and, though the singer denies it, it's known that he's harbored a grudge against Hope ever since.

Perhaps Hope had Marilyn Maxwell on his mind when he crashed his Cadillac into a ditch along Highway 60 on his way back to Toluca Lake from Palm Springs one dark night in the first week of January 1950. Or perhaps he was concerned, to the point of distraction, about his radio ratings, which had slipped to 13.9 in the last sampling. 13.9 was half of Jack Benny's rating. Adding insult to injury, Fibber McGee and Molly, who followed the Hope radio show on Tuesday nights, were now getting higher ratings than Hope.

Adding to his trouble was the rough cut of *Fancy Pants*. Hope was disappointed with the results. He insisted to the studio bosses that they shoot retakes of the scenes he felt didn't work.

✿ ✿ ✿ ✿

To get his mind off business, and a nasty cold he'd picked up entertaining troops in Alaska over Christmas, Hope had decided to chuck it all, go down to the desert, practice his golf for the Crosby Pro-Am tournament at Pebble Beach the next week, and perhaps refine changes he wished to make in *Fancy Pants*.

For company, he brought along his favorite writer, Fred Williams. Between rounds of golf, Hope planned to work on the script of *Fancy Pants* with Williams.

Hope didn't get in much golf that first week in January. It rained most of the time, and the weather was cold, damp and miserable.

While Hope was sitting around cursing the rain, Jimmy

Saphier paid him a surprise visit, and brought along Hugh Davis, an account executive with the Chicago-based advertising firm of Foote, Cone & Belding.

Davis handled the General Motors account. He came with an offer for Hope to go into television, for the Frigidaire Division of General Motors.

Hope was still leery of getting into television. When Davis broached the subject, Hope said he wasn't interested.

David persisted. "How much do you want?" he asked.

To quell the man's proposition before it could go any further, Hope gave him a figure that he felt was completely out of the question:

"Fifty thousand a show," he told Davis.

At the time, the entire budget for Milton Berle's *Texaco Star Theater*, which was America's top TV program, was only $15,000 a show, and that included everything: Berle's salary, the cast salaries and all the production costs.

To Hope's great relief, the subject was dropped and, apparently forgotten, for there was no further mention of television during the round of golf the four of them played after the weather cleared and before Saphier and Davis drove back to Los Angeles.

Traffic was light that evening, and as there were no cops around, Hope felt free to open up his Cadillac to its maximum speed. He was in the habit of driving fast on Interstate 60, but this night the highway was slippery from the rain and oil slicks, and Hope must have been wearier than he thought.

As the speedometer hit 75, Hope dozed for a moment and the car lurched out of control. It swerved into the ditch at the side of the road, turned over and slammed into a tree. Both doors of the automobile opened simultaneously upon impact, hurling Hope and Williams out of the car and into the muddy ditch.

Hope was unconscious but Williams, who was drunk, remained awake. Except for a bruised leg, he was unhurt and alert enough to pull his boss, who by then had opened his eyes, away from the wrecked Cadillac, which he feared might catch fire and explode.

As the muddied pair stood by the side of the highway trying to thumb a ride, a truck with a "No Hitchhikers" sign on its windshield, came around the bend and into view. Recognizing the world's favorite comedian, even under a layer of mud, the trucker slammed on the brakes, picked up the pair and drove them to Riverside Community Hospital.

Williams suffered just a few bruises, but Hope wasn't as lucky. The emergency room X rays showed that he had a broken collar bone. It wasn't life-threatening but it was painful, and he wouldn't have the use of one of his arms for at least a month, for it would have to be strapped to his body.

Not only was there no chance of his competing in the Crosby Pro-Am at Pebble Beach, but he'd be unable to complete the retakes for *Fancy Pants*.

While Hope was recuperating, Hugh Davis came back to him with a counter-offer: Forty thousand dollars for one ninety minute television show, to be broadcast on Easter Sunday.

Forty thousand dollars was not to be sneezed at.

That was so much more money than anyone in television was getting, including Uncle Miltie, that Hope accepted the offer. When Jimmy Saphier negotiated the deal he made arrangements for Hope to do three additional television shows for $150,000.

A hitch in the deal was that Frigidaire had contracted to do all of its TV advertising on CBS, while Hope's radio contract with Lever Brothers called for him to be exclusive to NBC. Frigidaire worked it out with CBS, and Hope was able to make his television debut on NBC. The date was Easter Sunday, April 10, 1950.

Soon after signing his first television deal, Hope accepted $100,000 for two weeks at the Paramount Theater on Broadway.

Although the money was good, Hope had been warned by Bob Weitman, the manager of the theater, not to expect full houses, because business around Times Square was generally bad, and the film on the bill was a turkey called *Captain China*. It starred John Payne and Gail Russell.

Feeling that bad business would be a reflection on his own drawing power, and already upset by his fallen radio ratings, Hope decided to enlist all the help he could get. So he added Jane Russell to his act, and brought in Les Brown and his Band of Renown.

For further insurance, Hope put his two personal publicity men, Frank Liberman and Mack Miller, to work. This resulted in a publicity blitz across the country that filled the print media with photos of Hope, along with human interest puff pieces about him and his family.

As part of this campaign, the Hope camp also persuaded the New York *Journal-American* to sponsor a "Laugh-A-Day" contest in which readers would submit jokes and comedy routines. These would be judged by Jane Russell, Bob Hope and Arthur Godfrey on Godfrey's daily radio program.

On his way east, Hope stopped off in Washington to pick up another medal—this one from the Air Force—and to emcee the White House correspondents' annual Gridiron Dinner.

As usual, Hope was the hit of the evening, cracking jokes about the government, the press and even Charles Luckman, a former vice-president of Lever Brothers, who was also at the dinner.

Hope was having difficulties with Lever Brothers at the time. The soap-maker was concerned both with his falling ratings and his intention to keep "traveling" the show. They announced they were going to drop him at the end of the season. It had been Luckman who had been responsible for Hope getting the boot but, ironically, Luckman left the soap company ahead of Hope.

Whether it was the massive publicity or just the magic of Bob Hope's name, all worry about the amount of business he'd do at the Paramount Theater proved unwarranted. His six-shows-a day for two weeks, eighty-four appearances in all, smashed every attendance record. Customers queued up at the box office early in the morning and the lines snaked around the block by midday.

The critics loved Hope, too.

"Bob had mellowed considerably in the decade he had been away from Broadway stages," wrote the *Daily Mirror's* Alton Cook. "He no longer is so strenuously eager to please. His charm has increased with his new casual air. The test is that he stays on the stage without much assistance for forty whole minutes, a very long time for anyone to remain the life of the party, and get away with it."

With an undistinguished picture attached, Hope did $141,000 worth of business the first week, and almost equaled that the second week.

Hope's name was now so big that he was offered the chance to have his own "disease," just as Jerry Lewis would several years later. Bob Goldenson, who ran the Paramount Theater chain, and Bob Weitman asked Hope to head the national fund drive for cerebral palsy.

With his first TV show on the horizon, Hope told them that he didn't see how he would have the time to give justice to the cerebral palsy drive. But after Goldenson took him to P.S. 135, on West 51st Street in Manhattan, where they observed special classes for stricken kids, Hope posed with the children for some publicity stills. His entire attitude changed. And when a five-year-old girl, with heavy braces on her legs, climbed up on Hope's lap, to have her picture taken hugging him, he could no more turn Goldenson down than he could have said "no" to any eighteen-year-old chick without braces who wished to climb on his lap.

In the spirit of the thing, he immediately scheduled cerebral palsy appearances in the towns where he would tour before returning to California. These were Rochester, New York; Cincinnati, Ohio; Owensboro, Kentucky; Kansas City, Missouri; St. Louis, Missouri, and Wichita, Kansas.

Hope wanted to feature Jane Russell at the cerebral palsy benefits, but she wasn't available, so he replaced her with Marilyn Maxwell.

That marked the first time Marilyn Maxwell's name turned

up in Hope's cast. It was 1950 and their friendship blossomed into romance.

At the time Marilyn was married to Andy McIntyre, a Beverly Hills restaurateur. They had tied the knot on January 2, 1950, in Santa Barbara, where dancer Dan Dailey was the groom's best man. "Man" may not be quite the name for the role at the wedding Dailey played, for he subsequently turned out to be a transvestite. "Marilyn Maxwell had a crush on Dailey as well as Hope," according to agent Al Melnick.

In this respect, Maxwell was a little like Will Rogers; there was hardly a man she met whom she didn't like.

At the height of her affair with Bob Hope, she confessed to her New York hairdresser, "I'd marry Bob, and I believe he'd marry me, but I'd be such a heavy around Hollywood for stealing him away from Dolores and breaking up that allegedly happy family that I believe someone would kill me."

In the summer of 1950, Hope emceed a cerebral palsy fund-raiser at the Hollywood Bowl for 16,000 Angelenos. It was called *Once in a Lifetime*—no relation to the Kaufman-Hart play of the same name—and it featured a number of Hollywood stars: Dinah Shore, Dean Martin, Eddie Bracken, Peggy Lee, Dan Dailey, Gordon MacRae, Gene Tierney, Lloyd Nolan, Betty Hutton, Jane Russell, Marge and Gower Champion, the Skinnay Ennis Orchestra, and of course Marilyn Maxwell.

The morning after the show, the *Los Angeles Times* published a large picture of Bob Hope, with actress Gene Tierney on one side and Marilyn Maxwell on the other. The picture reveals how Marilyn felt about Hope. Her right arm is draped around his neck, her left arm is resting on his left arm, and her chin is on his shoulder. Her wedding ring is prominent on the fourth finger of her left hand, but she's looking at Hope with adoration in her eyes.

Shortly after she returned from Korea with the Hope troupe in 1951, she divorced Andy McIntyre.

27

For the first time since he'd become a superstar, Bob Hope was nervous about doing a show—his first television special for Frigidaire. This was scheduled to be telecast from the roof of Manhattan's New Amsterdam Theater, which had been converted into a TV studio.

For the momentous occasion, NBC hired as producer Max Liebman, who had created the successful Sid Caesar-Imogene Coca *Show of Shows*. Hal Keith was chosen to direct what was to be called *The Star Spangled Revue*. It was spangled with stars all right: Bea Lillie, Douglas Fairbanks, Jr., Dinah Shore, dancer Hal LeRoy, novelty pianist Maurice Rocco, vocalist Bill Hayes, and the Mexico City Boys Choir.

The ninety-minute show would be telecast live to the twenty-seven stations of the NBC network east of the Rockies and kinescoped for rebroadcast a week later to eighteen other NBC affiliates west of the Rockies. In the infancy of television, there was no such thing as a direct broadcast from coast to coast, hence the delayed kinescope transmission.

What made Hope nervous were two things: He'd been on top for so long, and had become such a worldwide name, that most of his competitors would be happy to see him fail, and the physical requirements of doing live TV were so much more arduous than doing radio or a stage appearances, or even shooting a film.

In live TV during a scene, there were several cameras shooting simultaneously and moving around the set, trying to capture different angles. As Hope said after his second show, "It's like trying to do a nightclub act with three waiters with trays walking in front of you every time you reached the punch line." Then there was the question of having to commit as much as sixty pages of dialogue to memory. One wrong line, one wrong cue, and the whole show could look like amateur night.

For security, Hope decided to do what other TV comedians were trying—display his lines on cue cards out of camera range, but in such large print he could read them at a distance. But that was hazardous too. The man working the cue cards had to be in tune with your timing and your style and not get ahead of you or fall behind.

In the beginning it was hit or miss with the cue card, but after he'd been in television for a couple of years, Hope found Barney McNulty. McNulty was so good at coordinating the changing of the cards with Hope's unique style of rapid-fire delivery that Hope took him everywhere he performed—even to such remote spots as Korea and Vietnam.

"I can remember a perfect example of Hope's dependency on McNulty," recalls humorist Steve Allen today. "It was about fifteen years ago. Bill Larkin, one of Hope's writers, called to invite Jayne [Meadows] and me to a party at his house, here in the Valley, that he was giving for his daughter who was getting married in a few days. It was to be an informal evening, he said. Dress any way you like. . . . Lots of your friends will be there . . . musicians, writers, etc. Well, we went and it was a typical Valley party, in the backyard, under the stars. Lots of people milling around. Good food and drink . . . guacamole dip . . . you know the kind. Anyway, late in the evening, about ten thirty, the buzz went through the crowd that Bob Hope was there, and would say a few words.

"Well, we all looked around, and sure enough, there was Bob coming out of the kitchen, onto a little landing off the back door.

He was about five feet above the rest of us, like Mussolini's platform. He waved and went into a typical Bob Hope monologue . . . about eight minutes long . . . on the subject of marriage, kids leaving the nest, etc. . . . Typical Hope jokes . . . 'You know what San Fernando Valley is. . . . It's Cleveland with palm trees . . . but I want to tell you, folks . . . there's not a nicer guy than Bill Larkin . . . good writer, but a little cheap. . . . You know I usually get paid for doing parties . . . and not in guacamole dip.' Well, during all this I noticed Bob looking out into the crowd, beyond all of us. I turned around. And who do you think I saw, kneeling down in the mud . . . behind some bushes? Barney McNulty flipping the cue cards, with a flashlight shining on them."

✿ ✿ ✿ ✿

In the beginning, besides the worry about whether the cue card boys could keep up with him, there was the usual concern about whether the written material would play as well visually as it did on radio. As Hope later recalled for the media, "I couldn't believe how nervous and jumpy I was that first night. You'd have thought I was some green kid the way I reacted."

Not normally superstitious, "Hope phoned me at his office in Toluca Lake," said Marjorie Hughes, his personal secretary at the time, "and asked me to send him his top hat, the one he wore in *Roberta*, by the next plane out. He wanted to wear it for good luck in the opening sequence, with his white tie and tails."

A messenger picked up the top hat at La Guardia airport the following afternoon, and it arrived at the site of the broadcast on the roof of the New Amsterdam theater in time for Hope to go on.

His opening monologue was sprinkled with jokes about television, his sponsor, and the amount of money he was being paid.

> This is a fine looking audience . . . [HE LOOKS THE AUDI-ENCE OVER AND COUNTS WITH HIS FINGERS] . . . Oh, excuse me . . . I thought I was still at the Paramount working on

271

a percentage. . . . Now, ladies and gentlemen . . . this is a high point for me . . . doing this big special on Easter Sunday . . . for years I've been on radio. . . . You remember radio . . . blind television. . . . But I want to tell you that Frigidaire has been a brick about the whole thing . . . especially where the money is concerned . . . ah, the money, are you listening, Washington?. . . . Yes, Frigidaire has been very generous . . . they told me I could have my salary any way I wanted it . . . in big or little cubes . . .

After the monologue, and his appearance in a couple of short blackout sketches, Hope and Dinah Shore sang and danced in a comical version of "Baby, It's Cold Outside", Frank Loesser's Oscar-winning hit. Then came a sketch with Hope, Douglas Fairbanks, Jr. and Bea Lillie. Lillie, who for years had been a favorite in London music halls, did a solo routine of her own. And this was followed by the funniest sketch of the evening . . . a takeoff of Hope signing his first television contract, in a plush NBC executive suite. Without letup Hope kidded himself, and the rivalry between NBC and CBS over who would sign Jack Benny to a long-term contract. After each mention of CBS a group of NBC junior executives appeared, and in a pantomime of fumigation, they scampered around the suite spraying the air with a flit gun.

The reviews of Hope's first national TV appearance were mixed. The New York *Journal American* said that Hope appeared "too subdued." *Variety* was "disappointed." And John Crosby, the *Herald-Tribune's* TV maven, wrote that Hope had not yet found "the middle ground between movie technique and radio." But Jack Gould's review in *The New York Times* couldn't have been more positive.

Judging by *Star Spangled Revue*, there's nothing wrong with television that Bob Hope and a $135,000 cast can't cure. Sprightly Robert, making his debut before the network's TV cameras last Sunday, put on ninety minutes of capital amusement that had all the zing and style of the real big time.

By his performance, Bob became the first top-flight film star to take the TV plunge, and by now the moguls of Hollywood must really know what a competitive wallop television can carry.

In general Hope was pleased with his reception, but believed he could do better once he got the feel of the new medium and felt comfortable with the cameras and cue cards.

Hope's second TV appearance was scheduled for Mother's Day, one month later. For this show, he hired Frank Sinatra (in his TV debut), Peggy Lee, dancer Michael Kidd, and nasal-voiced comedian Arnold Stang. He brought back Bea Lillie because she'd been such a hit on his first show.

The format of the Mother's Day special was similar to the first one: monologue, songs, sketches, dance numbers and double-entendre jokes about pretty girls.

To make certain there would be no unnecessary camera movement during a scene, Hope took over the direction himself, and tied down the cameras to one place. As he later wrote, "The only way not to get killed on television is to set up the scene the way you want it, and not the way *they*, the technicians and the director, want it."

As usual Hope kidded himself and TV in his monologue:

It's amazing how many people see you on TV. I did my first television show a month ago, and the next day five million television sets were sold. . . . The people who couldn't sell theirs threw them away.

His self-deprecating manner was an approach his audience couldn't resist, and the reviews were better overall the second time around, the consensus being that Hope looked more at ease in front of the cameras, and therefore was funnier.

After his second special, Hope flew back to Hollywood for pre-production meetings on *The Lemon Drop Kid*, based on a Damon Runyon story.

There were problems. The writers, Ed Hartman and Robert O'Brien, couldn't seem to get it right. Also, Hope was unable to hire the leading lady he wanted: Jan Sterling. She was a

Broadway actress of renown, and the wife of actor Paul Douglas. Being a serious actress from the New York "theatuh," Sterling couldn't see herself playing wild Bob Hopian kind of comedy. Bob turned to his favorite backup: Marilyn Maxwell.

He liked the way she performed comedy with him at his cerebral palsy functions. He persuaded the Paramount big-wigs that though Marilyn was not a big name on her own, her dumb blond sexiness had a lot of appeal. He was convinced, if given a chance, her career might take off.

This seemed unlikely, inasmuch as Miss Maxwell had been in Hollywood approximately ten years, without making much impact outside of her appeal to men.

At any rate, Hope got his wish, and once more Marilyn Maxwell was within hugging range whenever he got the urge.

Just days before starting filming *The Lemon Drop Kid*, Hope terminated his twelve-year relationship with Lever Brothers.

Hope wanted to record his shows but his contract specified that he do them "live." The soap company insisted that he adhere to the terms of the contract so Hope took the matter to court. When a judge in the L.A. County Superior Court ruled against Hope, he announced to Lever Brothers that, notwithstanding, he would prerecord his radio show when he wished. The bitterness that followed made cancellation of Hope's radio contract inevitable.

This wasn't much of a tragedy. Jimmy Saphier got a deal with NBC. The NBC deal was a more lucrative contract than the one he had with Lever Brothers, which paid him $25,000 a broadcast, or approximately $875,000 a year. NBC agreed to pay Hope twice that. Moreover, Saphier worked out such a favorable-to-Hope deal that the network had to guarantee him air time even if he didn't have a sponsor.

❊❊❊❊

Just a few days after the start of filming *The Lemon Drop Kid* on June 25, 1950, the armies of North Korea swarmed across the 38th parallel and invaded South Korea. Because Gen.

Douglas MacArthur was in command of the United Nations forces, the United States got sucked into another war.

The first shot had barely been fired before Hope was on the phone making plans to take a USO unit to the fighting front.

There was an ulterior motive behind this move, and it wasn't just to get Marilyn Maxwell on a slow boat to Korea. Hope wanted to make personal appearances in Tokyo to shore up the attendance for *The Paleface*.

In the meantime, he had to complete *The Lemon Drop Kid*, do a third *Star Spangled Revue* for Frigidaire, and please a new radio sponsor, the Liggett & Meyers Tobacco Company. Liggett & Meyers agreed to let him prerecord his thirty-minute radio show from the various locations of the troop-entertaining tour he was planning.

❈ ❈ ❈ ❈

When *The Lemon Drop Kid* director Sidney Lanfield, called the film a "wrap," Hope saw a rough cut. He wasn't amused. In fact, he refused to let Barney Balaban, the studio head, release it for the Christmas trade until several scenes were rewritten and then reshot, particularly the Christmas sequence, which was the climactic and most important one in the film.

Balaban reluctantly agreed, and Frank Tashlin was hired to do a rewrite of certain scenes, which he'd also direct. Livingston and Evans, who'd written "Buttons and Bows," came up with another hit song for the sequence, "Silver Bells."

"Originally we had called it 'Tinkle Bells,'" recalls Livingston with a grin, "but when my wife informed me that 'tinkle' stood for something else, which you do in the bathroom, we hurriedly switched tinkle to 'silver,' and miraculously it became one of the biggest hits we've ever written. It's still being played around the world at Christmas time every year."

Since Hope couldn't shoot the retakes until after he returned from his Frigidaire broadcast in New York, and his Korean troop entertaining tour after that, completion of *The Lemon Drop Kid* was put on the back burner.

Hope's third show for Frigidaire was better than the first two.

This time he had Lucille Ball costarring with him, along with Bob Crosby and Dinah Shore, the Jack Cole Dancers and Al Goodman's Orchestra to take care of the rest of the entertaining chores.

Stuart Symington, Secretary of the Air Force, had arranged for Hope to have the use of two C-54s on his trip to the Far East. This cleared the way for Hope to take a cast of fifty. Whereas on other USO trips he'd been limited to one guitarist to supply the music, now he had room on the two planes for the entire Les Brown orchestra, the technicians for his radio show, Charlie Cooley, his personal masseur, producer Al Capstaff, his NBC soundman Johnny Pawlek, his manager-brother Jack, and his writing staff, Larry Gelbart, Charlie Lee, Chet Castlehoff and Fred Williams.

The performing talent consisted of announcer Hy Averback, country-western singer Jimmy Wakely, a dancer named Judy Kelly, and a singing group called the Taylor Maids. For sex appeal he again called on Jane Russell. But Russell had to back out at the last minute because she was about to go into a film called *Macao* for Howard Hughes.

Again, Hope's second choice was Marilyn Maxwell. She was excited about the trip, but unfortunately she was in Pittsburgh doing an act with Dean Martin and Jerry Lewis. She couldn't join the Hope unit until she finished her current tour. She promised to catch up with Hope in Hawaii, where he'd be breaking the show in at several Army camps. Meanwhile, he booked Gloria DeHaven for the Hawaiian leg of the tour and to be on his first radio broadcast from out there.

With Gloria DeHaven substituting for Marilyn Maxwell, at the start and Maxwell taking over from DeHaven on the Far Eastern leg of the journey, there would be no shortage of extracurricular entertainment for the sexually active Mr. Hope.

✱✱✱✱

On Oahu, in the Hawaiian Islands, the Hope unit performed for the soldiers at Hickham Field, the sailors at Pearl Harbor, and the patients at an Army hospital in Honolulu. After that they proceeded through James Michener territory to Johnson Island, Kwajalein, Guam, and finally Okinawa, doing shows at every stop. By the time Marilyn Maxwell had joined the unit at Guam, and Gloria DeHaven had returned to Hollywood, all the rough spots in the show had been smoothed out.

Their next stop was Haneda Air Base, outside of Tokyo, in occupied Japan.

In Tokyo, Hope and nineteen members of his party were invited to lunch with General and Mrs. MacArthur at the American Embassy. Since there were fifty in Hope's party, and only twenty, including himself, were invited to the luncheon, Hope had to make the decision of who would go and who wouldn't. When it came down to his four writers, Hope decided that he could only take two of them, and that the fair way would be for the four to draw lots. Gelbart and Williams won. Charlie Lee took it calmly but Chet Castlehoff was bitterly disappointed, and said so to Hope, but to no avail.

The twenty in Hope's party were driven to the American Embassy in limousines. In the dining room inside the Embassy there was a long banquet table beautifully set for the twenty Hope entertainers plus MacArthur's staff, and the general and his wife. After everybody sat down, Hope noticed that one colonel was still standing up, looking for a chair.

"And then," recalled Hope, "I saw Chet Castlehoff sitting next to General MacArthur! I couldn't believe my eyes! I never did find out how Chet got there. He must have promised the general he'd write jokes for his speeches if he ever decided to run for President."

After the luncheon, Hope and company moved to the Ernie Pyle Theater, where, before an audience of three thousand grateful GIs, he recorded his radio show for consumption back in the States. It included his usual monologue and a comedy sketch between him and Marilyn Maxwell. That night they did an expanded version of the show in front of ten thousand soldiers in a huge civic auditorium.

After two more days of performing for the GIs around Tokyo, it was time for the Hope troupe to move on to Korea. There, in freezing cold weather and unpleasantly rugged conditions, they put on shows for the boys in Seoul, Teagu, and Taejon, all below the 38th parallel. In Taejon, Hope asked a Colonel Leyden, "Do you know where the Marines are? I promised to do a show for them."

"They're in Wonsan," replied the colonel.

"Can we go?" asked Hope.

"I guess so," the colonel came back. "We just took it."

But the colonel was a little premature. When the two C-54 transports flying the Hope company put down on the air strip in Wonsan, the place was completely deserted.

On October 27, the *Los Angeles Times* ran the following story on its front page:

BOB HOPE AND MARILYN MAXWELL IN WONSAN BEFORE LEATHERNECKS

The U.S. First Marine Division—20,000 strong—hit the beaches at Wonsan today, and the only casualty was a leatherneck who fell and dislocated his shoulder.

The Marines had been told several weeks ago they would have to fight their way ashore in one of the bloodiest amphibious landings in their history. But the Communist defenders of Wonsan couldn't wait for them.

South Korean forces captured this port fifteen days ago, and are still chasing the reds a hundred miles to the north.

Even Bob Hope and blond actress Marilyn Maxwell got into Wonsan before the Marines. And the leathernecks didn't know whether to be disgusted or thankful.

Grumbled one disgruntled Marine: 'The only thing we're going in for is to give Bob Hope an audience.'

After Wonsan, Hope and company did a couple of shows on the battleship *Missouri*, where he slept in the suite that had been MacArthur's, and the next day he performed for the crew on the flight deck of the carrier *Valley Forge*.

Following that, Hope and his troupe worked their way south to Pusan, and then all the way back north and across the 38th parallel. They did shows at Pyongyang, which had once been the capital of North Korea, but had been retaken in the fighting.

Larry Gelbart, Charlie Lee, Chet Castlehoff and Fred Williams were kept busy thinking up new topical gags for Hope's monologue. Easy laughers that they were, the soldiers got their kicks out of jokes like these . . .

> Some of these towns are changing hands so fast one soldier bought a lamp with three thousand won [Korean money] and got his change in rubles. . . . Seoul has changed hands so many times the towels are marked, HIS, HERS, and WHO'S SORRY NOW? . . . I asked a GI here how to tell a North Korean from a South Korean and he said, 'Turn your back.' . . . There are no psychiatrists in Korea . . . they know you're nuts or you wouldn't be here.

Although it was rough entertaining the GIs in outdoor theaters in midwinter in Korea, it was worth it for Hope just to see the smiles on the faces of those lonely GIs when he told jokes they could identify with, and to hear the approving wolf whistles when he introduced Marilyn Maxwell.

So everyone got something out of the trip: the troops, Hope and Maxwell, but the one it paid off for the most was Larry Gelbart. The trip afforded him the opportunity to pick up a lot of local color for the TV series, *M*A*S*H*, which in the future he would create and write.

*M*A*S*H* became such a hit on TV that it lasted nine years or six years longer than the Korean hostilities, which it was about.

✿ ✿ ✿ ✿

In early November, Hope and his troupe headed home. But not wanting to get home too soon he directed the pilots of his C-54s to detour through the Aleutian Islands and the Alaskan mainland. There Hope did shows at Adak and Amchitka in the Aleutians, and Anchorage and finally Fairbanks on the Alaskan mainland.

There he taped his fourth radio show of the tour for later broadcast in the States.

❀ ❀ ❀ ❀

Back home in Toluca Lake, Hope barely had time to kiss Dolores and the children "hello" before he was off to Paramount for the retakes of *The Lemon Drop Kid*.

Hope was satisfied with the Frank Tashlin rewrite, and the film was completed in time for a Christmas release.

In the Christmas sequence, Hope and Maxwell sang "Silver Bells" as a duet, but it was Bing Crosby's recording of the song that made both the picture and the song a success. "Silver Bells" was a gold platter hit, and has sold millions of records.

Prior to the release of *The Lemon Drop Kid* Hope did his fourth television show for Frigidaire. In this one, because he wanted his American audiences to see just what he'd been doing for the boys in Korea, he re-created the same shows he'd been doing for the GIs, and with the same cast—Marilyn Maxwell, Jimmy Wakely, Jimmy Kelly, and Taylor Maids, the High Hatters, and Les Brown's Band of Renown.

If not the most actively strenuous years in Hope's life, 1950 had been one of the busiest. But it had been a lonely one for Dolores, who'd been home alone so much of the time wondering precisely what it was that was going on between her husband and Maxwell.

According to those who knew her well, Dolores was beginning to seek more and more solace in the Catholic Church, sometimes attending Mass twice a day.

Hollywood gossip columnists were beginning to suggest that the Hope marriage wasn't too solid, and that the comedian and Maxwell, were an "item."

Louella Parsons, whose syndicated column appeared in over six hundred newspapers every day, alluded to the Hope-Maxwell romance in her usual cute way.

A LOUELLA PARSONS EXCLUSIVE
In an exclusive interview with Dolores Hope, I have learned that there's absolutely no truth to the current rumors that Bob Hope and his leading lady, Marilyn Maxwell, are serious about

280

each other just because they have been seen together so much. "Our marriage is stronger than ever," Mrs. Hope assured me.

If Louella's readers hadn't suspected anything prior to that, her disclaimer certainly brought it to their attention.

Friends and relatives of the Hopes liked to rationalize his behavior and his long and frequent absences from home as just his need to hear live audience's laughter. After all, "fish don't applaud."

The money never seemed to be enough. Besides his Paramount deal, he was now getting $45,000 a week for his radio show, $50,000 for each television appearance, and about $2 million a year for NBC just to remain exclusive to them.

Whenever he yearned for additional cash, he could always collect $20,000 for a single appearance in cities where movie stars rarely deigned to play—secondary ones like Kansas City or Minneapolis or Galveston.

But there was more to his roaming than just the love of money.

"It was pretty generally known around the studio," recalls former Paramount publicist Robert Slatzer, "that whenever Bob had to go off on one of his [personal appearance] tours or to play the Army camps, he'd have girls he wanted to boff sent ahead for him. Not name girls, like Joey Heatherton. Those he'd just use in his show. But sexy girls who hung around the set, waiting to be asked. Models, beauty contest winners, extras—that sort of broad. I remember a set of twins, the Corbett twins—Jeannie and Joan—who were on call for every Hope and Crosby picture. All the talk was that Hope was having an affair with Jeannie, because she lived across Riverside Drive from his house on Moorpark. But his favorites were beauty contest winners. He was always trying to get them on his show—not only to rev up the GIs in the audience, but because he wanted them for himself when he went on tour with them. I remember—it was either 1952 or '53—I was working doing publicity at Paramount. There was a Miss Universe contest down in Long Beach. And it was won by a very attractive brunette from Ohio. I don't remember her name—it's unimportant. Anyway, to show you how Bob operated, I was standing in front of Bob's dressing room when Jack Hope came out and said, 'I wonder if you'd be interested in doing Bob a favor?'"

"I told him, 'That depends on what it is.'

"Well, there's this girl, who just won the Miss Universe contest down in Long Beach," said Jack, handing Slatzer a picture of her. "Why don't you take the afternoon off and drive Bob's convertible down there and give her this note?"

"He handed me the note, which said, 'This is Jack Hope. I'm Bob Hope's manager. We'd like to talk to you about appearing on his TV show.'

It sounded like a pleasant way to spend the afternoon, so Slatzer drove down to Long Beach with his own girl, in Hope's Cadillac, located the new Miss Universe at the hotel where she was staying, and handed her the note.

"She was very flattered and excited about the prospect of doing the show," remembers Slatzer, "but then her mother suddenly appeared. She was a hard-looking, no-nonsense type woman. She grabbed the note, read it, and said to me very angrily, 'Well, she's not going.' 'Why not?' I asked her. 'He'd like to meet your daughter, and take her around and put her on his show.' Well, the mother glared at me and said, 'I'll tell you why not. I've heard of his philandering around with young girls from beauty contests, and NO WAY am I allowing my daughter to be on his show.'

"She handed the note back to me and as I was leaving, Miss Universe burst into tears, pounded her mother on the chest, and cried out, 'But mother, I want to be on his show.'"

She never was, however. "That's one time The Boss's plan to trick the innocent virgin didn't work out," states Slatzer.

✿✿✿✿

Hope finished filming his next picture, *My Favorite Spy*, during the spring of 1951 and immediately asked Lew Grade, his agent for Britain and Europe, to book him for a personal appearance tour of England and Scotland. If possible, he wanted to play London's Palladium.

But first he'd appear at a few military bases in the British Isles.

He had specified certain dates to Grade, because after his stage gigs, he had his heart set on competing in the British Amateur Golf Championships at Porthcawl, Wales.

Unfortunately the Palladium wasn't available when he wanted it, because Judy Garland had beat him to it, and was booked there for the two weeks Hope had requested. So in the end he had to settle for a two-week engagement at the Prince of Wales Theater in London.

According to Hope, he tried to get Jane Russell for his act, but when she turned him down, he was again "forced" to substitute Marilyn Maxwell. But that was probably just a red herring to throw Dolores off the track.

* * * *

Hope sailed for England with Marilyn aboard the *Queen Mary* on April 14. By that time, their affair had reached such a fever pitch that "Marilyn Maxwell was being referred to as 'Mrs. Bob Hope,'" recalls Robert Slatzer.

"That's what they called her on the Paramount lot," affirms composer Jay Livingston.

It was inevitable that the gossip would get back to Dolores and her mother, Theresa Defina. According to what Theresa later told Hope's secretary Jan King, Dolores was so upset over the Maxwell affair that she was sobbing most of the time at home.

"Finally," recalls Theresa, "Dolores phoned Bob on the *Queen Mary* and told him that he was publicly humiliating her, and that his adultery had to stop."

As usual, her complaint fell on deaf ears.

During his stay in England, where all his stage appearances were sold out, Hope was constantly in Maxwell's company, which was duly noted by the British tabloids.

After completing his stage work, and before playing in the British Amateur, Hope took off for a much-needed "rest" in

Ireland, and brought Marilyn Maxwell along to help him. Nothing too subtle about that. Whatever relaxation he had resting with Maxwell, it didn't help him in the golf championships.

Hope lost in the second round, to a middle-aged, pipe smoking, bespectacled Yorkshireman named Chris Fox.

But Hope didn't seem to mind, according to an account of his match in the sports section of the local newspaper.

> Munching a slice of homemade cake given him by a woman spectator, and with his free hand around his stage partner, Marilyn Maxwell, Bob Hope walked down the seventeenth fairway here, beaten but happy.

I asked Jean Greenberg, Maxwell's personal secretary of twenty-six years, about Hope and Maxwell's affair. She said, "I will tell you this much, Bob asked Marilyn to marry him when they were in Ireland together. But she turned him down because she knew Dolores would never give him a divorce, being so Catholic, you know."

Despite the official denials emanating from the Hope camp, Marilyn Maxwell remained a big part of the comedian's emotional life until she married writer/producer Jerry Davis in 1954.

And they went everywhere together. Hope's appetite for her was apparently insatiable.

Hy Steirman, publisher of the now-defunct *Confidential* magazine, tells of a time when Hope and Maxwell were flying back home from a golfing weekend in his private plane, when the comedian suddenly got the urge to have her perform oral sex on him while they were in the air.

She seemed agreeable to this until she discovered he had a bad case of poison ivy on his penis, which he had contracted while urinating in some deep rough on the golf course. Seeing his condition, Maxwell recoiled in horror. But Hope saw no problem. "I'll use a condom," he advised.

"I used to date Marilyn occasionally after she divorced Andy McIntyre in 1951," recalls Hollywood agent Peter Sabiston, "and she wasn't at all bashful about telling me that she and Hope were having an affair.

"Hope was ever-determined to conceal his secret life from his important Hollywood friends. In the fifties, some of the big stars around town and their wives used to throw formal sit-down dinner parties at their respective homes, in Beverly Hills and Brentwood. Black-tie affairs, with ten or twelve guests at the most. Rocky Cooper [Gary's wife], Ann Sothern, Merle Oberon would host these swanky dinner parties at least once a month. Being a bachelor, the extra man, I was invited to a number of them too. The guest lists were impressive. Peter Lawford, Tony Curtis and Janet Leigh, Martin and Lewis, and their wives, Sammy Davis, Jr. And I saw Bob Hope at a number of these affairs. He would always bring Dolores, and they'd appear happy together."

"Of course, it was different once they were alone," said George Hope to Robert Slatzer. "They haven't slept together in years."

❖ ❖ ❖ ❖

Whether Hope had a legitimate reason for going outside his marriage for sex is anybody's guess, and a question not likely to be answered until Dolores writes a tell-all book of her own. But one thing there's no denying: Hope had plenty of co-conspirators in keeping his love life secret.

In addition to Barney Dean and several favored writers bearding for Hope, his movie agent, Louis Shurr, himself a legendary womanizer, performed services for the comedian that weren't spelled out in their written artist-representative agreement.

"I remember when Louis Shurr's office was right across the street from Romanoff's on South Rodeo Drive," recalls Kurt Niklas, proprietor of the successful Bistro restaurant in Beverly Hills, and former maitre d' at Romanoff's in the Fifties. "Every once in a while I'd get a call from Shurr at Romanoff's ordering dinner for two to be delivered to his office when he closed for the day. He'd leave the door to his office unlocked, and we'd cart in the food in warming dishes, and lay the whole dinner out on a sideboard in the office, so that whoever was coming in would be able to get it buffet style. The office would always be empty when we delivered the dinner, but it was understood from Shurr that it was for Hope and 'a friend.'"

Producer Peter Vieira told me, "I was doing some post-production work for Hope for one of his overseas shows, in 1961. Hope came around a lot. He always took an interest in his work. I remember, we were using the screening room one night to look at the finished product. I was sitting right behind Hope and Louis Shurr, when one of his aides arrived. I believe it was Hope's brother Jack. He had three young ladies with him . . . two redheads and a blonde. I could see Hope and the doctor staring at them and talking . . . Very low . . . I couldn't hear what they were saying. Finally Shurr pointed to the three ladies and said to Jack, 'We'll take that one and that one.' The third girl, I believe it was the blonde, was dismissed.'"

28

Following his tax deductible European vacation with Marilyn Maxwell, Hope returned to Los Angeles, said hello to the wife and kids, finished his 1951 radio season for Chesterfield Cigarettes, and then checked onto the Paramount lot to begin some pre-production work on his next film, *Son of Paleface*.

Son of Paleface, was of course a sequel to *The Paleface*, which had been a big box-office success. In it Hope plays a Harvard graduate instead of a dentist, but it's the same fish-out-of-water or tenderfoot-out-west theme. Hope returns to Sawbuck Pass to reclaim the fortune he believes his father had stashed away for him. Jane Russell plays Mike, a saloon singer, concealing her true identity as the Torch, a lady bandit. When Miss Russell takes a fancy to Junior (Hope), the college boy becomes embroiled in several touchy scrapes with her, averting disaster only with the timely aid of Roy Rogers and his faithful horse, Trigger.

On December 27, 1951, Hope's most recent feature, *My Favorite Spy*, costarring him with Hedy Lamarr, opened in New York.

Bosley Crowther, of *The New York Times*, wrote: "*My Favorite Spy* is difficult to believe, but because of its harried hero's breezy delivery, it does generate a generous portion of laughs."

During the next five years, Hope would make seven more films for Paramount. After *Son of Paleface*, there would be *Road to Bali*, the fifth of the series, *Off Limits*, *Here Come the Girls*, *Casanova's Big Night*, *The Seven Little Foys*, *That Certain Feeling*, and *Beau James*. In addition he did gag bits in *The Greatest Show on Earth* with Bing Crosby and in Martin and Lewis's *Scared Stiff*, a remake of Hope's earlier *Ghost Breakers*.

He'd host a monthly television special for NBC eight months a year. He'd do thirty-nine weeks of radio, He'd squeeze in as many personal appearances as were necessary to promote his films. He's continue to emcee star-studded fund-raising benefits for cerebral palsy, and other charities. He'd do annual Christmas shows for the GIs. He'd take part in presidential politicking during the Eisenhower-Stevenson campaign in the summer of 1952.

❖❖❖❖

With all this, Bob Hope still had time to indulge in his favorite hobby, the pursuit of beautiful women. Sometimes, once they were caught, he would keep them in apartments around town, on which he paid the rent. Some of these apartments were within walking distance of his house in Toluca Lake, so that when he took his midnight strolls through the neighborhood, supposedly "just for the exercise," he wouldn't have far to go to get sexual satisfaction.

"Regarding the proximity of Bob's house to the apartments of some of the girls he was keeping," relates Robert Slatzer, "I've got to tell you about something that happened to me once, when I was working with George Hope, Bob's brother, at General Service Studios. I'd set up an independent film production company, and George was in it with me. Though he was still working for Bob as sort of a gofer. One of his jobs was to deliver the envelopes containing the cash for the rent to these girls Bob was keeping around Toluca Lake. Well, there came a time when George's wife caught him with one of the girls on Hope's TV show, and he became a little gun-shy about having anything to do with Bob's women. So for a period of a few months I made the money drop for George. George would swing by my office, pull some envelopes full of fifty and hundred dollar bills out of his pocket, hand them to me—they'd have the apartment numbers and addresses on them but no names of the girls—and say, 'Take care of this for The Boss, will you, Bob?' So it would be up to me, at my leisure, to drive out to Toluca Lake, stop at these apartments, push the doorbell, and when a pretty girl opened the door, hand her her envelope with the rent money. I remember, one of the girls was a redhead and another a pretty blond.

"Well, I made the money drop in place of George for a few months, being careful to get the money to the right girl, because I didn't want to get George in trouble with Bob. But the last time I made the drop, a couple of nights later, about three A.M., to be exact, I got a frantic call from George, who said, 'Get your fucking ass out of bed. You've fucked up this whole deal. Did you take the money and spend it on some broad or something?' And I said, 'What in hell are you talking about?' And he said, 'We're in deep shit. That girl in 301 . . . her landlord called Bob at his house and complained that the rent hadn't been paid. The girl claims she didn't get the money.' 'Well, I handed it to her,' I said. 'I even went in and had a cup of coffee with her.' Then George said I'd better get over to Bob's house 'right now,' because we're going to have a meeting in The Boss's office. So George and I drove over together. In the car George told me that The Boss was very upset, because the landlord had phoned Bob's house, and Dolores got the call. And now she wants to know what's going on.

"Well, in Bob's office, George and I were sitting together when Bob walked in, all dressed very natty, as if he were going to a business meeting or something. And Bob said to me, very icily, 'Did you give her the money or didn't you?'

"I insisted that I did, and I guess he believed me, because suddenly he changed his tune. He said, 'Well, sometimes these broads take the money and spend it, and they don't use it for rent like they're supposed to.' So I said, 'Bob, what do you want with those kind of girls in the first place?' I guess it was foolish of me to say, because he looked at me as if I were crazy and snapped, 'You take care of your business, and I'll take care of mine.'

"The bottom line is that he apologized to me for getting me up at such an hour, thanked me, then told me to go home get some sleep. Like I could sleep after all that.

"A couple of days later, George told me that the girl admitted she got the money, and that she had bought some clothes with it, because Bob was too cheap to give her clothes money. She figured she could stall paying the rent until the following month."

* * * *

Obviously Hope hadn't heeded Dolores's warning that he'd better quit two-timing her or there would be serious consequences.

After several such warnings, Dolores caught Hope in bed with one of his ladies. Out of control, she yanked the covers off Hope and his playmate of the night. Caught with the goods, Hope sat bolt upright in bed and exclaimed, "It isn't me!"

At least he had a sense of humor about it. However, he wasn't so amused when the shoe was on the other foot, according to one of his writers, the late Lester White, who worked for him in the fifties and sixties, but whose business relationship with him dated clear back to his vaudeville days.

"One time Hope was in Chicago at the same time Marilyn Maxwell was playing a nightclub there," White told me. "Figuring she'd be anxious to see him, Bob went to her hotel room around midnight without any warning, and knocked on the door. When she called out nervously, 'Who's there?' Bob replied, 'It's me, "Great Lover" Hope.' There was a long delay before she came to the door. Meanwhile, Bob could hear scrambling inside the room. When Maxwell finally opened the door, she wore a sexy negligee, but seemed flustered. Suspecting hanky panky, Bob yanked open the closet door, and there, huddled inside in polka dot undershorts, was Jimmy Durante."

White wasn't sure of the date, but he said it could have

happened in the summer of 1952, when the Republican and Democratic conventions were both held in Chicago and Hope was there, being paid by NBC to do a humorous commentary on them over radio every night. He'd also been commissioned to do a short daily newspaper column on the political goings-on for King Features, which, of course, was being ghosted by Hope's gang of writers.

If the humor in his newspaper columns seemed a little derivative of Will Rogers, it wasn't entirely by accident. Who better to steal from when you're doing political jokes? Sample joke:

"Chicago was known as the Windy City even before the politicians arrived."

And, "The hotels here are really luxurious, they have everything. Hot and cold running rumors on every floor."

Following both conventions, Hope took a few weeks off that summer to vacation in Vermont with Dolores, Linda and Tony. Then, after depositing his family back in Toluca Lake, where it was nearly time for Linda and Tony to begin their fall school semesters, Hope left on an extended business trip to New York, London and some cities on the Continent, to publicize *Son of Paleface*.

Son of Paleface opened in New York at the beginning of 1952 to reviews astonishingly good for a sequel—in fact, much better than had been accorded the original from which it had derived.

✿ ✿ ✿ ✿

Before leaving for Europe that summer, Hope had London agent Lew Grade obtain for him that booking at the Palladium that had been so elusive the year before.

Since the Palladium booking wasn't until mid-October, Hope spent a couple of weeks bouncing around the Continent in the company of an assortment of beautiful women.

Hope flew frequently to London, ostensibly for business, but actually for the other things that attracted him there. London was notorious for its beautiful, statuesquely built British showgirls.

Sabrina was one, Pamela Guard was another. Pamela, whose stage name was simply Yana, was considered around London as the Hildegarde of that period.

"Yana had her own variety show on the BBC," recalls producer-writer Digby Wolfe, one of the creators of *Laugh-In*. "I wrote it for her in the mid-fifties. She danced, sang and did comedy sketches, but she was known best for her legendary tits. Hope used her in his camp shows in Europe a lot, and the two of them traveled all over together. Yana told me that whenever Bob came to London that she'd have him over to her flat, work in his act whenever he needed her, and they tootled all over the Continent together."

Hope's two weeks at the Palladium drew raves from the tough London critics. One of the toughest was Peter Forester. But he was putty in Bob's hands.

A brilliant Palladium bill is headed by Bob Hope, surely the most endearing of the American comedians. His very entrance is a joy as he ambles on, jaw-shutting, eyes-roving, abounding in that old indefinable heart-warming quality of your true star comedian. Mr. Hope is funny to look at, funny to hear, funny without effort, and without flagging. What matter how many joke writers assist?

Hope was in a good mood by the time he returned to Hollywood to begin rehearsing for his first *Colgate Comedy Hour* for NBC.

Sid Caesar did a ninety-minute show every week but few comedians of that period, except Milton Berle were brave enough to undertake an hour-long television show every week. The *Colgate Comedy Hour* devised a format in which four different comedians would rotate in that same spot within a four-week period. Rotating with Hope were Martin & Lewis, Abbott & Costello, and Eddie Cantor.

✣ ✣ ✣ ✣

With the approach of the November presidential election pitting Dwight D. Eisenhower against Adlai Stevenson, Hope decided to get in the spirit of the season and loaded his opening monologue with political jokes. Jokes about the Gallup Poll ("The Gallup Poll is very positive this time . . . they've come up with a statement that there *will* be a president elected"). Jokes about Adlai Stevenson ("I'm so confused I don't know whether to join the Democrats who are voting for Eisenhower or the Republicans who are voting for Stevenson. Or Crosby who is still voting for John Quincy Adams"). Jokes about Pat Nixon's cloth coat and Richard Nixon's Checkers speech ("My aunt heard Richard Nixon's speech on television, but she got the whole thing confused . . . she said I feel sorry for Mrs. Nixon . . . imagine having to wear a cloth coat with a cocker spaniel collar"). Jokes about the Marshall Plan ("I'm happy to be back from Europe . . . I bring you regards from your money").

Wrote *Variety*:

> Bob Hope's turn . . . resulted in a mixed session in which the principal offenders were some sketches that lowered the caliber of the show. However, there were a couple of bits that hit its mark with room to spare. On this session, as with many others Hope left himself in the position where he would stand or fall on the strength of his various sketches.
>
> It seems Hope generally does better on his stand-up comedy. His opening remarks had charm and wit.

❖❖❖❖

Until the Eisenhower campaign Hope had always been chary of devoting too much of his comedy to politics. Even though he was a devout Republican, with a strong distaste for Communism, and an inherent suspicion of anyone even faintly on the Left, he tried to keep his political jokes from sounding biased for fear of offending people in his audience who might not believe in the same things he did: Mom, apple pie, baseball, "good" wars and the American flag. He'd long known that it would be dangerous to take a stand on a *controversial* subject and risk offending whole groups who might thereafter boycott the sponsor's product.

Even in his choice of movie material, Hope always sought to remain apolitical.

I once wrote a screen treatment called *The Man in the Back Seat*. It was about an aging Secret Service man who'd been assigned to guard the President's incorrigible teenage daughter. With her father in the White House she suffered from and resented her lack of freedom. How could she enjoy such simple pleasures as going on a date and necking with her boyfriend with a Secret Service man (Bob Hope) sitting in the back seat of her car?

It seemed a natural vehicle for Hope, and there was nothing political about the story, except that it took place in the White House. Louis Shurr liked it and handed it to Hope with the recommendation that he do it. But Hope turned it down on the basis that it was "too controversial."

Being more liberal than their boss, the Hope writers, led by Mort Lachman, urged him to start doing some jokes lampooning Joseph McCarthy, the controversial senator.

But Hope was afraid of offending even McCarthy and his Senate Un-American Activities Committee, for fear *he'd* be labeled a Communist. Hope knew that many in Hollywood, including Ronald Reagan and George Murphy and Cecil B. DeMille and John Wayne were all McCarthy supporters.

Though anything but a left winger, the newly elected President, Dwight Eisenhower, was as much against Senator McCarthy's demagoguery vis-a-vis the Communists in the U.S. Government as were the liberals. After Hope discovered that Eisenhower, who was one of his heroes, shared the same anti-McCarthy sentiments with his writers, Hope gave Lachman the green light to create jokes roasting the senator.

One of his earliest anti-McCarthy cracks showed up on his December 1952 *Colgate Comedy Hour*, which, of course, was devoted largely to Christmas and the holidays.

The joke was in the form of a letter from Santa Claus to Bob Hope:

"Dear Robert . . . Thank you for your nice letter, and the beautiful new brown suit you sent me . . . but tell Senator McCarthy I'm going to wear my old red one anyway . . . I had it first."

Even though he received mail from pro-McCarthy people, that called him a Communist sympathizer, Hope continued to needle McCarthy in his TV shows in 1953 and into 1954.

"Senator McCarthy got off the train in Washington, D.C., and spent two days at Union Station investigating redcaps. . . . And McCarthy is on a new type of television show. . . . It's sort of a soap opera where everything comes out tattletale gray . . . Even President Eisenhower is careful about what he says on the air these days. Senator McCarthy may demand equal time in the White House . . ."

President Eisenhower enjoyed Bob Hope's anti-McCarthy campaign as much as anybody. He also reacted favorably to Hope's defense of him on his television show after the media criticized the President for devoting more time to his golfing jaunts to Georgia than he did to national affairs. The defense of Eisenhower's golf came in the lyrics of a song Hope sang on his TV show in April 1953.

The lyrics weren't particularly witty, and Oscar Hammerstein had nothing to fear from whoever composed them.

> *Do what you do*
> *Putt when you putt*
> *Just follow through*
> *And we'll be happy.*
>
> *The White House lawn is all yorn*
> *Who cares if it is torn*
> *Just follow through*
> *And we'll be happy.*
>
> *Since you made Augusta, Georgia*
> *So very popular*
> *Those Dixie-Democrats*
> *Are wearing black homburg hats.*

As long as you've got that drive
We'll all survive
Just follow through
And we'll be happy.

Witty or not, Eisenhower was pleased that Hope stuck up for him. To repay the comedian, he invited Hope to play in a golf foursome with him, Gov. Dan Thornton of Colorado and Sen. Prescott Bush of Connecticut at Burning Tree Country Club in Maryland on Saturday, May 3, 1953.

The golf game with Ike provided grist for Hope's joke mill, and the following night, when Hope was emceeing the annual White House correspondents' dinner, he was prepared to spew them out in a rapid fire monologue.

> I knew the President when he was still a General and *really* had power. . . . I played golf with him yesterday, and it's hard to beat a guy who rattles his medals while you're putting. . . . Ike used a short Democrat for a tee . . . He was hitting the ball much farther than I . . . he had Senator McCarthy's picture painted on the ball.

In addition to affording Hope a target for his jokes for many months to come, the golf game with the President led to a strong bond between the two, which culminated with Hope being the White House court jester and confidant for future administrations and for most who followed Ike into that office—even Democrats.

His relationship with Ike and future presidents afforded him access to almost any important figure in the government he chose to speak with, by merely lifting up the telephone in his bedroom and placing a call to the White House switchboard.

"It's an unbelievable kind of access," believes TV documentary producer Andrew Solt, who worked on several projects with Hope in the early eighties.

"During the Carter administration, I was working on a documentary with Hope that was to be about his troop entertaining experiences. It was right after Iran had taken all those people at the embassy hostage. Well, Hope was very interested in this thing, absorbed, I would say, and very unhappy about it, and how it made America look. So much so that when we were working on this documentary at his house at Toluca Lake one night, about eleven o'clock, and running some tapes of his shows, he suddenly exclaimed, 'Stop the tape . . . stop the tape!'

"We stopped it, and he asked us if we knew anybody who could speak Iranian. When I asked him why, he said, 'I've got a number from President Carter, and I can call, and maybe I can do something about this hostage situation.'

"I didn't know what he was talking about, but I did know someone, a girl, who spoke Iranian. It was now past midnight and I didn't want to bother her. But Hope insisted, and I called her, and asked her if she'd come over to Hope's house. She did and so, at about one-thirty A.M. we all met in Hope's bedroom, on the second floor.

"I must say, it was an interesting bedroom. There was a huge desk . . . a big bed . . . and a lot of cushions on the floor which everybody sat around on. . . . And the walls were covered with framed photographs . . . of the Kennedys . . . Nixon . . . the Pope . . . but the one I really remember was one of General Patton, pissing in the Rhine. . . . His back was to the camera, and he was looking over his shoulder at the photographer. It was autographed to Hope, who told us he got it personally from Patton, who'd made a vow that the day the Germans surrendered, he would urinate in the Rhine.

"Anyway, to get back to Hope's power, he took a paper out of his desk drawer after we were all seated . . . dialed a number . . . and after he told them at the White House switchboard who he was, they immediately put him through to the State Department. It was about four-thirty A.M. in Washington.

"Well, someone high up got on the phone with Bob, and to my amazement, he was put directly through to the American Embassy in Teheran, where the hostages were being held. Until then I didn't know that anybody in Washington had any phone numbers directly to the hostage-takers.

"A forty-minute conversation ensued with this woman, Diti, the one I brought over, who spoke Iranian, with Bob telling her what he wanted to say, and she translating it to Iranian. It turned out she was talking to the radical dentist who was the ringleader of the group holding the American hostages.

"What Hope offered was to go over and entertain the Iranians and talk a deal with them whereby they'd release the hostages. Hope was sure they'd go for the idea. If not, at worst, he'd get some message from the hostages and bring them back to the folks back home.

"Hope was really serious that he could bring it off, when Carter couldn't. But eventually the dentist told Hope that he didn't think it would be right for him to get involved, but they said they appreciated his interest, and told him to 'stay in touch.'

"On my way home, I just couldn't believe what I'd witnessed . . . that Hope had actually been talking to the people holding the hostages, and that he had access to President Carter by a special hot line. That's the kind of thing I'm talking about . . . access . . . real power. Who else could do that? Not even the vice-president."

But 1953, the first of the Eisenhower years, was the beginning of that access. It was also the start of Bob Hope being perceived as more than just a comic. He had political power. He could pick up the phone and call anybody and make a request, and it would be granted. By the using this power, he's been able to suppress many of the damaging stories about him that were scheduled to appear in magazine articles or unauthorized biographies.

I personally know writers who've had portions of their manuscripts censored by book publishers in order to please Mr. Hope.

In the early seventies I had a contract to write a biography of Bob Hope for Norton. I signed it and deposited the advance, which was considerable. Then Evan Thomas, editor-in-chief at Norton at the time, called me to say, "A word of advice about the Hope book! Take it easy on the guy. If you knock him, the people who like him won't buy it, and the people who don't like him won't buy it anyway."

"Well, if I can't tell the truth about him, there's no point in writing it," I replied.

He agreed, and I wrote a biography of Sam Goldwyn instead for Norton.

✦ ✦ ✦ ✦

Except for the article in *Confidential* magazine detailing Hope's romance with Barbara Payton, and one in the same magazine in which he was accused of rigging a Miss Universe beauty contest so that he could sleep with the winner, Johnine Avery, no one has talked frankly about Bob Hope until Jan King. She worked for him as his personal secretary for fifteen years. She spoke about Hope's secret life to the *Globe* in two articles in 1991.

29

Until late in 1953, Marjorie Hughes, who'd started out as Hope's secretary right after she graduated from business school in 1942, had been able to handle his business correspondence, fan mail, and the sending out of five thousand or more Christmas cards every year. She organized his joke files with the aid of a pair of low-paid assistants.

But a man doing all that Hope was doing by 1953 could not possibly get along with just one executive secretary. Hope was no longer just a comedian or film star. He was big business. In addition to films, radio, TV, oil, real estate, frozen orange juice, charity fund-raising, golf, wholesale meat, personal appearances on both sides of the Atlantic, he was also involved in major league baseball. Not to be outdone by Bing Crosby, who owned a large share of the Pittsburgh Pirates, Hope bought a five percent interest in his favorite ball team, the Cleveland Indians, in 1949. He also was part owner of several radio and TV stations.

With so much going for him, it's difficult to imagine why Hope would have permitted, let alone encourage, his agent Jimmy Saphier to commit him to a deal to do a fifteen-minute network radio show, five-days-a-week, at 11:45 in the morning, beginning in November 1952. This was in addition to doing his weekly half-hour nighttime network radio show, which General Foods would sponsor starting in January 1953.

On the other hand, perhaps it isn't so hard to believe that Hope would take on this extra burden when you consider that he was to receive $2 million a year for the daytime series, and the million dollars-plus he was making on the nighttime show, and the $400,000 he received for the eight times a year *Colgate Comedy Hour*.

The nighttime show would be moved to Wednesday from Tuesday, which had been his broadcast night for all the years he was on for Lever Brothers. The new show would be sponsored by Jell-O, produced by Jack Hope, and announced by Bill Goodwin. Les Brown would supply the music, and Larry Marks and Norm Sullivan the jokes.

Hope's radio shows were a success during the 1952–53 season, which is a tribute to his staying power. Except for Edgar Bergen, Jack Benny and Bing Crosby, most variety radio programs were rapidly losing listeners to television by 1953. As a result, sponsors were deserting radio.

As if he didn't have enough on his schedule, Hope agreed to make several more films for Paramount: another "road" picture with Crosby and Lamour, *Road to Bali*, which was more of the same except it was the first of the series in technicolor; *Off Limits*, a service comedy about the military police, with Mickey Rooney and Marilyn Maxwell; and *Here Come the Girls*, a run-of-the-mill Hollywood film musical with nothing distinctive about it except Rosemary Clooney's singing and Arlene Dahl's red-haired ravishing looks.

❈ ❈ ❈ ❈

On February 27, 1953, the Friars Club honored Hope for the second time with a testimonial dinner. This was different from Hope's first roast in 1947 in that the proceedings were broadcast to the nation over NBC radio. The caliber of the guest speakers was impressive: Milton Berle, George Jessel, Fred Allen, Sen. Stuart Symington, Cleveland Mayor Tom Burke, aging financier and presidential advisor Bernard Baruch, former vice president

Alben Barkley, Gen. Rosie O'Donnell, Eric Johnson, RCA chief Frank Fulsom, NBC's top man Frank White, Paramount's ninety-year-old chairman Adolph Zukor. Also in attendance were important columnists such as Ed Sullivan and Bob Considine.

Unlike other Friars roasts where sometimes the jokes were too raunchy for a mixed audience, wives were invited to this affair, including Dolores, who, at one point in the proceedings, was asked by Hope to stand up and take a bow. Dolores timidly rose to her feet, and took a short body squeak. As she sat down hurriedly, Bob quipped, "Is that all you're going to show of that fashion investment?" He followed that with a joke about Dolores he's used many times since: "I suppose this is the first time Dolores knows what I do for a living. She probably thought I was a test pilot for United Airlines."

Before consenting to the roast, Hope had stipulated that the awards to himself be kept to a minimum. He agreed to be presented with just one statuette, which would be awarded to him by the Boy Scouts of America. Eleven other awards from various charities were sent to his office and presented to him in private.

The best jokes of the evening came from Milton Berle, who referred to Hope as "America's second greatest comedian," and the ailing Barney Baruch, who'd gotten up from a sick bed to attend. Baruch said to Hope, "May the Lord take a liking to you, but not too soon."

As Hope received his statuette from an Eagle Scout, who told him what a great American he was, Hope replied, "No man can be this great . . . but you've finally convinced me. . . . If I'd known you were going to eulogize me like this, I'd have done the decent thing and died first."

Among the no-shows that evening were Jack Benny, who was in Cedars of Lebanon Hospital in Los Angeles with a stomach-ache, and Bing Crosby, who begged off with his usual excuse: "I never go to those things."

Although he was somewhat of a loner who didn't enjoy black-tie affairs, perhaps there was another reason behind

Crosby's consistent refusals to attend functions honoring Hope. Knowing Hope as well as he did, quite possibly he believed it was hypocritical to eulogize a man who had such a dark underside to his character.

One thing for certain: Despite their surface friendship on display in their golf matches and "Road" pictures, a rivalry existed between the two men. Insiders would characterize it as "resentment." Crosby no doubt resented the fact that he'd been replaced by Hope in the box-office polls, and Hope, though he joked about it constantly, resented the fact that Crosby had won a Best Acting Oscar for *Going My Way*, while all his life he had to be content with "honorary" Oscars.

On March 19, 1953, the Academy Awards were televised for the first time, from the Pantages Theater in Hollywood, over NBC. The wedding of the film business and television was a milestone in the entertainment world. It marked the first time major studios officially acknowledged the existence of their greatest rival, TV.

For the seventh time, Bob Hope emceed the proceedings, and for the third time he picked up an honorary statuette—this time "for his contribution to the laughter of the world, his service to the motion picture industry, and his devotion to the American premise."

But it did not make up for the fact that Bing won *his* Oscar for dramatic acting.

So their one-upmanship continued, and became more strained, if anything, as the years passed.

For example, when Simon and Schuster published *Call Me Lucky*, Bing Crosby's 1953 autobiography, Hope decided he needed an autobiography, too, and immediately made arrangements with Jack Goodman, editor in chief of Simon and Schuster to publish one. The *Saturday Evening Post* agreed to serialize it weekly in nine installments.

Hope's book was called *Have Tux, Will Travel*. It was to be a more honest telling of his life than his other tomes that had been written by his gagwriters. To insure that the book would have some substance to it, *Saturday Evening Post* editor Ben

Hibbs assigned the magazine's top "as told to" autobiographer, Pete Martin, to the project.

After doing another *Colgate Comedy Hour* in the spring of 1953, and before going to work with Pete Martin, Hope went on the road again to fill some charity engagements. One was a golf exhibition at the Greenbriar Hotel, in White Sulphur Springs, with the Duke of Windsor as his partner.

Before leaving New York for Greenbriar, Hope phoned his newest girlfriend, Jeanne Carmen, who lived in Manhattan and asked her to go with him on the golf date. A model who'd migrated to New York from Arkansas, Jeannie was a gorgeous brunette, about twenty-one-years-old, with a figure that would make Marilyn Monroe envious. But more than just a pretty face, she could play golf in the low seventies and made a living as a trick-shot artist. Hope had met her in 1950 when he was doing his first television show for Frigidaire, and she was one of the bit-part girls.

"I was basically a model—not an actress," recalls Jeannie, "but I went on the audition, with about seven other girls. I had never acted before and I was pretty lousy. The director didn't want me, but Bob fought like a son-of-a-bitch for me. I don't know why. No matter who said, 'Forget her.' He kept saying, 'No, I want her.' And then he found out I could play golf. And that was it.

"He said to me, 'I hear you're a good golfer.' And I said, 'Well, I'm a trick-shot artist.' And that intrigued him, and he asked me if I wanted to go out and play sometime. So I said, 'Sure, why not?' I think I was seventeen or eighteen years old at the time, and I didn't realize that it wasn't necessarily golf that he wanted to play.

"I met him on the set, and he asked if I'd like to meet him for dinner. And I said, 'Sure.' Well, I didn't realize he didn't necessarily mean dinner at a restaurant, either, and that I was supposed to be the dinner when I said 'yes.'

"He said, 'Meet me at the Waldorf-Astoria.' That's where he was staying. And I thought he wanted me to meet him in the restaurant . . . I was as dumb as they come. So I got to the restaurant. I was a little early, and he wasn't there. So I asked the maitre d' if Bob Hope was there, and he said, 'I don't think he has a reservation. I'll seat you.' So he sat me at a front table. The maitre d' was kind of hovering around me, waiting for Bob. Then I see Bob walking by the doorway on his way to his room, and the maitre d' called out 'Mr. Hope, Mr. Hope, monsieur, monsieur . . . your lady is here.' I could see Bob's face fall down on his lap . . . except I was really too dumb to know what was going on. I just thought he looked very nervous, so he said, 'Wait here, wait here . . . I—uh—I, I have to go look for a beard.'

"I thought is this dumb-ass going to put a beard on? They've already seen him. How's he going to fake it with a beard? I didn't realize that in those days 'a beard' meant some guy to look like he was with me. So he goes out and comes back with some young guy . . . and his agent . . . and we all sat down and had dinner, which Hope wasn't expecting to do, I'm sure.

"By that time I was getting a little upset. So after we'd finished eating, I decided to go home. I didn't go upstairs with him, not that night.

"Anyway, after that I met him a few times when he was in New York. But he was so suave about it, I guess a young girl can be had without knowing it.

"And I didn't even know he was married. I didn't read anything much. I was just that 'Little Girl from Little Rock' that you hear about. I was a country girl. I wasn't from the intelligentsia. In fact, I was pretty stupid. But what I found fascinating about him . . . his humor was so great . . . I love that on-the-spot sense of humor, until I found out it wasn't on-the-spot sense of humor at all . . . he had writers. But he was really nice. Nobody was nicer than Bob. And he was nice looking, too, until he got his little tummy and his girdle and all that.

"So we started running around together, here, there and everywhere. But we still had not been intimate. He took me to a nightclub one time. We were with a lot of people. Except Dolores, who I didn't really know about, because when he came to New York, she never came with him. The minute we walked in they started playing "Thanks for the Memory." And Bob grabbed me and started waltzing with me. "I had ten left feet. I couldn't dance . . . I was tripping all over myself. I made a total fool of myself. But none of that bothered Bob. He just said, 'What's the matter, honey, you don't know how to dance?' And I said 'No.' So we sat down after he got tired of trying to teach me.

"After that he had me call him at the studio in California . . . I'd call him all the time and reverse the charges. I'd say to the operator, 'Reversing the charges to Robert Hope.' And the operator would gasp, 'You mean Robert Hope the movie star?' And I said, 'Fuck, no, Bob Hope the plumber!' Hoping they wouldn't listen in, but I'm sure they did.

"He was always trying to get me up to his room. I don't even remember the first time we had sex. That's how exciting it was. I can't remember . . . where it was or when. But I'm pretty sure it was at the Waldorf, on either his second or third trip. But it took a while, because he would be in and out of town . . . and there'd be a lot of time in between. As a lover, he wasn't very exciting.

"I think he might have been torching for Marilyn Maxwell by the time we first went to bed. He was quite taken with her.

"He was always trying to get me to travel with him. He wanted me to go on one of those junkets with the soldiers, but I never would . . . I never much cared for travel. I was doing a little TV . . . I was doing my golf exhibitions and getting a thousand-dollars-a-performance. I didn't want to be running around all over the world.

"I think the affair started around the time I went to Greenbriar with him in 1953, or immediately afterward. We went there . . . he was playing a match coupled with the Duke of Windsor . . . The Duchess was there too. It was a charity thing . . . We were staying at the main hotel at White Sulphur Springs. But he was such a cheap prick that he only got one room, because he didn't want to pay for two. He gave me my choice. I could sleep in the bed with him or I could sleep on the couch. He was too much of a tightwad to pay for two rooms.

"Thinking back, this was still before we had our first affair. I wasn't up to it. I slept in the bed with him, but there was no sex, until we were back in New York at the Waldorf. I mean, he didn't push it. He's not pushy.

"But some of the stupidest things happened to me when I was with Bob. Like I was really temperamental and crazy, and one night we're all down at the nightclub at Greenbriar. Bob was on my left, the Duke of Windsor was on my right . . . and the Duchess was there, but she had a young guy with her. . . . It was a long table . . . there were twelve people there . . . and we were eating and having champagne.

"I had a lot of pink champagne, and I got mean. Sometimes I get mean when I drink. All of a sudden, Bob said something to me, I don't remember what, probably just 'hi honey,' but it pissed me off, and I jumped up. And when I did, the whole table tipped over and drinks spilled all over the Duke and everybody else. And then I walked out like the Queen of Sheba and went back to the room. "Bob came up to the room and told me, 'You have to come back down. Change your clothes and come back down.' And I said, 'I'm never coming back down.' And then he gave me a long lecture on how I had to get along with people if I was going to be in show business. But he never got angry, never yelled, just gave me these lectures about how I should be nicer.

"Then . . . time went by. I refused to go on his junkets with him. He'd still call me. We'd still see each other once in a while when he came into New York. And we talked on the phone a lot when he was in Hollywood. And then I moved out to the Coast . . . in the early fifties.

"I used to go to those pro-celebrity tournaments with Bob . . . all over the country with him. . . . I'd walk around the course with him or ride on a golf cart . . . but the beard was always close by . . . Louis Shurr . . . Jimmy Saphier or maybe one of his writers.

"But I remember once, we had sex in his house in Toluca

Lake, upstairs in his bedroom when Dolores wasn't around. He talked me into that. . . . But only once. And now that I think of it, that was pretty nervy of me, doing it right there in another woman's house.

"I didn't see him much out here, but we talked a lot on the phone. And one day he said, 'Look, I want to make some bets on you. I want you to come to Lakeside, so get in shape, I've got some big bets going on.'

"By that time I was playing a lot of golf at Hillcrest Country Club . . . all the time. And I got the really hots for a kid who was club champion . . . I was dying to jump his bones, never mind Bob Hope. So the morning of the match at Lakeside that Bob had arranged, I got up real early and played thirty-six holes with this kid.

"Then we went to the back of his car and started kissing, hugging and making out. I spent so much time with this kid I was exhausted by the time I had to go to Lakeside. Worse luck my car died halfway there, so I hitched a ride in a laundry truck to Lakeside, and left my car somewhere there in the Valley.

"Bob met me at Lakeside. By that time I was so exhausted I didn't give a damn whether I ever played golf or not. It was around one o'clock, and everybody was there to watch the big match. And I could see Bob in the background, whispering to everybody when I got up to tee off. 'Wait'll you see this' because when I wasn't exhausted from all that screwing around with the kid, I could hit it two-twenty straight down the middle. But I swear to God, the best shot I hit that day probably went twenty yards. I mean I was going farther than the ball. Of course I blew the match, and Bob was pissed off, because he had a lot of money on it.

"When we got through, he put me in his car, refusing to speak to me, threw my clubs in the back seat, and we took off. He drove me to where my car was parked. Then he threw my clubs out on the street, along with me, and then got back in his car and proceeded to run over my clubs, and bent them double. And all the time he was laughing . . . he was laughing like hell. . . . I was too scared to explain to him the reason I was so bad, that I'd been making it with a sixteen-year-old . . . I was still only twenty-one or something.

"Then he drove away. And that more or less ended our affair . . . though we've spoken a few times since, and I still have his private telephone number."

✿✿✿✿

Pete Martin began his interview sessions with Hope for *Have Tux, Will Travel* in June 1953, after Hope came back from Greenbriar, and checked into Paramount to begin work on his next film. It was a costume picture starring Joan Fontaine and Basil Rathbone. It was called *Casanova's Big Night*, certainly an appropriate title, considering what Hope did in his spare time.

Although Pete Martin was the *Saturday Evening Post*'s most respected Boswell, what he came up with, when Hope's story finally appeared in print the following year, was more puff than fact. This wasn't Martin's fault entirely. The only facts he had to work with were the ones supplied by Hope, and the comedian, who had full control of the contents, wasn't about to do a mea culpa for the world.

✿✿✿✿

Certainly Jan King had no idea of the kind of person Hope was when she went to work for him as an executive secretary in November 1953.

A petite attractive blond of about thirty-five, Jan had been story editor at NBC's Burbank studios when she came to Hope's attention.

"I was walking down a flight of stairs at the time, and Hope saw me from below," remembers Jan. "Bob called up to me and told me I had very pretty ankles and how would I like to come and work for him. I must admit I was very flattered. I wasn't the old bag of seventy-five I am today. Anyway he said he wanted me to be his personal secretary and script girl in order to take some of the burden off Marjorie Hughes. He told me she was very efficient but that the work was snowballing and she could no longer handle everything herself. So I quit the story department."

Hope offered Jan the princely salary of $75 a week to take his personal dictation, handle his script work, and travel with him when he was doing personal appearances.

He didn't mention what else he had in mind for her before she reported to work for him in his Toluca Lake house one afternoon in November 1953. All Jan knew was that she was flattered by the offer and was anxious to work for the comedian she had heard so much about and admired.

Dolores evidently wasn't at home when Jan drove her station wagon through the gates at the Hope estate in Toluca Lake that afternoon. Hope appeared at the door in casual clothes and, with his usual jaunty manner, welcomed her. He gave her a quick tour of his trophy room, which one had to pass through on one's way from the door to his large attractive den-dining room, where he received most visitors. It was an attractive room, with a large round dining table, a huge coffee table in front of a ten-foot sofa, a piano, a small bar, and a view through a picture window of his one hole golf course in the back yard.

Hope whisked Jan past all his medals, plaques and portraits of himself with important political, show business and sporting figures, then maneuvered her onto one of the couches in the den, where, almost immediately, she had to fend off his amorous advances.

At first Jan thought he was clowning, but she realized it was the real thing when he suddenly grabbed her, pulled her very close in a bear-like hug, and made some intimate remarks.

"Mr. Hope, you're a married man!" exclaimed the surprised Jan, trying to pull out of his grasp. "What about Dolores?"

Hope didn't want to hear about Dolores as he pushed Jan over on her back on the sofa and held her beneath him as she tried to squirm away.

"Bob," she finally yelled. "You don't appeal to me. Now let go and zip your pants up. I want to work for you a long time, but not doing this."

Hope finally got the message.

"He took his arms from around me," recalls Jan, "and he never mentioned the incident again."

When I asked Jan why she hadn't just turned around and walked out after such a flagrant display of sexual harassment, she said, "Well, I wanted the job, so I decided I'd give Bob a trial. If it turned out that I'd have to shack up with him in order to take 150 words of dictation a minute, then I wouldn't work for him at any price."

But it never came to that.

Before she retired fifteen years later, however, Jan King had to perform a number of other duties anathema to her sensibilities. Being "confidential" secretary turned out to be one of the most important functions Jan was called upon to perform.

"It didn't take long after I joined Bob's Hollywood staff to find out that the man America loved, the man who promoted himself as an adoring husband and father, was a lech. He had women stashed away all over town, and part of my job was to help him conceal his secret harem from Dolores and the world. I also learned that his lavish dressing room-offices at the studio was a hotbed of intrigue, from which he carried out secret seductions and where members of his family spied on him. He finally barred Dolores from his office.

"His quarters at Universal Studios when he moved there after leaving Paramount were like a sexual command post. They were lavishly furnished with expensive carpeting, a king-size bed, mirrored walls, a stocked bar, and even a solid-gold coffee pot.

"His 'talent scouts' brought him a succession of beautiful young women. They all had stars in their eyes and were looking for their big break. Some of these women he gave bit parts to in his pictures, and others he just put on his payroll, so he could use them as tax deductions."

Jan felt guilty protecting her boss from exposure, but she rationalized her part because she was sure Dolores knew her husband was fooling around, since she had to make appointments a week in advance to go down to the Palm Springs chalet on El Alameda Street.

"That gave Bob enough time to get the place cleaned up and

to move out his bimbo-of-the-week," Jan explained. "He didn't want Dolores to catch him in any kind of a compromising situation. And Dolores went along with this charade. I know, because she always called me to make the appointment. She never just popped in on him down at the desert, for fear of what she would find."

While most people believe that the reason Hope spent so much time at the desert was for golf, sun and relaxation, Jan believes the main reason he had the place in the Springs was to set up a bachelor pad away from the prying eyes of Dolores and Hollywood gossips.

"The place was pretty tacky when I first saw it," recalls Palm Springs interior designer Gary Jon. "It had a lot of rooms— seven, I believe—and a swimming pool, but it was pretty run-down inside. It had been done a number of years before by Gladys Belzer, Loretta Young's mother, who was a pal of Dolores Hope. Another nice Catholic lady. But then Hope brought in Joan Billings, whom he knew from Cleveland, to do the whole place over, and I was assigned to work with her."

Joan Billings was a gorgeous, leggy, green-eyed blond of about thirty.

"Bob was having an affair with Joan when I first went to work for him," reveals Jan King.

That seemed to coincide with what Gary Jon remembers of his former partner's relationship with Hope. "Joan came from Cleveland, and Hope met her there on one of his frequent trips to his hometown to visit his relatives. He was introduced to Joan by a man named Max Mink, who'd run a vaudeville theater in Cleveland, and who was a longtime friend of Hope.

"At the time they met, Joan was married to a man named Joe Padera—who owned a beauty college and a number of beauty salons, and who had a local television show in Cleveland. Joe sold personal health care, and all that sort of thing. Then Max introduced Joan to Bob, and they started an affair. Joan divorced her husband and moved to Hollywood.

"She went into the dress business in Hollywood with a partner, and Hope helped her get started financially. She did well, and was able to build a house up on Mulholland Drive. I was introduced to her through a girlfriend from Cleveland that I worked with, whose name was Liz Braden. Liz had been a fashion director at Saks Fifth Avenue. Then Bob asked Joan to decorate his Palm Springs house, so she and I went down there and did it together. We liked Palm Springs so much that we decided to open a business down there, which Bob also helped us finance and get started."

According to both Gary Jon and Jan King, Hope's affair with Joan Billings lasted for at least six years.

What eventually broke them up, believes Jan, is that Bob was using the digs Joan had decorated for him to cheat on her with other women, and Joan couldn't take this two-timing. But they didn't end their affair until the sixties.

Hope's Palm Springs home was not just used for a love nest; he often worked on his scripts there, or held business meetings. Occasionally even his family would be welcome. Once-a-year during the Easter Spring break, Hope would allow daughter Linda, who seemed to be his favorite among his kids, to invite a few of her classmates from Immaculate Heart, a Catholic school in Hollywood, to spend their Easter vacations with her.

"A lot of the kids of famous people went to Immaculate Heart," remembers Ann Rapp, one of Linda's classmates. "Earl Warren's daughter, Gary Cooper's daughter, and John Wayne's daughter. On Friday nights Linda would take us to her house in Toluca Lake, and we'd also go down to Palm Springs for the Easter break and stay at the Hopes' house.

"We were all in our early teens, and quite innocent, but I can remember that Hope was a very lecherous man . . . beyond what you'd expect. I knew Maria Cooper [Gary's daughter] quite well. I grew up with her, and I knew from Maria that her father was a great rogue, too. He was a gentleman about it. But not Hope. Hope was actually repulsive around young girls. He had a dirty mouth, and he was kind of perverted. By perverted, I mean, like, well, he was an exhibitionist. At the Palm Springs house sometimes he'd come out without any clothes on, or if he was dressed, his fly would be open. And then he would pretend it was a mistake, like he didn't know we were in the room. He was actually pretty open about it. It finally got to the point where my father would tell me, 'No, darling, you're not going down to the Hope place at Easter again.' And being a typical dumb teenager, I would ask, 'Why? I want to.' And he'd reply, very sternly, 'Because Bob Hope is a very bad man.'"

Kay Dibels, who is now married to singer Frankie Avalon, also used to live in the Hopes' neighborhood when she was growing up. "Linda and I were great friends. We went to Immaculate Heart together. And very often during the school year Dolores would pick us up at school on Friday afternoon and drive us to their house in Palm Springs, to spend the weekend there. If Bob was there, you'd rarely see him, because he hardly ever came out of his room.

"I got to know him better on Sunday nights, in Toluca Lake, when Linda would invite me over to have dinner with them. Sunday was the maid's night off, and Dolores would do the cooking. The dinner would always be roast chicken. The menu never varied. It was always roast chicken. And Hope never changed either. He spent the whole dinner trying out his monologue jokes on us."

Being a neighbor of the Hopes in Toluca Lake, one was privy to all the gossip. "And there was plenty," adds Dana Thompson, an attractive blond housewife and former neighbor of the Hopes during the fifties. "In a small village like Toluca Lake, it was difficult to keep secrets very long, especially when one was as open as Bob Hope about his womanizing. Hope may well be the horniest guy I ever met. When I was working on a charity in Toluca Lake with Dolores, Bob used to phone me up all the time on the QT and try to get me to go out with him, even though I was married. Of course, I never did."

His real life and personality were so contrary to Hope's public image, that this is what might have attracted him to the story idea Mel Shavelson and Jack Rose pitched to him in 1954—a film based on the life of Eddie Foy. Foy was a top star in the heyday of vaudeville, but like so many of his brethren he was a son-of-a-bitch offstage.

Foy had been married to a beautiful Italian dancer, but he had been a rotten husband; he cheated on her constantly and paid little attention to their seven children. When his wife died suddenly, at a very young age, Foy was stuck with the task of raising seven kids, who ranged in age from three to thirteen. Not knowing what else to do with them, Foy turned them into a vaudeville act called *Eddie Foy and the Seven Little Foys*. They were a smash hit.

Hope sparked to the idea of playing Eddie Foy—not only because he identified with the character and was familiar with the vaudeville background, but because it would give him a chance to prove he could be a serious actor—at least one as good as Bing Crosby. The Foy story wasn't just a song-and-dance idea; it contained a number of dramatic, tear-jerking scenes. The most poignant was the sequence when the authorities stripped Foy of his kids because he'd exploited them in violation of the child labor laws and he had to plead for their custody in front of a judge. This culminated with Hope as Foy making a long dramatic speech in the courtroom, which was quite a change of pace for a fellow accustomed to delivering one-liners.

The only hitch in the negotiations: Mel Shavelson insisted on directing it. He had never directed a film before. When Shavelson broached this proviso to The Boss, Hope, surprisingly, agreed without argument.

"You don't mind?" exclaimed Shavelson.

"No big deal," replied Hope. "My last pictures were so bad I can't sink any lower."

Actually they weren't so bad as all that, and they did "okay business at the box office," according to *Variety*.

Hope had always jested about his acting ability, but deep inside he knew he had it in him to play a serious role, if given the opportunity. And true to his inner confidence, he pulled off the courtroom scene in *The Seven Little Foys* magnificently.

As he later recalled, "The night before I had to do the scene, Barney Dean died of cancer. Maybe that's how I got through it."

Hope had visited Dean at his deathbed in the hospital. In a

moment of consciousness, just before he closed his eyes forever, Dean looked up from his pillow at Hope and cracked, "Any messages for Jolie [Jolson]?"

Hope's never forgotten that moment. It's easy to see why he and Dean had been such close friends.

30

When *Have Tux, Will Travel* was published in the fall of 1954, it became an immediate bestseller, despite its superficiality.

One could learn very little about Hope's true character from its pages. Pete Martin did manage to set down in print most of the important milestone's in the comedian's life; his birth in England in 1903 as the sixth son of a hard-working, heavy-drinking stonemason and his mother Avis, whom he loved dearly; his upbringing as a poor but honest Horatio Alger figure in Cleveland, Ohio; his failed attempts at being a prizefighter; his early vaudeville days; his first big success on the New York stage in *Roberta*; his romancing and winning of Dolores, "the only woman in his life he ever loved"; his singing with Shirley Ross of "Thanks for the Memory" in *The Big Broadcast*, which made him a movie star; his success in movies and radio; his wartime travels with Frances Langford to entertain the troops, and his success in television.

Anyone who didn't know all that before, just wasn't paying attention to the press releases that poured out of Hope's publicity factory.

One of things that helped *Tux* become a bestseller was Hope's constant plugging of it on his radio and television shows. Plugging books over the air was a novelty in the early fifties, and when a book was mentioned on TV, its sales in the bookshops would sometimes rise dramatically. Jack Goodman, Simon & Schuster's editor-in-chief at the time, told me that Hope's constant plugging was responsible for the book selling five thousand hard-cover copies a day. That's more than some books sell in their lifetime.

My biography of my father, *Life With Groucho*, was published by Simon & Schuster in the same month as Hope's book. This prompted Jack Goodman to persuade both Hope and Groucho to agree to doing cross-plugs: Groucho would plug *Have Tux* on *You Bet Your Life*, in return for Hope giving *Life With Groucho* equal time on his TV show.

Being more or less a man of his word, Groucho did a very sincere sales pitch for *Have Tux* on his program, held the book up to the camera to show its cover, and told his viewers they'd be missing a great reading experience if they didn't run to their nearest bookstore and buy Hope's book.

Not knowing anything about Hope at the time, I figured he'd do as much for my book when I sat down in front of the set. I anticipated his turning *Life With Groucho* into an instant bestseller.

My expectations were too high. Hope brushed my book off with a gag that couldn't have sold three copies. His pitch went by so fast that if you blinked or the dog barked you would have missed it. It's been forty years since then, but the following is approximately how Hope plugged my book:

Hedda Hopper entered with a copy of *Life With Groucho* under her arm. After a few jokes about the flamboyant fruit-covered hat she was wearing, Hope asked, "What's that under your arm, Hedda?"

HEDDA: Oh, that's a new book—*Life With Groucho*.
HOPE: Well, you ought to read my book, *Have Tux, Will Travel*. You'll learn all about your favorite comedian.

A small mention is better than no mention, of course, but it's interesting how Hope was able to turn the pitch for my book into a plug for his book.

Bob Hope caught in his underwear in his dressing room in Boston for the Hollywood Victory Caravan. With him is Artie Jacobson, a stage manager, brought along from Hollywood to handle some of the production numbers. PHOTO BY GENE LESTER

Johnine Avery, one of Hope's numerous girlfriends, showing off the look that (with the comedian's assistance) won her the title Miss World of 1968.

Barbara Payton, another of Hope's mistresses. PHOTO COURTESY OF THE ACADEMY OF MOTION PICTURE ARTS AND SCIENCES

with
JEANNE CARME
AS *Felicity Comfort*

Jeanne Carmen showing off the golf form that caught Bob Hope's eye. This shot is from the cover of a humorous golf instruction record album called "The Reluctant Golf Pupil."

Hope and Marilyn Maxwell at the height of their affair. PHOTO BY GENE LESTER

Hope seated with Dolores (left) and Maria Alberghetti. PHOTO COURTESY OF THE ACADEMY OF MOTION PICTURE ARTS AND SCIENCES

Left to right: Agent Louis Shurr, company manager Emilio Prister, Bob Hope, and his attorney Martin Gang. PHOTO COURTESY OF THE ACADEMY OF MOTION PICTURE ARTS AND SCIENCES

Hope, with his long-time secretary, Miss Hughes. On the wall in the background are some of Hope's awards. PHOTO COURTESY OF THE ACADEMY OF MOTION PICTURE ARTS AND SCIENCES

Hope in Korea.

Hope in the South Pacific with Frances Langford, Tony Romano, and Jerry Colonna.
PHOTO COURTESY OF THE ACADEMY OF MOTION PICTURE ARTS AND SCIENCES

Bob Hope entertaining
the troops in England.
PHOTO COURTESY OF THE
ACADEMY OF MOTION PIC-
TURE ARTS AND SCIENCES

I want to thank
Morgan Brittany,
John Denver,
Howard Keel,
Miss Tahiti,
Susan Akin
(Miss America, 1986),
and that great clown,
Jonathan Winters .....
for a wonderful trip to
Tahiti, for their great
performances and a fine rating.

Bob Hope

"*'Bob Hope's Tropical Comedy Special From Tahiti' was a joy.*"
—Sam Schwartz, Chicago News

Spurious ad taken out by Bob Hope in *Variety* to refute a bad review given to his "Tahiti" special by Jane Galbraith in the same publication. The glowing quote was pure fiction, since at the time, March 6, 1987, there was no "Chicago News"; neither was there a "Sam Schwartz" reviewing TV for it.

This is but a hint of Hope's true character. Tony Romano, who was his guitarist on his camp show travels during World War II, told me when we lunched recently, "Hope's really a terrible guy. I once heard him say, 'The only way to get ahead in this world is to step on anybody who stands in your way.'"

If that's how Bob Hope conducted his business, it's no wonder he was able to bring Eddie Foy to life on the screen.

Although Hope's dramatic acting was surprisingly good, one of the highlights of *The Seven Little Foys* was a hoofing number featuring him with James Cagney. Cagney played a cameo role as George M. Cohan, briefly reprising his Oscar-winning portrayal of Cohan in *Yankee Doodle Dandy*. It was a brilliant piece of showmanship to have Cagney recreate his role in the short sequence.

Cagney made only one request as a condition to playing Cohan, and it was an unusual one for an actor: he asked *not to be paid* for the bit.

"Why not?" asked Mel Shavelson.

"Because when I was breaking in as an actor," replied Cagney, "I knew I could always get a square meal and a place to flop at the Foy's. This is my way of paying them back."

When *The Seven Little Foys* opened in New York at the end of June 1955, reviews were mixed, with some carping about Hope's lack of warmth.

Opinioned the *Times*'s Bosley Crowther:

The notion that the late Eddie Foy was a better comedian than he was a family man, even though he was the father of seven children and built a famous vaudeville act around them, is conveyed by Bob Hope in a manner that leaves no doubt of the comic's skill, but considerable question as to his intelligence.

The impression the viewer is likely to get of the popular card from this report, which Mel Shavelson and Jack Rose have written, directed and produced, is that he was just a bit of a nitwit, operating in a fog of conceit, shy of the normal compassions and wholly committed to the gag. He bore, in short, a

321

strong resemblance to the stock screen character of Mr. Hope . . .

The New York *Daily News* however, gave the picture the maximum four stars, and this glowing sendoff:

Hope doesn't have to take any more insults from Bing Crosby about his acting. Hope can now hold up his head with Holly-wood's dramatic thespians as for the first time in his career, Hope isn't playing Hope on the screen. He's acting and doing a commendable job.

Business in the nation's movie houses reflected the positive things about the film rather than the negative ones, with the result that everyone connected with *The Seven Little Foys* made money. However, there was still no acting Oscar in Hope's future. Despite the film's serious slant, *The Seven Little Foys*, struck out in every category when Oscar-nominating time rolled around.

****

Hope was less than ecstatic with his television show. While his ratings at the start of the fall season in 1954 were acceptable, he was no longer leading his competition the way he did when he was kingpin of radio.

The competition was pretty strong. There was the *Jackie Gleason Show*, featuring "The Honeymooners," with Gleason, Carney and Audrey Meadows; Milton Berle's *Texaco Star Theater*, and Groucho's *You Bet Your Life* at its most popular.

Unanimous good reviews were not absolutely essential to the success of a variety show like Hope's, but the critics bugged him with their constant references to the "sameness" of his humor.

One dig, by television critic John Crosby, in *Life* magazine, called "The Seven Deadly Sins of the Air," exacerbated his paranoia to such a degree that he actually brought a lawsuit against Time, Inc., seeking $2 million in damages. The comment that broke the comedian's back was: "Writers got two-thousand-dollars-a-week in Hollywood for copying down Fred Allen's jokes and putting them on Bob Hope's program."

Hope contended in his suit that "the article accused him of plagiarism, exposed him to hatred and ridicule by the public, which tended to damage his standing in the entertainment business."

He dropped the suit before it reached court, having been advised by his lawyer, Martin Gang, that it wasn't worth the expense to force a retraction. And besides, why bring it to the attention of the public in the first place?

Because of all the criticism, justified or not, Hope made up his mind to do something spectacular and different on his next TV show, scheduled for November 1954. He had nothing in mind, however, until he received an invitation from the King and Queen of England to emcee a royal Command Performance in London in November.

Accepting it would be in conflict with his scheduled regular television broadcast in November, over NBC, in the States. NBC said he couldn't leave with an unfilled primetime hour and besides, if he went to London he would be in violation of his contract. Hope didn't care. He told Jimmy Saphier to inform NBC that he was canceling his November broadcast in order to go to London.

He softened the mutinous act by promising that he would do something different for the network while he was in London—he would film his show abroad, with an entire new cast which he would assemble in London.

It would be shown back home in December at his regular broadcast time. At first NBC balked at the extra expense, but when they realized how determined Hope was, and that nothing would change his mind, Saphier was able to convince them that by letting Hope do his show his way, they would be making history.

Hope's Command Performance for the King and Queen was a huge success. Following that, Hope spent the next days gathering an international cast of stars and feature acts: Maurice Chevalier, Bea Lillie, a London choir, a French ballerina named

Laine Dayde, two gorgeous blonde showgirls, Moira Lister and
Shirley Eaton, and a local British newsman, McDonald Hobley,
to do the commercials for the General Foods products, Jell-O,
Swansdown and Minute Rice, after actor Reginald Gardiner
backed out as announcer.

The production was filmed by a British technical crew in
BBC's largest London studio.

Hope's writers didn't get to see much of the city. According to
one, Marty Ragaway, they were forced to spend most of the
time in a London hotel chained to their typewriters.

"On our third day there," recalled Ragaway, "Hope started to
feel guilty about the lousy time we were having, and he said,
'Gee, I've been very inconsiderate of you guys. You probably
haven't seen anything of London. Well, I'm going to do
something about that.' Then he went downstairs to the news-
stand and bought forty picture postcards of London scenes, and
sent them up to us."

❉❉❉❉

After wrapping things up in London, Hope returned to
Toluca Lake in time to watch his *International Revue* on
television on December 15. He wasn't the only one glued to the
tube. Because of NBC's publicity buildup telling Hope fans they
would be seeing history in the making, the *International Revue*
audience topped the Neilsen ratings that week.

The *Washington Star* wrote, "If this is history, Arnold
Toynbee has been ploughing a long furrow in the wrong field."
But *Variety* gave it a much warmer welcome.

Bob Hope's filmed show emanating from England proved that
it's not true what they say about British audiences. They do so
laugh, and in the right places. At least when Hope's on.

Hope, during his recent trip on the continent, filmed a show
with a truly international flavor, and one distinguished by the
telebow of Maurice Chevalier, and the presence of Bea Lillie.

Hope put on an excellent show for General Foods, his
sponsor. His opening remarks kidding Britain, American rela-

tions with that country and some topical references put a bright opening to the layout, and some good sketches helped put the show across on most counts.

Chevalier didn't really hit his peak until he donned the straw skimmer and sang "Louise." The sketch he performed with Hope had an ancient plot, and the bit he essayed on languages as they sound to those that do not understand their lingo was a zero effort.

31

By January of 1955, Hope's next film, *That Certain Feeling*, was ready to go before the Paramount cameras. This was an adaptation by the producer-director-writers Norman Panama and Mel Frank of the Broadway comedy, *King of Hearts*, which had been written by Jean Kerr and Eleanor Brooke.

In this story, Hope plays a neurotic newspaper cartoonist who is unable to work at home and simultaneously please his wife. Eva Marie Saint played the wife but not very effectively, because comedy is not her forte.

✿✿✿✿

Because Eva also came from Ohio—Bowling Green, to be exact—Paramount thought it would be a money-making idea to open the picture in Cleveland in June, and have the two stars make an appearance before each running of the film.

"So George Hope asked me if I would go back to Cleveland with him and do some advance publicity for the film," recalls Robert Slatzer, "since I knew the territory, having worked on a paper in Columbus. I agreed, and brought my wife and George brought his and we went to Cleveland in advance of Hope and Eva. That's when I saw firsthand why Bob was always so anxious to leave his wife and go on the road. After we had checked into the Carter Hotel, where Bob and Eva would also be staying,

George took me aside and whispered, 'Don't say anything about the girls in front of our wives.' I didn't know what he meant until I got to the rehearsal the first day and saw three pretty girls, who weren't in the act, hanging around backstage. They were gorgeous—like Vegas showgirls. Just to be friendly, I started to say hello, when George nudged me and said, 'Keep away. They belong to The Boss.'

"That night I discovered that the three of them also had rooms at the Carter Hotel, right near Bob's suite. One was on the same floor, one was on the floor below, and one was on the one above his. George told me they were Paramount extras, and that Bob had paid their way to Cleveland so he could have them for playmates while he was there."

❖❖❖❖

After *That Certain Feeling* opened, most of the critics agreed that Hope was miscast as the cartoonist, and that Eva Marie Saint didn't handle comedy very well.

Rumors began to circulate around Hollywood that Bob Hope was thinking of retiring. This may have had something to do with *That Certain Feeling*, but more likely were caused by a frightening experience he had while playing golf down on the desert with his first agent, Charlie Yates.

In the middle of the round, Yates fell over dead in the golf cart right beside Hope. "He was there for twenty minutes before they came for him," Hope later recalled. "He was a good friend. It happened so fast."

It happened so fast that the shock didn't really set in for three days. When it did, Hope suddenly began to feel all kinds of imaginary pains, and thought he was dying. "At that time NBC came to me about a new contract and I said, 'Nothing doing. I'm going to retire.'"

After telling them that, Hope became terribly depressed, and went to get a complete physical from his doctor, Tom Hearn. Hearn checked him over from head to toe and gave him a clean bill of health.

Hope was his old self again, with the result that in the following February, he signed a new deal with NBC.

A banner headline in *Variety* on February 6, 1957 announced:

HOPE, NBC IN $25 MILLION DEAL

Bob Hope and NBC yesterday concluded an unprecedented $25,000,000 contract for the comedian to star in 40 TV shows and five theatrical films over five years. Unprecedented pact is retroactive to 1955 and runs to 1960. What it amounts to is that the television network, in order to hold Hope, has become a partner in his motion picture enterprises . . .

So much for retirement.

✿ ✿ ✿ ✿

For a fellow who had just flirted with the idea of retiring, Hope set an ambitious schedule for himself in the coming months. Two of his eight television programs would be filmed in Europe. He had already committed to make two feature films there in the next eighteen months.

The first one starred Katharine Hepburn as his leading lady. It was a weary second cousin to *Ninotchka*. In its preparatory stages it was titled *Not for Money*, but ended up with the name *The Iron Petticoat*. It was Hope's first away from Paramount. The script had been written by Ben Hecht.

The Iron Petticoat was supposed to star Cary Grant, but he bowed out rather suddenly after he read the script. Hope was given the role instead. At first he had been flattered to be playing opposite Hepburn, but Hope couldn't get along with Ben Hecht during the script preparation stages. Hope expected a much more joke-filled script than Hecht delivered. Hecht was more of a serious writer and craftsman than a gagman.

At any rate, Hecht walked out on the project when it was about three-quarters through, insisting that his name be removed from the credits and that he be in no way associated with the project. Consequently Hope turned loose his army of writers on the script, for an overhaul.

The picture turned out to be just what you'd expect when too many cooks are involved—a mishmash that became a box-office dud. Even the two star names of Hope and Hepburn couldn't save it.

However, because the story involved a U.S. Air Force officer during the Cold War falling in love with a beautiful dedicated Communist, a seed was planted in Hope's fertile mind that it would be a good idea to film one of his television shows in the Soviet Union. Not only would it be a "first" for an American TV star, but the publicity he'd reap would be beyond what mere money could buy.

Getting approval for this project from the Soviet authorities seemed difficult. All attempts by Betty Box, the British producer of *The Iron Petticoat*, to get permission to shoot the Hope-Hepburn starrer behind the Iron Curtain were quickly nixed by the Communist bureaucrats.

But Hope didn't let a previous failure discourage him when he made up his mind to do a TV show from Russia. After all, he was Bob Hope. He wasn't just a comedian; he played golf with presidents. If he could do that, why not blinies and caviar with Khrushchev in the Kremlin?

Even if he could swing it, however, Hope's dream of filming a TV special in Moscow had to be put on the back burner until he finished his next two films, *Beau James,* the life of the colorful but corrupt New York mayor of the Roaring Twenties, Jimmy Walker, and *Paris Holiday*, his second film not produced by Paramount. This was a joint venture between Hope's company and United Artists. It was based on Hope's plot about an American movie star in Paris to buy a movie script for himself and have a vacation simultaneously.

It wasn't much of an idea, and it wasn't much of a picture. Hope's costar was the French comedian Fernandel, but neither he, nor Hope nor Anita Ekberg's brassiere-size could keep *Paris Holiday* (which went millions over budget) from being a fiasco financially and artistically.

Hope had an inspiration. He'd hold the world premiere of *Paris Holiday* in Moscow. And while there he'd film the TV special he wanted to do in Russia.

Hope himself went directly to the Russian Consulate in London, and applied for sixteen visas for himself, his technical crew and his writers. Then he phoned his New York press agent, Ursula Halloran, and told her to go to Washington and see if she could get some action on the visas from that end.

Fresh out of Penn State, where she had majored in public relations, Ursula was Hope's latest love. She was a petite brunette, as smart and as attractive as she was ambitious. Hope—who met her while doing a personal appearance in Pennsylvania, liked her looks, and her resumé—had hired her to be his New York publicity rep.

While he was waiting for Ursula to get some action, Hope contacted NBC's Moscow correspondent, Irving R. Levine, and asked his help. Then he phoned Jock Whitney, the United States Ambassador to England, to ask for help in pressuring the Soviet bureaucracy. The call paid off. Whitney told Hope that he would be seeing Jacob Malik, USSR Ambassador to Great Britain, at a cocktail party that very evening. Whitney promised to do his best, but when Hope didn't hear from him the next day, he returned to Los Angeles, somewhat discouraged, but clinging to the old adage that "no news is good news," he settled down in Toluca Lake for a few days to see what developed.

What developed was a message from Whitney informing him that Malik had said neither "nyet" nor "da." He merely had asked, "What does your Mr. Hope want to do—entertain our troops in Red Square?"

A few more weeks passed, with no further news. Ursula Halloran wasn't getting anywhere in Washington, despite her good looks, winning ways and famous boss.

Hope flew to London for the opening of *Paris Holiday*. While there, he dropped into the Russian Consulate to see what was cooking, and again got no satisfaction. Then he flew back to California.

Six days later he received a call from NBC's Washington

office, with the news he wanted to hear: There were visas waiting for him at the Soviet Embassy. Hope had applied for sixteen, but would have to settle for six. And these good for only seven days in the Soviet Union.

In addition to his own, there would be visas for Arthur Jacobs, who was the United Artists representative, who would try to arrange the Moscow premiere of *Paris Holiday* after they arrived there; the writers he intended to bring along, Mort Lachman and Bill Larkin; Ken Talbot, one of Britain's best cameramen; and of course Ursula Halloran, who'd be handling publicity, as well as other things.

With those cold winter nights in Russia, and inadequate heating in Moscow's hotel rooms, he definitely needed Ursula along to warm up his bed. In fact, the way things were going between the two of them, Ursula could have written her own book, *Have Nightie, Will Travel.*

32

Once the Russian trip junket was approved, Hope faced a problem to which he hadn't given much thought. What kind of a show could he put on from Moscow that would entertain American audiences and at the same time pass the Russian censors?

"I didn't really have an idea," Hope later recalled in a later autobiography *Don't Shoot, It's Only Me*, "but I had the tickets, and the publicity and what Barney Dean called chutzpah, so I had no choice. I had to go through with it."

Before embarking on the flight to Moscow, Hope had been coached on what would be expected of him and his party by the Russian authorities. It was explained that the visas were limited to Moscow *only*. He was told not to impress Moscow citizens with tales of how great it was to live in America, with TV sets, automobiles, and electric dishwashers. And finally he was told that all film he shot in Russia would have to be developed in Russia.

That would make difficult to sneak in any anti-Communist jokes in order to make the show more acceptable in America.

A week after he was given the green light, Hope, Ursula and Jacobs, boarded an SAS plane for Copenhagen. There the three took an Aeroflot jet to Moscow. For reasons never explained,

Hope's writers and the cameraman had to fly to Moscow by way of Prague in a different plane.

As Hope described it, "The interior of the Aeroflot jet was done in Russian-style, with material that looked as if it had been made from Mrs. Khrushchev's old shower curtains. But the lunch was great. They had taken it aboard in Denmark: delicious Danish beef and fresh vegetables. It was the last real beef we saw until we left Moscow."

But even if Moscow food was lousy, and its hotel rooms bleak and depressing, and the footage they filmed a bomb, Hope derived publicity enough out of the adventure to make the discomfort worthwhile.

Hope, Ursula and Jacobs were met at the Moscow airport by NBC correspondent Irving R. Levine, two reporters from *Look* magazine, who had been assigned to cover Hope's seven-day stay, and several free-lance photographers. He was also greeted by Larissa Soborova, who was assigned by the government to act as Hope's interpreter and guide.

Larissa was a personable, well-educated, well-built girl in her early twenties from the Soviet Republic of Georgia. She always wore boots, a sheared beaver coat, and a blue angora babushka. She was a quiet girl, who spoke Russian-accented English, and was proud of her country, but she was not the hard-core propagandist portrayed in *The Iron Petticoat*.

With Larissa as their guide, the Hope party checked into the Hotel Ukraine, which had a lobby that looked about five stories high, and furniture you couldn't tell much about since everything was covered with white sheets. On each floor a tough looking Russian matron sat at a desk near the elevator. This caused Hope to quip: "Evidently Russian hotel managers were aware that vaudevillians have a propensity for stealing towels and other things not nailed down."

The restaurant in the hotel was reserved for foreigners and VIP Russians only. The food was edible—barely. Hope never found out if his room was bugged, but if it was, the authorities listening in apparently never reported what went on to Dolores.

After a night's sleep and a bad breakfast laced with vodka,

Hope and his group scouted Moscow all the next day for colorful places to photograph.

According to Hope, his writers had come up with an inspirational idea for the show: all the talent would be Russian, except for the host, and the city itself would be the star.

After getting final approval from the authorities, who insisted on knowing beforehand everything he would be photographing, Hope was shot standing in front of the Kremlin wall, walking through Red Square, at the entrance to Lenin's tomb, in the stands at the Moscow circus, watching a fashion show at the GUM department store, and fronting an all-girl band at a Moscow nightclub.

The government also gave Hope film footage of Soviet violinist David Oistrakh, playing Tchaikovsky, ballerina Galina Ulanova dancing in *Swan Lake*, the Russian clown Popov, a comedian named Arkady Raikin, and the Ukrainian State Dancers doing their dancing.

As a warm-up to filming the TV program, Hope did an hour-long one-man show for the English-speaking community at Spasso House, the official residence of the United States Ambassador. This show was also filmed for possible inclusion of the best parts in the TV special. Hope was careful not to say things in Spasso House that the Russians might find objectionable.

"They have a national lottery here in Russia. It's called living," was one joke Hope cut.

As an example of just how paranoid the Russians were about what could and couldn't be said about their country, when Hope returned to his hotel room prior to doing his show, he found that his briefcases had been forced open and all of his gags spread out on the bed. Apparently the reason they made no effort to cover up their dirty work by putting things back in the same order in which they found them was to let Hope know they meant business.

To placate the censors, Hope confined most of his monologue jokes to kidding himself and the U.S. rather than taking pokes at the Russian lifestyle.

It's very exciting to be here in Moscow with all you
Democrats. . . . You must be Democrats or you wouldn't be
here. . . . I hope you people here at the embassy will be
cooperative tonight and laugh. On my passport I wrote "comedian." I'd hate to have the Russians think that I lied. But it's a
thrill to be in Russia. I know I'm in Russia. This morning my
stomach got up two hours before I did and had a bowl of
borscht. . . . It's amazing the way people can get the wrong
impression . . . one Russian official showed me a picture of
starving people in America . . . people without shoes and
nothing to eat, absolutely desperate. And I couldn't argue with
him . . . it was a picture of the bus station at Las Vegas . . .

Hope made references to Sputnik but the Russians insisted
on blue-penciling them. For example, "The Russians are over-
joyed with their Sputnik. . . . It's kind of weird being in a
country where every ninety minutes is a national
holiday . . . anybody without a stiff neck is a traitor . . ."

For some reason any mention of Sputnik was a no-no, in spite
of the fact that Hope told the censors that it was perfectly all
right in the U.S. for him to kid the American space program.
Hoping to change their minds, he gave them a sample joke from
his last TV show in America.

I guess you heard the big news from Cape Canaveral. Our
government has launched another submarine . . . actually the
test firing of missiles is going very well . . . they hit the target
every time . . . as a matter of fact, there's hardly anything left
of Bermuda.

The censors smiled but refused to back down on the Sputnik
issue, then they handed Hope a list of other jokes they found
offensive, and which would have to be excised before the film
could be released for its trip back to America.

* * * *

Hope's TV footage eventually made it to Hollywood, where it
was edited down to an hour and shown to American audiences
on the night of April 5, 1958, under the title of *Bob Hope in
Moscow.*

Variety loved it, and wrote, "Bob Hope translated his visit to Moscow into a fascinating and entertaining hour . . ."

Although a bit un-Hopian, Hope's sign-off speech pulled the whole thing together and gave the show a touch of class that had been absent from all his TV specials prior to that time:

> For five days and nights I have stared and walked and wondered. It's a strange city. I missed the street signs, the hubbub of traffic, the colorful clothing, the billboards, and the neon gleaming in the night. Yet there is much that is the same: people trying to make a living, people trying to keep their families together. And kids, wonderful kids, with great faces.
>
> It would be wonderful if someday their kids and our kids could grow up into a world that spoke the same language and respected the same things. Right now the world is busy building a bomb for every letter in the alphabet. That cannot be the answer. But there must be one. We must find some plan for peaceful coexistence, so that human beings don't become obsolete.

It was a beautiful touch to the finale, and although *Bob Hope in Moscow* didn't receive as high a Nielsen rating as was expected, it was appreciated where it counted: Hope was awarded both the Peabody and the Sylvania awards for 1958, two of TV's prestigious broadcasting honors. He put them in his already jam-packed trophy room.

33

Hope was fifty-five years old when the strain of his work, his nonstop travels and his high-tensity lovemaking with his virtual harem began to affect his health.

Hope was a little bit like the Ado Annie character in the musical *Oklahoma!* who "can't say no." This was true especially when the government begged him to entertain the troops. The United States wasn't engaged in war in the late fifties, but the Cold War was as hot as it had ever been, in spite of Hope's efforts to cement relations between the U.S. and the USSR by doing a goodwill show from Moscow in 1958.

To understand how Hope's televised Christmas shows for the troops all began, it is necessary to back up four years to 1954. At the time the U.S. had a Strategic Air Command base in Thule, Greenland, an early-warning station for a potential missile strike from the Russians. The most serious trouble at that remote outpost was from the low morale among the troops.

Hope's old friend, Gen. Rosie O'Donnell, was the C.O. at Thule. He asked Hope to bring a show to his men at Christmas, in 1954. Ever grateful for an excuse to get away from home, Hope agreed, provided the Air Force would give him transportation and technical assistance so he could film the show for later use as one of his television specials.

This would be the first of his televised Christmas shows, and although he didn't know it at the time, this practice of doing his broadcasts at government expense would continue for the next fifteen years.

As a treat for the boys at Thule, Hope had tried to enlist Marilyn Monroe for his cast, but she had other commitments. Late in the fall he was still seeking someone who could adequately fill her sweater when he was called upon to emcee a Big Ten Football Conference banquet. One of the guests was a Swedish import who had just won the title of Miss UCLA. "She was wearing a sweater with team letters, and the U and the L were outstanding," recalls Hope.

Actually she had more than enough to fill Marilyn Monroe's sweater, so he invited her to join his troupe that was going to Thule over Christmas.

Her name was Anita Ekberg, and she was a staple in Hope's USO shows, as well as some of his movies, for several years to come. Also along on this first trip were Bill Holden, Margaret Whiting, Jerry Colonna, Peter Leeds, Charlie Cooley, and columnist Hedda Hopper, plus Les Brown and his band.

At Thule that Christmas there were six thousand troops who laughed at Hope's one-liners, but were more appreciative of the lesson in female anatomy they got from Miss Ekberg. As she removed her coat, in the freezing cold, and stood there in a gown cut so low her nipples were practically exposed, the sex-starved men in the audience rose to their feet and cheered, stomped and whistled.

Hope did another show from Goose Bay, Labrador, on New Year's Eve, which he also photographed for later home audience consumption.

Nine days later, Hope's Christmas travels, edited down to an hour, were shown on NBC's *Colgate Comedy Hour*. As a reward for sacrificing a Christmas at home with his family in order to be with Anita Ekberg, Hope's rating on that particular Colgate show was the highest in his TV career to date: he swept the opposition with a 60 percent share of the available sets in use.

Moreover, *Variety* raved about him in its January 10, 1955 review:

The laughs rolled as Hope and Company panicked 'em with a succession of gags and tidbits on (1) Girls (2) Army and Air Force Brass (3) Girls (4) Girls. No performer of this age can do what this comic accomplishes before a uniformed crowd, having long since established himself as the one man for whom the Armed Forces have the highest regard.

Entertaining American troops during the holiday season in faraway lands was to become an annual obligation for Hope to have to cram into his overloaded work schedule. Those days when he could rest his body were dwindling down to a precious few.

Hope still got a charge out of hearing the roar of the GIs and their whoops and hollers as he stood at the mike on an open air stage with the likes of Anita Ekberg, Marie (The Body) McDonald, Jayne Mansfield, or Raquel Welch, and made not too subtle jokes about their bodies. He was particularly intrigued by their Grand Canyon-sized cleavages.

The strain caught up with him during his Christmas '58 trip. For some reason—either bad scheduling or inclement flying conditions—Hope was able to get only seven hours sleep in the first seventy-six-hours of his itinerary.

Arriving in Spain, a weary Hope was greeted by the host commanding officer, Col. Ernest Nance. As Hope stepped forward to shake his hand, he felt something snap inside his head. He suddenly was overcome with dizziness and the colonel's face became a blur. Believing he was going blind, he sagged onto a nearby bench. When he felt no improvement after a few minutes rest, he asked to be taken to the base hospital. There, two Air Force doctors examined him and medicated him to make him sleep. That night's show had to be canceled.

By next morning the dizziness and blurred vision were gone and Hope was his old bouncy self again. Attributing his dizziness to just plain lack of sleep, he flew with his cast to Madrid and put on a show that night, with Gina Lollobrigida heading his list of guest stars. After Madrid he played Naples, and on Christmas day, he appeared at the Rhine-Main Air Base outside of Frankfurt, West Germany. Following that performance he attended a cocktail reception, given by the base commander. There he became dizzy again, and collapsed to the floor.

Since columnist Hedda Hopper was present, the story of his collapse wound up on the front pages in the U.S. the next day. Dolores phoned frantically, imploring her husband to quit the show and come back home. But Hope was again feeling better so he assured Dolores he was just suffering from exhaustion. He promised her that when he came home he'd undergo a complete physical.

He felt okay during his next show, at Hanau, West Germany, but at Keflavik, Iceland, he again experienced dizziness.

By the time Hope returned home, Dolores had already made an appointment for him to be examined by Dr. Tom Hearn. But because the day of his arrival was New Year's, the exam had to wait until January 2.

In the meantime, as was Hope's custom, when he was away for the holidays, he held his Christmas party on New Year's night, sometimes with as many as two hundred guests. Occasionally the winning football team, from that afternoon's Rose Bowl game, would also be there to enjoy his and Dolores's hospitality.

They always had a huge Christmas tree in their playroom, with mountains of wrapped presents under it.

"One year," Robert Slatzer remembers, "George Hope got so drunk he knocked over the Christmas tree, smashing all the ornaments and nearly catching the place on fire. Hope was so embarrassed that he shipped George back to Cleveland the following day, and insisted that his brother Fred, with whom he was partners in the Ohio Provision Company, give George a job at their Columbus meat-packing plant."

***

Hope felt encouraged by the results of his physical. The only worrisome news was his blood pressure, which Hearn attributed to overwork. He prescribed that Hope take it easy for a few weeks.

To anyone else but Bob Hope "taking it easy" would mean just that. But to Hope, it meant spending the next few weeks at General Laboratories, editing the film he had shot on his USO Christmas tour and preparing it for television consumption.

No more eye problems developed until he tried to play golf at Lakeside one afternoon. He'd only played a couple of holes when he again became dizzy and had blurred vision. He called off the rest of the round, but when the eye seemed better by the next day, he decided it was okay to keep a date to play golf with golf pro Jimmy Demaret at Palm Springs on January 8.

He was all right during the drive to Palm Springs, but on the golf course, he played only two holes when he found himself stumbling and unable to focus his eyes on the teed-up ball. Apologizing to Demaret, Hope drove his golf cart back to the clubhouse, where he hoped some relaxation at the nineteenth hole would speed his recovery, but when the framed golfing prints on the wall started doing a ballet, Hope said he realized he had something seriously wrong.

He returned to L.A. immediately, and made an appointment to have his eyes examined by Maurice Beigelman, a top eye specialist.

Beigelman found a blood clot in the vein of Hope's left cornea. He cautioned Hope about working more than was absolutely necessary. He warned Hope that stress could cause the clot to move and completely destroy the vision in his left eye.

Hope promised to be good, but as soon as the dizziness disappeared, and he could again focus on a golf ball with his left eye, he decided to ignore the problem. But the eye acted up again during a rehearsal on his March television show. Hope phoned Beigelman, who immediately called another of the country's top eye specialist, Dr. Algernon Reese, at New York's Columbia Presbyterian Medical Center.

Hearing the symptoms, Reese suggested that Hope fly to New York immediately to be examined by him. As a result,

Hope and Dolores were on the next plane out of Los Angeles bound for the Big Apple.

Somehow the media got the story—probably from Hope's girlfriend-press agent-traveling companion Ursula Halloran. The result was a rash of headlines.

> BOB HOPE SERIOUSLY ILL— *New York Post*
> BOB HOPE FLYING HERE TO SAVE EYE—*Daily News*
> BOB HOPE SUFFERS HEART AND EYE TROUBLES—*Daily Mirror*

The newspapers exaggerated the situation but they weren't far from the mark. After Reese and his colleague, Stuart Cosgriff, examined Hope and put him through several days of tests, they came into Hope's hospital room and informed him that he had a circulatory problem that was causing his cornea to clot. Their recommendation: *complete rest*.

The word "rest" being anathema to Hope, he asked if there wasn't something else that could be done—something like an eye operation.

They told him that an operation would be the last resort.

"We think we can take care of it with tranquilizers and cortisone," said Reese, "but you have to do the rest. You—must—take it easy! Unless you want to wind up with a white cane and a seeing-eye dog."

Hope was fearful of losing his sight so he canceled all personal appearances for the next three months. He canceled anything involving work, except his television commitments.

Learning to take it easy was probably the most difficult thing Hope had ever attempted in his life. Fish don't applaud.

34

The best film of Hope's career, *The Facts of Life*, is about attempted adultery.

Concocted by Norman Panama and Mel Frank, the screenwriters of several of the best "Road" pictures, the story concerns a California suburban couple, not married to each other, who fall in love and attempt to have an adulterous affair.

In actuality it was a lighthearted version of Noel Coward's *Brief Encounter*, and rather daring for 1960, the year it was released. While it was a comedy, and a very funny one at that, there are a number of situations in the story that anyone who's ever had an affair would be able to identify with: family obligations, a kid getting sick, a car unwilling to start, in fact any circumstance that keeps the affair from actually becoming consummated.

In the end, weary of these frustrations, the would-be illicit lovers, return to their mates and eternal boredom.

When this bittersweet story was submitted to Hope, he said it was a little too straight. But after the two writers assured him that it would play funnier than it read, Hope agreed to do the film.

Lucille Ball liked the script after the first reading, but she agreed to play opposite Hope only if Panama and Frank didn't turn it into *The Road to Infidelity*.

With Hope and Ball (in their fourth film together) playing the frustrated middle-age lovers, there was hardly a way that this story, in the capable hands of director Norman Panama, could fail to be hilarious.

As Hope himself wrote in *Don't Shoot, It's Only Me*, "Adultery is very difficult, if you're not British."

I don't think he was speaking from experience, but those difficulties made for some very funny moments in *The Facts of Life*. One involved Hope checking into a San Fernando Valley motel with Lucy, but before they could get to the main event, Lucy suddenly is hungry. Playing the gallant lover, Hope speeds to a drive-in on Ventura Boulevard, picks up a hamburger and fries, and a malt in a container, and races back to the motel.

The problem was, in those days, the string of motels on Ventura all looked alike from the outside. Hope realizes he can't tell one motel from another. By the time he finds the motel where Lucy was waiting for him in bed, three hours later, he is so frustrated and disgusted—and Lucy is asleep—that all thoughts of sex are abandoned for the night.

The Facts of Life was shot on the MGM lot in Culver City, in 1959, and released in 1960 by United Artists.

The critics adored it.

While Hope was waiting for *The Facts of Life* to open, he managed to slip in another film, this one for MGM. It was called *Bachelor in Paradise*, and was a domestic comedy involving sex in the suburbs. Hope's costar was Lana Turner, who, though sexy, was not a Lucille Ball. Nor was the Hal Kanter—Valentine Davies script up to the quality of Panama and Frank's. The result was a film that Hope wasn't particularly proud of and the critics could take or leave.

Shooting two films in quick succession, and doing an hour television special once a month wasn't exactly the rest Dr. Reese had prescribed. But just remaining close to L.A. and eliminating most of his unnecessary traveling prevented Hope from having any serious flare-ups with his eye for a couple of years.

The elimination of his travels didn't hamper his extracurricular love life. In addition to Ursula Halloran and Joan Billings, a new girl entered the picture, named Joy Monroe. She was a redhead.

Joy was born in Bellingham, Washington, and had done some modeling in Seattle, Los Angeles and Paris before meeting Hope for the first time in Monte Carlo, in the sixties.

Recalls Joy Monroe, who today is the widow of David McConnell, the heir to the Avon cosmetic fortune, "We met through a mutual friend, John Mills, who owned a big hotel on the hills of Monaco. He also owned Les Ambassador, the private gambling club in London.

"Bob was in Monte Carlo vacationing and playing some golf with Mills. We met and he asked me to come to Hollywood to do some PR work for him. I worked out of L.A. and New York. And I also did some bit parts in a couple of his pictures—*A Global Affair* and *I'll Take Sweden*. I wasn't much of an actress. I just did those parts for the fun of it."

This seems to be Bob's standard *modus operandi*. Once he met a girl he was attracted to, and vice versa, he put her on his payroll.

"I first became aware of Joy," remembers Jan King, "after we left Paramount and moved to MGM, where Bob was making a picture. Joy would come around with a little girl named Donna, who was about five, and very cute and pixie-like."

At the time Jan was never sure what relation Donna was to Joy.

"Donna was my sister's daughter," explains Joy. "When my sister got remarried when Donna was still a child, her husband was jealous of Donna. So Donna came to Los Angeles to live with me."

Hope would bring Joy and Donna down to the set to watch him shoot. "What puzzled me about all this," states Jan, "was that Bob didn't ordinarily like having kids or dogs around. He didn't care about children hardly at all, and yet he was crazy about Donna. She had a personality that wouldn't quit."

Part of Jan's duties was to "baby-sit Donna whenever Bob and Joy went off together."

Another of her chores was to take care of Hope's travel

arrangements, hotel bookings, plane reservations, and all that sort of thing. According to Jan, Hope did a lot of traveling with Joy. For example he took her and Donna to the Seattle World's Fair in 1962 when he was making an appearance there. I know he went there with Joy and Donna because I'm the one who booked the reservations for the three of them. I remember that trip specifically, because when they got back, Donna told me that she had gotten airsick on the plane to Seattle and had thrown up all over Hope's good suit."

To throw people off the track, Bob assigned "code" names to his various girlfriends, reveals Jan. "When he wanted to talk to Joy, he'd say, 'Get Miss Phipps on the phone for me, will you, darling?' Or 'Get me the Crooner.' That's what he called Betsy Duncan, a blue-eyed, redheaded singer who was another one of his mistresses. And 'Miss Kent' was the code name for Rosemarie Frankland."

Rosemarie Frankland, a British girl, with a peaches and cream complexion and big blue eyes, was crowned Miss World, in London, in 1961, when Hope was there, shooting *The Road to Hong Kong*.

"Bob had been one of the judges of the Miss World contest, and lusted for Rosemarie immediately upon seeing her. He lobbied with the judges for her to win the title," relates Jan, "and Dolores unknowingly advanced Bob's amorous plans by taking a liking to Rosemarie and suggesting that he bring her back to America to appear in one of his movies."

To give her some acting experience, Hope added her to the cast of his camp show that he took to Newfoundland, Labrador and Greenland that Christmas. Christmas '61 was the first time Hope did a camp show since he promised to take it easy and give his eye a chance to recover.

Judging by the looks of Rosemarie in a swim suit, his bum eye must have been back in focus by the time he became one of the judges of the Miss World contest.

To please Dolores, Hope eventually did bring Rosemarie Frankland back to Hollywood where he rewarded her with a bit part in his 1964 film, *I'll Take Sweden*, that I wrote for him with my partner, Bob Fisher, and Nat Perrin.

"But she wasn't much of an actress, so when her film career fizzled, Bob kept her in a Los Angeles apartment, which he visited regularly," states Jan King. "I also used to make reservations for them when the two of them traveled together."

For a man who was supposed to be taking it easy during 1961 and 1962, Hope couldn't have been busier. Not that it took much out of him to judge a Miss World contest, in London. But producing and acting in *The Road to Hong Kong*, seventh and last of the "Road" pictures, was fairly exhausting work.

The filming took four months at London's Shepperton Studios, and because Hope had known in advance how long he would have to be away from Southern California, he brought Dolores and their four children along.

The Road to Hong Kong was the only "Road" picture not made under Paramount's auspices. It was produced independently for United Artists. It had been ten years since *Road to Bali* and in that time the picture business had changed. Its stars were ten years older. In the cases of Hope and Crosby, this didn't make too much difference, but Dorothy Lamour, at forty-seven, was no longer the sexy jungle princess in a sarong of old. As a result, Crosby wanted to replace her with one of the younger leading ladies who were a little more *au courant*—a Brigitte Bardot or Sophia Loren or Gina Lollobrigida. Hope, on the other hand, felt it wouldn't be a "Road" picture without Lamour. So they effected a compromise that pleased no one. They hired Joan Collins to play the love interest, and wrote a smaller part for Lamour.

After reading the script, Lamour (more or less in retirement at this time) attempted to back out. She couldn't understand why she was "too old" when both Hope and Crosby were ten years older than she was. But after Hope assuaged her by promising to fatten her part, give her more money and an additional musical number to do in the picture, she reluctantly acquiesced. But she remained distant toward Hope and Crosby for many years that followed. Not just because of the size of her role, but that aggravated her complaint that Hope and Crosby had never given her what she felt was her due: a percentage of the profits from the "Road" pictures.

Lamour or no Lamour. *The Road to Hong Kong* was not a success, and while the critics thought it contained some funny moments, the consensus was, that it was "tired."

You can't go home again, as Hope, Crosby and Lamour discovered, after reading the reviews and totaling up the disappointing theater grosses.

Bosley Crowther's review in *The New York Times* wasn't so much a knock as it was an assessment of what age can do, even to one's favorites:

> Age may have withered somewhat the glossy hides of Bing Crosby and Bob Hope, and custom may have done something to stale their brand of vaudeville. But the old boys still come through nicely in another turn in the "old" road act.
>
> Even their old touring partner Dorothy Lamour is come upon towards the end of this current excursion, *The Road to Hong Kong*. And though she is a bit long in the tooth and a trifle too thick around the middle for any more than one quick shot in a sarong, she is there with her old no-talent bungling to make the sentimental journey complete.

Although Hope was nagged by eye troubles all through 1962 and '63, he maintained a pace that would have exhausted the average thirty-year-old.

In addition to producing and appearing in his monthly television broadcasts, performing to enthusiastic crowds at a string of universities across the nation—Duke, Tulane, Notre Dame, the Universities of Indiana, Texas, Oklahoma and Maryland—doing another Command Performance before the Royal Family in England, making yet another movie in London, and publishing a book about his experiences putting on the show in the Soviet Union, called *I Owe Russia $1,200*, he found time, in June of 1962 to take Dolores and Linda to Georgetown

University so he could be in the audience for his oldest son Tony's graduation.

An additional inducement to get him to Georgetown was that he to was to be given an honorary doctorate in Humane Letters, for "unstinting generosity with his gift of laughter."

This, of course, made Tony's graduation a newsworthy event, with photographs of Hope in cap and gown and holding onto a diploma, in the newspapers and on the wire services.

No matter how big Hope became, he always believed that self-promotion was at least as important as talent, and he worked at it constantly.

✦ ✦ ✦ ✦

Following the doings at Georgetown University, Hope took Dolores, Nora and Kelly on a fishing vacation on a yacht off the coast of Alaska. In early July, Hope received word that his brother Jack had been hospitalized in a Boston clinic for acute hepatitis. It turned out to be cancer of the liver. It was serious. Jack was operated on and then went into a coma.

Hope flew to Boston on August 3 in time to see Jack come out of the coma and to exchange a few words with him. But Jack's illness was terminal. Hope remained at Jack's bedside, except for a few hours, until Jack died three days later.

Because he had the most experience of all of Hope's writers, Mort Lachman inherited the job of being Hope's line producer after Jack's death.

Call Me Bwana was the brainchild of producer Harry Saltzman. He had a script, written by Johanna Harwood and Nate Monaster, about an inept explorer, hired by the United States Government to find an American moon-probe missile that had landed in darkest Africa by mistake. In the course of things, the explorer becomes involved with Anita Ekberg, an enemy spy, who's in the jungle for the same purpose—to find the misfired missile.

Saltzman planned to shoot the film at the Mount Kenya Safari Club in Africa in 1962.

It sounded good to Hope. Being anywhere with stacked Anita

Ekberg sounded good to Hope. But seven-thousand-miles from Toluca Lake with her was even better.

Then, because of political unrest in Africa, the Kenya location had to be called off and the picture was shot at Pinewood Studios, outside of London, in a fake jungle. This was a setback, but as long as Anita Ekberg's bosom was real, Hope had no complaints.

During the shooting of *Call Me Bwana* Hope was reminded of his own mortality, when two more people close to him succumbed unexpectedly.

On November 8, Monty Brice, Fanny Brice's brother, who had taken over the spot on the Hope staff left vacant when Barney Dean died, had a heart attack on the set and died before the day was over. He was seventy-one.

That evening, back in his suite at the Dorchester, Hope received bad news from the States. Mack Millar, his ever-so-loyal publicity man, also died of a heart attack that night, in his home on Coldwater Canyon in Beverly Hills. Millar had only been fifty-seven.

Jimmy Saphier negotiated a long-term, multimillion-dollar deal for Hope to be Chrysler's principle spokesman. It was Hope's most ambitious undertaking to date: it would be an hour-long (and sometimes ninety minutes) weekly series of comedy, drama and variety shows, under the umbrella title *Bob Hope Presents the Chrysler Theater.*

Hope would be paid the incredible sum of $500,000 each time he starred in a production, and $25,000 each time he filmed an introduction to a weekly drama that he didn't appear in.

The dramas were yet another attempt to bring good writing and acting back to TV, not unlike the high standards set by *Playhouse 90* and *Philco Playhouse* and *Studio One* before it.

It would be produced at Universal Studios by Dick Berg, who would engage the best dramatists available—Budd Schulberg, Don Mankiewicz, Rod Sterling, William Inge, and Paddy Chayefsky—to write the teleplays. It was believed that those writers would attract top actors and actresses from the New

York stage. People like Anne Bancroft, Jason Robards, Henry Fonda, Helen Hayes, and others of their stature.

Hope could have used one of those top writers himself, judging from the reception *Call Me Bwana* received when it opened on July 4, 1963.

"Bob Hope, one of the world's most celebrated traveling men, undoubtedly took the wrong turn when he hit the trail toward Africa for *Call Me Bwana*," wrote A.H. Weiler, in *The New York Times*, the morning after it opened. "Mr. Hope has been called many things in films, but tired must be the word for him, his writers, and his cast in this pseudo safari."

❊ ❊ ❊ ❊

Fortunately, Hope's admirers on Capitol Hill couldn't have cared less what film critics said about him.

On September 11, 1963, in a ceremony in the White House Rose Garden Bob Hope received a Medal of Freedom from President Kennedy, "In recognition of having rendered outstanding service to the cause of Democracy throughout the world."

This was the highest civilian award a person could get, and only two other entertainers had received it previously: George M. Cohan and Irving Berlin.

In accepting the award Hope quipped to the President, "This is a great thing. There is only one sobering thought. I received this for going out of the country. I think they are trying to tell me something."

❊ ❊ ❊ ❊

For his first Chrysler Special, broadcast on Friday September 27, 1963, Hope enlisted Barbra Streisand, James Garner, Dean Martin, and Tuesday Weld to assist him. In the writing department he had his regulars: Lester White, Johnny Rapp, Norman Sullivan, and Mort Lachman, who also produced.

Variety's review said:

Bob Hope, who is giving his all for Chrysler this season as host of an anthology series, and star of a monthly variety, teed off with one of his own crackerjack comedy stanzas. It remains to be seen whether the dramatic entries can sustain this momentum, but in any case Hope's own specials can be counted on to be sure-fire winners . . .

Hope's high-powered, publicity-minded agent, Jimmy Saphier, urged Hope to replace Mack Millar with a new and younger high-powered press agent, in order to publicize *Chrysler Theater*. Saphier didn't believe that Ursula Halloran, who was trying to cover both coasts, had the clout or the connections to do a first-rate job. As a matter of fact, he didn't believe she'd ever been any good. "Keep her for recreational sex if you want, but let's get a new press agent who really can do the job."

Hope fired her, and replaced her with Allan Kalmus, a young PR man from New York. Kalmus was a veteran of the NBC publicity staff, had good contacts and knew his way around show business's inner circles and the network's executive suites. He also had a Harvard background, and the veneer of one of President Kennedy's "best and the brightest."

That's the official Hope camp version of why Hope fired Ursula. The real story, according to Jan King, is that Hope was beginning to get tired of her as a lover and found this was the easiest way to get rid of her.

Ursula refused to go quietly.

"[She] told me that she was angry over her firing," states Jan King. "Bob didn't know just how really desperate Ursula was. She started hitting the bottle and constantly quarreled with him over his failure to divorce Dolores and marry her.

"Eventually Bob had the studio guard bar her from entering the lot. Once however she managed to get past the guard. She confronted Bob in his office. He told her she was fired, and simply walked away."

Ursula retreated to her apartment in New York City, where she drank heavily.

Meanwhile, Hope had begun to sound like the official spokesman for Chrysler Motors. And he was no longer taking it easy.

On October 4, he flew to Dallas to put on a show for the students at Southern Methodist University. He announced he'd make a donation of $300,000 for the establishment of a Bob Hope Theater on the campus.

This was the first step in a campaign to establish his immortality, by getting buildings and streets named after him.

After Dallas he returned to Hollywood, where he filmed a special and also some Chrysler commercials together with introductions to the dramatic series. He appeared at some bookstores to autograph his latest book, *I Owe Russia $1,200*, which *Variety* described as "the longest stand-up monologue in history." He attended a baseball writers luncheon. He made a personal appearance in Indianapolis.

And then he flew back to Hollywood to attend a dinner honoring Cecil B. DeMille.

His eye doctor was concerned, but Hope wasn't. He hadn't had a recurrence of his eye trouble in several months. In fact, his eye seemed to be improving, which convinced the ubiquitous Hope that it was work that was good for him, and not the other way around.

But then, at the end of October, he was played golf at the Springs his eye suddenly started hemorrhaging.

He put in a hurried call to Dr. Beigelman who told him that the only way he could save sight in his bad eye was give it total rest. Moreover, by resting it, he didn't mean doing a benefit for three eskimos in front of an igloo at the South Pole. He told Hope to lie flat on his back, in a darkened room, for three weeks.

Hope was so frightened that he actually did stay still in a darkened room for three weeks. Toward the end of that period, Hope received a disturbing phone call from Allan Kalmus in New York, that Ursula Halloran had been found dead in her apartment, of an apparent overdose of barbiturates and liquor.

"Bob got the news when he was having all that eye trouble, and he was terribly afraid the details of their affair would be dragged through the newspapers," remembers Jan King. "But

Ursula left no suicide note. All that was left to face was the funeral."

Using a trip to Manhattan to see Dr. Reese as a cover, Hope flew East two days later to attend Ursula's funeral service in Pittsburgh.

"Ursula's sister, who was a nun, went berserk at the sight of her dead sister's lover," continues King. "She rolled in the church aisle and vowed to get even with Bob."

To avoid a scene, Hope beat a hasty retreat back to New York.

"The Boss was very embarrassed about Ursula's death, and also that brouhaha at the church," George Hope confided to Robert Slatzer a couple of days later. "He's trying to explain it away by telling all his friends that Ursula was a very-mixed-up, sick girl. He hopes people believe him."

Apparently nobody questioned what Hope was doing in Pittsburgh at the funeral of his fired press agent, and why he looked so shook up. As a result his public image remained unsullied, and Ursula Hallaron took her secret to the grave.

35

If there's such a thing as retribution, Hope must have felt that "someone up there" was trying to warn him about the double life he was leading after he spoke with Dr. Reese in New York City the day after Ursula's funeral.

The bad news was that his eye problem could not be corrected by surgery; the good news was that a Swiss surgeon named Dr. Dohrmann Pischel, at Children's Hospital in San Francisco, had recently developed a process called photocoagulation, which could be the answer to Hope's eye hemorrhaging. Reese couldn't guarantee that Pischel could help him, but at least it was worth a try.

Hope was ambivalent about undergoing more treatment. For a few days after he returned home, he delayed meeting with Pischel. But when the eye didn't improve after three days, he was depressed. News of President Kennedy's assassination, on November 22, added further to his gloom.

Like many millions in the country during the next three days, Hope was glued to the television screen. That didn't help his ailing eye. Consequently he phoned Pischel, and made an appointment.

Pischel didn't think Hope's eye was ready for the photocoagulation treatment after the first examination, and sent him home with the same advice—"Take it easy."

But "taking it easy" wasn't the answer. So on December 6, Bob and Dolores flew to San Francisco to undergo the photocoagulation treatment at Children's Hospital.

It was probably the most suspenseful moment of Hope's life when he was placed on an operating table and his head was locked in a vice-like contraption to keep him perfectly still when the treatment began. Then the photocoagulation gun was positioned above him and the beam aimed at the cornea to coagulate the bleeding cells behind the eye.

What would happen if this treatment failed? Hope asked himself. Would he be able to work again? Or was this his finish as an entertainer? A bon vivant? A lover?

The first treatment failed. So Pischel tried a second time on December 10. The results were encouraging, and Pischel gave him special dark glasses to wear. These contained tiny pinholes, so that his eyes would focus in a straight path.

Hope was then released from the hospital, but Pischel cautioned him that he would have to wear the glasses at all times. He would have to remain in a darkened room, remaining as motionless as he possibly could, during the ten or twelve days it would take his eye to heal.

Taking it easy, in a dark room, behind black pinhole glasses, was torture to a man as active as Hope. Worse, it seemed that he would have to forgo his annual USO Christmas tour. He'd been scheduled to go to Europe, Turkey and North Africa.

But there were problems with calling it off. Two members of his production staff, Sil Caranchini and John Pawlek, who were in charge of the sound system, were already in Turkey preparing the stages for his arrival.

Hope's new producer, Mort Lachman, was in the process of locating Caranchini and Pawlek to inform them that The Boss was too ill to tour, when Hope phoned him and said that all systems were on "go."

"What about your eye?"

Hope said he would go to Palm Springs to rest for about ten days. Then he'd meet the troupe in Ankara. Informed of the plans, Dr. Pischel said he thought Hope was foolish and that he wouldn't be responsible if the comedian's eye had a relapse.

But Hope said he was going regardless; he was not about to disappoint "the boys."

His cast, which consisted of Tuesday Weld, Anita Bryant, beauty contest winner Michele Metrinko, John Bubbles of the legendary Buck & Bubbles dance team, Jerry Colonna, the Earl Twins, Les Brown and his band, took off for Istanbul, as scheduled.

The troupe, arrived in Turkey several days before Christmas and put on two shows, with Jerry Colonna supplanting Hope as emcee.

Meanwhile, Hope, hidden behind dark pinhole glasses, flew to New York via TWA on December 22. Then he boarded a Lufthansa flight for Frankfurt, West Germany, where a U.S. fighter jet met him and flew him to Ankara. The Defense Department not only had arranged for his VIP transportation, but also had sent along, as his traveling companion, one of the best opthalmologists in the service to keep an eye on Hope's eye.

When Hope arrived at the site of his first show, which was in Ankara, and alighted from the army jet still wearing the pinhole glasses, few who were watching his uncertain steps believed he'd ever be able to pull himself together to perform. But there was no keeping Bob Hope away from hearing that laughter and applause. They were his life's blood.

Hope didn't plan to emcee the entire Christmas show, or was he about to do anything terribly physical, like a challenge dance with John Bubbles, which had originally been part of the proposed show.

As a matter of fact, he took a short nap during the opening twenty minutes of the show. Then awaking, and feeling some-what refreshed, he strolled out onto the stage, with the intention of just telling a few one-liners to prove that he was there, after which he would again retreat to his cot.

But the reaction from the GIs upon seeing him and hearing that familiar voice saying, "Hi, ya, fellahs . . . this is Bob

'Ankara' Hope telling you I'm glad I could make it . . . I just thought you'd like to see a new kind of turkey . . ." was so electric that Hope immediately forgot his eye troubles.

As he later described the feeling "I stood there, feeling stronger and stronger with every laugh."

With each show Hope became braver and stronger, and, of course, funnier. By the time of his last one, in Naples, ten days later, Hope was in such fine fettle that he told Mort Lachman to get out the dancing shoes; he would do the challenge dance with John Bubbles.

Everyone thought he was crazy to attempt such a strenuous routine—one that he and Bubbles hadn't even rehearsed. But Hope, throwing all caution to the Neapolitan wind, said he didn't care; he and Bubbles would "wing" the routine.

They did. And it brought down the house.

Reminiscing later about that moment, Hope maintained that it was "the most important comeback" of his life.

36

Part of that comeback was fulfilling his television commitments to Chrysler and making at least one feature film a year for Hope Enterprises.

Since the actual producing for *Chrysler Theater* was to be done by Dick Berg at Universal Studios, one of the first things Hope did after signing with the automobile company was to set up a lavish suite of offices on the Universal lot. Universal was on Lankersham Boulevard, in North Hollywood, just a five minute drive from Toluca Lake.

"Because he liked the way Joan [Billings] and I did his Palm Springs house," remembers Gary Jon, "he asked us to decorate his new offices at Universal. This was a triplex bungalow that had been moved onto the lot especially for him. When we got through with it, it was like a second home: king-sized bed, mirrored walls, sofas, a well-stocked bar, and carpeted wall-to-wall with a thick shag rug. It was the perfect place for him to have his liaisons with women. And Chrysler paid for everything.

"Anyway, after we'd finished that, and the Palm Springs house, Bob said to me, 'I'd like you to go and work with Dolores on the Toluca Lake house. She's let it go pretty badly.'

"The whole place needed freshening up, but what bothered Bob most was the butler's pantry. It was huge, and that's how you entered the house through the rear when he didn't want to come in the front door. But Dolores had ripped up the original linoleum a couple of years before that, and she couldn't make up her mind what to put down in its place. So she had just covered the bare cement with a large sheet of plywood, which Bob had to walk over every time he entered the house, and he was getting pretty sick of it, he told me.

"I said I'd do the place, so he told Dolores that she had to use me, and to listen to me. Joan Billings stayed pretty much in the background on this job, because by then Dolores was suspicious of her relationship with Hope. That was the summer of the 1962 World's Fair in Seattle. Bob had gone there to entertain, which was why he picked that time to do over the house.

"As I said, Joan stayed away, because of Dolores's suspicions. Dolores didn't know anything for sure, but she knew something was going on. Of course she knew about Bob's fooling around. But she was devoutly Catholic and very determined not to divorce him, because of the children."

Dolores told friends she continually sought God's assistance in helping her deal with Hope's philandering, and went to St. Charles Church on Lankersham Boulevard and Moorpark, in North Hollywood, every day. There she'd fall to her knees, and pray that Bob would change his ways and turn into a good husband. "But Hope wasn't at all religious, and thought that praying for his redemption was a huge joke," says Jan King.

At any rate, he wasn't about to be converted to Catholicism, though he told *TV Guide* he was religious in his own way.

According to neighbor Kay Avalon, "Dolores had every kind of devotive candle and religious statue around the house. Every time you walked by one, you had to genuflect and say a prayer. That's how Catholic she was."

Ed Lasker, whose accounts at Lord & Thomas included Lever Brothers at the beginning of Hope's radio career, said to me recently that he believed Dolores is "psychopathically Catholic."

And Jay Burton told me about a dinner he had with Bob and Dolores in the Toluca Lake house when he was still working for Hope.

"I'll never forget this scene," recalled Burton. "There were just the three of us at the table."

During dinner, Hope asked Jay, "Did you bring the monologue for the show?"

"Oh, for Christ's sake, I must have left it in the car," exclaimed Burton, feeling in his pocket for the missing script.

"What did you say?" snapped Dolores angrily.

"I said, I must have left the monologue in my car," replied Burton.

"No, before that," she insisted, in the manner of a district attorney grilling a witness on the stand. "You said something else."

"Oh," Burton suddenly remembered. "I guess I said 'Oh, for Christ's sake!'"

Dolores eyed Burton coldly, and told him sternly, "Don't you ever say that in front of me again."

Sensing a fight, Hope immediately jumped up from the table without finishing dinner, and said, "Come on, Jay, let's get over to rehearsal."

❋❋❋❋

Dolores somehow managed to maintain the façade of being a happily married Toluca Lake housewife.

"Whenever Bob wasn't around the house on Moorpark it was always full of people," recalls Gary Jon. "Important people. Politicians from Washington. Dignitaries from the church. Hollywood actors and actresses who might have been working with her on her various charities. And priests. There were always lots of Catholic priests around."

According to an article about Hope in a January 1964 issue of *TV Guide*, Hope became accustomed to arriving at his home in Palm Springs late at night and finding one or more strange priests roaming the grounds. The men would introduce themselves, pass a little time together, and then go to bed—separately, of course. Today Bob and Dolores reside in separate houses in Palm Springs—she in the new big one that resembles the TWA terminal in New York's Kennedy Airport in the South Ridge area, and he in the old one on El Alameda.

****

"One thing I thought was interesting about Hope," continues Gary Jon. "I did Bob's suite of bedrooms upstairs, at Moorpark. And stuck to his bathroom mirror every morning, would be little tabs of paper with reminders written on them that he'd see when he was shaving. Mrs. Hughes had stuck them there. There'd be things like, 'The Pope called at nine o'clock. Wants you to call' . . . 'The Vice President wants you to play golf with him next Tuesday' . . . 'Charlton Heston phoned . . . wants you to make a speech at the Screen Actors Guild . . .' I loved to read these little notes. It was as if the world had phoned in while he was asleep.

"But Bob and Dolores did lead separate lives, as far as I could tell. He had his suite, she had hers. And Bob had his own separate entrance and telephone line, so he could phone out to make his dates."

From what Jan King said, Dolores was "haunted by Hope's infidelity," and though she pretended not to be, she was consumed by an agonizing curiosity about her rivals. She and her mother, Theresa Defina, would sit for hours listening to reports on Hope's illicit love life, from spies they had hired. Members of the family and his two daughters also spied on him. Hope was not amused by this and became expert at avoiding family members. He became paranoid about strangers, thinking they might be detectives, checking on him.

"Although Bob hated being alone, he liked to keep his family away from his office at Universal," states Jan. "Dolores had strict orders not to come to the studio without an invitation. And the same applied to his four children.

"But Bob's oldest daughter, Linda, broke the rule and nearly caught him in the act with a beautiful young 'Deb Star.' Bob was having one of his traditional 'nooners' when Linda surprised me by popping up in the outer office.

"I told her Bob wasn't in, but she was too smart to fall for that.

'I know he's here—his car is outside,' she said, and headed for the door to the inner office.

"I cut her off before she reached the door, I told her he was napping and didn't want to disturbed. I told her that I was supposed to wake him in a half-an-hour, and that she should come back then. Then I alerted Bob. I saw Linda returning down the long corridor minutes later. I quickly punched the intercom and told Bob I was desperate.

"The starlet hadn't left yet, and he ordered me to do anything I could to delay his daughter. I quickly shut the office door, locked the outer office door, and hid behind the curtains so that Linda couldn't see me. She banged and banged for what seemed like an eternity before storming off.

"Bob hustled his companion out the back door and told me the coast was clear. When Linda returned again, which of course she did, he was sweet and charming to her. He even told her it was my fault for not waking him up!"

On another occasion, Dolores's mother, while standing on the upstairs landing in the Moorpark house, tried to eavesdrop on Hope's phone conversations behind the locked door to his private bedroom. She became so engrossed that she lost her balance, slipped, fell down the stairs, and broke her hip.

Nora, Hope's youngest daughter, also got into the spying act when she was fifteen. She once told Jan, "When I get my driver's license, I'm going to find out where he goes at night. He never comes home."

By the time Nora was almost sixteen, Hope knew what to expect. Weeks before Nora got her driver's license he started making jokes about how she'd soon join the ranks of the spies he was raising.

She didn't disappoint him. "After she got her new Chrysler convertible, Nora began to follow her father all over Hollywood in it," reports Jan. "Hope was usually able to lose her in traffic, but he became really alarmed when Nora followed him to Joy Monroe's apartment. Bob often complained to me about having to pay the bill for the family spy operations."

By the summer of 1962 Joan Billings grew increasingly bitter over the fact that Hope was using the love nest she had designed in his Universal studio triplex to entertain her rivals. The last straw came when Hope went to the Seattle World's Fair with Joy Monroe. After putting up with Bob's bed-hopping for six years, Joan, who thought she was the true love of his life, had finally had all she could take. After Hope returned from Seattle, he refused to take Joan's phone calls.

As unhappy as she was over this, and she was in tears a good deal of the time, Joan was not going to let him ruin her life the way he did Ursula Halloran's. She had a plan. She warned Hope she would tell the world about their relationship.

To quiet her, Hope agreed to buy two motels for her in Palm Springs. "They cost between $200,000 and $300,000" reports Jan. "He sputtered with rage when it came time to spend it—he just didn't spend that kind of money on his women. Joan was the only mistress to eventually get her revenge."

Gary Jon prefers not to think of Joan's request as "blackmail." "It was more like a financial settlement that a husband would make with his wife when he was divorcing her."

If that's so, he was getting off a hell of a lot cheaper than he would have if Joan had been Dolores—at least according to the following story I heard from actress Jayne Meadows, the lovely and talented wife of Steve Allen.

She told me, "Steve and I were doing a telethon for flood relief at the Mechanic Theater in Baltimore in July of 1972. It was the year of the Wilkes-Barre, Pennsylvania flood. A whole bunch of other stars and ourselves were flown to Maryland in the same plane, including Bob and Dolores Hope.

"It was during Richard Nixon's first term, and he and Pat were there, too. It was late at night, backstage at the theater. Everyone was milling nervously around, waiting to do their thing. I happened to be standing near Hope and Dolores who were over in a darkened corner, having a terrific fight.

"Being a woman, I was dying to hear what the fight was about. So I moved closer, just in time to hear Hope saying, 'I want a divorce!' Dolores, whose back was to him, wheeled around suddenly facing him and spat out, 'All right, Bob, you can have your divorce. Just give me fifty million dollars cash, and I'll give you your freedom.'"

Obviously, Hope decided it was cheaper to remain married.

❖ ❖ ❖ ❖

Joan Billings died in Palm Springs, on July 24, 1989, due to complications from a brain tumor operation. At the time she had rewed and her married name was Joan Gortz. She was fifty-two.

37

Eight on the Lam was one of four films my sometimes collaborator, Robert Fisher, and I wrote for Bob Hope. How Hope decided to turn it into a vehicle for himself is an indication of the hit-or-miss way he was beginning to handle his film career after he left Paramount.

In 1962 Fisher and I wrote a film treatment based on a story that appeared in *Life* magazine about the trials and tribulations of a small-town bank teller. He was a widower with seven children, who started embezzling funds from his bank in order to feed his family. When the authorities started to close in on him, the teller went to Arizona with his seven children. He hid out for many months in a housing development under an assumed name.

It's difficult to keep small children from talking, especially when you don't want them to. That being so, we decided the bank teller's story should be based on the problems he had keeping his kids from blabbing out the truth about who they were, and why they were hiding out. It could be turned into a funny comedy. ("Hey, doesn't that look like Dad's picture hanging up in the Post Office!") It was all there; it just needed one minor change: the teller had been falsely accused, and was actually innocent.

As a result, we dashed off a twenty-page screen treatment

based on that premise and gave it to our agent at MCA. Because we had written it in such brief form, we didn't succeed in selling it, until I suggested he give it to Louis Shurr for Bob Hope. He did, and Shurr told us that he liked the premise and would show it to Hope.

Some weeks later, Hope strolled into Shurr's office on Rodeo Drive. He glanced at a large pile of movie scripts on Shurr's desk that had been submitted for his consideration, and asked, "Got anything good for me to read?"

Being a rather laissez-faire type agent, Shurr nodded toward the pile, in the middle of which was our slim offering.

Hope studied the pile, I was later told by Shurr, then reached out and selected *Eight on the Lam* saying, "I think I'll take this one—it's the thinnest."

Then he walked out with our story under his arm.

Several more weeks passed. Then we heard from Shurr that Hope liked the story, and would pay us $50,000 to develop it into a shootable screenplay. Before we'd see any of that green stuff, however, Hope would first have to get a major studio— probably Paramount or United Artists—to finance the project. This sounded like a sure sale to us. After all, Hope was a major film star, and we believed that when he spoke, studios listened.

Unfortunately, after his last couple of films, Hope wasn't as "bankable" as he once had been, and none of the studios showed interest. Shurr told us not to be discouraged. Hope wasn't going to give up. He liked our story. With seven kids, it had many of the same qualities as one of his film hits, *The Seven Little Foys*.

Shurr assured us that if worst came to worst, Hope might even come up with his own money to pay us to develop the screenplay. Meanwhile, Hope was committed to play in *A Global Affair* which Charlie Lederer was writing for Ray Stark's Seven Arts Productions, so there wasn't any hurry.

We figured that was the end of it. But shortly after the new year, we received word from Shurr that although Hope was unsuccessful in getting a studio to finance *Eight on the Lam*, he had faith enough in the project to pay us himself to write the screenplay, for the same figure agreed to before: $10,000 for the story, which we'd be paid upon signing the contract with Hope Enterprises; $30,000 upon completion of the first draft; and the final $10,000 after we'd done any needed rewriting and polishing.

We weren't worried about getting paid. We were sure Hope was a responsible fellow. All that mattered to us was that we write a good screenplay that could be turned into a Bob Hope comedy as successful as *The Seven Little Foys*.

Before we went to work, Louis Shurr insisted that we sit through a screening of *The Seven Little Foys* in a projection room so we'd know the kind of "schmaltzy" treatment to give our screenplay.

In four weeks we finished a first draft. Shurr read it, liked it, and gave it to Hope for final approval.

Later in the week we received a call from Shurr. He told us that Hope hadn't read our script yet, but that he was taking it with him on his trip east where he would play some colleges.

During the next eight weeks, Fisher and I waited for some word as to whether Hope liked our script. Since Shurr never phoned us, we called him at the end of each week with the question, "any news?"

"I spoke to Bob in Minneapolis," replied Shurr, during our first conversation. "He likes the first ten pages."

"What about the rest of it?" I asked, worried.

"He hasn't had time to read any more of it than that, but he'll get around to it."

Another week passed, and Shurr told me, "Bob's read the first twenty pages. He likes them a lot."

Three more weeks passed, with Bob reading and liking ten new pages a week, I finally asked Shurr, "How come Bob only reads ten pages a week?"

Shurr laughed, and said, "Well, actually, Bob doesn't read at all. He's got a bad eye, you know."

"Well, who's reading it?" I asked. "A seeing-eye dog?"

Shurr laughed again and said, "No, this broad he took with him is reading it to him. She reads to him every night in bed."

"Well, how does the girl like it?" I asked.

"She thinks it's very funny," said Shurr, without telling me who she was. "She just wishes there was a part in it for her."

In all probability the girl doing the reading was Rosemarie Frankland. She was with Hope in the summer of 1964, when he gave her a small part in another film we wrote for him, *I'll Take Sweden*.

At any rate, when Hope returned to Hollywood later in the spring, he had good news for us. Shurr told us, "Bob likes the script so much he doesn't even want a rewrite."

We were delighted until we received the balance of our payment for the screenplay, which we expected to be the $40,000 still owed us. To our surprise, the check was for only $30,000.

When our agent complained about this to Shurr, he was informed that since "the boys" (writers were always referred to as "the boys" in those days) didn't do a second draft, they weren't entitled to the last payment.

"But Hope didn't want a second draft," our agent reminded him.

That didn't matter, according to their interpretation of the contract. "Hope says you don't get the last ten grand until you do a second draft."

"But he doesn't want one," we repeated.

"Well, he may someday, after he makes a deal with a studio."

"That could take years," we pointed out.

"That's life," laughed Shurr.

Since we knew that wasn't the intent of the contract, and that it was against the Writers Guild's rules, we had to take this sticky little problem to an attorney. Hope's lawyer, Martin Gang, who'd drawn up the contract in the first place, finally admitted we were right.

We were paid the money.

The Bob Hope philosophy of spending seemed to be: $10,000 saved is $10,000 earned.

Another interesting thing about the Bob Hope mentality: even though he was annoyed with us for insisting on getting the money rightfully due us contractually, his anger was short-lived.

Since he'd made such a fuss about not paying us, we figured that was the end of our relationship with Hope. Not that it was much of a relationship. To that point we'd never had a single meeting with him, or even a phone call.

But Hope fooled us. Several weeks after we received our money, our agent told Fisher and me that Hope was so delighted with the job we'd done with *Eight on the Lam* that he wanted us to rewrite the screenplay for *A Global Affair*, which he was supposed to shoot next.

Charlie Lederer, one of the most experienced screenwriters in the business, had done the original screenplay but Hope decided it wasn't funny enough for him and wanted a complete overhaul. He also wanted Seven Arts Studios to pay for it.

A Global Affair already had a production date set that couldn't be changed, because of Hope's schedule, which was four weeks from the time we agreed to rewrite the script. So we worked fast, and somewhat in the dark, because Hope was too busy to meet with us to tell us exactly what he wanted. We had to guess. Working for Bob Hope was akin to working for the Phantom of the Opera.

Because of our television experience, Fisher and I were used to meeting tight deadlines. Our new version of *A Global Affair* was in the hands of producer Hal Bartlett in time for it to go before the cameras on the summer date originally planned.

Yvonne De Carlo played opposite Hope, and there was an ensemble of beautiful young women of various nationalities in the other female roles. Having a cast of sexy creatures to play with was one of the serendipitous things that attracted Hope to *A Global Affair* in the first place.

The story was about a minor American diplomat, working at the United Nations, who finds an infant boy outside his office door and has to care for the tot until his mother can be found. The sub-plot has all the foreign beauties at the UN vying for custody of the baby, for their respective countries. Hope falls in love with the infant, but, being a bachelor, has to prove he's worthy of parenthood before the Security Council will allow him to keep the infant.

Hope winds up in a number of compromising situations with single women, which causes an international crisis. In the end he not only gets to keep the baby, but winds up with a wife.

There were some amusing moments in the film, including one where the baby gives the chickenpox to all the members of the UN. But perhaps the funniest moment wasn't in the film at all.

"Occasionally, Bob brought Joy Monroe and little Donna down to the set to watch him shoot," says Jan King. "Well, sometimes Dolores would be sitting in a director's chair opposite them. Dolores would eye Joy and try to figure out who she was and just what she was doing there, but never dared to ask Hope who these friends were."

38

While some of the best drama in *A Global Affair* may have been going on behind the cameras, the film, when it was completed, fared surprisingly well at the pen of *The New York Times*'s Bosley Crowther in May 1964.

> It's a pip of an idea to have Bob Hope at the United Nations, where he probably belongs, come to think of it. In *A Global Affair* he's a minor functionary, who scoops up an abandoned foundling and fends off 111 determined countries, via their representatives, mostly female, all of whom want the child. Furthermore, the scenes of Mr. Hope and the little charmer have genuine appeal.

Crowther also found plenty to complain about, including a "middle that sagged." But Hope was pleased enough with the picture's reception to contact me and my collaborator, via our agent, in the spring of 1964, and ask us to do another fast rewrite on a script he had half committed to doing, but which he wasn't entirely pleased with in its present version.

I'll Take Sweden was its name, and it was an original screenplay by Nat Perrin, a collaborator on some early Marx Brothers films; it was meant to hone in on the sexual revolution that was sweeping 1964, with the emphasis on unmarried couples living together.

The story was about a widower, whose teenage daughter, Tuesday Weld, seemed on the verge of giving herself to her boyfriend, Frankie Avalon. In an effort to get Tuesday away from Frankie, of whom he doesn't approve, Hope takes her on a vacation to Sweden. There, to his shock, he discovers that in Sweden, sex without marriage is an acceptable thing. Consequently his daughter is in more danger of losing her virginity in Sweden than she was in Southern California. Moreover, he becomes involved with a Swedish beauty, Dina Merrill, whose morals are also questionable.

Hope was all for the idea of doing a film that would appeal to the flower children generation, because he was striving for a more "with it" image on the screen.

However he wouldn't commit to producer Edward Small until the script was completely overhauled. And since Hope had to shoot in the summer, so there would be no conflict with his TV schedule, we were asked to do a rewrite in three weeks.

Because we were in the throes of writing and producing a new ABC-TV sitcom for Mickey Rooney that we had created and was already slotted into the network's fall schedule, the three-week time limit fit right in with our schedule. We'd have to start writing scripts for the Rooney series when we finished *I'll Take Sweden*—if we expected to get on the air in the fall, that is.

Again we couldn't get a meeting with the busy Hope in order to find out what he liked and didn't like about the Perrin script. But since Freddy DeCordova was already signed to direct the film, and he had a close relationship with Hope dating back to their Broadway days, he acted as an intermediary between us and our star.

We also had a couple of story conferences with producer Eddie Small. Small was one of those old-style Hollywooders who wasn't very articulate about what he wanted in a script. He was like Harry Cohn, who judged everything by the seat of his pants. Interpretation: if he started squirming while watching a movie, he knew it wasn't any good.

DeCordova was better at explaining what Hope wanted, because he'd been able to meet with Hope.

Three weeks later, we turned in the completed script. DeCordova got it to Hope, who probably had his current bed partner read it to him.

Whoever did the reading, when Hope got back to us he said it was a big improvement, but he wasn't completely satisfied with it. He kept asking for new scenes, more line changes, and bigger jokes. We gave him these, but he still wasn't sure that the script was right. He couldn't quite pinpoint the problem. Meanwhile, the three weeks were up and his demands were eating into the time we should have been spending on our Mickey Rooney series. Finally I suggested to Freddy, "Let's get a meeting with him, and maybe we can figure out what he wants."

Hope agreed and a meeting was set for 8:30 in the evening, at his house in Toluca Lake.

It wasn't the best time for me, because my wife Lois had taken ill with a female problem and was in great pain. Nevertheless she urged me to go to the meeting, saying she'd get her aunt to stay with her.

My partner and I drove out to Hope's place. We stopped at the gate leading to the Hope compound, and identified ourselves to the guard, who then directed us to the main house. Someone, I believe it was a butler, let us in and we walked through the trophy room and into the den-sitting room, where, I later discovered, Hope ate his meals and had most of his business meetings. DeCordova was already there. Hope hadn't come from his upstairs bedroom yet. Ten minutes later Hope strolled down the stairs. He was his usual jaunty self, and dressed in slacks and a sport jacket. He motioned for us to take our places at the large round dining table at one side of the room. Not that he was offering us anything to eat or drink; it just doubled as a conference table.

As we started to go through the script, Hope said that the script needed a "block" comedy scene in the first half. He envisioned a scene where the father goes to visit his daughter's boyfriend who lives in a tiny trailer, to talk him out of shacking up with his daughter. The trailer is so tiny that the three of them can barely stand or sit down in it. It would have echoes of the classic stateroom scene in the Marx Brothers' film, *A Night at the Opera*.

We admitted it could be funny, but were about to tell him it had nothing to do with the story and would throw the entire construction off if we tried to fit it in. At that moment I received a call from my wife's aunt, summoning me back home; Lois had taken a turn for the worse and had to call in her gynecologist.

I thought to myself, "How can I not go home now? And yet, we've waited three years for this face to face meeting with Hope."

Hope solved my dilemma by dismissing us with, "There's nothing more to talk about, boys. I want that scene."

By the time I arrived home, the crisis was over. The doctor had given Lois a shot to relieve the pain. What it didn't do was solve Robert Fisher's and my problem of how to keep Hope from wanting a duplication of the stateroom scene.

The next morning we were back in our office on the MGM lot, where we had another meeting with DeCordova. We insisted that the scene Hope wanted didn't fit, and that we wanted another meeting with Hope to see if we could talk him out of it. But DeCordova said he'd already gone back to the desert.

It was then arranged that Hope would phone us the following afternoon at 2:00. But the next day, 2:00 came and went with no call. Then DeCordova told us the reason Hope didn't call us was because he passed out after playing golf in the 120 degree desert heat.

Two days later Hope got back to us, but he still hadn't changed his mind about the trailer scene. By then we were two weeks past the three we allotted ourselves to rewriting *I'll Take Sweden*, so we told him we might have to sign off on the project, because we had to get back to the Mickey Rooney series.

I'll Take Sweden went into production on the old Sam Goldwyn lot on July 21, 1964. Rosemarie Frankland, the Miss

World whom Dolores had insisted Hope bring back to the States from England, was also a member of the cast in the minor role of Uta, a Swedish sexpot.

After Fisher and I finished our job on *Sweden*, Hope put his gag writers to work on the script, to punch up some of the lines, and, oh, yes, to add a scene in a trailer.

It had long been a practice of Hope's to give his movie scripts to his writers to add jokes, and, incidentally, for no extra compensation, so I wasn't surprised when I saw the film at the preview and heard many lines I didn't recognize. The trailer scene was in the picture, with a number of double-entendre bed jokes. To paraphrase a song in the musical *Damn Yankees*, whatever Bob Hope wants Bob Hope gets.

But I was surprised at the amount of bad taste that had been injected into the script. The critics weren't too pleased with all the double-entendre lines.

In *The New York Times*, A.H. Weiler wrote:

Bob Hope should get some soap and scrub out that blue humor. *I'll Take Sweden* . . . is altogether unworthy of a beloved sunshine man who has cheered millions.

Although in most instances Hope was astute in recognizing good movie material for himself, he made a large judgment error in the late fifties, when screenwriter Stanley Shapiro approached him with a screenplay he had written that he thought would be perfect for him.

"Bob was scared to death of it," recalls his former agent, Al Melnick. "He felt it wasn't funny enough. He told me to tell Shapiro that he'd consider it only if his writers could punch it up. But Shapiro said no way were Hope's writers going to put their hands on it."

As a result, Hope turned it down, and *Operation Petticoat* became an enormous hit, with Cary Grant and Tony Curtis in the leading roles. It was nominated by the Academy of Motion Picture Arts and Sciences the following year for "Best Original Screenplay."

In the fall of 1964, after he'd finished filming *I'll Take Sweden*, Hope learned from the Defense Department that he had been cleared to take his entertainment unit to Vietnam for the Christmas holidays. However, he was told to keep his impending trip quiet for security reasons."

Since very little can be kept under wraps in Hollywood except the names of Academy Award winners, news of the trip leaked out before Hope and his company flew to Vietnam in an Air Force transport plane, in mid-December.

In addition to his mainstays, Jerry Colonna and Les Brown, he took along Anita Bryant, Janis Paige, Jill St. John, Anna Marie Alberghetti, Peter Leeds, and Ann Sidney, of Australia, the 1964 Miss World.

Before arriving in Vietnam on Christmas Eve, Hope and his troupe performed in Korea, Okinawa, and Thailand. In Bangkok they were all invited to a sit down dinner at the Grand Palace with the King and Queen of Thailand.

Hope had met the royal couple in Hollywood when they visited the set of *The Facts of Life*. At that time they had told Hope that if he was ever in their neighborhood to drop in.

Hope's Christmas Eve show was at Bien Ho Air Base, a few miles from Saigon. The stage was about as close to the war as one could be without being in a foxhole. At Bien Ho, security measures were taken to insure the safety of Hope and his cast. Every enlisted man and officer in the area carried a rifle or a sidearm, including all of those in the audience.

Hope's monologue, of course, was timely: "Here I am in Bien Ho. That's Vietnamese for 'duck'. . . . Nice to be here in sniper valley. . . . I remember Vietnam . . . it's the place Huntley and Brinkley are always talking about . . ."

Because the show was so well received by the troops, it lasted longer than usual. This still didn't deter Hope from touring a local hospital ward after the show. Then he and his troupe had a quick drink at the officer's club before boarding the Army buses that would carry them back to the Caravelle Hotel in Saigon.

The trip back to the hotel was delayed by an hour, because of reports that enemy snipers were in the brush alongside the dirt road that wound its way through the jungle back to Saigon.

The delay may have saved Hope's life.

Ten minutes before the buses arrived at the Caravelle, a Viet Cong bomb exploded in the Brinks Hotel directly across the street where the American officers were billeted. Two officers were killed and fifty Americans were injured along with thirteen Vietnamese. The blast gutted the Brinks and caused damage to surrounding buildings, including the Caravelle where Hope and his cast were staying. Fragments of glass from shattered windows were everywhere, especially the Caravelle's lobby, which was also filled with smoke.

It was revealed in documents years later that the bomb had been intended for Hope as punishment for helping keep up GI morale. If the bomb had exploded ten minutes later, Hope might not have lived to celebrate his ninetieth birthday.

It was the closest brush with death Hope experienced during his many years of putting on USO shows in war zones.

"I remember that night we checked into the Caravelle, after the bombing," says Peter Leeds, who played Hope's second banana on several of those tours. "They told us to keep our windows and curtains closed in our rooms after we checked in, in case there were snipers in the neighborhood. Which I did. Then, after I'd unpacked, I was about to take a nap when I got a call from Bob from his room. He said, 'Meet me in the lobby.' So I did, and so did Les Brown and Jerry Colonna. From there we were driven to a hospital, where they were bringing in the wounded from the front. The hospital was seven stories high. After we went through the first floor, with Hope doing his best to cheer up the wounded, I said, 'Well, let's get back to the hotel and get some shut-eye.' But Bob said, 'Not on your life. We have to go through the whole hospital.' And we did. He insisted on visiting the wards on every floor . . . even the seventh floor, where they were operating on the wounded. That's how seriously Bob took that stuff."

Leeds remembered that it rained a good deal in Vietnam, and usually on the afternoon or evening Hope was scheduled to do an open air show. But "someone up there" must have been looking out for us. "We had a joke about that. It could be pouring rain, coming down in buckets, as it only can in the tropics. And then, about twenty minutes before the show, the sky would suddenly clear and the sun would come pouring out. When that happened, we used to say, 'Dolores must be on her knees with the beads in her hand.'"

Leeds believed that Hope led a charmed life.

But charmed or not, the War Department decided that on Hope's subsequent visits to Vietnam, they'd rather not have him spend the night at the Caravelle. For his own safety, they whisked him and his cast away in an Army helicopter to the Erawan Hotel in Bangkok, which was about an hour's flight. There, Hope was relatively safe.

The following January, when Hope's *Christmas in Vietnam* Chrysler TV special was shown, its ratings went through the roof. This was the first time the American public got a firsthand glimpse of the kinds of places our GIs were living in in Vietnam.

In fact, there was such interest in the show that Hope decided to do a sequel on his March 24 special, with the film that was left over from the earlier broadcast.

When his Chrysler sponsor heard of his plans, they immediately objected, claiming they had hired Hope to be a comedian, not a deliverer of hawkish messages to American audiences. (Hope had gotten carried away on his first special and in one or two instances did some serious propagandizing.) In answer to Hope's rejoinder that his ratings had never been higher, Chrysler said, yes, but they were antagonizing that part of the public that no longer believed that we were participating in a "good" war in Vietnam. Already anti-Vietnam protests were happening all over the country, especially on college campuses. Draft card burning demonstrations were becoming the order of the day in many locales frequented by the young.

But Hope wasn't to be deterred. In March, he did his sequel to the Christmas show with the same gratifying results in the Nielsens.

✿ ✿ ✿ ✿

Whether it was the ratings on his Vietnam shows that made him that way or the result of his constant hob-nobbing with high officials in the Defense Department and Army and Navy brass, Hope was a genuine Hawk.

In an interview with Associated Press feature writer Bob Thomas, Hope said, "This is important to the world, Bob. Listen—if the Commies ever thought we weren't going to protect the Vietnamese, there would be Vietnams everywhere. That would be a lot worse than what we're facing now. Like it or not, we're the Big Daddy in the Free World."

Whatever Hollywood liberals thought of him, Hope was certainly a favorite among the military, and that included Dwight D. Eisenhower.

Their relationship dated back to World War II, but after Eisenhower retired from the presidency he made Palm Springs his second home, and he and Hope became even closer, because of their mutual love of golf. Eisenhower believed as Hope did—that it was wrong to be engaged in a war which you weren't going all-out to win. You either pulled back completely, or you went for broke.

✿ ✿ ✿ ✿

After the Oscar telecast on April 5, which Hope emceed for the thirteenth time, he repaired to Palm Springs for a rest. While golfing with Eisenhower at the El Dorado Country Club, Hope and the former President discussed plans for the erecting of an Eisenhower Medical Center, for "the study and treatment of respiratory heart diseases" for which Bob and Dolores were raising money. Hope had already donated property for the project—forty acres of choice sand and sagebrush in Rancho Mirage.

At age sixty-two, Hope wanted to be known as more than just the richest, most successful comedian ever. It was more important for him to be known as a philanthropist, an intimate of presidents and kings and queens and statesman, spokesman for the GIs, and also a great family man.

❖❖❖❖

As a family man Hope was seeing to it that his children, now that they were growing up, hewed the straight and narrow, got good grades, stayed away from pot, and had all the benefits he never had when he was their age. Fortunately he had Dolores to do the supervising when he was flitting around the globe.

Following his graduation from Georgetown, son Tony expressed a desire to become a lawyer. Hope sent him to Harvard to earn a law degree.

While still at Georgetown, Tony met and fell in love with Geraldine Gertrude Burke, whose well-to-do parents lived in Port Washington, New York. Geraldine was studying to be a nurse, and graduated at the same time Tony did. The two planned to marry soon after their graduation in June of 1962.

Linda Hope, the comedian's number-one daughter, didn't start life with ambitions to be in show business. When she finished high school at Immaculate Heart, she became an English major at St. Louis University. There she performed in a few college plays, but after realizing that "I was not too spectacular," she decided to become a clinical psychologist.

After four years at the university, Linda came back to L.A. and accepted a job teaching English to Mexican children at Our Lady of Queen of Angels High School in the barrio district downtown. "I knew there was a need for teachers, so I decided to do some teaching until I went back to school in the fall to study for my Master's Degree, and maybe my Doctorate," Linda told a reporter. "I'd always been interested in people and what made them tick. I'd like everyone to know, however, that I am doing this because I like it, but that I'm also being paid for it, like any other teacher. It's not just some philanthropic thing I'm doing."

Linda admitted she was interested in clinical psychology, which deals in actual case histories, but said she hadn't been

384

practicing on her family, including her father. "I don't guess he'd like it," she laughed.

Hope may not have liked it, but he was proud of how well his children were doing. On June 3, 1965, he attended younger son, Kelly's high school graduation from St. John's Vianey in Los Angeles at the Wilshire Ebell Theater and delivered a commencement address. Because he was the principal speaker, the place was packed.

Although Hope's commencement words were geared for laughs, he took a few moments in the middle to address something that had been troubling him—the current uprisings on college and university campuses, with their sit-ins, unruly demonstrations and draft card burnings.

"I think it's great," he said, "that our young men and women are concerned about people's rights, because that's the American way, and that's why the world looks to us for help. Americans need the new ideas of its young people . . . it needs their idealism, and I only hope that they aren't all hoarse when it's time for them to be heard."

Hope sounded like a spokesman for the United States Government.

Although his largely hawkish attitude was later to turn him off with students, the antiwar movement was in its earliest days—not large enough yet to make him an unwelcome speaker on the nation's campuses.

In June he picked up another honorary doctorate, this one at Monmouth College in West Long Branch, New Jersey. It was his fourth. He also appeared at Southern Methodist University where he handed over a check for $300,000 as a contribution toward the Bob Hope Theater.

In 1968 he made *Fortune* magazine's list of sixty-six Americans in the $150–$200 million class. Commenting on this, James Bacon, columnist on the *Herald-Examiner*, wrote, "He should read *Time* magazine—he's much richer there."

Several years earlier *Time* had estimated Hope's wealth to be somewhere around $400 million. Hope has always disputed both these estimates, claiming that in reality he's property poor, and that he wouldn't have cash close to these amounts until he sold off everything he owned.

Moreover, he frequently complained that property taxes on his enormous land holdings were killing him. Other people complained, however, that much of his acreage was *under-*assessed by the county tax collector, particularly three thousand acres he owned in the Malibu Mountain area. When Hope went to sell off the land in 1968, he asked $34 million, but county tax assessor Phillip Watson, had assessed the property at only $7.5, the amount on which Hope was paying property taxes. That sale didn't go through at the time.

On the other hand, one can't fault Bob Hope for trying to save as much money as he possibly could when you consider the cost of all the women he was keeping on the side.

❂ ❂ ❂ ❂

Bob Hope has probably given more "free" performances than any entertainer in history. He's never been too busy to become affiliated with another worthy cause.

One of his favorite affiliations was with the annual Miss World contest, for which he had been acting as an honorary judge since its inauguration in the early sixties.

Why anybody as busy as Hope would spend time going to San Diego to judge a Miss World contest, is a mystery that might never have been solved had it not been for Miss Johnine Leigh Avery. She was crowned Miss World USA in 1968.

Bob Hope was one of the judges.

Johnine Avery, a Navy chief's daughter, was nineteen, blonde, five-foot- six, with just the kind of body you'd expect of a Miss World winner. She is not reticent about admitting that Hope rigged the contest in her favor.

According to Miss Avery, the story of her relationship with Hope began three years earlier, in May of 1965. At the time Johnine was living in Hollywood, working as an actress, doing small parts, mostly for "scale."

"When I met Bob, I was making $350-a-week on a regular

contract, and for two weeks I could get as much as seven-fifty or a thousand a week."

It was her agent, Miles Engles, who arranged her first meeting with Hope. Engles was apparently one of Bob's "talent" scouts. "He gave me a real bulldozer job, to get me to fly down to San Diego and meet Hope for a film he was doing. I doubted that there was a film, so I didn't want to go, but everyone was very clever, and manipulating a nineteen-year-old is not that difficult. Anyway, Engles arranged this meeting in San Diego at the Mission Inn, where Hope always stayed. He arranged it as if it had something to do with a movie, which we both really knew it didn't. It was just that Bob was having a holiday in San Diego, and he wanted company."

According to Johnine, the "company" became Hope's mistress, with the affair beginning that weekend in his room at the Mission Inn.

Less than a month later, on June 14, Hope set Johnine up in an apartment at 12946 Valleyheart Drive, in Sherman Oaks, in the San Fernando Valley. This was right behind the Sportsman's Lodge, and just a few miles from Hope's house in Toluca Lake.

This arrangement went on until March of '69.

"Not being a reader of movie magazines, I didn't even know he was married for the first six months of our affair," states Johnine. "A friend finally told me."

Once Johnine became Hope's full-time live-in mistress, he forbade her to work. He wanted her totally dependent on him. "Over a period of many years, this destroyed my instinct to work and I lost my ambition," continues Johnine. "He even had me blackballed, quietly, at all the studios, because he didn't want me working.

"Once, when he was traveling without me—I think he had gone to Vietnam or something—I did a show with Bing Crosby. And when Bob came back and discovered this, he went into hysterics. He couldn't stand that I was working, and that I had seen Bing, or that Bing liked me. It really threw him out of his mind. He was very, very jealous, really."

Since Hope didn't want Johnine to work, he felt obligated to support her. He gave her the use of a Chrysler, which he, of course, got for nothing from his sponsor. But as for money, what he gave her was "a lot smaller than any money I ever earned," relates Johnine. "He's tight. To give you an idea, he once told me during our relationship that it was stupid to waste money on rent for the apartment. That it was ridiculous, year-after-year, laying out all that money for rent, and that I should go out and find a house and he'd buy it for me.

"I looked at houses for six months. I was out of my head with delight. I was a kid, and I'd never had a house or anything that belonged to me in my life. I'm a Navy brat. So it was very heavy to me. But after I had found this house—it was close to Jerry Colonna's Laurel Canyon house —Bob started talking about taxes and cracks in the wall and termites.

That's when he asked, 'What's the rent?' And I said, 'What do you mean?' and he just copped out after that. It was his suggestion. I didn't ask for a house. It was completely his idea. And so I stayed with him a while longer after that, but I was so pissed off that I just realized that he was just using my youth."

By the spring of 1967, Johnine was discouraged. Not only was she not getting the house Hope promised her, but she was still prevented by him from working. To make up for it, Hope told her to enter the 1967 Miss World contest in San Diego. Being one of the judges, he told her he was sure he could arrange for her to win. "But what happened," says Johnine, "in 1967 I lost by one vote because Bob didn't come in until the second night of the voting. This time, this other girl had a rig in, and her judges were ready. But the following year, 1968, I gave him an ultimatum—I had to win. So Hope came both nights of judging, and like, with everybody you can imagine. His agents . . . his managers . . . he even brought all his writers. This time Bob made sure I won."

A long account of this event appeared on the front page of the *Los Angeles Times* on August 19, along with a large photo of Bob Hope crowning Johnine Avery Miss World and giving her a kiss on her forehead.

The story was headlined:

LOSERS WALK OUT ON NEW
MISS WORLD

San Diego. UPI . . . The climatic moment had come. The crown was being lowered by Bob Hope on the lovely blond head of Miss World USA, 1968. And right then the losers began walking off the stage in a tizzy.

Miss Kansas, Jade Hagen, claimed that it was a fraud. She and four other also-rans said that they were going to get a lawyer . . .

Whether it was possible for Hope to have rigged the contest in favor of his girlfriend, or whether she was the most beautiful of the lot, really didn't matter in the larger scheme of things.

During Hope's relationship with Johnine, he never took her on any of his trips to Vietnam, as he had other beauty contest winners. He sent her postcards from there, however.

"I still have a couple of them," relates Johnine. "Also, I did go on lots of trips with him. Hundreds. And I was on his TV show a lot."

To prove it, she has photographs of herself doing comedy sketches with Hope, with Hope and Jimmy Durante; with Hope, Bing Crosby and Peter Leeds; and with Hope and Lee Marvin.

In New York City Johnine stayed with Hope in Room 610 of Hampshire house on Central Park South.

Hope became extremely jealous because she dated Bing Crosby a couple of times when Hope was out of the country. So Johnine broke off the relationship in March of '69, and went her own way without his assistance for about a year.

In June 1970, she married a man named Van Den Heever. This union ended eight months later. Because Johnine left him, she received no support money from him, and consequently was having financial troubles. "When I realized that I was in trouble, I went to Bob for help," says Johnine, "but he didn't want to be bothered, and neither did Mark Anthony, who was running his company."

In 1972 Johnine moved to Italy, where she got a job with a film distribution company. Today Johnine lives in a little villa in Rome. She operates as an independent film distributor. But until 1981, she would often rendezvous with Hope at his request in London or Paris or whatever European city he was visiting.

And on a number of occasions, when she had reasons to come to the States they'd get together and be intimate again. As of 1981, she had been with him four or five times since their breakup.

"We'd have dinner, and a drink, and a show or something," she reported. This would be a one-night stand, of course. The last time I really had it with him. He had me meet him in San Diego, which I did. He reserved a room at the Hilton, which used to be the Mission Inn, when we first used to meet down there. Anyway, this time he checked out without me, and without paying the hotel bill. I was really pissed off."

39

Lest anyone get the idea that Bob Hope stopped all his other activities in order to play Casanova to Johnine Avery after he spent the night with her at the Mission Inn in 1965, this brief summary of his activities between then and 1970 ought to dispel any such notions.

In the summer of 1965, soon after he and Johnine got together, he shot the fifty-first film of his career. *Boy, Did I Get a Wrong Number*, at the Producer's Studio (actually the former Sam Goldwyn lot), on Santa Monica and Formosa Avenue in Hollywood. This film was produced by Eddie Small, directed by George Marshall, and costarred Elke Sommer and Phyllis Diller.

It was Phyllis Diller's first movie, and "I was green as grass," relates the comedienne who's apparently no innovator when it comes to originating similes. "I knew of Hope's reputation for using cue cards and that he couldn't get along without them, so I assumed there'd be cue cards for everyone in the cast. Consequently I didn't bother to memorize my lines. Well, I got on the set and there were no cue cards for anyone. Bob, it turned out, never used them when he was making a picture, because picture-making is serious acting! Ha! So there I am in the first scene and no cue cards. Panic, panic, panic. Geez, that was the fastest memorization job I ever did in my life."

The plot of *Boy, Did I Get a Wrong Number* had to do with a real estate agent who, while trying to phone his wife, accidentally becomes involved with a knockout runaway actress. It wasn't much of a script, and the reviews it received helped to explain why Hope was having such a difficult time getting financing and distribution for the story my collaborator, Bob Fisher and I had sold him.

Leonard Maltin, in his *Movie and Video Guide*, was succinct about *Boy, Did I Get a Wrong Number*: "They sure did. The result is a worthless film that should be avoided. Absolutely painful."

✿ ✿ ✿ ✿

The problem with Hope as a screen personality in 1965 was that he could no longer play the comic romantic leads of yesteryear. Girl chasing, girl ogling wasn't becoming to a sixty-two-year-old man who was on the verge of becoming a grandfather. Instead of being sympathetic in those parts, he came off as a buffoonish aging roue.

Tony Hope was already engaged, and would be married to his fiancée, Geraldine, in December of 1967. And Linda would become engaged in 1968.

Obviously Hope didn't face the fact that he was growing older, and could not do it too gracefully.

NBC was aware of this, so that when it renewed Hope's contract, it stipulated that in any films it financed, Hope was not to play the "romantic lead who gets the girl."

The aging process might have altered the formula of Hope's movie plots, but it didn't curtail his sexual drive.

After his affair with Marilyn Maxwell became public, Hope attempted to be more discreet. "Bob bedded lots of Las Vegas showgirls, but tried to keep a low profile," Jan King told the *Globe*. "After Marilyn Maxwell, Bob made sure that his celebrity lovers were kept under tight wraps.
While traveling, Hope preferred to pick up exotic local ladies instead.

"I was with him on several of his Vietnam Christmas trips, doing his secretarial work. Once he invited me and a couple of other staff members to have a drink in a Saigon bar. As soon as he walked in, one of the bar girls approached Bob, not knowing who he was. She did her usual playing up to the American, sitting on his lap and asking him to buy her a drink. And Bob behaved like thousands of other GIs, cuddling with her at a table.

"The Vietnamese woman was seductively dressed in a skin tight miniskirt and a low cut blouse that revealed most of her bosom. The girl eventually took Bob by the hand and led him out the back door of the bar and to her room upstairs."

✿ ✿ ✿ ✿

Hope finally got around to filming *Eight on the Lam* in the summer of 1966, but because he was no longer a "bankable" name by himself, before United Artists would take on the picture new characters had to be written into our script to accommodate additional marquee names. Jonathan Winters, Phyllis Diller and and Jill St. John were those stars.

Because my collaborator and I were in England at the time, opening our first play in London's West End, the rewrite chore was given to Al Lewin and Burt Styler. They were responsible for Hope's most recent film, *Boy, Did I Get a Wrong Number.*

After reading the revised script when the Writers Guild was determining the writing credits, I didn't bother to see the finished film because it was so different from our original. After reading the reviews when the film was released, I was sorry I had allowed my name to remain on it.

It was obvious from the reviews that Hope's film career was approaching the end.

All was not lost. Hope still had Vietnam, which a general referred to as "Hope's War," and there was his lucrative television deal with Chrysler and NBC.

For the 1966 Christmas tour of Southeast Asia including Vietnam, Hope had to do without Jerry Colonna, who had suffered a stroke. Eventually, partially paralyzed and with his

393

speech impaired, he was hospitalized at the Motion Picture Country Home and Hospital in California's Woodland Hills.

To replace Colonna, Hope hired Phyllis Diller. She joined Joey Heatherton, Anita Bryant and Vic Damone, and of course Les Brown and his Band. Hope also brought along Dolores and his two younger children, Nora and Kelly, so they wouldn't have to spend another Christmas without him.

Phyllis Diller was a hit with the troops, as she competed with Joey Heatherton's sexy good looks. But Dolores's appearance was the smash of the Christmas night show. Originally she was only expected to take a bow, but after she stood up and was acknowledged by the audience with a loud enthusiastic cheer, Bob asked her, "How about singing 'White Christmas' for the guys?"

Dolores replied that she wasn't sure that she remembered the lyrics, but when Bob said he'd cue her if she forgot them, she complied and handled the assignment like an old pro.

She got a standing ovation from the GIs.

When that show was aired on *Chrysler Theater* in February of 1967, it again topped the Nielsen ratings, and won Hope a Peabody Award the following April. It was his second.

Chrysler was pleased with the Hope specials, but not with the rest of the anthology series, consequently the following *Variety* headline appeared on the day that the Nielsen ratings were published.

CHRYSLER AXES ONLY ANTHOLOGY FILM SERIES
ON TV—KEEPS HOPE NBC SPEX

Hope remained popular with television audiences, but there was a bothersome incident at his 1967 Christmas show in Vietnam.

Hope became more and more publicly outspoken about his warlike feelings. And these feelings were beginning to infiltrate his comedy monologues. Consequently he was starting to lose laughs, instead of getting the big yaks from the GIs that he was used to. Based on his first two performances in Vietnam in '67, the soldiers to whom he was playing apparently didn't appreciate Hope's controversial quips, especially about home-front problems. They were more concerned with ducking Viet Cong and Hanoi's anti-aircraft fire.

As always there were wolf whistles and howls of appreciation when Hope unveiled such dazzling beauties as Raquel Welch and Maedle Hartog Bell of Peru, who was Miss World of 1967. But when he started cracking jokes about the demonstrators and draft card burners back in the States, the Marines at DeNang were strangely silent. Moreover, at another air base the following night there was only mild response to such Hope patter as: "I bring you great news from the land of liberty . . . It's still there even if you have to cross a picket line to enjoy it."

Some of his former sure-fire gags missed completely. Gags about Lyndon Johnson, Charles De Gaulle and Ronald Reagan, "the only man who doesn't know he's running for President."

Because of the controversy raging over the war back in the States, GIs found it no laughing matter. Resentment toward Hope was beginning to grow—possibly because the GIs were beginning to feel he was having fun and making a profit from the war, while they were suffering and risking their lives.

In 1967 there was even anti-Bob Hope propaganda coming from the Soviet Union official newspaper *Izvestia*. It was quoted in the Hollywood *Citizen News:*

[February 16, 1967]

REDS SAY HOPE TAKES NAKED GIRLS TO GIs

The Soviet government newspaper *Izvestia* has charged that comedian Bob Hope, "a Pentagon clown," and a "salesman for aggression," had taken a troupe of naked women to Vietnam simply to publicize a "dirty war."

While Hope's official reason for going to Vietnam was to raise troop morale, *Izvestia* said, his actual purpose is publicity for the Pentagon, publicity for the "dirty war."

The paper said that in Hope's shows "half naked girls" were

singing. More naked girls were dancing. And in between, Bob Hope, the Pentagon's worthy jester, was clowning.

"Bob Hope plays the unattractive role of a comedian without principles, a salesman of aggression and a Pentagon clown," *Izvestia* said.

The paper illustrated its article with two photographs of Hope, one in Vietnam and one advertising luggage.

It is easier to advertise luggage than to "advertise the dirty war," *Izvestia* said.

Was Hope losing touch with the GI sense of humor? Or had he failed to recognize what other big name entertainers had already realized: nobody wanted to be associated with the war in any way.

As the war became increasingly unpopular the really big names bowed out as far as entertaining troops was concerned. (Jane Fonda had even joined the other side.)

Consequently the USO eventually had to rely on bush-league acts like "The Sig Sockowich Show" or Manny Fuller and his Nebraska Playboys, and a handful of faithful, outspokenly patriotic personalities such as Sebastian Cabot, Raymond Burr, Martha Raye, George Jessel and, of course, "Rapid Robert Hope."

Through the late sixties, Hope became even more outspoken. In an interview with *Variety*, on January 11, 1968, there was this:

Hope said that he shared the belief of General Westmoreland that the war should be escalated . . . While admitting he was talking for himself and not the generals, Hope said he was expecting something big to happen soon. Maybe not THE BOMB, but crippling air strikes in hot pursuit of the enemy into bordering neutral countries. He doesn't share the beliefs that this being a presidential election year has anything to do with military strategy. 'We are out to win it, and as soon as we can, to save American lives. The thinking in Washington is getting more hawkish.'"

That interview came out the week before the airing of his January 18 special about his 1967 Christmas trip to Vietnam.

Again his Nielsen ratings were high, but not what they'd been in previous years. The public was tiring of his Christmas shows.

Hope may have had strong feelings about the war and questioned anyone's patriotism who opposed it, but he kept a large degree of separation from most other current matters of controversy. The civil rights movement, for example. When a reporter asked him in 1966 whether he'd been involved in it, he replied, almost proudly, "not at all."

Mort Sahl recalls Hope rushing up to him during that period to tell him the latest Martin Luther King joke: "Have you heard—L.B.J. is making Martin Luther King pope so he doesn't have to kiss anything but his ring."

Jokes about King weren't popular after the civil rights leader was assassinated on April 4, 1968. The King murder postponed for two days the Academy Awards show which Hope was emceeing. Undeterred by the assassination, Hope led off his monologue with, "About the delay of two days . . . it didn't affect me, but it's been tough on the nominees. How would you like to spend two days in a crouch?"

Not funny. Socially conscious Academy members greeted it with silence.

What some critics were now saying about Bob Hope was that his disinclination to probe beneath the surface of life produced a prefabricated humor which simply wasn't funny anymore in a world that had so many serious problems.

"Some audiences laugh even before Hope's punch lines, as if they were responding not to the joke but to the man," wrote one critic. "We're programmed to laugh at certain people. For more than a generation we've been told Bob Hope is one of the funniest men alive. So we laugh even when it isn't funny any more."

While being interviewed for an article about Hope for *The New York Times Magazine* in 1970, Mort Lachman, Hope's head writer and sometime producer, conceded that his boss was a "limited comedian. He can't do faces or pantomime. He's not a physical comic at all. He doesn't tell stories particularly well. He's the worst dialect-man I've ever heard. But he just happens to be the greatest monologist in the business."

Phyllis Diller, on the other hand, disagrees with Lachman about Hope's inability to do dialects. "He does two great dialects—Negro and fag—he just can't do them in public!"

✿ ✿ ✿ ✿

Hope may have lost favor with the public over his Vietnam stand, but in government circles within the so-called "loop," his approval rating was high. He was a favorite of Lyndon Johnson, who by 1968 had lost so much popularity that he had dropped out of the presidential race.

But when Nixon and Agnew were elected in 1968, Hope, a Republican, had an even closer tie to the White House. Nixon, of course, was trying to end the war with his well-publicized "secret plan." Or at any rate, that was the platform on which he ran for the presidency. But Agnew was as big a hawk as anyone, and in addition he hated the press. He and Hope had a great deal in common.

The two of them had met for the first time in 1968 when Agnew was still governor of Maryland, and Hope had gone to Baltimore to accept the Humanitarian Award from Variety Clubs International. They sat next to each other on the dais and apparently they hit it off immediately. The governor made what Hope recalled as a "nice little speech"; in response, Hope cracked that "Agnew could make it in our racket. With the right kind of makeup man he could really move."

But Agnew's favorite Hope joke of the evening was, "I used to play a little football, but I had to quit because I was ticklish. I played center and I kept laughing when the quarterback put his hands between my legs."

Agnew left that banquet believing that Bob Hope was the most "wonderful guy I ever met."

Barely two months later Agnew was nominated for the vice-presidency in Miami, and Hope sent him a telegram:

SEE WHAT ONE DINNER WITH ME WILL DO.
BOB HOPE

That cemented the relationship.

✿✿✿✿

During the campaign, Hope and Agnew spoke frequently on the telephone. Sometimes Agnew would call to ask for a joke to use as an opener for one of his speeches. Ever ready to oblige a fellow hawk, Hope would direct his gag men to get right on it.

Sometimes the two men talked at midnight to trade the latest joke. Agnew loved jokes of any kind—especially dirty ones, and no one enjoyed telling them more than Hope did.

✿✿✿✿

On the home front, there were some interesting developments. Not all good. The week after Hope returned home from Baltimore where he met Agnew for the first time, he was to start his next picture, *How to Commit Marriage*, a costarring vehicle with Jackie Gleason. However he had a recurrence of the eye ailment, his third since 1958. Hope was confined to his home by Doc Hearn. After a couple of weeks' rest, hiding behind dark glasses, Hope's left eye improved and he was able to again go before the cameras.

How to Commit Marriage was a generation gap comedy. It focused on the changing morality in the sixties in general with emphasis on sex. The story was written by Ben Starr and the late Mike Kanin, and directed by Norman Panama. In a nut-shell the plot was: Hope and Jane Wyman, who played his wife, were about to divorce when their daughter announced plans to marry Jackie Gleason's son.

✿✿✿✿

Although it had an imaginative premise, *How to Commit Marriage* turned out to be the last Hope film to make a profit at the box office. And unfortunately Louis Shurr, who was responsible for calling the story to Hope's attention, never got to see the finished product.

In November of 1968, Shurr died of pancreatic cancer at Cedars-Sinai Hospital in Los Angeles. He'd been ill for a year, and in and out of the hospital a good portion of that time. During the final months of Shurr's hospitalization, and whenever he was in town, Hope would leave his home around two A.M., drive to Cedars, and sit by Doc Shurr's bedside to keep him company. They'd sit and talk and discuss the old show biz days.

Since Shurr spent every nickel he earned, according to his partner, Al Melnick, he died broke. There were no funds for his hospital stay or his doctor bills or even his funeral. Hope paid for everything.

On a happier note, Linda Hope became engaged to Nathaniel Greenblatt, a former creative project director at Time Inc., on October 21, 1968. Nat was the son of a prominent Augusta, Georgia doctor. He was an alumnus of Duke University and had done graduate work at Oxford.

Linda and Nat met on the Universal Studios lot, where Greenblatt was a producer. "But before Bob would approve the match," recalls Kay Avalon, who was one of the bridesmaids when the lavish wedding took place two months later, "Bob insisted that Nat change his name from Greenblatt to Lande. I was at the dinner table one night when heard them discussing this."

There can be only one possible explanation for Hope's insistence on the name change. But as Shakespeare might have put it, "A Greenblatt by any other name is still a Jew."

However there was no attempt to fool God at the wedding, on January 11, 1969, at St. Charles Church in North Hollywood. After a Catholic monsignor married Nathaniel and Linda, a rabbi gave the couple a rabbinical blessing. Apparently this was a concession to the groom's parents.

Bob Hope, in tails, ascot tie and gray vest, gave the bride away as Dolores, her mother, and Dr. and Mrs. Greenblatt watched. A family portrait showing the entire group in formal attire graced the social page of the *Los Angeles Times* the next day.

The groom looked like a character out of the Ascot scene in *My Fair Lady*. He wore a gray silk topper, tails and morning trousers. Greenblatt, six-foot-six, towered above everybody in the photo, this caused Hope to remark, "I'm glad we're finally getting a control tower in the family."

The reception was held on Hope's estate a few miles away. A white silk circus tent was set up in the garden. It was probably the glitziest social event that the hamlet of Toluca Lake had ever witnessed.

Among the name guests, feasting on champagne and cracked crab, were Vice President Spiro Agnew and his wife Judy; Governor Ronald Reagan and Nancy; Ohio's Governor Jim Rhodes; former California Governor Goodwin Knight; and former Senator George Murphy, who was responsible for Hope and Dolores's "storybook" marriage. And, indeed, storybook is the proper adjective, since at the time Murphy allegedly got those two together, Hope was still married to Grace Louise Troxell.

Among the other important guests were Generals Jimmy Doolittle and Omar Bradley; Cardinal McIntyre of Los Angeles; MCA founder Jules Stein; MCA President Lew Wasserman; MCA Vice-President Jennings Lang; plus Danny Kaye, Gregory Peck, Jack and Mary Benny, Danny Thomas, Loretta Young, Irene Dunne, Dorothy Lamour, Bing and Kathy Crosby. Kay Avalon and Ann Rapp were bridesmaids.

There was a dance floor built over the swimming pool, with two rotating bands for nonstop dancing. There was also a mountain of wedding gifts.

At the height of the festivities, Hope strode to the bandstand and quieted the guests with a wave of his hand. Nodding toward the bride and groom, Hope said, "When Linda was young I traveled so much she rarely saw me. When she did, she thought I was the gas meter man trying to get fresh with her mother." Then turning to Nora, who was standing with her fiancé, Sam

McCullagh, he suggested, "Why don't you two get married now before we have to strike the set?"

✿ ✿ ✿ ✿

There are no figures available as to how many thousands this little shindig set back the father of the bride, but no doubt much of it was probably deductible as a business expense. But dollars don't a marriage make. This one lasted six years. Linda's close friend Kay Avalon believes "Linda was never really in love with Nat. She just married him because she felt that at twenty-nine, she ought to be married. And I don't believe he loved her either. He was just using her and her connections."

It's also been rumored that Lande tried to pull some financial chicanery involving Linda's money at the time of the separation that didn't sit too well with Hope. "I heard that Hope used his connections with a couple of hoods who ran a restaurant on the Sunset Strip to run Nat out of town when he started to become a nuisance to the family," reports another close girlfriend of Linda's who knew them both.

✿ ✿ ✿ ✿

Since her divorce, and much to her conservative father's displeasure, Linda surfaced as a lesbian.

40

Shortly after the reception, Linda and Nat went on a six-week honeymoon that took them to the Caribbean and South America.

Hope, meanwhile, having had his fill of family life, took off in the vice-president's private jet, with Spiro and Judy Agnew to attend the Super Bowl game the next day, in Miami.

He was back in Toluca Lake in time to watch the broadcast on January 16, 1969, of his fifth Vietnam Christmas show. His ratings were higher than his previous Christmas special, which convinced him that the public appreciated what he was doing for our fighting men, even if certain liberals did not.

Spurred on by this vote of confidence, he flew to Oakland to appear at a benefit with astronaut Walt Cunningham at a Youth of America show. His high didn't last for long. During his performance, his vision became blurry again.

Knowing this was the start of more eye hemorrhaging, he phoned Dr. Reese and was told to check into the Jules Stein Eye Clinic at UCLA for observation and possible treatment.

The treatment again consisted of rest in a dark room, this time for three days. The attending eye specialist instructed him to take it easy for at least a month.

His eye responded to the rest. As soon as vision returned, he was back doing the only thing that made him happy: doing benefits and college shows all over the country and golfing with bigwigs, including a round with former Air Force secretary Stuart Symington at Burning Tree Country Club. He used that occasion to drop into the Walter Reed Hospital to visit former President Eisenhower, whose health, according to Mamie, was failing fast.

Then it was back to California to prepare for his April 11 television show. He had just settled down to work when Eisenhower died, on March 28. He and Dolores flew to Washington to attend the funeral service at Arlington.

Except for Nora's engagement to Sam McCullagh, an administrator at the University of San Francisco, at the beginning of April and their subsequent marriage in August, the rest of 1969 seemed to be filled with illness and death in Bob Hope's circle.

The funeral services for Eisenhower were barely over when Hope received word that his brother George had been hospitalized with a life-threatening stomach ailment at Cedars-Sinai in Los Angeles. Hurrying back to the coast with Dolores, Bob went straight to the hospital from the airport. George seemed out of danger. So Hope took another plane to Palm Springs to be at Nora's engagement party the following day.

After taping his television special, he attended an engagement party for Mort Lachman and his fianceé, spent the night in Toluca Lake, and drove to Palm Springs the next day to be with Dolores, who was being made Honorary Mayor.

On April 14 he was at the annual Academy Awards bash, but only to make a brief appearance as a presenter. He gave the Jean Hersholt Humanitarian Award to old Paramount pal and Vietnam stalwart, Martha Raye.

The Oscar show changed its location that year, moving from the Pantages Theater to the 3,400 seat Dorothy Chandler Pavilion at the Music Center in downtown Los Angeles. For the first time there was no single emcee, which was the reason Hope's appearance was brief. A new era of Academy Award shows was ushered in. Most opinion is that they've never been as good as when Hope did them as a single.

On April 27, he was at the University of Miami in Oxford,

Ohio, accepting another honorary degree. Feeling dizzy again he went straight to New York City where, according to a wire service story: "Bob Hope underwent light coagulation treatment at the Institute of Opthalmolgy at Columbia Presbyterian Medical Center here over the weekend. Hope entered the hospital after a recurrence of an old ailment in his left eye. The treatment is known as xemomarc photocoagulation, designed to cauterize hemorrhaging vessels in the eye."

That story appeared on May 5, 1969. Now Hope got the fright of his life. After five days in the hospital Hope was told by Dr. Reese that he had had his last photocoagulation treatment. There was nothing left to work with but scar tissue, so the only treatment that could possibly do him any good in the future was not to work so hard.

Hope was not up to taking it easy.

In June he traveled to West Point to entertain at the senior class's graduation eve banquet; three days later he appeared at Madison Square Garden at a Republican fund raiser for Nelson Rockefeller. Then he flew to Columbus, Ohio, to attend another commencement banquet, this one for the Ohio State graduating class, where he also received another honorary degree.

Following that he flew to Portland, Oregon, to make an appearance at that city's annual Rose Festival. He took off for Chicago the next day to attend the premiere of *How to Commit Marriage.*

Business was good, due to the pairing of Hope with Jackie Gleason. And so that he shouldn't have a spare minute on his hands, he dropped down to Bowling Green University in Ohio, to receive his thirteenth honorary degree and do a little off-the-cuff entertaining.

While he was on the stage doing his act, his brother, Ivor, the oldest of the seven brothers, died of a heart attack in Gate's Mills, Ohio. He had spent his last years, running, in partnership with Bob, the Hope Metal Products Company—which stamped out metal partitions for toilets.

Of the original seven brothers, only Bob and Fred, who was still in the wholesale meat business, were standing at the grave site to say good-bye to Ivor. Both George, who was recuperating from his stomach operation, and Jim, who was suffering from severe emphysema, remained in California.

But death was still not taking a holiday in Hope's life in the first half of 1969. No sooner did Hope return to Palm Springs than he was informed by Mary Hope, George's wife, that George was terminally ill with throat cancer.

Since there was no telling how long George could hang on—weeks, months, maybe even a year—Hope left L.A. in June, after visiting his brother in the hospital, for a four-day engagement at the Pike's Peak Festival in Colorado Springs. His playing dates were from June 21 to 25.

The Air Force flew Hope, for free, to Colorado Springs as part payment for all the good work he'd done for the armed forces.

When he arrived at Colorado Springs he learned that the advance ticket sale for his show was disappointing. Nothing can make an entertainer less enthusiastic about doing a show than playing to half-filled houses. As a result, he gave his first performance there very little of his well-known energy.

During the show he received word that George had died. This was less than a week after Ivor's death.

Between the attendance and the news about George, Hope had had his fill of Pike's Peak. He told the management he was sorry, but he had to return to Los Angeles for his brother's burial. Even a funeral was preferable to playing to empty houses in Pike's Peak.

The manager threatened to sue him for breach of contract. Hope told him not to worry; he'd get Danny Thomas to fill in for him. And he did. But that didn't satisfy the manager, who felt that Hope could have worked until the 24th, and then flown back for the funeral on the 25th.

Hope left anyway, and on October 19 the manager of the Turf Club of Pike's Peak sued him for $112,000, charging breach of contract.

The suit never reached court. Hope settled by sending the night club owners a check for $12,500. He'd received an advance of $37,000.

41

Despite the antiwar feeling spreading like an out-of-control forest fire, by the fall of 1969, Hope didn't believe we should pull out of Vietnam at any price.

Albert Lasker, president of Lord & Thomas when Hope started on the air for Pepsodent, once cautioned him, "Never take sides in a political issue because both Republicans and Democrats buy toothpaste."

Hope had lived by that advice for most of his career, but by 1969 he had become so hysterically emotional about Vietnam that he threw caution to the wind. After all, he had $400 million to protect from the Communists.

He supported the sentiments of his newest pal in the White House, Richard Nixon, who after being sworn in to office said, "I don't intend to be the first President to lose a war."

Hope was far to the right politically, and he condemned those who believed otherwise. He believed that people objecting to the war were giving comfort to the enemy.

More than half of Hope's appearances during Nixon's first term were on college and university campuses, where, according to reports he brought back home, his "reception was just marvelous."

Most of the colleges he played couldn't very well be considered bastions of liberalism. They were Arkansas, South Caro-

lina, Georgia, Clemson, Bradley, Auburn, and SMU, where in
October he appeared in a revival of *Roberta* on the stage of the
newly-built Bob Hope Theater.

His co-stars for that one were John Davidson and Janis Paige.
The latter was a veteran of several of his Vietnam tours, and,
according to Jan King, one of the few name actresses he was
intimate with on his tours.

Opening night tickets at SMU sold for $500 each to wealthy
Texans, who made up most of the audience, and the profits from
that two-week engagement went to the Bob Hope Scholarship
Fund at SMU.

Later in the month, Hope and Dolores arrived in Washington
for an Eisenhower birthday dinner—another high-powered
fund-raising event to help perpetuate Eisenhower College.

On the podium, Hope's anti-Democratic remarks naturally hit
their mark: "Good evening Republicans . . . and Democrats. I
like to include the help . . . Eisenhower College . . . it'll be the
first school to offer a degree in golf . . . I'm delighted to be here
for a fine cause . . . I think it's a great idea . . . Our future
Republicans have to come from somewhere . . ."

After that, Hope embarked on his fall college tour. At
Clemson on October 25, Hope did another show for the
students. In an interview with a female reporter before the
performance, Hope was asked why he opposed immediate
withdrawal from Vietnam. He replied "Because it's not a good
answer." The reporter persisted, "Don't you find more and
more students opposing that view?"

"I've found very little of that. It's just small minorities on
campus who make headlines. And the news media is guilty of
blowing every antiwar event way out of proportion."

Later he was asked by the president of Clemson, Robert
Edwards, to attend a reception to meet with the wives and
widows of fighter pilots who had been shot down over North
Vietnam, and were either missing or prisoners.

In his enthusiasm, Hope sounded like one of those flag-
waving politicians that you might find in an Oliver Stone movie.
To lend this credence, the setting for his appearance at Bradley

University in November looked like a scene straight out of one of those films. Hope was brought out to a platform in the center of the Bradley gymnasium by an honor guard of eight pompom cheerleaders. A blue gray spotlight followed him out as a band blared out "Thanks for the Memory," and the crowd rose to its feet and remained there cheering. Behind Hope, on the wall, was a huge American flag.

His monologue was filled with jokes that Hope and his writers knew would get big laughs. They did. But one line, though few in the audience realized it, was the height of hypocrisy coming from such a womanizer as Hope.

"I don't believe in all that sexual permissiveness you hear about today. Maybe it's because I'm at the age when my bag is my lunch."

In reality Hope was at least fifteen years away from the time when he'd stop his wide and varied extramarital activity. As recently as the mid-eighties, he still had a mistress living in Burbank, whom he visited regularly.

Jeanne Carmen, Hope's trick golfing playmate with whom he'd been intimate in the fifties, was living in Phoenix in 1972, when she read that Bob was in town, staying at the Camelback Inn.

Since they were still friendly, but hadn't been in touch with each other for a while, Jeanne decided to give him a call at the hotel and say, "hello."

He took her call as soon as the operator told him who was on the line. Remember me? This is Jeanne Carmen."

"Gee, Jeanne, I'm on my way to the airport now. You should have called earlier," he exclaimed. "I woke up this morning with the biggest hard-on you ever saw. I had to drop the window on it."

"It must have been a small window," she retorted. "It's not that big."

42

In November of 1969, Hope reprised his SMU production of *Roberta* as a television special, with the cast he'd used at SMU: Janis Paige, John Davidson and Michele Lee. (This was his second TV *Roberta*.) Shortly after that, as a favor to Davidson, he flew to Las Vegas, to introduce the singer at the Riviera, where he was opening on the same bill with comedienne Joan Rivers.

Since she was costarring, Rivers thought it would be appropriate if Hope introduced her, too, but Hope refused. "My manager was furious," wrote Rivers in her book, *Still Talking*, and he said to Hope, 'You must introduce her. You are implying that Joan is just a little warm-up opening act, and here's the real show now with John.' But word came back from Hope, 'No way.'

"Well, I came onto that stage opening night with my adrenalin pumping—furious that a man of such stature could be so mean. In the front row were June Haver and Fred MacMurray, and on my first line, June fell apart. What joy. I felt the whole audience was with me.

"Backstage Bob Hope was pacing up and down saying, 'Get her off. She's wearing them out.' Angry. Pacing. 'Get her off!' When I came off, high from that audience, he stalked past me, went to the microphone and said, 'That girl is too funny for her own good,' then did a whole routine of his own to make them forget me, to show that he was better."

Hope finished out 1969 by taking a troupe of performers on a tour to entertain America's servicemen—only this time the tour would circle the globe.

He put on his first show in the Blue Room at the White House for Pat and Richard Nixon. That was followed by a dinner with the President and First Lady, to which everyone in Hope's cast was invited. Hope sat at one end of the long table, with Pat, while Connie Stevens, his female star of the show, sat on the other end alongside the President. Also at the dinner were Attorney General John Mitchell and Martha, Maj. Charles Robb and Lynda Bird, David and Julie Eisenhower, Henry and Christina Ford, and cartoonist Al Capp.

❉ ❉ ❉ ❉

From Washington the Air Force plane carried Hope and his group to Berlin, Rome, Ankara, Bangkok, and finally Vietnam. Along the way sexy German film star Romy Schneider joined the cast as did astronaut Neil Armstrong, the first man to walk on the moon.

Hope's alignment with the extreme right wing, and his public pronouncements that there should be no end of the war without total victory by the United States, got him in trouble with GI audiences.

An early indication of this was when he told the troops at Lai Khe in Vietnam that the President had assured him personally that he had a plan for peace. Instead of the customary cheers, he was greeted by boos. (The booing, of course, was cut when the show was edited for home TV consumption, on January 15.)

Except for his television commitments to Chrysler, Hope spent the most of 1970 helping to raise the $7 million needed to construct the Eisenhower Medical Center in Palm Desert, and trying to get his "don't pull out of the war" message across to college audiences.

On January 20, Hope picked up the $70,000 tab at a

Waldorf-Astoria banquet. Fifteen hundred guests in black tie paid $1,000 each to attend. The $1.5 million raised was earmarked for the Eisenhower Building Fund. Entertainment was donated by Raquel Welch, Bing Crosby, Johnny Cash, Ray Bolger, and of course, Hope.

There were other fund-raising luncheons and dinners throughout the rest of 1970. In addition, Hope received pledges of $125,000 each from Frank Sinatra, Irving Berlin and composer Fritz (*My Fair Lady*) Loewe, who also willed to the hospital all his royalties from that hit musical after his death.

In the fall of 1970 *Life* magazine assigned writer Joan Barthel to accompany Hope on a three-day swing of paid appearances in the midwest. It started in Chicago, then encompassed Flint, Michigan, and finally South Bend, Indiana, in Notre Dame's new twelve-hundred-seat convocation center.

At South Bend he was invited to attend the Notre Dame-Georgia Tech football game as the guest of honor and to receive, at half-time, a "Salute to Bob Hope."

The salute was arranged by Edward "Moose" Krause, the school's athletic director.

"At half-time," wrote the *Life* reporter, "Moose Krause and a guard of ushers escorted Hope from the president's box down a ramp and onto the field. The band swung into Hope's theme, and he grabbed a baton, clowning to cheers and applause.

"Krause introduced him as a great American, and Hope stepped to the microphone. As he did, booing suddenly came from the upper stand—long, loud, drawn-out booing. Spectators turned, and everyone on the field looked up toward the students standing in a block, gesturing thumbs down. Krause glared in anger; Hope just looked up at the stands, eyes narrowed, in a tight half-smile . . ."

After the game, in the limousine that took them from the stadium, Hope was plainly embarrassed about the booing. He said to Joan Barthel, "That wasn't booing, you know. They saw Moose Krause on the field with me, and they were cheering him. They were saying 'Moo—mooooo—mooooo.'

"The night before, at Flint, Michigan, Hope had called the war 'a beautiful thing—we paid in a lot of gorgeous American lives, but we're not sorry for it.'"

The "beautiful thing" line stirred up bad publicity for Hope, who denied ever saying that the war was a "beautiful thing." "What I did say was that I thought the guys doing the fighting were beautiful, because they were serving their country and doing their duty," Hope insisted, in an interview with the *Los Angeles Times* on March 17, 1971.

Joan Barthel, however, wasn't buying his assertion that she had misquoted him in *Life*, because she had been with him at Flint the night before and had taped the entire show and could prove that he said what she said he did.

A couple of weeks after Barthel's cover story on Hope, in which she recounted his hostile college receptions, *Life* carried a number of angry letters:

Sirs:

I find it sadly ironic that your Jan. 29th issue features both an article on the horrors of war and an article on a man who calls this abominable conflict "a beautiful thing." Perhaps Mr. Hope is correct in saying the Notre Dame students were cheering "Moooooo, Mooooo." However, to this great American who says we paid in a lot of gorgeous American lives, but we're not sorry for it, I would only like to say—loudly and clearly—Boooooo, Boooooo, Booooo.

James Johnson
Jamaica, N.Y.

Sirs:

Having lost my son in Vietnam, God save us from the likes of Bob Hope. What a misery they have caused.

Mrs. John Modderman
Grand Rapids, Michigan

Sirs:

Thank you for giving me an insight into what Bob Hope really thinks. I can see now that he is as much a double talker as the men in the Administration.

Deborah McDonald
Plains, Ohio

Sirs:

I wonder if Joan Barthel could script a "Road to Nowhere" for Bob Hope with Spiro Agnew as costar.

Judy Anderson
Arlington, Texas

Another criticism now leveled at Hope because of his pro-war stance was that his Vietnam Christmas shows (from which he profited enormously when they were shown as regular programming on television) were only made possible by substantial logistical support from the Department of Defense. The Pentagon supplied a C-140 transport to fly Hope, his cast and film crew—seventy-three persons in all. It supplied helicopters to ferry them from base to base and from base to hotel in Vietnam. It furnished ground transportation at every stop. Other incidental expenses such as for food while in the field, stages and sound systems, and the time of escort and Special Service men assigned to the troupe, ran the cost to the taxpayer up into six figures.

✿ ✿ ✿ ✿

I was with Bob Hope during some of this controversy, because my collaborator Bob Fisher and I were writing our fourth picture for him called *Cancel My Reservation*. I remember meeting him in his dressing room at NBC in Burbank to get approval of our story just after the *Life* article appeared. Hope kept insisting he'd been misquoted.

As Groucho Marx might have put it, "Who are you going to believe—Hope or that crooked tape recorder?"

Although Hope's last film, *How to Commit Marriage*, had

turned a small profit, he had no luck in getting another project off the ground. His contract with NBC called for them to advance $1 million toward the production of any film his company made with them. The million dollars wasn't cumulative however. This meant that if he didn't make a movie for a year, as happened in 1970, he didn't get to put that million towards his next film, should there be a next film. NBC kept it.

Since Hope Enterprises hadn't been able to find a suitable script for him in 1970, Hope was talked into buying the rights to a Louis L'Amour novel and have his company produce it as a serious Western. That way Hope wouldn't be tossing the million dollars down the drain by not making any film. Never mind that he wasn't going to be in it.

But whoever wrote the screenplay was unable to come up with a draft that pleased either Hope or Tom Sarnoff, who was the NBC rep on all Hope Enterprise projects. Consequently Bob Fisher and I received a call from our agent in the beginning of 1971 advising us to run out to Hope Enterprises in the Valley and take a meeting with a man named Mark Anthony who was working for Hope in some undefined capacity. "He may have a picture for you guys to write," said our agent.

Since we had nothing else to do, we drove out to see Anthony who was holed up in a small office in the Hope Enterprise Building on Riverside Drive in Burbank. We'd never met Anthony before, but we'd heard of him, and that he'd worked for Hope for twenty years.

"Mark used to book girlie shows out of San Francisco," says Robert Slatzer. "That's how Hope met him and why he put him on his payroll."

A pleasant man, who seemed dwarfed behind the big flattop desk that took up most of the office, Anthony shook our hands, offered us coffee, and said Hope Enterprises owned a script that he wanted us to turn into a comedy for "The Boss." It was based on a Louis L'Amour Western, and Hope planned to produce it, with a serious actor playing the part. But since no one liked the script, he didn't want to waste the money he'd already spent acquiring the rights.

"Take it home and read it and come back and tell us what you think," said Anthony, handing us both the novel and a script, which was bound in a blue cover. "Hope thinks you're the boys to do it."

Never ones to turn down an opportunity to get a feature writing credit, we felt we were "the boys to do it" too, until we went home and read the script.

We returned to Anthony's office for another meeting. We told him that there was no way the L'Amour story could be turned into a Bob Hope vehicle. It wasn't constructed for comedy and just putting some funny lines into the mouth of the main character wasn't going to help. You needed a story that led to comedic situations. We suggested that they deep-six the script and assign us to write an original new story suited to fit Bob Hope's style.

But Mark Anthony replied that Hope didn't want to throw out the L'Amour book, and that "if you want the job you'll have to make something out of this pile of shit."

We said we'd try to come up with a concept. Anthony cautioned us that Hope want wouldn't to pay for it until he saw and liked it.

The L'Amour book was about a tribe of poor Indians who lived on a reservation in Arizona. They claimed that a white man had stolen a parcel of land that belonged to them and was trying to turn it into a real estate development. In the course of things, an Indian maiden has the papers to prove tribal claim to the land. She gets murdered. In a convoluted story line the hero gets blamed for it.

Realizing there wasn't much comedy in that premise, we concocted a whole new plot about a New York TV talk show host and his wife who are having martial trouble. The couple decides that the only way to save the marriage is for him to go out West and take a rest away from his wife. He'd spend a couple of weeks in a cabin they own in Arizona, which happens to be on the land the Indians believe belonged to the tribe.

The morning after his first night in the cabin, our hero wakes up with a dead Indian girl beside him. From that moment on he's the prime murder suspect. So instead of getting a much needed rest, he has to play detective and at the same time explain to his wife what he was doing in bed with a beautiful Indian maiden.

In the course of our scenario there were some comedy sequences, with Hope riding on the back of a motorcycle, and Hope on a mountain peak talking with an ancient Indian who has the answer to the mystery but who, unfortunately, doesn't speak or understand English. We had Hope trapped in a cave with his wife, with the heavies trying to knock him off, and Hope falling out of a helicopter into a lake.

We thought we'd done a pretty good job of writing a comedy for Hope, but after reading it, Tom Sarnoff threatened to throw it out because "it's not the Louis L'Amour novel."

We explained to Sarnoff why it wasn't, but he didn't have any instinct for comedy, and particularly what made a Bob Hope comedy. He got his job not through *The New York Times* but because his father was David Sarnoff, who founded NBC.

He stuck to his opinion and we stuck to ours—that before he reject our story, he should at least let Hope read it. He consented to this, but we expected that this film would be stillborn for Hope was somewhere in the U.S. and Sarnoff wasn't really sure where.

Two weeks later we heard from Sarnoff. Hope liked our concept and wanted us to turn it into a vehicle for him. So while Hope was traveling around the country to raise more dollars for the Eisenhower Medical Center, we spent our time writing a movie script called *Cancel My Reservation*. Along the way we'd discarded the Louis L'Amour title.

That spring we met twice with Hope at his home. He was cordial to us despite the reviews of the last film we'd done for him. Once, when we were having a meeting with him at his breakfast table overlooking his one-hole golf course, he even offered us tuna fish sandwiches.

I found Hope's suggestions for changes in the script were helpful and insightful. So were his casting ideas. Eva Marie Saint (who'd starred with him in the fifties in *That Certain*

Feeling) as his wife, Ralph Bellamy as the heavy, Keenan Wynn as the sheriff, Forrest Tucker as a policeman, and Chief Dan George, a real Indian as the Indian Chief. He also put a young girl in it named Anne Archer, who hadn't had much experience acting, but she was to play the beautiful Indian maiden.

Our problems stemmed from Hope's choice of director. Because critics were beginning to believe Hope's brand of comedy was old-timey—not like the new comics such as Woody Allen and Mel Brooks—Warner Brothers would only agree to make the film if Hope hired one of the new *au courant* directors instead of an established name like Jack Arnold or George Marshall, who'd done his latest films.

Hope hired Paul Bogart, who had worked mostly in television with credits on hit shows like *All in the Family*. He was an excellent director. The problem was he and Hope didn't agree on what was funny. Bogart had not directed a stand-up comic before, especially one that was a living legend.

"When I first read the script," recalls Bogart, "I said to myself, 'Oh, what fun it would be to make one of these pictures, with Bob Hope, with that kind of easy going attitude of his.' And the script had a certain simple charm.

"There wasn't a hell of a lot going on there but there was enough to drape his character on, and even Eva Marie's. So I called Eva Marie first and said, 'I understand you're going to do this picture, and I've been asked to direct it. What do you think? It might not be the right thing for me. I've never done this kind of comedy before, a comedy film that's wrapped around a personality.' And she told me, 'Oh, you'll love it . . . the set with Bob around it . . . is relaxed and easy and everyone's in a happy mood. And Bob's delightful to work with. He's so nice.'

"So I said 'yes' to my agent, I'll do it, and I signed the papers."

"The first thing I found," complains Bogart, "was that the script kept changing. Apparently Hope had writers all over the globe and he had sent them the script and every day new punch-up lines would come in, and they would go into the script at Hope's insistence. The script kept getting thicker and thicker until it was about the size of a Manhattan phone directory.

"The jokes came by mail, and I'd look at them and say, 'This is terrible. These jokes have nothing to do with the story. This is becoming all one gag.'

"I got so disconcerted, I tried to wriggle out of the assignment, right away, before the picture got started. But my agent warned me that if I walked, my film career would be over. So reluctantly I stayed. My relationship with Hope became cooler and cooler. Which is more than could be said for the trailers we all had to live in on the Arizona desert in mid-summer. The only one who had an air-conditioned trailer was Hope. He refused to spring for air-conditioned trailers for the rest of us.

"Hope and I disagreed on everything that had to do with the picture. We disagreed on Anne Archer, who was a beautiful young girl, very young in fact, and very healthy, a sexy young broad. But Hope didn't like what she was doing in the scenes with him. He complained to me that she wasn't sexy enough. She played the young Indian girl that he wakes up in bed with. We'd get into endless arguments about her. I'd say, 'What's she doing that's not sexy?' and he'd indicate the she should stick her chest out, wiggle her ass more. And I'd ask, 'Who the hell does that?' and he'd say, 'That's what Zsa Zsa and Eva Gabor do.' And I'd say, 'They aren't sexy. Kiss one of those women and you get a face full of makeup.'

"There were a lot of things about that production that were dark and ugly. For example, the cameraman was Russell Metty, who had a great reputation as a photographer. He was cool to me. He didn't like me. He and Forrest Tucker were like the classic Jew-haters of all time. I had this strong feeling, and I'm not terribly sensitive to this sort of thing unless it's dumped on me—I had this terrible feeling that they *were* Jew-haters.

"Tucker would make those sly remarks about Rosh Hashanah and Yom Kippur since part of the time we were shooting during the Jewish high holidays. Hope, of course, is not as unsubtle as Forrest Tucker was, but for some reason I felt he was part of that attitude.

"Then there was Keenan Wynn. He was drunk all the time and while we were in Arizona, he had an accident. He slammed his car into a tree or a lamppost on the corner and he had to go into the hospital for three weeks. We arranged to shoot around him."

After the accident, Hope referred to the place where Wynn wrapped his car around a tree as Keenan's Corner.

"Meanwhile," continues Bogart, "Hope kept changing everything. Nobody I ever knew had such disrespect for a script. Chief Dan George was in the picture, a very dignified Indian, and he was required to say some dialogue to Eva Marie. Hope had his writers write funny translations of what he was saying, subtitles, to put on the screen. Bad taste Indian jokes that were so offensive to the old man he almost quit.

"Like a lot of stars, too, Hope had to make you wait, not be ready, not show up. He doesn't wear a watch because he claims someone else will tell him the time when he wants to know. Evidently he didn't want to know. Before he arrived I'd set up a scene and we'd go through a rehearsal without him. Then he would turn up, and I'd say, 'Okay, Bob, here's what we're going to do. You're over here, and Eva's over there.' And he'd say, 'Oh, I hadn't thought of it that way.' And then I'd grit my teeth and say, 'Well, how have you thought of it, Bob?' and then he'd give me his concept, and we'd argue and argue in the hot sun because I felt he was all wrong.

"There were times when Hope could be charming . . . usually late at night when he was lonely and wanted someone to talk to. But most of the time he was damned difficult, and he could get really angry. I remember we were doing this scene where he presumably falls into a lake out of a helicopter. A stunt man did the fall of course, but then we needed shots of Bob floundering around in the water, which he was not very happy to do. I reminded him that we had to do them, and then lunch was called and he left the set to have a conversation with Dick Van Dyke who would come over to visit from Carefree, where he had a studio. Finally I said, 'Let's get back to work, Bob. You have to get in the water again,' and he asked, 'What for?' 'I don't have a shot of you getting out of the water,' I explained. He looked at me as if he wanted to kill me. Finally he got back in the water.

"His least attractive aspect is that he has no respect for his coworkers . . . especially his writers and directors. Unless they are the 'good old boys' who belong to his club, like Forrest Tucker.

"I remember the last days . . . we were shooting in Rockefeller Plaza in New York. It was the last scene of the picture. It took place at the skating rink. There were crowds forming to see what was going on, and they were held back by policemen and ropes. Meanwhile Hope kept us waiting for several hours.

"Anyway, he finally shows up, and I'm starting to feel feverish. I was coming down with something. I was actually very close to pneumonia. I started to explain to him, 'This is what we're going to do, Bob,' and he said, 'I don't see it that way.' Well, I completely lost my cool and started to scream, 'Well, how do you see it, Bob? Tell-me-how-you-fucking-well-see-it, Bob.' And before he could even answer I said, 'You know what, Bob, you're boring. This whole thing is fucking boring.' I could hear myself saying that over and over again, 'You're boring, you're BORING, FUCKING BORING!'

"Meanwhile, the crowd was hanging on every word and gaping. I don't know how we ever finished the scene, but we finally did and I went back to my hotel and called my doctor, and he said, 'You go to the hospital.' So I checked into the New York Hospital and was there for three weeks, recovering from the ordeal."

Bogart didn't know which one of the girls in the cast was Hope's, but he did say, "It was generally known around the set when we were in Arizona that Hope was having girls brought in all the time for his own pleasure."

My collaborator, Fisher, went to Sedona one week when they were down there to watch the shooting. When he came back he told me that one Friday evening Dolores showed up on the set unannounced and surprised Hope, who, until that moment had no plans to go away for the weekend. But one look at Dolores, and Hope suddenly remembered he had a charity golf match to play in Chicago on Saturday, and off he went, leaving Dolores in Sedona with egg on her face."

Cancel My Reservation previewed in Woodland Hills in the San Fernando Valley later that year. Fisher and I got there first, and Hope and his group arrived a short time later, followed by Paul Bogart. None of us was too happy about what we saw, but strangely enough, the picture was considered by Warners to be worthy of being booked into the Radio City Music Hall when it opened in 1972. It was Hope's one and only Radio City Music Hall movie.

"When I heard that, I went into a decline," remembers Bogart. "Because this was the worst work I'd ever had anything to do with. I couldn't imagine this turkey playing in that beautiful theater. The only thing that saved me was that two days after it opened, the Rockettes went on strike and the theater management used that as an excuse to close the theater down. It went dark for the first time in its history. I was so glad. And wouldn't you know? Pauline Kael actually reviewed it! She said, 'It was a new low.'"

❋ ❋ ❋ ❋

Paul Bogart was one of the first people I interviewed in connection with this book, and when he talked about Hope he expressed the rage he still felt twenty-two years later.

43

By the time he finished his last film, Hope had personally collected $4 million for the Eisenhower Medical Center. This, combined with what others had raised, enabled the hospital to open its doors in November of 1971. The dedication ceremony attracted big names. In addition to Hope's celebrity friends, there were Governor Ronald Reagan, Vice President Spiro Agnew, and President Richard Nixon and his wife Pat who flew into Palm Springs on Air Force One.

In December Hope took a show to Southwest Asia. This was to be his next to his last Christmas tour, and it had a twist to it. While in Bangkok, Hope got the notion that he could do something to help free the American POWs held in North Vietnam.

He phoned U.S. Ambassador Leonard Unger, and asked that he arrange a meeting to discuss his going to Hanoi to entertain the POWs. While there he felt he could get friendly with Hanoi's top officials and talk them into releasing the American men they were holding.

It was a daring move on Hope's part, possibly even a grandstand play for the benefit of his fans back in the States, because it was unlikely that anything would come of it. To almost everyone's surprise, the North Vietnamese agreed to see him in Vientiane, and he was flown to there in a CIA airplane.

He was given an interpreter, a Reverend Roffe, and the two of them were then taken to the North Vietnamese embassy, a modest, French Colonial house on the outskirts of the city.

Hope was not his usual confident self when he met with First Secretary Nguyen Van Tranh. The official was a polite man in his early thirties and pleasant when he and Hope engaged in preliminary small talk. But he lacked the authority to approve either a show for the POWs or their release.

In essence, Hope's proposal was that America would come up with lots of money for the release of the prisoners of war. Hope would also sponsor a Vietnam children's relief fund in the United States. Everyone of school age in America would contribute their nickels and dimes which would be given in turn to those Vietnamese children who'd been made homeless and parentless by the American presence.

Van Tranh was sympathetic but his final word was, "Nixon knows well that the prisoners will be released when your government agrees to a withdrawal date."

That was that, but when the news got to the American public about what Hope had tried to do for the POWs he again made the Gallop Poll list of the world's "Ten Most Admired Men." He'd dropped from it in recent years because of his hawkish propagandizing.

****

The new year started off promisingly enough for Hope, with his 1971 Christmas in Vietnam special again getting high Nielsen numbers. But then his world—at least an important part of his secret life—caved in on him, when he received word on March 21 that Marilyn Maxwell had been found dead in her Beverly Hills home. Her body was discovered by Mathew Davis, her fifteen-year-old son by writer Jerry Davis, from whom she had been divorced for a number of years.

According to the obituary in *The Hollywood Reporter*, the next day, "Miss Maxwell was last seen by her son Sunday night when she told him she was planning to go to the movies. Authorities said she apparently died of natural causes during the night. She is said to have been under a doctor's care for high blood pressure and pulmonary disease."

Actor John Conte, Marilyn Maxwell's first husband, told me recently that Marilyn had a congenital heart problem. "She used to say she knew she was going to die young. Her mother had died at an early age."

Marilyn Maxwell was forty-nine. Her funeral was held at the Beverly Hills Community Presbyterian Church on North Rodeo Drive, the following Friday. It was attended by a number of show business luminaries, including Rock Hudson, Jimmy Durante, and Dorothy Lamour. Bob Hope delivered the eulogy with misty eyes.

"'If all her friends were here today we'd have to use the Colosseum," Hope told a packed house from the pulpit. "Marilyn had an inner warmth and love for people . . . and the thousands of servicemen she entertained over the years felt this. Who would have thought that this little girl from Clarinda, Iowa, would do this much and go as far as she did?

"Who knows why some of us are called earlier than others? Maybe God needed a lovely gal to sing and cheer him up, and so he called her . . . I must say it was a great job of casting."

Hope was pale and shaken when he left the church, wearing a dark suit, black tie, with a white carnation in his buttonhole, and made his way through the crowd to a waiting limousine.

Dolores, usually at his side to bolster his spirits on such somber occasions, was conspicuous by her absence.

❊ ❊ ❊ ❊

Dolores was with him, however, during his highly publicized two-week tour for the GIs the following Christmas, 1972. Since the United States had withdrawn all of its ground combat troops from Vietnam four months earlier this was to be the last of his Christmas tours for the government. The cast included Redd Foxx, dancer Lola Falana, L.A. Rams quarterback Roman Gabriel, Dolores and a bevy of beauty contest winners called "The American Beauties."

Though the ground fighting was over, there was still Air

Force personnel in South Vietnam to whom Hope brought Christmas cheer. According to the *Detroit Free Press*, "The hit of the final show was Dolores singing "White Christmas" to six thousand marines and sailors aboard a battleship."

When the filmed version of Hope's *Last Christmas Show* was broadcast in January of 1973, it was well received.

Hope followed this triumph by entertaining at Richard Nixon's second inaugural festivities in Washington.

44

Steve Allen has, and always has had, a great admiration for Bob Hope as a performer, and has written glowingly about him in several books on comedians. But he said to me the last time I was with him, "I've always maintained that Bob Hope is never as popular as when there is a war going on. I don't mean that to be a wisecrack so much as a plain statement of truth."

Whether it was his last few films, the ending of the war, or the fact that there were other young comedians vying for the public's attention, the Bob Hope brand of comedy was showing its age. It's hard to jest about twenty-year-old girls when you're seventy without looking like a dirty old man.

Hope's television ratings remained in the top ten most of the time, but Chrysler no longer was a regular sponsor. Chrysler dropped him when its original contract had expired. Now Hope had a different sponsor for each show. This was okay, but it wasn't as good as being identified with a regular product.

"After Chrysler dropped him," says Robert Slatzer, "I was over at Hope's house one night to pick up George—this was probably 1968 . . . anyway Hope still used two Chryslers that the company had given him when they sponsored him. While I was standing with George in the driveway, two guys walked in—they looked like the tough guys you'd see at a collection agency—and asked for Bob.

"George said, 'You can't see him—he's busy. What do you want?' They explained that they were from Chrysler, and 'we're here to pick up two cars.'

"Well, George ran into the house to tell Bob. He came back minutes later and told them to forget it. 'I talked to Bob and he says those cars belong to him.'

"The men went away, but the argument about who owned the cars went on for a year. Once while Hope was over at Lakeside playing golf Chrysler again sent some guys over there to pick up his car. But Hope made such a stink about it in front of the other members, calling Chrysler 'fucking Indian givers' and everything else you can think of, even threatening to take them to court, that the repossession men retreated. In the end Chrysler let Bob use the cars until they were worn out."

****

Ever since Hope had started entertaining the troops at March Field in 1941 he had an increasing sense that "the boys" in his audience were actually a part of his own family. He believed this so sincerely that when he'd come home from one of his Christmas tours overseas, he'd take the time to sit down with his secretary and start phoning relatives of the men he'd met in Southeast Asia and deliver the messages they'd given to him.

Now that he'd done his last Christmas show that sense of family was missing. To regain it, Hope reached out to his own family, and on July 3, 1973, there was a gathering of the entire Hope clan on his Toluca Lake estate. This was to be a Fourth of July celebration that lasted a full week. Dolores had invited every member of the Hope family and her own. The children and grandchildren alone numbered more than fifty.

To entertain them, Hope and Dolores spent liberally. They chartered a school bus, and during the week they took them to Disneyland, the San Diego Zoo, Knotts Berry Farm, the Universal Studios Tour, and even to colorful Olivera Street in downtown L.A.

At age seventy, Hope decided he would slow down. To him, slowing down meant only working 250 days a year. As he told

UPI reporter Vernon Scott, "You can't just say I'm a certain age and I'm going to sit still for the rest of my life. When you're living you've got to live it your way. You can't just say I'm going to slouch it out for the next ten years."

Some Hollywood wit said about Hope, "He's afraid if he stops running he'll die."

Hope once told a reporter, "I'm never going to retire. I intend to be cracking jokes on my way to the grave."

✵ ✵ ✵ ✵

In the summer of 1973, while Hope was on hiatus from his multi-sponsored television shows, a man named Bill Eliscu, a former employee of the CIA whom Hope had on salary to negotiate foreign movie deals for his more recent films, met a Benton & Bowles ad man at a party. The agency man asked Eliscu, "So you know Bob Hope?"

Eliscu replied, "I work for him."

"Well, ask him if he'd like to do some commercials for Texaco?"

When Eliscu put the proposition to Hope, his response was "Why should I do commercials? If Texaco wants to sponsor my television shows, I'll talk business."

Eliscu relayed this message to Benton & Bowles, and a meeting with Hope was arranged.

Out of this came a deal for Hope to produce and star in seven hours of television programming a year, for three years, at $3.15 million a year. He would also be paid $250,000 more to do commercials as Texaco's chief spokesman.

Soon after that Hope's lawyer negotiated a new deal with NBC. In recent years, the network had been dissatisfied with the movies produced by Hope Enterprises. Not only because profits were disappointing but because they were unhappy with the films artistically. And Hope resented the advice he'd been getting from Tom Sarnoff and other NBC executives who thought they knew better than he how to produce movies.

So the Hope Enterprises–NBC deal came to an end. ABC and CBS showed interest in signing him. With the competition in the market for Hope's services, NBC decided to retain him. They offered Hope $18 million for three years, just to stay with them after his present contract expired in 1975.

That was an offer Hope couldn't refuse.

Ordinarily Hope's longtime agent Jimmy Saphier would negotiate his deals, but in June Saphier fell over in his office, the victim of a stroke. The stroke was the result of a brain tumor which took his life in April 1974.

The Saphier agency was closed, and Hope hired Elliot Kozak, Saphier's assistant, to run Hope Enterprises and produce his television specials.

It hadn't been all that easy for Hope to make these big deals with Texaco and NBC. They didn't balk at the money, but they were insistent that Hope's show take on a "new look." The public was tired, they said, of what looked like the same show month after month, and year after year.

Hope promised to revamp his show. But Texaco said they didn't see how that could be done unless he replaced his creative talent, and put new minds to work writing for him.

Bob Hope wasn't the kind of fellow who would let his loyalty to anyone stand in the way of an $18-million deal.

Neither did he want to be the one to break the news to Mort Lachman, who'd been with him for twenty-eight years, or Lester White, who had joined him during his vaudeville days, or Norman Sullivan, who was one of the original Pepsodent writers.

"So he turned the hatchet job over to me," says Elliot Kozak. "I had to tell Mort, Lester and Norm that they were finished after being with Hope all those years."

To save money, Hope also fired Allan Kalmus and Frank Liberman, who'd gotten him marvelous publicity for so many years. Why pay them when Texaco had its own publicity department?

Hope not only lost his agent, his writing staff and his publicity men that year, but the 29,000 square foot house he was building on five acres of ground overlooking all of Palm Springs, in the South Ridge area, burned to the ground on July 25, 1973.

The house, designed by an architect named Lauter, had a mushroom shaped roof that reached a height of forty feet, and was modeled to resemble the TWA terminal at New York's Kennedy airport. Only the vast dome of the roof had been finished, but its cost alone was approximately $500,000.

Every fireman in the city had been dispatched to the site to help put out the blaze. In the end all that was left standing of this monument to Bob Hope were some upright steel supports that were left jutting into the air.

Nobody was injured in the conflagration, because nobody was near the house except a guard the Hopes had stationed at the construction site. Obviously he wasn't paying attention when the fire broke out.

The cause of the blaze was under investigation, but a city spokesman declared that there was no evidence of arson. There was speculation, however, that the fire was started by a disgruntled member of the IATSE theatrical union, which, at the time, was striking all three major broadcasting networks.

Why destroy Hope's house?

Hope, anti-union as part of his "conservative" credo, had threatened to do his first TV special of the coming season from Las Vegas if the strike shutdown NBC in Hollywood.

Bob and Dolores had hoped to have the house completed by the following February, in time for the 1974 Bob Hope Desert Classic.

Hope still had his seven room shack on El Alameda in Palm Springs to rattle around in, however, until the burned-out establishment could be rebuilt, but that would take five years.

El Alameda is where Hope spent his Christmas that year. He was home with Dolores for the first time in twelve years. When asked how he thought it would feel to be at home that Christmas instead of on the stage in a jungle, Hope replied, "It'll seem strange. I may eat some Spam and hire three or four Marines to come up from 29 Palms and yell, 'Bring on the girls!'"

45

Hope may have cut down his work schedule, his travel time, and the number of benefits he was doing, beginning in 1974, but he still had a sharp eye for business deals and land accumulation.

In 1955 he'd bought a seven-hundred-acre ranch in Newberry Park, Ventura County, for $275,000. Later that year he purchased the Jordan Ranch from Jim and Marian Jordan (Fibber McGee and Molly of radio days), in Agoura, just north of the Los Angeles County line. About this land purchase, more later.

In this deal he bought 2,324 acres for $400,000.

In 1974 he bought radio station KRLA, in Pasadena, one of the most successful "rock" stations on the West Coast. The story in the *Los Angeles Times* reported:

> Comedian Bob Hope has been granted a license to own and run station KRLA, in Pasadena.
>
> Hope is the principle stockholder of Western Broadcasting Corporation, which was granted the License by the FCC, which is dominated by Nixon appointees.
>
> Hope, incidentally, contributed $50,000 to Nixon's presidential campaign in 1972.

There's no reason to believe Hope wouldn't have been granted the license if he hadn't contributed fifty grand to

Nixon's campaign, but a contribution of that size certainly helped get the approval.

By this time Hope's land holdings in the San Fernando Valley, exclusive of his own estate in Toluca Lake and all the property he had accumulated since he made his original purchase in 1938, was beginning to make him seem like an old-time land baron. As of 1968, his holdings, at cost, in the West San Fernando Valley, and up to Ventura County, were as follows:

NEWHALL	35 acres at $7,500 per acre	$ 262,500
RUNKLE RANCH	3200 acres at $5,000 per acre	$16,000,000
HOPETOWN	1500 acres at $7,500 per acre	$11,250,000
JORDAN RANCH	2324 acres at $5,000 per acre	$11,628,000
MALIBU HEIGHTS	1984 acres at $10,000 per acre	$19,840,000
CORRAL CANYON	327 acres at $12,500 per acre	$ 4,087,500
AUDIE MURPHY RANCH	1004 acres at $5,000 per acre	$ 5,020,000
	TOTAL	$68,079,000

That list was given to Robert Slatzer by Hope's young brother Jim, who until his death lived on the Hope ranch near Malibu Canyon and handled his brother's real estate.

But it wasn't Jim who talked him into buying all that acreage. The man responsible was Joe Rosenberg, who'd been the loan officer at the Toluca Lake branch of the Bank of America when Hope first moved to the Valley.

After retiring from the bank in the early fifties, Rosenberg joined a large real estate brokerage firm in the area. When Hope sold his shares in the Kelly-Snyder Oil Company, in Texas, in 1954, he profited approximately $3.6 million from his $100,000 original investment. Now he was cash-rich and he didn't know what to do with the money. He invited Joe Rosenberg to lunch with him.

Rosenberg didn't have much to say at lunch. They talked generalities. Then, after they'd eaten, Rosenberg said to Bob, "Let's take a drive."

They drove along Ventura Boulevard to Malibu Canyon. Then they drove through the Canyon to the Pacific Coast

Highway. They continued up the coast to Ventura County. All the time they chatted about everything except land investment.

In fact, nothing had been said about what Hope should do with his nearly four million until the two men returned to Hope's home that afternoon. As Rosenberg started to alight from the car, Hope said, "Wait a minute, Joe. I asked you to lunch because I wanted you to advise me on what to do with my money. You haven't mentioned it."

Rosenberg smiled, and said, "Did you notice all that land we passed by this afternoon?"

"Yeah," replied Hope. "What about it?"

"Well, take those profits you just made and buy all the property that you can between here and Ventura," advised Rosenberg.

And so he did.

Hope told that story personally to John Beck, a close friend of his for many years, and the producer of his 1968 film, *The Private Navy of Sergeant O'Farrell*, a dated service comedy.

"I heard that from Hope one night when we were sitting around in Puerto Rico where we'd gone on location for the picture," Beck told me.

With real estate holdings of that magnitude, plus his Texaco and NBC deals, Hope could well afford to have been a high numbers contributor to Richard Nixon's campaign.

But it was his connection to Nixon, now in deep trouble over Watergate, and to Agnew, who'd been forced to resign the vice-presidency because he was a crook in his home state of Maryland when he was governor, that hurt Hope with the critics and the public.

Despite the fact that both Nixon and Agnew had been exposed as thieves and liars, Hope remained loyal to both men.

When asked one night by talk-show host Lou Gordon, "How can you remain friends with a thief and a scoundrel?" Hope replied, without a moment's hesitation, "Lou, if you were my friend in the same position I would still be your friend."

Not everyone admired that kind of loyalty. Especially those media critics who found the ammunition they needed to fire away at Hope for the kind of comedy he was doing after twenty-five years in television.

Hope's first show for Texaco was broadcast on October 24, 1975 over NBC. It had a huge cast of 97 stars, but they were mostly on black and white film or color tape, though there were live appearances by Bing Crosby, John Wayne, Frank Sinatra and of course Hope.

This special was called *A Quarter Century of Bob Hope on Television*, and it was offered as the best of everything Bob Hope had done on his television shows for the past twenty-five years. The stars whom he was able to resurrect from his film vault were Maurice Chevalier, Bea Lillie, Ethel Merman, Jimmy Durante, Ernie Kovacs, Jack Benny, Gloria Swanson, Jimmy Cagney, Ed Wynn, Dinah Shore, Rex Harrison, Mickey Rooney, Martha Raye, Betty Grable, Lana Turner, Joan Crawford, Lucille Ball, Steve Allen, Jack Paar, Barbra Streisand, William Holden, Phil Silvers, James Garner, Ginger Rogers, Fernandel, Ken Murray, Shirley MacLaine, Shelley Winters, Natalie Wood, Perry Como, Danny Thomas, Gina Lollobrigida, Fred MacMurray, Andy Williams, Sammy Davis, Jr., Milton Berle, and Carol Burnett.

In pre-broadcast publicity releases, Hope claimed he spent two weeks reading old scripts and looking for the best material out of eight hundred or more sketches he performed over the years. He added that every writer who had contributed to those sketches would be paid, and all the performers would work for scale. With so much talent, there had to be great moments on the two-hour show. In fact, the most difficult part was deciding what he should discard.

Ratings were high. But *New York Times* television critic John J. O'Connor found that

Hope's open courting of the establishment status quo had blunted his ability to produce pungent comedy. Some proof of this is on display, ironically, in tonight's tribute. Almost invariably material from the earlier TV years is superior stuff. It has more energy, zaniness and pure sass. Earlier routines with Crosby are still marvelous. Too frequently the later sketches rely heavily on extraneous gimmicks, on silly drag costumes, on the mere presence of celebrities.

Still it can hardly be denied that Bob Hope is a performer of immense stature, and an outstanding humanitarian in every way, and there are enough good moments scattered throughout the two hours to demonstrate splendidly what all the fuss is about.

One of the most amusing things about the Hope mystique is that after he agreed with Texaco to make a clean sweep of his writing staff and come up with a fresh format as part of the deal, he had the gall to lead off on the first show of the season with two-hours of film clips from past twenty-five years. Even more astonishing, the public bought it, and would continue to buy more or less the same old formula, for the next eighteen years, or until death do them part.

✦✦✦✦

At the Thalian's Ball in the fall of 1976, Hope, Crosby and Dorothy Lamour were the guests of honor, and it was the first time they'd been together since *The Road to Hong Kong* in 1962.

By then, all three were in trouble with their picture careers. Crosby's last feature appearance had been in a remake of the classic *Stagecoach* in 1966. Lamour's last feature had been a turkey called *Pajama Party* in 1964. And Hope's *Cancel My Reservation* became famous for being able to do something no other film in the history of the business had been able to do—close down New York's Radio City Music Hall.

So when Ben Starr, coauthor of *How to Commit Marriage*, approached them with an idea for a new "road" picture, featuring Hope, Crosby and Lamour playing their real ages as grandparents, Hope and Crosby reached into their own pockets and paid for an option on it. They changed Starr's title from *The Road to Tomorrow* to the *Road to the Fountain of Youth*.

The plot led off with Hope and Crosby bumping into each

other at the airport, where they had come with their respective grandchildren to embark on European vacations. They wind up on the same plane to London and become involved in a mystery. Along the way they bump into grandmother Lamour.

Crosby was spending time traveling around Europe with a show he had put together called *Bing Crosby and Friends* featuring Rosemary Clooney and the Joe Bushkin Combo. There was nothing Hope liked better than a chance to visit the country of his birth, while earning money at the same time. He pitched the idea of another "Road" picture to English producer Sir Lew Grade.

Grade seemed amenable, and the wheels were set in motion for the film to be shot in England in the fall of 1977, after Crosby finished a summer tour.

Unhappily, even the best laid plans of superstars sometimes go awry.

On the evening of March 3, 1977, Bing Crosby taped a CBS special commemorating his fiftieth anniversary in show business. The show took place at the Ambassador Auditorium in Pasadena in front of an audience of 1,200. With him on the show were Pearl Bailey and Bob Hope. Music that evening was played by the Joe Bushkin Combo, seated on a band platform between the stage and the audience which could be raised from the basement to stage level.

The taping took three hours and the band platform was raised and lowered a number of times during the evening in order to accommodate the action on the stage. There was some good-natured joking between the performers about the dangers of working in front of a twenty-foot-deep orchestra pit when the platform had been lowered to the basement level.

"The third time that the Bushkin Combo was lowered during the taping," wrote Robert Slatzer in his biography of Bing, "Bushkin quipped 'We're going down for the third time—like the Titanic.' Bing peered down into the gloom of the pit and joked, 'I hope they don't get lost down there.'

"At the end of the taping, Bing apparently believed the band platform had been raised again, which it hadn't. As he took his bows after his final song, he backed into the pit. Instinctively, he grabbed for a piece of scenery that had masked the pit from his sight, but it was too flimsy to hold him and he crashed through into the pit below."

Hope was the first to get to Crosby's side. He was followed by Katharine Crosby and Paul Anka.

Three doctors from the audience, including Dr. J. DeWitt Fox, also hurried to Crosby's side to attend him.

He was conscious, but badly bruised. Blood gushed from his forehead. While lying on the floor, Bing joked about the fall, saying "I'll have to get a new finish to my act." The medics who attended him in the ambulance that took him to Pasadena's Huntington Memorial Hospital told the press that the crooner had sung to them on the way.

At the hospital, it was determined that there were no fractures, but Crosby had ruptured a disc at the base of his spine between the fifth lumbar and the sacrum.

After three weeks at Huntington Memorial, Bing was flown by special air ambulance to the Peninsula Hospital, at Mill Brae, California, near Hillsborough, where he spent another two weeks in bed before he was released to his home.

It pained him very much to stand, and he could have had an operation to correct the problem but he and his doctor decided to wait. At his age, seventy-three, an operation was to be avoided if possible. Crosby was soon getting around with the aid of a cane, and worried aloud about whether he'd be able to play golf well again.

Because Crosby's recovery was slow, the new "Road" picture was delayed indefinitely.

While he was waiting to start the new film, Hope filled in his time playing golf benefits, making guest television appearances and picking up four more honorary degrees from colleges.

By mid-August Bing Crosby appeared to be his old self again. He was playing golf, and did a one-night *Bing Crosby and Friends* concert at Concord, California, across the bay from his Hillsborough home. This was a warm-up for the show he planned to take to London's Palladium the following month.

The Palladium show was a smash. When the engagement ended on October 10, Crosby left for Spain to hunt and play golf. Being an indoor girl, Katharine flew back to Northern California.

Four days later, on Friday, October 14, 1977, Crosby was playing golf at the La Moralejo Golf Club outside of Madrid. He was teeing off on the eighteenth hole when he keeled over from a massive heart attack. His golfing partners thought he had just slipped and fallen, but realized their error when he didn't get up. He never regained consciousness. The most famous crooner in the world died in route to the Red Cross Hospital in Madrid.

Hope was on tour to plug his new autobiography, *The Road to Hollywood*. He was in his suite at the Waldorf Towers in New York when the telephone rang and he was given the news.

Hope was so shocked that he cancelled a performance that was to have been given in Morristown, New Jersey, that night. He also canceled all appearances for the next few days, and flew back to Burbank's Lockheed Airport in a private jet.

Hope remained in seclusion until the funeral, but through his publicity man Ward Grant he released a statement to the press:

> The whole world loved Bing with a devotion that not only crossed international boundaries but erased them. He made the world a single place through his music, spoke to it in a language that everybody understands—the language of the heart.
>
> No matter where you were in the world, because of Bing, every Christmas was white, and because we had him with us—it'll always seem a little whiter.
>
> The world put Bing on a pedestal, but somehow I don't think he ever really knew it. Bing asked the world "Going my way?" and we all were.
>
> Yesterday a heart may have stopped, and a voice stilled, but the real melody Bing sang will linger on as long as there is a phonograph to be played . . . and a heart to be lifted.

Although there had been a period of coolness between Crosby and Hope for a number of years, the two had drawn closer again as they grew older. Hope felt a great loss. Notwithstanding, he did not attend the old-fashioned wake that was held for Bing at a West Los Angeles hotel the night before the funeral. Katharine had leased an entire floor of the hotel to accommodate Bing's many friends and relatives.

According to Rosemary Clooney, all of Bing's old drinking, golfing, hunting and fishing pals attended the wake, including Phil Harris. Bob Hope was prominent by his absence.

Hope did turn up at the funeral the next day at St. Paul's Church near the UCLA campus in Westwood Village. According to a member of the Crosby family, Bing had left instructions in his will that only Katharine and his seven children were to attend his funeral. But because Katharine felt that would be insulting to some of his closest friends, including Bob and Dolores Hope, she disregarded Bing's orders by not only inviting the Hopes but also the Phil Harrises (Alice Faye), Rosemary Clooney, and John O'Melveney, Crosby's attorney.

Crosby was buried at Holy Cross Cemetery, five miles away across town, near Loyola University, where the rest of his family were buried, including his first wife, Dixie. Because there were no more plots left in that section of the cemetery occupied by the Crosby family, he'd been unable to purchase a plot for Katharine. Consequently he left instructions to be buried nine feet deep instead of the usual six, so that if Katharine wished, her coffin could be placed on top of his.

Later, when asked what she thought of being buried in the same grave as her husband, Katharine replied, "Why should I be buried there? I was never that close to him when he was alive."

46

If Bing's sudden death in 1977 was a low point in Bob Hope's life, 1978 is remembered by him for two high points:

First, Howard Koch, who produced the Oscar show that year, invited Hope to again be the sole emcee at the Academy Awards at the Dorothy Chandler Pavilion. It was a particular honor, because Oscar was celebrating its fiftieth anniversary. To make the evening more memorable a host of previous Oscar winners and other names lined the staircase at various levels when Hope descended to make his entrance. Fred Astaire, Michael Caine, Kirk Douglas, Joan Fontaine, Greer Garson, Goldie Hawn, William Holden, Walter Matthau, Jack Nicholson, Gregory Peck, Eva Marie Saint, Maggie Smith, Barbara Stanwyck, Cicely Tyson, Jon Voight, Raquel Welch, and Natalie Wood.

Hope's opening monologue led off with, "Hey, can you believe this group? . . . all on the same stage at the same time . . . it looks like the clearance sale at the Hollywood Wax Museum . . . nine Oscar winners. I'm the only one who has to show my American Express card to get on the stage . . . anyway, good evening and welcome to the real star wars."

As had been the case more and more in recent years, someone used the occasion for some serious propagandizing.

A producer named Bert Schneider won an Oscar for an anti-Vietnam war documentary. While accepting his statuette,

Schneider pulled a telegram from his pocket and blasted American involvement in the Vietnam war.

Later Frank Sinatra read a disclaimer from the Academy Board saying, "The Academy is expressly forbidden from concerning itself with economic, political or labor issues on occasions such as this."

When it was Hope's turn to speak he attacked Schneider. He said that Academy members didn't agree with his views. Hope was wrong, which was pointed out to him the next morning by writer Ben Starr.

When Ben Starr phoned Hope the following morning to pitch his "road" picture ideas, "Bob got on the phone with me," relates Starr, "and his opening words to me were: 'What did you think of that cocksucker Schneider?' Now my whole life passes in front of me. I was a navigator in B-17s during World War II, I flew thirty-five missions, I was shot down, I've been president of two writers unions, and I've always tried to teach my kids integrity. So I said to myself, 'Fuck it! I'm not going to sell out. It's only money. I'm going to tell Hope what I think.' So I said to him, 'Bob, I think Schneider had a right to say what he said.' There was a long pause and then Hope answered, 'You think that cocksucker was right?' Well, I was now into it, so I had to keep going. So I said, 'Listen, Bob, I'm a member of the Academy too. Now you came out on the stage and said to Schneider that the Academy members didn't agree with him. Now you didn't call me . . . you don't represent the whole Academy. The right thing for you to have done was to come out and say, 'I, Bob Hope, don't agree with you. I don't know what the rest of the Academy thinks, but I don't agree with you.'

"There was a long pause, and finally Bob said, rather coldly, 'What did you call me about?' I said, 'I have an idea for a picture. Want to hear it?' And he said, 'I'm too busy. Call me in a couple of weeks.' And he hung up. Well, I did, and this time I got his secretary, who told me, 'Bob is busy. Call him in a couple of weeks.' "This went on for months. But finally he forgave me for what I said or he was in need of some picture material. So the next time I talked to him he said, 'How long will it take you to get to the house'?"

❋ ❋ ❋ ❋

In 1978, with Hope acting as sole emcee again, the awards ceremony was again marred by a propagandist, Vanessa Redgrave, who won the prize for Best Supporting Actress in *Julia*. As she clutched her gold Oscar, she chose her moment in the spotlight to call the Israelis, "militant Zionist hoodlums."

Her unexpected words shocked and then were greeted by boos. Many in the audience happened to be Jewish.

The other high-point in 1978 was Bob Hope's seventy-fifth birthday, on May 29. Like a Polish wedding, the festivities seemed to go on forever, in many different locales.

Actually, it only went on for a couple of days, and of course it was inevitable that the main part of the celebration would wind up as one of Hope's specials for Texaco, over NBC.

That part of the celebration was a collaborative effort involving Hope, network and sponsor. It was to be a three-hour star-studded show performed on the stage of the Kennedy Center in Washington. The concept was that the set was to be an "animated birthday card" featuring some of the glitziest names in show business: Pearl Bailey, Lucille Ball, George Burns, Sammy Davis, Jr., Redd Foxx, Elliott Gould, Alan King, Dorothy Lamour, Carol Lawrence, Fred MacMurray, Donny and Marie Osmond, Telly Savalas, George C. Scott, Elizabeth Taylor, Danny Thomas, and John Wayne.

Kathy Crosby and Dolores would also entertain. And the President of the United States, Jimmy Carter, would appear but his segment would be on film.

Before the show, Bob and Dolores were given a luncheon by a group of congressional wives, and then went to the White House for a reception in the East Room. Some five hundred guests from Washington and Hollywood were gathered to pay tribute to the one and only Bob Hope on his seventy-fifth, the actual date of which was a week off.

Jimmy Carter, the First Lady and daughter Amy were on hand to congratulate Hope. Carter delivered a short speech, which sounded as if it could have been written by Bob's writers: "I've been in office four hundred and eighty-nine days . . . three weeks more and I'll have stayed in the White House as many times as Bob Hope has. Bob has a second career making commercials, but it's not true that he sold Pepsodent to George Washington. We all knew he had wooden teeth. He was a Lemon Pledge man."

Hope responded with a monologue of his own:

"I've never seen so many freeloaders in my life . . . what a kick it is to shake hands with the President and the First Lady . . . thank you, President and Mrs. Carter, for loaning us your house. God knows we've paid for it."

Following the party with the Carters, Hope and Dolores hosted one of their own at an Italian restaurant in Alexandria, Virginia, called Peter's Place. The purpose was to thank the forty celebrities who would appear with Hope's on his three-hour extravaganza. There was some extemporaneous entertainment at the dinner. Pearl Bailey did a parody of "Hello, Dolly!" called "Hello, Bobby"; Dolores sang "'S Wonderful," and Hope cut the first slice from an oversize birthday cake.

As he put the first slice on a plate, he said, "I'm pretty sure I'm seventy-five. But I've lied to so many girls. Of course they always find out about one A.M.—Dolores!—that's a joke."

The climax of the birthday celebration occurred the following morning when Hope received a fifty-minute tribute from various members of the House of Representatives, including Speaker Tip O'Neil. Seated with Hope in the VIP seats in the House's visitors' gallery were Dolores, Linda and Nora, Tony, Judy, Kelly, Hope's four grandchildren, and his one remaining brother, Fred.

Missing were Linda and Nora's husbands. Linda had divorced Nat Greenblatt Lande in 1976, and Nora was just in the process of separating from her husband, Sam McCullagh.

At least twenty congressmen got up on the floor to speak about how Bob Hope was a great American. Jim Wright of Texas got a laugh when he declared, "I would not want to suggest that Bob Hope has been entertaining American troops a long time, but it seems only fair to report that there is no other entertainer who has fan letters from Lexington and Concord."

47

The saga of Bob Hope—and it is indeed a saga, of mythical proportions—continued through his ninetieth birthday, which he celebrated early on May 14, 1993. Again there was tribute to him on NBC in a three-hour special devoted to his career.

The documentary was called *Bob Hope, The First Ninety Years*. It consisted of film clips, with live portions cut in. Johnny Carson acted as emcee and delivered an opening monologue that caused some viewers to wonder whether this was the beginning of a comeback for Carson. This was Carson's first TV appearance since his retirement the year before.

Hope's oldest daughter, Linda, fifty-four, produced this tribute to her father, as she had produced a number of other Hope TV specials for him since her divorce from Nathaniel (Greenblatt) Lande in 1976.

At that crossroads in her life Hope gave Linda, his favorite of his four adopted children, a job developing new projects for Hope Enterprises. She studied film at USC, UCLA, and in Paris, and took an unsuccessful fling at acting while she was at the University of St. Louis.

Like a number of other scions of famous parents, Linda didn't exactly have an easy time of it when she was a youngster—mainly because her father was rarely around.

"I think we missed him a lot when we were growing up,"

Linda confessed in 1987. "The thing about him was that when he was there, the quality of the time was so terrific that it did make you miss him when he wasn't there."

Linda's fondest memories of her childhood were when her father was working at Paramount.

"We had a breakfast room on the ground floor that looked out on the patio. Every morning after breakfast he'd go out the glass door, do a 'Shuffle Off to Buffalo,' and then he'd be gone."

But as she grew up, and realized her father wasn't being exactly true to her mother, she began to see him in a different light, as did Nora.

Jan King, who left the Hope organization in 1969 because Hope wouldn't raise her salary, alluded to Linda and Nora's disillusionment when she told of Linda almost catching Hope in the act of infidelity in his office at Universal and Nora tailing him in her car to Joy Monroe's apartment, as related earlier.

Incidents such as these can cause considerable trauma. A youngster gets a different perspective of a parent the whole world loves. Whether these images of their father had anything to do with their sexual preferences or not, Nora, like her sister, announced she was gay after her marriage ended.

According to Melinda Manos, one of a long list of personal secretaries who have worked for the comedian since Marjorie Hughes and Jan King left him, "Hope was so disgusted with Nora that when I worked for him he didn't even have her phone number on his Rolodex."

Hope, despite having two lesbian daughters, is not a supporter of the Gay Rights movement. Too often, his jokes reflect that. At a $1,000-a-plate charity affair aboard the yacht *Princess* in New York harbor, he told assembled guests, "You know, the Statue of Liberty has AIDS. Nobody knows if she got it from the mouth of the Hudson or the Staten Island ferry."

He could get away with a joke like that at a Friars roast, but when he said it in mixed company that included important dignitaries such as Governor Hugh Carey of New York and General William Westmoreland, one wonders where Hope's good judgment is. On the other hand questionable taste has never kept him from telling a joke.

❊❊❊❊

Tony Hope also had his differences with his father.

At one point in his career, Hope wanted to immortalize himself through a theme park, much like Disneyland. According to Jan King, it was to be called Hopetown. "Bob wanted Tony to oversee this money-making monument to his ego, but Tony flatly turned the job down. This enraged Hope," says King. As a result, Tony left Universal Pictures and moved to Washington, D.C. where he has a successful law practice.

Over the years, Hope has had creative differences with Linda when she produced his TV shows. He has fired her, and rehired her, on several occasions.

Sometimes the firing was over how Linda was running the show. "I remember one time he fired Linda," says gag man Seaman Jacobs, who's collaborated on a number of recent Hope specials.

According to Jacobs, Hope was standing outside the studio at NBC talking to Linda when a stretch limo pulled up to the entrance and one of the actors—a no-name—got out.

"Who ordered that limo?" Hope demanded of Linda.

"I did," she replied.

"How much did it cost?" he demanded.

"Fifty-dollars-an-hour."

Is that a necessary? He's just a bit player. The limo's getting more than he's getting."

"Look, Dad—" Linda started to protest.

"No wonder we're over budget," said an enraged Hope. "You're fired!"

But Hope's anger didn't last long, as indicated by his hiring her to produce his ninetieth birthday gala for TV.

Linda is evidently quick to forget, too. In an interview when her father was eighty-four, and she was producing one of his specials, being taped on the South Pacific island of Moorea, Linda envisioned a project she wanted to do with her father.

The scenario would be about an aging man who makes desperate attempts to attract younger women to boost his failing ego.

"I would like to see him expose the softer gentler side of himself," she told the reporter. "I would like to see him take risks. His image is very much that of the lady killer—your basic Loni Andersons and Brooke Shieldses and all those young girls kissing him. That's not something that really happens to most people who are eighty-three or eighty-four. It could certainly have humor, but for it to work you'd have to be able to see the underbelly, see the pain."

Elliot Kozak, Bob's producer, until he got dropped unceremoniously by Hope in 1987, reports that Hope "regularly rejected such roles. As soon as he got a script like that he said, 'No, that's not for me.' He was eighty-three, but looked and acted like sixty."

Kozak may have failed to notice Hope's sagging flesh around his jowls, his sagging belly, his failing eyesight, his poor hearing, his thinning hair dyed an unnatural red, certainly suggest a man over eighty.

The energy of his Casanova days was still in evidence in 1986, however, when he filmed a movie of the week for NBC, with Jayne Meadows and Don Ameche in Vancouver. It was called *A Masterpiece of Murder*.

"We were living in a hotel in Vancouver and shooting about an hour away by limo," recalls Jayne Meadows. "Don Ameche always knew his lines, and I knew mine. But Bob never knew his. He had to rely on Barney McNulty, his cue card guy. We shot all week, and had the weekends off. Dolores would arrive on Friday, and sit on the set. But when Friday evening came Hope would take off in a plane 'to play a club date' somewhere, leaving Dolores behind. He'd fly back on Saturday. He'd play golf on Sunday, even in the pouring rain. The poor man: he can't sit still.

"Monday morning he'd be on the set. Not only didn't he know his lines, but I always had the impression he didn't know what he was saying. He won't even look at you. We'd be playing a scene and he'd be looking at the cue cards. He didn't know what the hell he was saying. He was awful. And he got awful reviews. And he was very upset about them.

"But he did have a young girl with him, when Dolores wasn't there. She was passed off as his secretary. She was around twenty-eight, and attractive, and a brunette . . . skinny . . . looked like a model. When Dolores was on the set she spent the whole time saying to me, 'Jayne, Jayne, who's that girl over there?' There were a couple of beautiful young girls playing parts in the picture, and Dolores was jealous of all of them. Even at her age, she had her eyes out for any potential rival."

❊❊❊❊

That was Hope's first and last made-for-TV movie.

It was about an over-the-hill gumshoe (Hope) who reluctantly teams up with a retired master-thief (Ameche) to solve a string of art thefts and murders.

"A tired walk-through by Hope, who used to toss off this kind of vehicle with relish in years gone by," was how it was described in Leonard Maltin's *Movie and Video Guide* by a critic named Alvin Marill.

Hope Enterprises made another attempt to star Bob in a feature film, in 1987, when it optioned a screenplay, written by veteran writer Charles Isaacs, called *The Snitch*. This one involved a married man who sees a murder, and after becoming a government witness, is forced to leave town and assume a new identity so the bad guy can't find him and kill him. He has to get a new face, a new way of dressing, a new hairstyle—and he even has to change the color of his dog from white to red.

Isaacs wrote it for a man of forty, but Hope thought he was still young enough, at the age of eighty-four, to play it. So Hope Enterprises tried to get a studio to make it.

Sadly, with Hope's name attached to it *The Snitch* couldn't be sold, either for a feature or a TV movie. The project, was dropped. (This was shortly before Nora Ephron wrote virtually the same plot for Steve Martin.)

For years Hope had wanted to do a film based on the life of

Walter Winchell. Hope figured he could play Winchell, because early in his radio career he had fashioned his rapid-fire way of delivering his radio monologue after the rat-a-tat way the columnist delivered the news on his fifteen-minute Sunday night show.

Hope paid to have a screenplay written on Winchell's life. But even that failed to spark any interest among the studios or networks.

In short, Hope's movie star career was over.

This isn't to say that Hope didn't still have plenty to keep him occupied or a way of raking in the bucks.

Between his personal appearances, for which he was getting $50,000 for a night's work (unless it was for one of his favorite charities, in which case he does it for nothing), and his TV specials and answering his fan mail and receiving honorary college degrees—at last count he had about forty, plus a high school diploma given belatedly to him in 1977 by his alma mater in Cleveland Heights—he had schedules that would exhaust ordinary mortals.

Even without movies, Hope estimated that his income from personal appearances and TV specials was in the neighborhood of $7 million a year.

Hope once said that the secret to his continued success in television is that, "We never do the same show twice." But by the eighties, critics were complaining that he was doing just that. His shows had monologue (very carefully edited to get rid of jokes that bomb), song, comedy sketch, number or dialogue with pretty girl or girls, second sketch, and close with theme song. Critics puzzled over the enduring appeal to the average fan.

Even NBC worried about Hope's popularity. "We've had to be extremely careful in the last few years about where to schedule his specials," admits an NBC executive who wishes to remain anonymous. "There once was a time when you could broadcast a Bob Hope special any day of the week, anytime of the night, and pull in a huge audience regardless of the competition. Now we're looking at protective time frames."

✿ ✿ ✿ ✿

Protective time frames or not, Hope still keeps eight secretaries on duty eight hours daily in a separate building on his Toluca Lake estate. They answer his fan mail and keep his joke files updated.

Melinda Manos, an attractive twenty-eight-year-old brunette, worked for Hope from 1987 to 1989. She said that Hope keeps his jokes and scripts in old-fashioned filing cabinets. He refuses to computerize the system.

According to Melinda, when Hope was away his personal mail would pile up. He'd come in the morning after he returned from his trip, and say, 'Okay, let's hit the mail, darling.' Often we'd work 'til late at night—always in the main house or his bedroom. And I'd always be on call. He gets lots of requests for money from strangers. Sometimes he would send somebody a check for schooling.

"He also loved to accept phone calls from fans, if he wasn't too busy.

"I spent a lot of time with him during the two years I was with him, and he was fun to work for. He loved to watch the TV show *Jeopardy*. If we were still working when it went on, he'd wheel a huge TV set over to where we were sitting, and play it very loud because he was so hard-of-hearing. I could hardly sit in the same room, it was so loud."

Melinda came in one morning with a new permanent. "It was pretty wild, I guess," she told me.

She said Hope always noticed those things. He said, "Melinda, what did you do to your hair—it looks like a bomb went off."

"It's the new Jane Russell-look," she explained.

Hope ogled her modest-sized breasts and quipped, "You have to have the right equipment for that."

Hope never made a pass at Melinda, however, she said.

From what Melinda observed, Hope and Dolores were leading separate lives when she was working for him. She remembers Hope glancing out the window one day and being surprised to see a brand new Chrysler convertible standing in his driveway.

"Who's here?" he asked.

"Your wife," replied Melinda.

"But that's a new car."

"Yeah," said Melinda. "Lee Iacocca just gave it to her."

During that period, Hope was in the habit of going to the movies by himself in the evenings. "He'd sit in the back row of a theater over in Burbank, all alone, and watch the latest movie," remembers Melinda. "He felt he had to keep up on current events and the latest movies because he satirized them on his specials. He didn't read much. He had a lot of books around the house and on shelves in his bedroom. The latest best-sellers that publishers would send him. But he read the newspaper and trades more. He was too busy answering mail and keeping up with business to read books."

When Robert Slatzer's book on Bing Crosby was published, Hope said on one of the late-night talk shows that "every word in it is a lie." But when pressed by the host he was forced to admit that he had not read the book.

"One of his favorite eating places was a fast food joint called the In-And-Out-Burger on Lankersham," says Melinda. "On the way to Palm Springs he'd have his chauffeur drive him there so he could eat it in the back seat during the ride."

For a time Hope had his own small plane for travel between Toluca Lake and Palm Springs. It was a Jet Star. "Before he bought it," says Melinda, "he had his pilot examine the plane and give it an okay. Then it turned out to have a cracked fuselage, which cost $200,000 to be repaired. He was furious with the pilot. It's the first time I ever saw him get really mad. He decided it was cheaper to sell the plane and fly commercially.

"The other time I saw him really upset was when Lucille Ball died in 1989."

Although Melinda got along well with Hope personally, she found she could no longer live on the $500-a-week salary he was paying her. "There was so much overtime involved, which I didn't get reimbursed for—he was always calling me late at night when he suddenly blew into town, to come over and work on his correspondence. So I finally asked for a raise at the end of 1989. He said 'no' and he wouldn't give me any medical benefits either, so I quit and took a job with a legal firm in Beverly Hills that gave me all those things. Bob did give me a nice letter of recommendation, though."

❈ ❈ ❈ ❈

Hope can be surprisingly ruthless about firing people in his employ no matter how long they'd served him.

Elliot Kozak, for example, had worked for Hope for more than twenty years.

"I had a yearly contract that ran from September 1st to June 1st," says Kozak. "Hope was supposed to let me know thirty days in advance—on May 1st—if he was picking up my option. He would always wait to the last minute to let me know, and frequently it would be after the deadline. He'd leave me dangling, unable to accept another job.

"After this happened a number of times I got disgusted and took a job at ICM, where I stayed for six years. After I quit, Hope gave my job to Linda. But she screwed it up—nearly ran the show into bankruptcy—and he fired her—threw her out of the office—and brought in Bob Hussey, who knew nothing about the operation, either.

"Then Hope asked me to come back, and I did, and I stayed until 1991. Then Hope pulled his old stunt again. He failed to let me know about my option and went off on a trip. I finally tracked him down in Alaska and asked him over the phone, 'Look, Bob, are you picking me up or not? I have to know. I have to start preparing the first show for next season.'"

There was a long pause and then Hope said, "Forget the first show. Mel Shavelson is going to put it together."

"Well, what about the second show? Shall I begin work on that?"

"Let's forget that, too," said Hope. "As a matter of fact, I don't think I need you at all any more."

"But, Bob, after all these years, you can't just—"

"Well, we had some laughs," Hope interrupted him callously, and hung up.

When it became apparent that Hope's popularity with the public was on the wane, NBC cut down the number of TV specials to four a year, including his annual Christmas show. Consequently Hope pared down his writing staff, several of whom had been with him for years on forty-weeks-a-year contracts. He replaced them with new free-lance writers. That way he didn't have to contribute anything to their retirement and medical benefits, which he'd have to do if they worked for him forty weeks a year.

With his performance income down to six-or-seven million annually, and the taxes on his real estate holdings eating into his capital by a couple of million a year, Hope decided to economize on his mistresses. By the mid-eighties his handful of mistresses had been cut to one. Her name was Sandy Vinger, and according to one of Hope's masseurs, she was thirty-eight years old, and lived in a tiny bungalow at 212 N. California Street in Burbank, not far from Hope's home.

Hope put Miss Vinger on his payroll as a writer (and she might well have performed those services, too). The masseur, who revealed all this to a well-known actress who also was a client, said that Hope used to visit Ms. Vinger about ten in the evening, after he'd had his nightly massage. This was confirmed by Ritchie, one of the gate guards, who said that Hope used to drive out the gate by himself, after he'd had his rubdown, and return a couple of hours later.

Ms. Vinger was unavailable for comment. However, according to her father, Milford B. Vinger, who owns the house in La Cresenta, California, which she gave as her place of residence, her whereabouts at the moment is a mystery, even to him. "She comes and goes," he told me, "and I don't know when, if ever, she'll be back, or how to get in touch with her." Vinger told me that his daughter did "some writing" for Hope during the eighties.

None of his current crop of writers, however, remembers anyone of Sandy's description contributing jokes to the show.

✿ ✿ ✿ ✿

If Hope didn't have enough on his mind to keep an 85-year-old man from dying of boredom, he found himself in 1988 at the center of a heated controversy over the sale of a 2,329 acres of his land in the Santa Monica Mountains.

The property was still known as the Jordan Ranch, even though Hope had purchased it years before from Jim and Marian Jordan of *Fibber McGee and Molly* radio fame.

In the mid-eighties Hope had the opportunity to sell the Jordan Ranch to the Potomac Investment Associates, a Maryland-based developer that, among other endeavors, built golf courses for the Professional Golf Association.

Originally Potomac intended to build a PGA tour "stadium" golf course and a 1,150 house real estate development on the oak-studded 2,329 acres. If the deal had gone through, Hope would have realized approximately $50-million out of his partnership.

It had been Hope's lifelong passion for golf, and his thirty-year friendship with PGA commissioner, Dean Beman, that had led to the PGA's interest in his property in the first place. And if the course were ever built, it would have been Hope's golf memorabilia that would decorate the clubhouse—yet another gold-plated monument to him.

However, there were such loud howls of protest from environmental groups—chiefly Save Open Space/Santa Monica Mountains—over the size of the development, that Hope and his potential investor-partners agreed to cut their announced housing project to only 750 homes.

All of this hinged on whether or not the National Park Service would be willing to trade 59.4 acres of Cheeseboro Canyon, which it had purchased for parkland in 1985, for 864.4 acres of Hope's Jordan Ranch property, in order to provide an access road into The Jordan Ranch for the Potomac developers.

Despite Hope's reputation as an astute businessman, he had overlooked that major drawback when he purchased the Jordan Ranch. For the twenty-eight years he had owned it, the only connection between Jordan and civilization was a dirt easement across someone else's pasture. While that provided all the access necessary for a fallow ranch, it would strangle any attempt to develop the land commercially. Hope tried several times to sell; but potential buyers took one look at the rutted dirt road leading to it and quickly lost interest.

The last realistic chance to turn Jordan into a developable parcel vanished in 1985 when the Santa Monica Mountains Conservancy (a state agency mandated to acquire land for preservation) engineered the purchase of Cheeseboro Canyon, just east of Jordan Ranch, for the National Park Service. Included in the newly designated Cheeseboro Canyon Park was a series of hills directly between Jordan Ranch and Cheeseboro Road which connects to the freeway.

When Cheeseboro Canyon became a park in 1985, Jordan Ranch virtually became an island. Though it was possible to stand at the bottom of what was Hope's property and hear traffic passing on the Ventura freeway, Cheeseboro Canyon Park cut off Jordan Ranch so effectively that, as one local wag gloated, "It was as if someone had hoisted Hope's land by helicopter to Bakersfield."

So without the Cheeseboro Canyon acreage for an access road there was no way Jordan Ranch could be developed or sold to Potomac.

The 864 acres Hope was willing to trade for only fifty-nine acres was steep, rocky mountainside that would be utterly worthless for housing anything but mountain goats. In addition, "The trade would be establishing a bad precedent," states Margo Feuer, president of the Save Open Space/Santa Monica Mountains Society, who, along with the then-senator from California, Alan Cranston, was trying to acquire Jordan Ranch for the Park Service. "Trading parkland to help a commercial developer just wasn't a wise thing to do for the country. If that could be done in this park, developers could get away with it or something similar in every public park throughout the nation."

Notwithstanding, the trade was about to happen—probably, believes Feuer, because of pressure put on Secretary of the

Interior Manuel Lujan by Hope's lobbying friends in Washington—when news of another proposed mammoth housing and golf course project in the area reached the ears of local residents.

This proposed project was to be on the 5,400 acre ranch owned by the Ahmanson Land Company, located on the east side of Cheeseboro Canyon. This was the same Ahmanson group who had started Home Savings & Loan, had assets of $45 billion, and were major contributors to the development of the Ahmanson Music Center in downtown Los Angeles.

The announcement of the Ahmanson project at the very time that Hope was negotiating for the acreage for the access road to Jordan Ranch killed the proposed trade. The Wilderness Society, a national environmental organization, along with Senator Cranston and Save Open Space raised such protests that the Ventura County board of supervisors, who had to approve both projects before they could go forward, decided to retract the temporary approval they had granted the developers earlier in the proceedings.

"The fact that a developer was going to get his hands on existing parkland in order to accommodate a commercial project was what caused the shit to really hit the fan," recalls Margo Feuer. "And besides, the park service couldn't just rubber stamp the whole trade. It first had to go through what's called an 'environmental impact study.'"

While it was doing that, it became evident that the Jordan Ranch project wouldn't fly in the face of public reaction. (Environmental groups, including Save Open Space, were even picketing Hope's house in Toluca Lake.)

"But then Maria VanderKolk, whom our group helped get elected to the Ventura County board of supervisors because we thought she was sympathetic to our cause, did a complete reversal," says Feuer. "She recommended that the Potomac/Hope people and the Ahmanson Ranch group combine forces and put both housing and golf course developing projects on the 5,400 acres owned by the Ahmanson Land Company."

Ahmanson Ranch, it should be noted, was not within the

boundaries of what the Public Service intended to turn into public parking. But Jordan Ranch was totally within the boundaries, and was the prize the Park Service was trying to acquire.

The one condition of the new deal was that Hope would agree to sell all his properties in the area—Jordan Ranch, Corral Canyon and Runkle Ranch—to the Park Service. That, of course, would lay to rest the whole question of access to Jordan Ranch.

The price agreed upon was $29.5 million. The deal was approved by the Ventura County board of supervisors in December of 1992. But within the thirty day period allotted to filing objections after the approval vote, nine lawsuits were filed to try to stop the Ahmanson Land Company project from becoming a reality. Among the suers were the County of Los Angeles, the City of Los Angeles, the City of Calabasas, the City of Malibu, Save Open Space, the Wilderness Society, and several influential citizens who lived in the area.

As a result, Hope announced that the deal was "off, because I don't know when I'll ever be able to get my money on account of all the lawsuits."

In addition, according to a *Los Angeles Times* story, Potomac and Ahmanson Land and Hope could not agree on how to split the profits from the Ahmanson Ranch project, which would create a mini-city of 8,600 residents and two PGA-approved golf courses in the rolling Simi Hills.

Although both projects appeared to be dead at the beginning of 1993, there was still considerable behind-the-scenes negotiating between Hope's lawyers and the Park Service. The latter still wanted to acquire Jordan Ranch.

On Saturday, March 27, 1993, the Park Service offered Hope $19.5 million for the Jordan Ranch and Corral Canyon. They gave him until the following Wednesday to accept the offer. Wednesday came and went with no response from Hope so the whole thing seemed to be off again.

"I feared Hope decided to heck with you all—I'll take this property to the grave," said David Gackenbach, regional director of the National Park Service, upon not hearing further from the comedian.

But Hope had no intention of taking Jordan Ranch with him to the grave. Being a shrewd negotiator he decided to wait out the National Park Service. And just as he felt they would, they finally came back to him in June with still another offer. $16.7 million for just the Jordan Ranch. Since this allowed him to retain ownership of Corral Canyon and Runkle Ranch, the $16.7 million was actually a better deal than the $19 million he had turned down in March.

"So Hope actually came out like Gangbusters," Margo Feuer says today. "You see, the Park Service is required to pay only 'fair market value.' If you judge landlocked Jordan Ranch on the basis of its having no access, it would be worth a lot less than sixteen-point-seven million, because who would want it? For some reason, the Park Service was willing to overpay. So Hope actually gave the shaft to the public once again."

But that's not the end of Hope's real-estate saga. Under the conditions laid down by the Ventura County board of supervisors, the Ahmanson Ranch project still cannot proceed until Hope's other two properties, Corral Canyon and Runkle Ranch, become public parkland. They've given the Ahmanson Land Company two-and-a-half years to transfer the other properties to park agencies. Since Ahmanson doesn't own Hope's properties, they will have to buy them from him for God-only-knows how many more millions of dollars in order to donate Corral Canyon and Runkle to the Park Service, so they can get their project approved. Or else Hope will give the properties to Ahmanson in exchange for a large chunk of the action from their two golf courses and their housing project.

Either way Hope will add to his fortune.

As far as the Save Open Space and the Wilderness Society are concerned, they hope the situation will remain as is, *without* the Ahmanson deal going forward. They view Hope as a "heavy" who is rich enough, and that further attempt to profit from his land would be proof of his "amoral" greed.

Hope himself fails to understand why anyone would object to

his making a profit from his property. He risked his money investing in it. "After all, I've given plenty of property away in my time," he said plaintively in answer to his critics.

Just what property he referred to isn't clear. Perhaps it was the acreage in Palm Desert that he donated to the Eisenhower Medical Center.

✿ ✿ ✿ ✿

It's often been rumored that Hope's Toluca Lake establishment is already owned by the local Catholic diocese, and so the Hopes don't have to pay any taxes on it. The story adds that he and Dolores are just allowed to reside there until they die.

I checked. The tale is a myth. According to the Equity Title Co. of Los Angeles, the Hope estate in Toluca Lake is still under the joint ownership of Leslie T. and Dolores Hope.

It's not known what disposition will be made of the 29,000-square-foot mushroom shaped edifice that, like the Phoenix, rose out of its ashes by 1979 to become the Hopes' second desert retreat. It's a spectacular tourist attraction. But if Dolores has anything to say about it, you can bet your crucifix that the church will wind up with that too.

In 1980 the Hopes hosted a $2,500-a-couple soiree in the new house, proceeds from which went to the Bob Hope Cultural Center (whatever that is). Probably the new house *is* the Bob Hope Cultural Center.

Sitting atop five large city lots, it certainly isn't the kind of place the average person would want to call "home." Even Bob Hope admitted the night of the gala that he didn't spend much time in it.

48

By the time Hope turned eighty-eight, he had done about everything one man in one lifetime could possibly do. From his humble beginnings he had pulled himself up by his proverbial bootstraps to become a star of vaudeville, Broadway, radio, films, and television. He'd traveled and entertained the world over.

Scuttlebut is that he has made love to more beautiful women than Errol Flynn, Chico Marx, and Bing Crosby, all put together. He'd raised more money for charity than any other living American. He'd made a hole-in-one. He'd become a mighty land baron. He'd been buddies with presidents, kings and queens, prime ministers, and five-star generals. He was in the Guinness Book of Records for being the "Most Decorated Civilian."

He was given a fourth star on the Hollywood Boulevard Walk of Fame. And he was the last big name performer to entertain the troops in America's last (we hope) war—Operation Desert Storm. In December of 1990 Hope took a troupe of entertainers consisting of Ann Jillian, Marie Osmond, Johnny Bench, The Pointer Sisters, country singer Aaron Tippon, and wife Dolores to Saudi Arabia, where he spent seven days over Christmas putting on shows for the Army, Navy, and Air Force staff stationed in the area. As usual, whenever Dolores appeared on one of his Christmas shows she wowed the troops with her rendition of "White Christmas."

Two weeks later, on January 12, 1991, highlights of his Middle Eastern tour were telecast on NBC under the title *Bob Hope's Christmas Cheer in Saudi Arabia.*

❄ ❄ ❄ ❄

Larry Klein, one of Hope's writers, once said to him, "If you had your whole life to live over again, Bob, you wouldn't have time to do it."

The one thing he didn't achieve was becoming President of the United States (ineligible, of course, as not being native born) although he'd been offered the opportunity by a consortium of friends and conservative businessmen in 1973. He turned it down saying, "I don't have the time."

Actually he didn't need to be president. He had power and influence and access to the White House without ever having to risk defeat at the polls.

But on November 4, 1991, at the grand opening of the Ronald Reagan Library, he discovered he didn't still have the clout he believed he had.

According to Jim Brown, who was NBC's Hollywood correspondent, and in charge of the "pool" camera for all the networks, the invited guests and dignitaries, including the four former presidents—Reagan, Carter, Nixon and Ford—were to gather in the parking lot, and at the proper moment proceed from there up the hill to the entrance of the Reagan library, where bleachers had been set up for the general public. The four were given their own limousines for the short drive. President Bush would arrive by helicopter.

Lesser guests—movie stars, city officials, and studio execs like Lew Wasserman and Michael Eisner—were to ride up the hill in open-air trams such as the ones used for transporting tourists around on the Universal Studio Tours. These trams had been provided by Universal so that the aging guests wouldn't have exhaust themselves by having to walk up the hill in the hot sun.

Bob Hope apparently thought he would be invited to ride in a limousine with one of the former presidents. Says NBC's Jim Brown, "When he found out it wasn't to be he caused quite a ruckus."

"The whole affair had been carefully orchestrated, and everyone had to go where he or she was assigned," adds Jane Galbraith, who was covering the affair for Monitor Television. "Bob Hope had to use a tram like everyone else."

He couldn't believe it. "I'm Bob Hope," he complained to the people in charge of the arrangements. "I'm sure I'm on the limo list."

"Look, Mr. Hope," said the official. "There are important people here who are riding in limousines, but you don't happen to be one of them."

Hope had to suffer the indignity of riding up to the library entrance in a tram with other commoners, like MCA's Wasserman and Disney's Eisner.

"I saw him come through from the bleachers," remembers Jane Galbraith, "and he really looked pathetic, because he's clearly an old man now. Not much hair, and the way he dyes it red, with big shocks of it on each side of his head, he looked like Bozo the Clown. That was the big joke among everybody from NBC. Bozo the Clown, and a very old one."

✿✿✿✿

At ninety Bob Hope has earned the right not to look like a young leading man, but not the right to inflict his faltering talent on the public, believes comedian David Letterman.

"If you consider ways to end up very successful careers," Letterman was quoted in the February 1993 issue of *Rolling Stone*, "Bob Hope could have done a similar version of what Johnny Carson did—a kind of step aside. I watched a lot of his early films over the holidays, and, Jesus, talk about a guy who was sharp and on the money and appealing and fresh and charismatic. Then I saw *Bob Hope's Kodak All-American Special* and it was tough to watch. If it had been a funeral you would've preferred the coffin be closed. It was sad. I mean, can he be gratified by that?"

✿ ✿ ✿ ✿

In May of 1992 Hope filmed a special in Columbus, Ohio, at the International Flower Show. First Lady Barbara Bush, who was sponsoring the flower show, was one of Hope's guests.

The show was held in Columbus in honor of the five hundredth anniversary of Christopher Columbus's discovery of America. There was also a swimsuit number, because as one of the writers said, "Hope needed some sex on the show. Swimsuits, Columbus, flowers, and Barbara Bush didn't really go together, but that's how Hope operates."

At one point in the taping, Hope was supposed to be interviewing the First Lady about her interest in flowers.

Barbara Bush knew her lines. But Hope couldn't do the spot even with help from his cue cards, because he couldn't read the large print. After several aborted attempts, she came up with a suggestion. She volunteered to feed the questions to Hope that he was supposed to ask her. Then he'd repeat the question, and she'd answer it. Her cue lines to him would be cut in the editing. The problem was, Hope couldn't hear Barbara Bush, either, because he refused to wear his hearing aide.

✿ ✿ ✿ ✿

In April of 1993, Hope taped an interview with NBC's late-night talk-show host Bob Costas. His purpose was to plug his May forthcoming birthday special, *Bob Hope, The First Ninety Years*. But staffers on the Costas show reported after the taping that Hope's spot turned out to be unusable. Because of his inability to hear, Hope responded to most of Costas's questions with "Huh?"

In an effort to funnel more audio to Hope, the producers then put a speaker behind his chair. It didn't help. As the interview progressed, Costas was forced to raise his voice to unacceptable levels when he asked questions.

To compound the problem, when Costas asked for Hope's impressions of his famous friends and coworkers, such as Bing

Crosby, he responded more than once with short answers along the lines of "He was a good fella."

In the end, the Hope segment had to be trashed.

✿ ✿ ✿ ✿

Early in 1993, while putting together the aforementioned special, Linda Hope decided that it would be a good idea to include a segment of still-photographs taken of Hope with other celebrities—celebrities who are no longer around to appear on the live portion of the show.

"So Linda came to my house," reports Gene Lester, one of Hollywood's sought-after still photographers during the thirties, forties and fifties. "We started going through all my Hope pictures together. When Linda came to a big close-up of her father kissing Marilyn Maxwell, a funny expression appeared on her face, then passed over it quickly." (See photo in this book.)

✿ ✿ ✿

Bob Hope, The First Ninety Years, emceed by Johnny Carson, seemed overlong to many in the TV audience who endured the finished product when it aired. Three hours of mostly film clips is a little too much to take, even from your favorite comedian, even if you have a hankering to see all his old friends who turned up at his ninety birthday bash to wish him "Happy Birthday" and to hear him sing "Thanks for the Memory."

Johnny Carson, John Denver, George Burns, Milton Berle, Tom Selleck, Angela Lansbury, Dorothy Lamour, Walter Cronkite, President Gerald Ford, Ginger Rogers (in a wheelchair), Lucy Arnaz, Whoopi Goldberg, Chevy Chase, and Paula Abdul were just some of the celebrities. The special presented Hope birthday greetings from four former presidents—Richard Nixon, Jimmy Carter, Ronald Reagan and George Bush—and one sitting president, Bill Clinton.

"During the filming of his routine with Hope, George Burns lost his place on the cue cards, and after floundering around, had to be pointed in the right direction," reported actress Jane

Wyatt, one of the guests. "But what do you expect of someone ninety-seven?"

At ninety, Hope was comparatively alert, "but the letters on his cue cards were at least a foot high," relates Gene Lester, "in order for him to be able to see them ten feet away."

Hope spent most of the live portion of the show being photographed seated, waving to his well-wishers, applauding what little live entertainment there was, and looking a little overcome by it all. He came close to tears when a flag-waving honor guard from all four services, the army, navy, marines, and air force, marched onto the stage to sing "Happy Birthday."

He was also genuinely moved when Dolores stood up near the end of the three hours to sing "It's Only a Paper Moon."

❊❊❊❊

Loyal Hope fans have diminished in number. *Bob Hope, The First Ninety Years* finished a disappointing seventeenth in the weekly ratings, though it had virtually no opposition on the other networks. Will Bob Hope do as that other famous old soldier, Douglas MacArthur, did, and simply fade away? Don't count on it. He's already planning another personal appearance tour.

Several years ago while being interviewed on *The Larry King Show*, King said to him, "Bob, and I want you to be truthful. You've worked with beautiful women all your life. Didn't you ever find it tempting?"

Hope squirmed uncomfortably in his chair at the directness of the question. This was once when he couldn't phone his writers for the quips that would get him out of that corner. He finally replied, "Yes, but I always wind up coming back to Dolores."

From all appearances he's back for good. Today the couple goes everywhere together—on the road, on pleasure trips, even home. So we have our happy ending. And Dolores, at the age of eight-four, is cutting her first album of her favorite songs, which Hope Enterprises is producing. Let's hope that among those songs is the one she sings to Bob on sentimental occasions:

"I Love You Just the Way You Are"

BIBLIOGRAPHY

BOOKS

Have Tux, Will Travel by Bob Hope, as told to Pete Martin. Simon & Schuster, 1954.

Don't Shoot, It's Only Me by Bob Hope, with Melville Shavelson. G.P. Putnam, 1990.

Call Me Lucky by Bing Crosby, as told to Pete Martin. Simon & Schuster, 1953.

Bob Hope by Joe Morella, Edward Z. Epstein and Eleanor Clark. Arlington House, 1973.

Bob Hope: A Life In Comedy by William Faith. G.P. Putnam, 1982.

Bing Crosby: The Hollow Man by Donald Shepherd and Robert Slatzer. St. Martin's Press, 1981.

My Side of the Road by Dorothy Lamour, as told to Dick McInnes. Prentice-Hall, 1980.

The Funny Men by Steve Allen. Simon & Schuster, 1956.

More Funny People by Steve Allen. Stein & Day, 1982.

Doris Day by A.E. Hotchner. William Morrow, 1976.

Still Talking by Joan Rivers, with Richard Meryman. Turtle Bay Books (Random House), 1991.

Bob Hope: A Comic Life by Pamela Trescott. Acropolis, 1985.

I Never Left Home by Bob Hope, with Carroll Carroll. Simon & Schuster, 1944.

MAGAZINES

"This is Bob (Politician-Patriot-Publicist) Hope" by J. Anthony Lukas. *New York Times Magazine*, Oct. 4, 1970.

"Bob Hope" by Joan Barthel. *Life*, Jan. 29, 1971.

"This is Bob (Legend In His Own Time) Hope" by Robert Jennings. *West*, May 14, 1972.

"Bob Hope's Scrapbook: Thanks for the Memories" by Joseph N. Bell. *Good Housekeeping*, Jan., 1974.

"Bob Hope Turns Serious" (Part 1) by Neil Hickey. *TV Guide*, Jan. 19, 1977.

"Bob Hope Turns Serious" (Part 2) by Neil Hickey. *TV Guide*, Jan. 26, 1977.

"Funny Man" by Margy Rochlin. *Los Angeles Times Magazine*, Feb. 1, 1987.

"Hope's Last Road Show" by Tom Johnson. *Los Angeles Magazine*, March, 1991.

ACKNOWLEDGMENTS

My thanks to the following, who so graciously granted me interviews or spoke with me on the subject over the years I have been preparing this book:

Elliot Alexander
Johnnie Avery
Steve Allen
Kay Avalon
Hy Averback
John Beck
Milton Berle
Paul Bogart
Walter Bunker
Jay Burton
Joanna Cameron
Jeanne Carmen
Rita Chandler
John Conte
Gary Crosby
Mathew Davis
Jerry Davis
Freddy DeCordova
Phyllis Diller

Frances Langford Evinrude
William Faith
Irving Fein
Margot Feuer
Ralph Fields
Fred Fox
Jane Galbraith
Larry Gelbart
Hal Goodman
Tim Gray
Everett Greenbaum
Jean Greenberg
Steve Greenberg
Joyce Haber
Jack Haley, Jr.
Bill Harbach
Edmund Hartman
Patricia (Honey Chile) Wilder
    Hohenlohe

473

Charles Isaacs
Seaman Jacobs
Gary Jon
Ruby Keeler
Jan King
Elliot Kozak
Howard Leeds
Peter Leeds
Gene Lester
Jay Livingston
Mannie Manheim
Melinda Manos
Joy Monroe McConnell
Fay McKenzie
Jayne Meadows
Al Melnick
Senator Howard Metzenbaum
Farlan Meyer
Kurt Niklas
Gabe Paul
Nat Perrin
Sam Perrin

Sally Presley
Anthony Quinn
Ann Rapp
Tony Romano
Peter Sabiston
Andrew Salt
Arna Saphier
Al Schwartz
Sherwood Schwartz
Stanley Shapiro
Robert Slatzer
Ben Starr
Hy Steirman
Phillip Stern
Peter Vieira
Milford B. Vinger
Bea Wayne
Dick Weiner
Lester White
Lorraine White
Digby Wolfe

INDEX